PENGUIN REFERENCE

The Penguin Pocket Spelling Dictionary

David Crystal was born in 1941 and spent the early years of his life in Holyhead, North Wales. He went to St Mary's College, Liverpool, and University College, London, where he read English and obtained his Ph.D. in 1966. He was a lecturer in linguistics at the universities of Bangor and Reading, becoming Professor of Linguistic Science at Reading in 1975, and is now Honorary Professor of Linguistics at the University of Wales, Bangor. He is editor of *The Penguin Encyclopedia* and related publications, the former editor of the Cambridge family of general encyclopedias, compiler of several dictionaries, and author of publications on the theory and practice of reference works. He currently directs a company which manages a large reference database and which is developing systems for improving document classification and internet search. A past president of the Society of Indexers, in 2001 his book *Words on Words* (co-authored with Hilary Crystal) was awarded the Wheatley Medal for an outstanding index. In 1995 he was awarded the OBE for services to the English language.

THE PENGUIN POCKET SPELLING DICTIONARY

Edited by David Crystal

PENGUIN BOOKS

PENGUIN BOOKS

Published by the Penguin Group
Penguin Books Ltd, 80 Strand, London WC2R 0RL, England
Penguin Group (USA) Inc., 375 Hudson Street, New York, New York 10014, USA
Penguin Group (Canada), 90 Eglinton Avenue East, Suite 700, Toronto, Ontario, Canada M4P 2Y3
(a division of Pearson Penguin Canada Inc.)
Penguin Ireland, 25 St Stephen's Green, Dublin 2, Ireland (a division of Penguin Books Ltd)
Penguin Group (Australia), 250 Camberwell Road, Camberwell, Victoria 3124, Australia
(a division of Pearson Australia Group Pty Ltd)
Penguin Books India Pvt Ltd, 11 Community Centre, Panchsheel Park, New Delhi – 110 017, India
Penguin Group (NZ), cnr Airborne and Rosedale Roads, Albany, Auckland 1310, New Zealand
(a division of Pearson New Zealand Ltd)
Penguin Books (South Africa) (Pty) Ltd, 24 Sturdee Avenue, Rosebank 2196, South Africa

Penguin Books Ltd, Registered Offices: 80 Strand, London WC2R 0RL, England

www.penguin.com

First published 2005
1

Copyright © Crystal Reference Systems Ltd, 2005
All rights reserved

The moral right of the author has been asserted

Set in 7/7.75 pt Stone Serif
Typeset by Rowland Phototypesetting Ltd, Bury St Edmunds, Suffolk
Printed in England by Clays Ltd, St Ives plc

Contents

Crystal Reference

GENERAL EDITOR
David Crystal

ASSISTANT EDITOR
Todd Warden-Owen

EDITORIAL MANAGER
Hilary Crystal

EDITORIAL ASSISTANCE
Peter Preston

DATABASE MANAGEMENT
Tony McNicholl

CRYSTAL REFERENCE ADMINISTRATION
Ian Saunders
Rob Phillips

Penguin Books

PUBLISHER
Nigel Wilcockson

EDITORIAL ASSISTANCE
Ellie Smith

PRODUCTION
Andrew Henty

DESIGN
Richard Marston

TYPESETTING
Rowland Phototypesetting Ltd

Introduction

The notion of a spelling dictionary, at first sight, seems paradoxical – for how can one look up a word to see how it is spelled if one does not know the spelling in the first place? But this is to misunderstand what a spelling dictionary is for. It is not for people who do not know how to spell. It is for people who *have* learned to spell, but who are uncertain about particular points in particular words. The problem with *diarrhoea* is not how it begins: it is what happens after we get to *diar-*.

There is a second reason for using a spelling dictionary. Spelling does not stand still. It changes with the times, as do other features of language, such as vocabulary and grammar. People are often surprised when they hear that around a *quarter* of the words in a general dictionary vary in the way they can be written: is it *moon* or *Moon*, *flowerpot* or *flower-pot*, *advertise* or *advertize*, *judgment* or *judgement* . . . ? Despite the best efforts of lexicographers, publishers, and printers since the end of the eighteenth century, the 'standard language' has been standardized only to a certain extent.

There are many languages for which a spelling dictionary would be pointless, because the relationship between sounds and letters is largely one-to-one. But such a degree of regularity has not been seen in English since Anglo-Saxon times. The present-day spelling system is the result of a process of development that has been going on for over 1,000 years. The complications we encounter now are the result of the major linguistic and social events which have taken place during this period.

The origin of the problem lies in the attempt by Christian missionaries to use their 23-letter Roman alphabet for the 35 or so distinctive sounds (phonemes) of Old English, spoken in Britain between the sixth and the eleventh centuries AD. Despite borrowing some runic letters and adding the symbol *æ*, it still proved necessary to use some letters (such as *c* and *g*) to represent more than one sound, and to represent some sounds by combinations of letters (such as *sc* – the equivalent of modern *sh*).

After the Norman Conquest, French scribes introduced several new spelling conventions. A number of Old English forms were replaced, such as *cw* by *qu* in such words as *quick* and *queen*. Other replacements included *h* by *gh* (*might*, *enough*), *c* by *ch* (*church*), and *u* by *ou* (*house*). They began to use *c* before *e* and *i* in such words as *cell* and *city*. Because the letter *u* was handwritten in a very similar way to some other letters (*v, i, n, m*), they tried to ease the reading task in some sequences of these letters by replacing it with *o* (*come, love, one, son*), thereby initiating a set of spelling exceptions (the handwriting problem disappeared after printing became routine, but the spellings stayed). By the beginning of the 15th century, English spelling was a mixture of two systems – Old English and French.

The introduction of printing caused several problems. Many early printers came from the Continent, and brought their own spelling norms with them. The distinctive *gh-* in such words as *ghost* is Dutch in origin. A major beneficial effect of printing, however, was to impose order on the many alternative spellings found in manuscripts. A word like *might* is found in over 30 spellings during the Middle English period.

Although spelling thereafter was much more stable, speech was not. There was a major change in the pronunciation of vowel sounds during the fifteenth century (the so-called 'great vowel shift'), but the spellings remained the same. Modern spellings thus in many respects more accurately reflect the way people spoke in Chaucer's time: *name*, for instance, would have sounded something like 'nah-muh'. Similarly, because of pronunciation change, we are left with many silent letters, as in *knee* and *knight*. The *k* ceased to be sounded after the writing conventions were established.

Another kind of complication emerged in the 16th century, when scholars tried to introduce a knowledge of a word's history (etymology) into its spelling. The *b* in *debt*, for example, was added by people who thought it was important to know that the word comes from *debitum* in Latin. Similarly, a *b* was added to *doubt* (from *dubitare*) and a *g* to *reign* (from *regnare*). The attempt by some spelling reformers to 'tidy up' the spelling was often helpful, but it also increased the number of irregular forms – the *gh* of *night* and *light*, for example, was extended to such words as *delight* and *tight*.

In the late 16th and early 17th centuries, a new wave of loan words arrived in English from such languages as French, Latin, Greek, Spanish, Italian, and Portuguese. They brought with them a host of alien spellings which greatly complicated the learning of longer words. Examples include *bizarre, brusque, caustic, cocoa, epitome, gazette, grotto, idiosyncrasy, intrigue,* and *pneumonia*. The loan-word situation continues to the present day, with such forms as *intifada, perestroika, arbitrageur,* and *chlamydia*.

A new dimension was added to the spelling system in the early 18th century, when Noah Webster altered the spellings of many words as part of his aim to introduce an American standard. An independent nation, he felt, needed an independent system, 'in language as well as government'. On this basis, he advocated the deletion of *u* in *-our* endings (*color*) and *k* from those ending in *-ick* (*music*), and such replacements as *-re* by *-er* (*theater*), *-ce* by *-se* (*defense*), and *ll* by single *l* before a suffix, when the stress is on the first syllable (*traveling*, but not in *excelling*). Several of his other proposals, such as the dropping of silent letters (*fether*, *ile*) or final *e* (*definit*, *examin*) never caught on. But the dropping of *-k* in such words as *music* became standard everywhere.

The result is a system which is an amalgam of several traditions – chiefly Anglo-Saxon, French, and Classical Latin/Greek. However, these are but the chief sources feeding the English habit of borrowing words and their spellings from anywhere and everywhere. It is said to be one of the strengths of the language that it has such a large and varied lexicon, but this is bought at the expense of an increasingly diversified spelling system.

It is moreover a system that continues to change. During the twentieth century American English usage increasingly influenced British, and the arrival of the Internet caused further changes (especially the dropping of diacritics). The result has been an increase in the number of alternative forms used by educated people in different countries. The main US and UK trends are reflected in the present book, but readers should be aware that practice varies around the English-speaking world.

A noticeable feature of this variation is the practice of hyphenation. A compound word first introduced with a space will in due course usually become hyphenated, and eventually be written solid (as in *flower pot*, *flower-pot*, *flowerpot*). This book represents the most frequently used forms, but there is a great deal of variation, especially since the arrival of the Internet, where software has made hyphenation largely a thing of the past.

David Crystal

Conventions

The following regular word-endings are not shown:

- noun plurals formed by adding -s or -es, e.g. *cat / cats, horse / horses, box / boxes, scratch / scratches*
- verb endings formed by adding -s, -ed, and -ing, e.g. *walk / walks / walked / walking*
- verbs ending in -ify, which change to -ifies, -ified, and -ifying, e.g. *deify / deifies / deified / deifying*
- verbs ending in -e, which drop the -e when adding -ed and -ing, e.g. *smile / smiled / smiling*
- adjective endings formed by adding -er and -est, e.g. *tall / taller / tallest*
- adjectives ending in -e, which drop the e when adding -er and -est, e.g. *wise / wiser / wisest*
- adjectives ending in -y, where -y changes to -i, e.g. *happy / happier / happiest*

All irregular forms are shown in parentheses. We also show cases where there is consonant doubling after a short vowel in a monosyllabic word, as the omission of the doubled consonant is a common spelling error, e.g. *big (~gger, ~ggest), fit (~tted, ~tting)*.

Compound words are listed only when the two elements are usually written solid (as in *nightshirt*) or hyphenated (*night-time*). Compounds or affixed forms are not included when the spelling can be easily deduced from the constituent parts (e.g. most words beginning with *non* or *over*). Common two-word foreign phrases (such as *sub judice*) are given in full.

The word *or* precedes an alternative spelling. When a word is also written with a capital, this is shown in parenthesis.

The abbreviations *UK* (for British English) and *US* (for American English) indicate preferred usage in parts of the world which follow these standards.

In cases where an originally US usage has become established in the UK (as with many scientific terms, such as *pediatrics* alongside *paediatrics*), the usage is simply shown as an alternative, preceded by *or*.

The tilde (~) represents part of a word given in full earlier in an entry:

persona (*pl* ~nae) = persona (*pl* personae)
personalising (*or* ~iz~) = personalising (*or* personalizing)
leviathan (L~) = leviathan (Leviathan)

Words which are commonly confused are given an exclamation mark, along with a cue-word (not a definition) which indicates the meaning distinction:

lessen (! lesson) *reduce*
lesson (! lessen) *teaching*

Abbreviations

adj	adjective
anat	anatomy
astron	astronomy
bot	botany
cf	compare
comp	computing
esp	especially
hera	heraldry
lit	literature
math	mathematics
med	medicine
n	noun
occ	occasional, occasionally
phar	pharmacology
phys	physics
pl	plural
pol	politics
pub	publishing
rel	religion
sg	singular
tab	taboo, offensive, or coarse
tech	technical
tr	trade mark
UK	used in British English
US	used in American English
usu	usually
v	verb

a posteriori
a priori
aardvark
Aaron
abaca
aback
abacus (*pl* ~ci, ~uses)
abaft
abalone
abandon
abandoned
abandonment
abase
abasement
abash
abashed
abashedly
abate
abatement
abatis (*or* ~ttis)
abattoir
Abba
abbacy
Abbasid
abbatial
abbé
abbess
abbey
abbot
abbreviate
abbreviated
abbreviation
abdicate
abdication
abdicator
abdomen
abdominal
abdominally
abduct

abductee
abduction
abductor
abeam
abecedarian
Abel
Aberdeen
Aberdonian
aberrance
aberrancy
aberrant
aberrantly
aberration
abet (~tted, ~tting)
abetment
abetter (*or* ~ttor)
abeyance
abeyant
abhor (~rred, ~rring)
abhorrence
abhorrent
abhorrer
abide
ability
abject
abjection
abjectly
abjectness
abjuration
abjure
Abkhaz
Abkhazia
ablate
ablation
ablative
ablaut
ablaze
able
abled
abloom
ablution
ablutionary
ablutions
ably
abnegate
abnegation
abnegator
abnormal
abnormality
abnormally

aboard
abode
abolish
abolishable
abolisher
abolition
abolitionism
abolitionist
abominable
abominably
abominate
abomination
aboriginal (A~)
aboriginality (A~)
aborigine (A~)
abort
abortifacient
abortion
abortionist
abortive
abortively
aboulia (*or* abul~)
abound
about
above
abracadabra
abrade
abrader
Abraham
abrasion
abrasive
abreact
abreaction
abreactive
abreast
abridge
abridgeable
abridgement
abridger
abroad
abrogate
abrogation
abrogator
abrupt
abruption
abruptly
abruptness
abscess
abscessed
abscond

absconder
abseil
abseiler
abseiling
absence
absent
absentee
absenteeism
absently
absent-minded
absent-mindedly
absent-mindedness
absinth *shrub*
absinthe (*or* ~th) *liqueur*
absolute
absolutely
absolution
absolutism
absolutist
absolve
absorb
absorbability
absorbable
absorbance
absorbed
absorbency
absorbent
absorbing
absorption
absorptive
abstain
abstainer
abstemious
abstemiously
abstemiousness
abstention
abstentionism
abstinence
abstinent
abstinently
abstract
abstracted
abstractedly
abstraction
abstractionism
abstractly
abstractor
abstruse
abstrusely
abstruseness

absurd
absurdism
absurdist
absurdity
abulia (*or* abou~)
abulic
abundance
abundant
abundantly
abuse
abuser
abusive
abusively
abusiveness
abut (~tted, ~tting)
abutment
abuzz
abysm
abysmal
abysmally
abyss
abyssal
Abyssinia
Abyssinian
acacia
academe
academia
academic
academical
academically
academician
academicism
academism
academy (A~)
Acadia
Acadian
acajou
acalculia
acanthus
Acari
acaricide
acarid
acarine
acarology
acausal
acausality
acausally
accede
accelerant
accelerate

acceleration
accelerative
accelerator
accent
accented
accentual
accentuate
accentuation
accept
acceptability
acceptable
acceptableness
acceptably
acceptance
acceptation
accepted
acceptedly
acceptor
Access (*tr*) *credit card*
access *reach*
accessibility
accessible
accessibly
accession
accessorial
accessorise (*or* ~ize)
accessorising (*or* ~iz~)
accessory (*or* ~ary)
acciaccatura
accident
accidental
accidentally
accidie
acclaim
acclaimed
acclamation
acclimation
acclimatisation (*or* ~iz~)
acclimatise (*or* ~ize)
acclivitous
acclivity
accolade
accommodate
accommodating
accommodatingly
accommodation
accommodative
accompaniment
accompanist

accompany
accomplice
accomplish
accomplishment
accord
accordance
accordant
accordingly
according to
accordion
accordionist
accost
account
accountability
accountable
accountably
accountancy
accountant
accounting
accoutre (*US* ~ter)
accoutrement (*US*
  ~ter~)
Accra
accredit
accrete
accretion
accretionary
accretive
accrual
accrue
accrued
acculturate
acculturation
acculturative
accumulate
accumulation
accumulative
accumulator
accuracy
accurate
accurately
accursed
accusal
accusation
accusative
accusatorial
accusatory
accuse
accused
accusing

accusingly
accustom
accustomed
ace
acentric
acerbic
acetate
acetone
acetous
acetyl
acetylene
achar (*or* ~aar)
ache
Acheron
achievability
achievable
achieve
achievement
achiever
Achilles
achiness
aching
achingly
achiote
achondroplasia
achromatic
achromaticity
achromatism
achy
acid
acidic
acidification
acidify
acidity
acidly
acidophilus
acidosis
acidotic
acidulate
acidulous
acidy
ackee (*or* akee)
acknowledge
acknowledgeable (*or*
  ~dga~)
acknowledgement (*or*
  ~dgm~)
acme
acne
acned

acolyte
Aconcagua
aconite
acorn
acoustic
acoustical
acoustically
acoustician
acoustics
acquaint
acquaintance
acquaintanceship
acquainted
acquiesce
acquiescence
acquiescent
acquire
acquired
acquirement
acquirer
acquisition
acquisitive
acquisitively
acquisitiveness
acquit (~tted, ~tting)
acquittal
acquittance
acre
acreage
acrid
acridity
acridly
acrimonious
acrimoniously
acrimony
acrobat
acrobatic
acrobatics
acrocyanosis
acromegaly
acronym
acrophobia
acrophobic
Acropolis *citadel of
  Athens*
acropolis (A~) *ancient
  Greek citadel*
across
acrostic
acrylic

act
acting
actinium
action
actionable
activate
activation
activator
active
actively
activeness
activism
activist
activity
actor
actress
actressy
actual
actualisation (*or* ~iz~)
actualise (*or* ~ize)
actuality
actually
actuarial
actuarially
actuary
actuate
actuation
actuator
acuity
aculeate
acumen
acuminate
acupressure
acupuncture
acupuncturist
acute
acutely
acuteness
acyclic
adage
adagio (*pl* ~os)
Adam
adamance
adamancy
adamant
adamantine
adamantly
adapt
adaptability
adaptable

adaptably
adaptation
adapter (*esp US*)
adaptive
adaptor (*esp UK*)
add
addendum (*pl* ~da, ~ums)
adder
addict
addicted
addiction
addictive
addition
additional
additionally
additive
addle
addled
address
addressable
addressed
addressee
addresser
adduce
adducible
adduct
adduction
adductor
Adelaide
Aden
adenine
adenoidal
adenoids
adept
adeptly
adeptness
adequacy
adequate
adequately
adhere
adherence
adherent
adhesion
adhesive
adhibit
adieu (*pl* ~us, ~ux)
adipose
adjacency
adjacent

adjectival
adjectivally
adjective
adjoin
adjoining
adjourn
adjournment
adjudge
adjudged
adjudgement (*or* ~dgm~)
adjudicate
adjudication
adjudicative
adjudicator
adjunct
adjunction
adjunctive
adjuration
adjuratory
adjure
adjust
adjustability
adjustable
adjuster
adjustment
adjutancy
adjutant
ad-lib (~bbed, ~bbing)
admin
administer
administrable
administrate
administration
administrative
administratively
administrator
admirable
admirably
admiral (A~)
admiralty (A~)
admiration
admire
admirer
admiring
admiringly
admissibility
admissible
admission
admit (~tted, ~tting)

admittance
admittedly
admix
admixture
admonish
admonishment
admonition
admonitory
adnate
ado
adobe
adolescence
adolescent
Adonai
Adonis
adopt
adoptable
adopted
adoptee
adopter
adoption
adoptive
adoptively
adorability
adorable
adorableness
adorably
adoration
adore
adorer
adoringly
adorn
adorner
adornment
adrenal
adrenaline (*or* ~lin)
adrenocorticotrophic
  (*US* ~opic)
adret
Adriatic
adrift
adroit
adroitly
adroitness
adsorb
adsorbability
adsorbable
adsorbent
adsorption
adsorptive

aduki
adulate
adulation
adulator
adulatory
adult
adulterant
adulterate
adulteration
adulterator
adulterer
adulteress (*or* ~tress)
adulterous
adulterously
adultery
adulthood
adultly
adultress (*or* ~teress)
adumbrate
advance
advanced
advancement
advancing
advantage
advantaged
advantageous
advantageously
advent (A~)
Adventism
Adventist
adventitious
adventitiously
adventure
adventurer
adventuress
adventurism
adventurist
adventurous
adventurously
adventurousness
adverb
adverbial
adverbially
adversarial
adversarially
adversary
adverse
adversely
adversity
advert

advertise (*occ* ~ize)
advertisement (*occ*
  ~ize~)
advertiser (*occ* ~iz~)
advertising (*occ* ~iz~)
advertorial
advice
advisability
advisable
advisably
advise
advised
advisedly
adviser (*or* ~or)
advising
advisor (*or* ~er)
advisory
advocaat
advocacy
advocate
advocateship
advocation
adze
adzuki
Aegean
aegis
aegrotat
aeolian (A~; *US* eolian)
aeon (*or* eon; *US* eon)
aerate
aeration
aerator
aerial
aerialist
aeriality
aerially
aerie (*US*; *UK* eyrie)
aerobatic
aerobatics
aerobe
aerobic
aerobically
aerobics
aerodrome (*UK*)
aerodynamic
aerodynamically
aerodynamics
aerofoil (*UK*)
aerogel
aerogramme (*or* ~gram)

aerology
aeronaut
aeronautic
aeronautical
aeronautically
aeronautics
aeroplane
aerosol
aerospace
aesthete (*esp UK; or* es~)
aesthetic (*esp UK; or*
  es~)
aesthetician (*esp UK; or*
  es~)
aestival (*esp UK; or* es~)
aestivate (*esp UK; or* es~)
aestivation (*esp UK; or*
  es~)
aether (*esp UK; or* eth~)
aetiology (*esp UK; or*
  et~)
afar
afebrile
affability
affable
affably
affair
affect (! effect) (*v*) *have*
  an effect; (*n*) *emotion*
affectation
affected
affecting
affectingly
affection
affectionate
affective
affectless
affectlessness
affenpinscher
afferent
affidavit
affiliate
affiliated
affiliation
affiliative
affinity
affirm
affirmation
affirmative
affirmatory

affirmer
affix
affixation
afflatus
afflict
afflicted
affliction
afflictive
affluence
affluent
affluently
afford
afforest
afforestation
affray
affricate
affront
Afghan
Afghanistan
aficionado (*pl* ~os)
afield
aflame
afloat
afoot
aforementioned
aforesaid
aforethought
afraid
afresh
Africa
African
Africana
Africanise (*or* ~ize)
Afrikaans
Afrikaner
Afro
aft
after
afterbirth
afterburner
aftercare
afterdamp
afterglow
after-image
afterlife
aftermath
afternoon
afters (*UK*)
aftersales
aftershock

aftersun
aftertaste
afterthought
afterwards (*US also*
  ~ward)
Aga
again
against
Agamemnon
agapanthus
agape *wide*
agape (A~) *love*
agar
agaric
agate
agave
age
aged
ageing (*esp UK; US esp*
  aging)
ageism (*esp UK; US esp*
  agism)
ageist (*esp UK; US esp*
  agist)
ageless
agency
agenda
agent
agglomerate
agglomeration
agglomerative
agglutinate
agglutinated
agglutinating
agglutination
agglutinative
aggradation
aggrandise (*or* ~ize)
aggrandisement (*or*
  ~ize~)
aggrandiser (*or* ~iz~)
aggravate
aggravated
aggravating
aggravatingly
aggravation
aggregate
aggregation
aggregative
aggression

aggressive
aggressively
aggressiveness
aggressor
aggro
aghast
agile
agilely
agility
aging *see* ageing
agism *see* ageism
agist *see* ageist
agitate
agitated
agitatedly
agitation
agitator
agitprop
agleam
aglet
aglow
agnate
agnosia
agnostic
agnosticism
ago
agog
agonise (*or* ~ize)
agonised (*or* ~ized)
agonising (*or* ~iz~)
agonisingly (*or* ~iz~)
agonistic
agony
agoraphobe
agoraphobia
agoraphobic
agraphia
agrarian
agree
agreeability
agreeable
agreeableness
agreeably
agreement
agribusiness (*or* agro~)
agrichemical
agricultural
agriculturalist
agriculturally
agriculture

agriculturist
agrimony
agrobusiness (*or* agri~)
agronomic
agronomical
agronomically
agronomist
agronomy
aground
ague
ahead
ahimsa
ahistorical
ahoy
ai (*pl* ais)
aid (! aide) *assistance*
aide (! aid) *assistant*
aide-de-camp (*pl* aides~)
Aids (*or* AIDS)
aiguille
aiguillette
aikido
ail
aileron
ailing
ailment
aim
aimless
aimlessly
aimlessness
air
airborne
airbrush
Airbus
aircraft
aircrew
airdrop
Airedale
airer
airfield
airfoil (*US*)
airframe
airgun
airhead
airhole
airily
airiness
airing
airless
airlift

airline
airliner
airlock
airmail
airman (~men)
airplane (*US*)
airplay
airport
airship
airsick
airspace
airspeed
airstrip
airtight
airtime
airwaves
airway
airworthy
airy
aisle
aisled
aitch (*or* haitch)
Ajaccio
ajar
Ajax
akee *see* ackee
akimbo
akin
akvavit (*or* aqua~)
Alabama
alabaster
alack
alacritous
alacrity
alarm
alarmed
alarming
alarmingly
alarmism
alarmist
alas
Alaska
alb
albacore
Albania
Albanian
albatross
albeit
albinic
albinism

albinistic
albino (*pl* ~os)
Albion
album
albumen
alchemic
alchemical
alchemise (*or* ~ize)
alchemist
alchemy
alcohol
alcoholic
alcoholicity
alcoholism
alcopop (A~)
alcove
Aldebaran
aldehyde
alder
alderman (*UK; pl* ~men)
aldis (A~)
ale
aleatoric
aleatory
alehouse
alert
alertly
alertness
Aleut
Aleutian
alevin
alewife
Alexander
Alexandria
alexandrine
alexia
alfalfa
alfresco (*esp UK; US esp*
  al fresco)
alga (*pl* ~ae)
algebra
algebraic
algebraical
algebraically
algebraist
Algeria
Algerian
Algonquian (*or* ~nkian)
Algonquin (*or* ~nkin)
algorithm

alias
alibi (*pl* ~bis)
alien
alienability
alienable
alienate
alienated
alienation
alienness
aliform
alight
align
aligned
alignment
alike
alimentary
alimentation
alimony
aliphatic
aliteracy
aliterate
alive
alkali (*pl* ~lis)
alkaline
alkalinity
alkalisation (*or* ~iz~)
alkalise (*or* ~ize)
alkaliser (*or* ~iz~)
alkaloid
alkalosis
all
all right (*or* alright)
Allah
allay
allegation
allege
alleged
allegedly
allegiance
allegoric
allegorical
allegorically
allegorisation (*or* ~iz~)
allegorise (*or* ~ize)
allegorist
allegory
allegretto (*pl* ~tti)
allegro (*pl* ~ri)
allele
allelomorph

alleluia (*or* hallelujah)
allergen
allergenic
allergenicity
allergic
allergy
alleviate
alleviation
alleviative
alleviator
alley (*pl* ~eys)
alleyway
alliance
allied
alligator
alliterate
alliteration
alliterative
allocatable
allocate
allocation
allocative
allocator
allocution
allosaurus
allot (~tted, ~tting)
allotment
allotrope
allotropy
allottee
allow
allowable
allowably
allowance
allowedly
alloy
allspice
allude
allure
allurement
alluring
alluringly
allusion
allusive (! elusive)
  referring
allusively (! elusively)
allusiveness
  (! elusiveness)
alluvium
ally

almanac
almandine
Almaty
almightily
almightiness
almighty
almond
almoner
almost
alms
almshouse
aloe
aloft
aloha
alone
along
alongside
aloof
aloofness
alopecia
aloud
alp
alpaca
alpenhorn
alpenstick
alpha
alphabet
alphabetic
alphabetical
alphabetically
alphabetise (or ~ize)
alphameric
alphanumeric
alphorn
alpine (A~)
alpinist (A~)
Alps
already
alright (or all right)
Alsace
Alsatian
also
Altaic
Altair
altar (n; ! alter) table
altarpiece
alter (v; ! altar) change
alter ego
alterable
alteration

altercate
altercation
altered
alternate
alternately
alternating
alternation
alternative
alternator
althorn
although
altimeter
altimetry
Altiplano
altissimo
altitude
alto
altocumulus
altogether
altostratus
altruism
altruist
altruistic
altruistically
alum
alumina
aluminium (US ~inum)
alumna (pl ~ae)
alumnus (pl ~ni)
alveolar
alveolus (pl ~li)
always
alyssum
Alzheimer's
amalgam
amalgamate
amalgamated
amalgamation
amanuensis (pl ~nses)
amaranth
amaretti
amaretto
amaryllis
amass
amasser
amateur
amateurish
amateurishly
amateurishness
amatory

amaurosis
amaurotic
amaze
amazement
amazing
amazingly
amazingness
Amazon
Amazonian
ambassador
ambassadorial
ambassadorship
ambassadress
amber
ambergris
ambiance see ambience
ambidexterity
ambidextrous
ambidextrously
ambidextrousness
ambience (esp UK; US
  esp ~iance)
ambient
ambiguity
ambiguous
ambiguously
ambiguousness
ambisexual
ambisonics
ambit
ambition
ambitious
ambitiously
ambitiousness
ambivalence
ambivalent
ambivalently
ambiversion
ambivert
amble
ambler
ambrosia
ambulance
ambulant
ambulate
ambulation
ambulatory
ambuscade
ambush
ameba see amoeba

amebic (*esp US; cf*
  amoebic)
ameliorate
amelioration
ameliorative
ameliorator
amen (A~)
amenability
amenable
amenably
amend (! emend) *change*
  content
amendable
amender
amendment
amends
amenity
amenorrhoea (*or*
  ~rrhea)
amentia
Amerasian
America
American
Americana
Americanisation (*or*
  ~iz~)
Americanise (*or* ~ize)
Americanism
americium
Amerindian
Ameslan
amethyst
amethystine
Amex
Amharic
amiability
amiable
amiableness
amiably
amicability
amicable
amicableness
amicably
amid
amide
amidships (*US also*
  ~ship)
amigo
amine
amino

amir (*or* em~)
amirate (*or* em~)
Amish
amiss
amity
ammeter
ammo
ammonia
ammoniacal
ammonite
ammonium
ammunition
amnesia
amnesiac
amnesic
amnesty
amniocentesis (*pl* ~eses)
amnion (*pl* ~ia, ~ions)
amniotic
amoeba (*pl* ~ae, ~as; *or*
  ameba)
amoebic (*or* amebic)
amok (*occ* amuck)
among
amongst
amontillado (A~, *pl*
  ~os)
amoral
amoralism
amoralist
amorality
amoroso (A~, *pl* ~os)
amorous
amorously
amorousness
amorphous
amorphously
amorphousness
amortisation (*or* ~iz~)
amortise (*or* ~ize)
Amos
amount
amour
amperage
ampere (*or* ~ère)
ampersand
amphetamine
amphibian
amphibious
amphibiously

amphibole
amphisbaena (A~, *pl*
  ~as, ~ae; *or* ~bena~)
amphitheatre (*US* ~ter)
amphora (*pl* ~ae, ~as)
amphoteric
ampicillin (A~)
ample
ampleness
amplification
amplifier
amplify
amplitude
amply
ampoule (*US also* ~pule,
  ~pul)
ampulla
amputate
amputation
amputator
amputee
Amsterdam
Amtrak
amuck *see* amok
amulet
amuse
amused
amusedly
amusement
amusing
amusingly
amygdala (*pl* ~ae)
amygdaloid
amylase
amytal (A~, *tr*)
Anabaptism
Anabaptist
anabatic
anabolic
anabolism
anachronic
anachronism
anachronistic
anachronistically
anacoluthon (*pl* ~tha)
anaconda
anacrusis (*pl* ~uses)
anaemia (*or* ~nem~)
anaemic (*or* ~nem~)
anaerobe (*or* ~er~)

anaerobic (or ~er~)
anaerobically (or ~er~)
anaesthesia (or anes~)
anaesthesiology (or
    anes~)
anaesthetic (or anes~)
anaesthetics (or anes~)
anaesthetisation (or
    anes~, ~iz~)
anaesthetise (or anes~,
    ~ize)
anaesthetised (or anes~,
    ~ized)
anaesthetist (or anes~)
anaglyph
anaglyphic
anaglypta (A~, tr)
anagram (~mmed,
    ~mming)
anagrammatise (or ~ize)
anal
analectic
analects (or ~cta)
analeptic
analgesia
analgesic
analgia
anally
analog (US comp; or
    ~logue)
analogical
analogically
analogise (or ~ize)
analogous
analogously
analogue (UK; ~log
    comp)
analogy
analphabetic
analysable
analyse (US ~yze)
analyser (US ~yzer)
analysis (pl ~ses)
analyst
analytic
analytical
analytically
anamorphic
anamorphosis
ananda

anapaest (or ~pest)
anaphrodisiac
anaphylactic
anaphylaxis
anarchic
anarchical
anarchically
anarchism
anarchist
anarchistic
anarchy
anathema
anathematise (or ~ize)
Anatolian
anatomical
anatomically
anatomise (or ~ize)
anatomising (or ~iz~)
anatomist
anatomy
ancestor
ancestral
ancestry
anchor
anchorage
anchorite
anchorman (pl ~men)
anchorwoman (pl
    ~women)
anchovy
anchylosis (or ankyl~)
anchylotic (or ankyl~)
ancient (A~ for a
    particular location or
    period)
anciently
ancientness
ancillary
andalusite
andante
andantino
Andean
Andes
andiron
Andorra
androecium (pl ~ia)
androgen
androgenic
androgenisation (or
    ~iz~)

androgenise (or ~ize)
androgyne
androgynous
androgyny
android
Andromeda
andromeda
anecdotage
anecdotal
anecdotalist
anecdotally
anecdote
anechoic
anemia see anaemia
anemic see anaemic
anemone
anergia
anerobe and related
    forms, see anaerobe
aneroid
anesthesia and related
    forms, see anaesthesia
aneurysm (or ~ism)
anew
anfractuosity
anfractuous
angel
angelfish
angelic
angelica
angelical
angelically
angelology
anger
angered
angina
angiogram
angiography
angiosperm
Angle (n) tribe
angle (n) shape,
    viewpoint, (v) fish
angled
angler
Anglesey
Anglican
anglicisation (or
    ~iz~)
anglicise (or ~ize)
Anglicism

Anglo
anglophile (A~, *occ*
 ~phil)
anglophobe (A~)
anglophobia (A~)
anglophobic (A~)
anglophone (A~)
Anglo-Saxon
Angola
Angolan
angora (A~)
Angostura
angostura
angrily
angry
angst
angstrom (*occ* ång~)
anguilliform
anguish
anguished
angular
angularity
angularly
angulate
angulated
angulation
anhydrous
aniline
animal
animalise (*or* ~ize)
animalism
animalistic
animality
animate
animated
animation
animator
animatronics
anime
animism
animist
animistic
animosity
animus
anion
anise
aniseed
Ankara
ankh
ankle

anklet
ankylosaur
ankylosis (*or* anchyl~)
ankylotic (*or* anchyl~)
annal
annalist
annalistic
annatto (*occ* ana~)
anneal
annealer
annelid
annex (*UK also* ~xe *as a
 noun*)
annexation
annexationist
annihilate
annihilation
annihilator
anniversary
Anno Domini (*or* a~
 d~)
annotatable
annotate
annotation
annotative
annotator
announce
announcement
announcer
annoy
annoyance
annoyed
annoyer
annoying
annoyingly
annual
annually
annuity
annul (~lled, ~lling)
annular
annularly
annulment
annunciate
Annunciation
annunciator
annus horribilis
annus mirabilis
anode
anodise (*or* ~ize)
anodyne

anoint
anointed
anomalous
anomalously
anomalousness
anomaly
anomie (*or* ~my)
anon
anonym
anonymity
anonymous
anonymously
anopheles (A~)
anorak
anorexia
anorexic (*or* ~ectic)
anosmia
another
anoxia
anoxic
anserine
answer
answerable
answering
answerphone
ant
antacid
antagonise (*or* ~ize)
antagonism
antagonist
antagonistic
antagonistically
Antarctic
Antarctica
Antares
antbear
antbird
ante *stake in card
 gambling*
ante (! anti-) *before*
anteater
antecedence
antecedent
antecedently
antechamber
antedate
antediluvian
antelope
antenatal
antenatally

antenna (*pl insects* ~ae,
  pl aerials also ~as)
antepenultimate
anterior
anteriority
anteriorly
ante-room
anthelion (*pl* ~ia)
anthem
anthemic
anther
anthill
anthocyanin
anthologise (*or* ~ize)
anthology
anthracite
anthracitic
anthrax
anthropoid
anthropological
anthropologist
anthropology
anthropomorphic
anthropomorphise (*or*
  ~ize)
anthropomorphism
anthropomorphous
anthropophagous
anthropophagy
anti (! ante) *against,
  opposed to*
antibiosis
antibiotic
antibiotics
antibody
antic
antichrist (A~)
anticipate
anticipation
anticipative
anticipator
anticipatory
anticlerical
anticlericalism
anticlimax
anticline
anticlockwise
anticoagulant
anticyclone
antidepressant

antidote
antifreeze
antigen
antigenic
antigravity
Antigua
antihero
antihistamine
anti-lock
antimacassar
antimatter
antimony
antinomian (A~)
antinomy
antinuclear
antioxidant
antiparticle
antipasto (*pl* ~sti)
antipathetic
antipathy
anti-personnel
antiperspirant (*occ*
  anti-~)
antiphon
antiphonal
antiphonally
antiphony
Antipodean
antipodes (A~)
antipruritic
antipsychotic
antipyretic
antiquarian
antiquarianism
antiquary
antiquated
antique
antiquity
antiracism
antirrhinum
anti-semite (*or* ~S~)
antisemitic (*or* anti-~,
  ~S~)
antisemitism (*or* anti-~,
  ~S~)
antisepsis
antiseptic
antiseptically
antiserum (*pl* ~ra)
antisexist

antisocial
antispasmodic
antistatic
antithesis (*pl* ~eses)
antithetical
antithetically
antitrust
antitype
antivenin
antivenom
antiviral
antivirus
antivivisection
antivivisectionist
antler
antlered
antonym
antonymy
anus
anvil
anxiety
anxious
anxiously
anxiousness
anybody
anyhow
anymore
anyone
anyplace
anything
anytime
anyway
anywhere
Anzac (ANZAC)
aorta (*pl* ~ae, ~as)
Apache
apart
apartheid
apartment
apartness
apathetic
apathetically
apathy
apatosaurus (*pl* ~ri,
  ~uses)
ape
aperient
aperitif
aperture
APEX (*or* Apex) *ticketing*

apex (*pl* apices, apexes)
  highest part
aphasia
aphelion
aphid
aphorism
aphrodisiac
apiarist
apiary
apical
apiculture
apiece
apish
apishly
apishness
aplenty
aplomb
apnoea (*or* ~nea)
Apocalypse *biblical book*
apocalypse *revelation*
  about the future
apocalyptic
apocalyptically
apocope
Apocrypha *biblical book*
Apocryphal *relating to*
  the biblical book
apocryphal *rumours*
apogee
Apollo *god; spacecraft*
apollo *handsome man*
Apollyon
apologetic
apologetically
apologetics
apologia
apologise (*or* ~ize)
apologist
apology
apoplectic
apoplectically
apoplexy
apostasy
apostate
apostatise (*or* ~ize)
apostle (A~)
apostolate
apostolic
apostrophe
apothecary

apothegm (*or*
  apophth~)
apotheosis (*pl* ~oses)
apotheosise (*or* ~ize)
appal (*US* appall; ~lled,
  ~lling)
Appaloosa
apparatchik (*pl* ~ks,
  ~ki)
apparatus (*pl* ~uses, *occ*
  ~us)
apparel (*v esp US* ~led,
  ~ling; *esp UK* ~lled,
  ~lling)
apparent
apparently
apparition
apparitional
appeal
appealable
appealer
appealing
appear
appearance
appease
appeasement
appeaser
appellant
appellation
append
appendage
appendectomy (*UK also*
  ~dicec~)
appendicitis
appendix (*pl med* ~ixes;
  pl pub UK ~ices; *US*
  ~ixes *or* ~ices *for both*)
appertain
appetiser (*or* ~izer)
appetising (*or* ~iz~)
appetite
applaud
applause
apple
applet
Appleton
appliance
applicability
applicable
applicably

applicant
application
applicational
applicative
applicator
applied
appliqué
apply
appoggiatura (*pl* ~ras,
  ~re)
appoint
appointed
appointee
appointer
appointment
apportion
apportionable
apportionment
appose
apposite
appositely
appositeness
apposition
appositional
appositive
appraisable
appraisal
appraisee
appraisement
appraiser
appraisingly
appraisive
appreciable
appreciably
appreciate
appreciation
appreciative
appreciatively
appreciativeness
appreciator
appreciatory
apprehend
apprehensible
apprehension
apprehensive
apprehensively
apprehensiveness
apprentice
apprenticed
apprenticeship

apprise (*or* ~ize)
approach
approachability
approachable
approbation
appropriate
appropriately
appropriateness
appropriation
appropriator
approval
approve
approved
approving
approvingly
approximate
approximately
approximation
approximative
appurtenance
appurtenant
apraxia
après-ski
apricot
April
apron
aproned
apropos
apse
apsidal
apt
apterous
apteryx
aptitude
aptly
aptness
aqua-
aqua vitae
aquaculture (*occ* aqui~)
aqualung
aquamarine
aquanaut
aquaplane
aquaplaning
aquarelle
aquarist
aquarium (*pl* ~ia,
  ~iums)
Aquarius
aquarobics

aquatic
aquatics
aquatint
aquavit (*or* akva~)
aqueduct (*occ* aqua~)
aqueous
aquiculture (*or* aqua~)
aquifer
aquiline
Arab
arabesque
Arabia
Arabian
Arabic
arabica
Arabisation (*or* ~iz~)
Arabise (*or* ~ize)
Arabism
arable
arachnid
arachnoid
arachnophobia
aragonite
Aramaean (*or* ~mean)
Aramaic
Arapaho
Aran
Ararat
arbalest (*or* arblast)
arbiter
arbitrage
arbitrageur (*or* ~ger)
arbitraging
arbitrament
arbitrarily
arbitrariness
arbitrary
arbitrate
arbitration
arbitrator
arbor (*UK* ~our)
arboreal
arboreality
arborescence
arborescent
arbour (*US* ~or)
arboured (*US* ~or ~)
arc (arced, arcing; *or*
  arcked, arcking)
arcade

arcana
arcane
arch
Archaean (*or* ~ean)
archaeology (*or* arche~)
archaeopteryx (A~; *or*
  arche~)
archaic
archaically
archaising (*or* ~iz~)
archaism
archaistic
archangel (A~)
archbishop
archbishopric
archdeacon
archdiocese
archduchess
archduchy
archduke
arched
archegonium
archeology *see*
  archaeology
archer
archerfish
archery
archetypal
archetype
archimandrite
Archimedes
archipelago (*pl* ~os)
architect
architectonic
architectural
architecturally
architecture
architrave
archive
archivist
archly
archness
archway
Arctic
Arcturus
ardency
ardent
ardently
ardour (*US* ~or)
arduous

arduously
arduousness
area
areca
arena
areola
arête
argent
Argentina
Argentine
Argentinian
argillaceous
argon
argot
arguable
arguably
argue
argument
argumentation
argumentative
argumentatively
argumentativeness
argyle (*occ* A~) *knitting*
Argyll *Scotland*
aria
Arian
Arianism
arid
aridity
aridly
aridness
Aries
aright
arise (arose, arisen, arising)
aristocracy
aristocrat
aristocratic
aristocratically
Aristotelian (*or* ~ean)
Aristotle
arithmetic
arithmetical
arithmetically
arithmetician
Arizona
ark
arm
armada (A~)
armadillo (*pl* ~os)

Armageddon
Armagnac
Armalite (*tr*)
armament
armature
armband
armchair
armed
Armenia
Armenian
armful
armhole
armiger
armistice
armlock
armorial
armour (*US* ~or)
armoured (*US* ~or~)
armourer (*US* ~or~)
armoury (*US* ~ory)
armpit
armrest
army
arnica
aroma
aromatherapeutic
aromatherapist
aromatherapy
aromatic
aromatically
aromatisation (*or* ~iz~)
aromatise (*or* ~ize)
around
arousal
arouse
arousing
arpeggiation
arpeggio
arquebus
arraign
arraigned
arraignment
arrange
arranged
arrangement
arrant
arrantly
arras
array
arrears

arrest
arrestable
arrestee (*US*)
arrester (*or* ~or)
arresting
arrhythmia
arrival
arrive
arrivisme
arriviste
arrogance
arrogant
arrogantly
arrogate
arrow
arrowed
arrowgrass
arrowhead
arrowroot
arse
arsehole
arsenal
arsenic
arsenical
arsenide
arsine
art
Artaxerxes
artefact (*or* arti~)
artemisia
arterial
arterialisation (*or* ~iz~)
arterialise (*or* ~ize)
arterialised (*or* ~ized)
arterialising (*or* ~iz~)
arteriole
arteriosclerosis (*pl* ~oses)
artery
artesian
artful
artfully
artfulness
arthralgia
arthritic
arthritis
arthropod
artichoke
article
articulate

articulated
articulating
articulation
articulator
artifact *see* artefact
artifice
artificer
artificial
artificiality
artillery
artisan
artist
artiste
artistic
artistically
artistry
artless
artlessness
artwork
arty
Aruba
arum
Aryan
arytenoid
asafoetida (*US* ~fe~)
Asam
asbestos
asbestosis
ascend
ascendancy (*or* ~ency)
ascendant (*or* ~ent)
ascender
Ascension *feast*
ascension (*astron, hera*)
ascent
ascertain
ascetic
ascorbic
ascribe
ascribing
ascription
asepsis
aseptic
asepticism
asexual
asexuality
asexually
ash
ashamed
ashamedly

ashcan
ashen
Ashes
ashore
ashram
ashtray
ashy
Asia
Asian
Asiatic
aside
asinine
asininity
ask
askance
askant
askew
asking
aslant
asleep
asocial
asocially
asp
asparagine
asparagus
aspartame
aspect
aspectual
Asperger's
asperity
aspersion
asphalt
asphaltic
aspheric
aspherical
asphodel
asphyxia
asphyxiate
asphyxiation
asphyxiator
aspic
aspidistra
aspirant
aspirate
aspirated
aspiration
aspirator
aspiratory
aspire
aspirin

aspiring
asprawl
ass
assail
assailable
assailant
Assamese
assassin
assassinate
assassinated
assassination
assault
assay
assayer
assegai (*or* ~sa~)
assemblage
assemblance
assemble
assembler
assembling
assembly
assent
assenter (*or* ~or)
assentient
assert
assertion
assertive
assertively
assertiveness
assess
assessment
assessor
asset
asseverate
assiduity
assiduous
assiduously
assiduousness
assign
assignable
assignation
assigned
assignee
assigner
assignment
assimilate
assimilated
assimilation
assimilative
assimilator

assimilatory
assist
assistance
assistant
assisted
assize (A~)
associability
associable
associate
associated
association
associative
associativeness
associativity
assonance
assonant
assonate
assort
assorted
assortment
assuage
assuagement
assume
assumed
assumedly
assuming
Assumption *feast*
assumption *principle*
assumptive
assurance
assure
assured
assuredly
assuring
assymmetric
assymmetrical
Assyrian
Assyriology
astatine
aster
asterisk
astern
asteroid
asthenia
asthenic
asthenosphere
asthma
asthmatic
astigmatic
astigmatism

astir
astonish
astonishing
astonishingly
astonishment
astound
astounding
Astrakhan *city*
astrakhan *fur*
astral
astray
astride
astringency
astringent
astringently
astrochemical
astrochemist
astrochemistry
astrodome (*US*)
astrolabe
astrologer
astrological
astrologist
astrology
astrometric
astrometry
astronaut
astronautical
astronautics
astronomer
astronomic
astronomical
astronomically
astronomy
astrophysical
astrophysicist
astrophysics
Astroturf (*tr*)
astute
astutely
astuteness
asunder
asylum
asymmetric
asymmetrical
asymmetrically
asymmetry
asymptote
ataractic (*or* ~axic)
ataraxia

ataraxy
atavism
atavist
atavistic
atavistically
ataxia
ataxic (*or* ~actic)
ataxy
ate
atelier
atemporal
atemporality
atheism
atheist
atheistic
atheistical
atheroma
atherosclerosis
athlete
athletic
athleticism
Atlantic
atlas
atman
atmosphere
atmospheric
atoll
atom
atomic
atomically
atomicity
atomisation (*or* ~iz~)
atomise (*or* ~ize)
atomiser (*or* ~iz~)
atonal
atonalism
atonality
atone
atonement
atonic
atonicity
atony
atop
atrioventricular
atrium (*pl* ~ia, ~iums)
atrocious
atrociously
atrociousness
atrocity
atrophy

atropine
attach
attachable
attaché
attached
attachment
attack
attacker
attacking
attain
attainability
attainable
attainableness
attainment
attar
attempt
attemptable
attempter
attend
attendance
attendant
attended
attender
attention
attentive
attentively
attentiveness
attenuate
attenuated
attenuating
attenuation
attenuator
attest
attestable
attestation
attestor
Attic *of ancient Athens*
attic *room under a roof*
attire
attired
attitude
attitudinal
attitudinisation (or
  ~iz~)
attitudinise (or ~ize)
attitudiniser (or ~iz~)
attorney
attract
attraction
attractive

attractiveness
attributable
attribute
attribution
attributive
attributively
attrition
attritional
attritive
attune
attuned
attunement
attuning
atypical
atypically
au fait
au lait
au naturel
au pair
au revoir
aubade
aubergine
aubrietia (or ~ret~)
auburn
Auckland
auction
auctioned
auctioneer
auctioneering
audacious
audaciously
audaciousness
audacity
audibility
audible
audibly
audience
audio
audiogram
audiometer
audiometry
audiotape
audiovisual
audit
audition
auditive
auditor
auditorial
auditorium (*pl* ~ia,
  ~iums)

auditory
auger (! augur) *tool*
aught (! ought)
augment
augmentation
augmentative
augmented
augmenter (or ~or)
augur (! auger) *portend*
augury
August *month*
august *noble, imposing*
Augustan *of emperor
  Augustus*
Augustine *Christian saint*
Augustinian
augustly
augustness
auk
auklet
auld lang syne
aunt
auntie (or ~ty; A~ *as
  title*)
aura (*pl* ~as, ~ae)
aural (! oral) *of the ear*
aurally (! orally)
aureate
aureole (or ~la)
auricle
auricula (*pl* ~ae, ~as)
auricular
auriculate
auriculated
auriferous
aurochs
aurora (*pl* ~ae, ~as)
auscultation
auspices
auspicious
auspiciousness
Aussie
austere
austerity
austral
Australasia
Australasian
Australia
Australian
Australiana

Australianism
australopithecine
Austria
Austrian
Austronesia
Austronesian
auteur
auteurism
authentic
authentically
authenticate
authenticated
authenticating
authentication
authenticator
authenticity
author
authoress
authorial
authoring
authorisation (or ~iz~)
authorise (or ~ize)
authoriser (or ~iz~)
authoritarian
authoritarianism
authoritative
authoritativeness
authority
authorship
autism
autistic
auto
autobahn
autobiographer
autobiographic
autobiographical
autobiography
autochthon (pl ~ns,
 ~nes)
autochthonous
autoclave
autocracy
autocrat
autocratic
autocratically
autocross
autocue (A~, tr)
auto-da-fé (pl autos~)
auto-destruct
auto-destruction

autodidact
autodidactic
autofocus
autofocusing (or ~ssing)
autogiro (or ~gyro; pl
 ~os)
autograph
autographic
autoharp
autoimmune
autoimmunity
autolysis
autolytic
automat
automate
automated
automatic
automatically
automation
automaton (pl ~ta,
 ~tons)
automobile
automobilia
automobilist
automotive
autonomic
autonomically
autonomous
autonomously
autonomy
autopilot
autopsy
autorickshaw
autoroute
autostrada
auto-suggestion
autumn
autumnal
auxiliary
auxin
avail
availability
available
availableness
availably
avalanche
avant-garde
avarice
avaricious
avariciously

avariciousness
avascular
avast
avatar
Ave
avenge
avenger
avenue (A~ for a named
 street)
aver (~rred, ~rring)
average
averagely
averse
aversion
aversive
avert
avertable
averted
Avesta
Avestan
avian
aviary
aviation
aviator
aviatrix
avicultural
aviculturalism
aviculturalist
aviculture
avid
avidity
avidly
avionic
avionics
avirulent
avitaminosis (pl ~oses)
avocado (pl ~os, ~oes)
avocation
avocational
avocet (or ~oset)
Avogadro
avoid
avoidability
avoidable
avoidably
avoidance
avoider
avoirdupois
avouch
avouchment

avow
avowal
avowedly
avulse
avuncular
await
awaited
awake (awoke, awoken, awaking)
awaken
awakening
award
awardee
awarder
aware
awareness
awash
away
awe
awed
aweigh
awesome
awesomely
awesomeness
awestricken
awestruck
awful
awfully
awfulness
awhile
awhirl
awkward
awkwardly
awkwardness
awl
awn
awning
awoke
awry
axe (*US* ax)
axel (! axil, axle) *ice-skating jump*
axial
axially
axil (! axel, axle) *part of plant*
axilla (*pl* ~ae, ~as)
axillary
axiom
axiomatic

axiomatically
axiomatise (*or* ~ize)
axis (*pl* axes)
axle (! axel, axil) *device for carrying a wheel*
Axminster
axolotl
axon
ayahuasca
ayatollah (A~)
aye-aye
Ayers *rock*
Ayrshire
ayurveda (A~)
ayurvedic (A~)
azalea
Azerbaijan
Azerbaijani
Azeri
azimuth
azimuthal
azoic
azonal
Azores
Aztec
azure
azurite

b B

baa
Baal
Baath (*or* Ba'ath, Ba'th)
Baathism (*or* Ba'ath~, Ba'th~)
Baathist (*or* Ba'ath~, Ba'th~)
baba
babassu (*occ* ~açu)
babble
babbler

babe
Babel *biblical tower*
babel *confused sound*
babelicious
babiche
Babinski
baboon
babouche
babu (*or* ~boo; *pl* ~us, ~boos)
babushka
Babuyan
baby
Babygro
babyhood
babyish
babyishly
babyishness
babyism
babykins
Babylon
Babylonia
Babylonian
baby-sit (~sat, ~sitting)
babysitter
bacalao
Bacardi
baccalaureate (B~)
baccarat
Bacchae
bacchanal (B~)
bacchanalia (B~)
bacchanalian (B~)
bacchant
Bacchic
Bacchus
baccy
Bach *composer, flower remedy*
bachelor (B~ *in name of degree*)
bachelorhood
bacillar
bacillary
bacillus (*pl* ~lli)
back
backache
backbeat
backbench
backbencher

backbite (~bit, ~bitten,
~biting)
backbiter
backboard
backbone
backbreaker
backbreaking
backchannel (or back-~)
backchannelling (or
back-~; US ~eling)
backchat
backcloth
backcomb (or back-~)
backcountry (adj)
backcrawl (or back-~)
backcross
backdate (or back-~)
backdoor (or back-~;
adj)
backdown (or back-~; n)
backdraught (US ~draft)
backdrop (or back-~)
backer
backfill (or back-~)
backfire (or back-~)
backflip (or back-~; v
~pped, ~pping)
backformation
backfriend (or back-~)
backgammon
background
backhand
backhandedly
backhandedness
backhander
backheel
backing
backlash
backless
backlight (v ~lighted or
~lit)
backlist
backlog (or back-~)
backmarker (or back-~)
backmost
backpack
backpacker
back-pedal (~lled,
~lling; US ~led,
~ling)

back-projection
backrest (or back-~)
backscratcher (or back-
~)
backscratching
backside
backslapping (or back-~)
backslash (or back-~)
backslide (~slid,
~sliding)
backslider
backspace (or back-~)
backspin (or back-~)
back-stabber
back-stabbing
backstage (or back-~)
backstairs (or back-~)
backstay (or back-~)
backstop (or back-~)
backstreet (or back-~)
backstroke
backswept (or back-~)
backtrack (or back-~)
backup (or back-~)
backveld
backward
backwardly
backwardness
backwards
backwash (or back-~)
backwater (or back-~)
backwoods
backwoodsman (pl
~men)
backyard (or back-~)
bacon
bacterial
bactericidal
bactericide
bacteriological
bacteriologist
bacteriology
bacterium (pl ~ia)
Bactrian
bad
baddy (or ~die)
bade
Baden
badge

badger
badger-baiting
badinage
badlands (B~)
badly
badman
badminton game (B~ for
the location)
badmouth (v)
badness
Baedeker
Baffin
baffle
bafflement
baffler
baffling
bafflingly
bafta fabric
BAFTA (or Bafta) film
award
bag (~gged, ~gging)
bagatelle
bagel (occ beig~)
bagful
baggage
baggily
bagginess
baggy
Baghdad (or Bagdad)
bagman
bagpiper
bagpipes
baguette
bagworm
bahadur
Bahai (or ~ha'i)
Bahaism (or ~'ism)
Bahaist (or ~'ist)
Bahamas
Bahamian
Bahasa
Bahrain (or ~rein)
Bahraini (or ~reini)
baht
Baikal (or Bay~)
bail (! bale) (law) release;
(UK) cricket; (US) help
bail (or bale) scoop, jump
bailable
bailee

bailer (*or* baler)
bailey *castle*
bailie *magistrate*
bailiff
bailiwick
bailor
bailout (*n*)
Bairam
bait
baize
bake
bakehouse
Bakelite (*tr*)
baker
bakery
bakeshop
baklava (*or* bac~)
baksheesh (*or* back~)
Baku
balaclava
balalaika
balance
balanceable
balanced
balancer
balancing
balconied
balcony
bald
baldacchino (*pl* ~os)
Balder
balderdash
baldheaded
baldness
baldric
baldy (*or* ~die)
bale (! bail) *bundle*; (*UK*) *help*
Balearic
baleen
baleful
balefully
balefulness
baler
Bali
Balinese
balk (*v, UK also* baulk) *resist*
Balkan
Balkanisation (~iz~)

Balkanise (~ize)
balker (*UK also* baul~)
Balkhash (*or* ~lqash)
ball
ballad *song*, (*occ*) *poetry*
ballade *poetry*, *instrumental music*
balladeer
balladry
Ballarat
ballast
ball-bearing
ballboy (*or* ball-~)
ballcock
ballerina
ballet
balletic
ballgirl (*or* ball-~)
ballistics
ballon
balloon
balloonist
ballot
ballpark
ballpoint
ballroom
balls
balls-up
ballyhoo
balm
balminess
Balmoral *residence*
balmoral *bonnet*
balmy *of warm air*
balmy (*US; UK* barmy) *crazy*
baloney (*occ* bol~)
Balqash (*or* ~lkhash)
balsa
balsam
balsamic
Balt
Balthasar (*or* ~zar)
Balti *style of cooking*
balti *curry*
Baltic
Baltimore
Baltistan
Baluchi (*or* Balo~)
Baluchistan

baluster
balustrade
Balzac
bambino (*pl* ~ni)
bamboo
bamboozle
Bamian
ban (~nned, ~nning)
banal
banalise (*or* ~ize)
banality
banana
Banbury
band
bandage
Band-Aid *music concert*
Band-aid (*tr*) *plaster*
bandana (*or* ~anna)
Bandar
bandbox
bandeau (*pl* ~ux, ~us)
banderole
bandicoot
bandiness
bandit (*pl* ~its, ~itti)
banditry
bandmaster
bandog
bandolier (*or* ~leer)
bandpass (*or* band-~)
bandsaw (*or* band-~)
bandsman
bandstand (*or* band-~)
bandswoman
bandwagon
bandy
bane
baneful
bang
Bangalore
banger
Bangkok
Bangla
Bangladesh
Bangladeshi
bangle
banish
banister (*or* bann~)
banjo (*pl* ~os, ~oes)
bank

bankable
banker
banking
bankroll
bankrupt
bankruptcy
banner
bannerette
bannister (*or* bani~)
banns
banoffi
banquet
banquette
banshee
bantam
banter
banyan (*or* ~nian)
banzai
baobab
bap
baptism
baptist (B~)
baptistery (*or* ~try)
baptize (*or* ~ise)
bar (~rred, ~rring)
bar mitzvah (B~, M~)
barb
Barbadian
Barbados
barbarian
barbaric
barbarise (*or* ~ize)
barbarism
barbarity
Barbarossa
barbarous
barbarousness
Barbary
barbasco
barbecue
barbecued
barbecuing
barbel
barbell
barber
barberry
barbershop
barbet
Barbican *London*
barbican *tower*

Barbie (*tr*) *doll*
barbie *barbecue*
barbiturate
Barbudan
barcarole
Barcelona
bard
bardic
bare
bareback
barefaced
barefoot
bareheaded
barelegged
barely
Barents
barfly
bargain
barge
bargeboard
bargee
bargepole
baritone
barium
bark
barley
barm
barmaid
barman
barminess
barmy (*US* balmy)
barn
barnacle
Barnardo
barnstorm
barnyard
barogram
barograph
barometer
barometric
barometry
baron
baronage
baroness
baronet
baronetage
baronetcy
baronial
barony
baroque (B~)

barque
barrack
barracks
barracuda
barrage
barramundi
barrel
barren
barrenness
barricade
barrier
barring
barrister
barrow
barter
Bartholomew
barycentre (*US* ~ter)
barycentric
baryon
barysphere
basal
basalt
bascinet *see* bassinet
base
baseball
base-court
baseless
baselessness
baseline
baseman
basement
basenji
baseplate
bash
bashful
bashfulness
BASIC (or Basic)
    computing
basic *level*
basil
basilar
basilica (*pl* ~as, ~ae)
basilisk
basin
basinet *see* bassinet
basis (*pl* ~ses)
bask
Baskerville
basket
basketball

basketful
basketwork
basmati
basnet *see* bassinet
Basotho
Basque *people*
basque *clothing*
Basquish
bas-relief
bass (! base) *music*
basset
bassinet (*or* basinet, basnet, bascinet)
bassist
basso (*pl* ~os, ~ssi)
bassoon
bastard
bastardisation (*or* ~iz~)
bastardise (*or* ~ize)
baste
bastille (B~)
bastion
bat
bat mitzvah (B~, M~)
batch
bated
Bath *city*
bath (bathed, bathing) *wash*
bathe (bathed, bathing)
bather
bathing
bathos
bathyscaphe (*occ* ~scape)
bathysphere
batik
batiste
Batman *character*
batman *servant*
baton
batsman (*pl* ~men)
batsmanship
batt (! bat) *textile*
battalion
batten
batter
battered
battering
Battersea

battery
batting
battle
battle-axe (*US esp* ~ax)
battle-cruiser
battledress
battlefield
battleground
battlement
battleship
batty
batwing
bauble
baud
Baudelaire
Bauhaus
baulk (*n, UK; US* balk) *beam*
baulk (*resist*) *see* balk
bauxite
bavardage
Bavaria
Bavarian
bavaroise (B~)
bavian
bawbee
bawd
bawdily
bawdiness
bawdry
bawdy
bawl
bay
bayberry
bayonet
bayou
bazaar
bazooka
bdellium
beach
beachcomber
beachhead
beacon
bead
beading
beadle
beadsman (*pl* ~men)
beagle
beak
beaker

be-all
beam
beaminess
beamy
bean (! been) *food*
beanpole
beanshoot
beanstalk
bear
bearable
bear-baiting
beard
bearded
bearer
bearing
bearish
Béarnaise (*or* Be~)
bearskin
beast
beastliness
beastly
beat (! beet) *strike; rhythm*
beaten
beater
beatific
beatification
beatify
beating
beatitude
Beatle (! beetle) *pop music*
beatnik
beatster
beau (*pl* ~us, ~ux)
Beaufort
Beaujolais
beauteous
beautician
beautiful
beautify
beauty
Beaver *scout*
beaver *animal*
bebop
becalm
became
because
béchamel (*or* be~)
Bechstein

beck
beckon
becloud
become (became, becoming)
becoming (*adj*)
becquerel (B~)
bed
bedabble
bedaub
bedazzle
bedbath
bedbug
bedclothes
bedding
Bede
bedeck
bedevil (~lled, ~lling; US ~led, ~ling)
bedew
bedfellow
Bedfordshire
bedim (~mmed, ~mming)
bedlam
Bedlington
Bedouin (*occ* ~duin)
bedpan
bedpost
bedraggled
bed-rest
bedridden
bedrock
bedroll
bedroom
bedside
bedsit
bedsore
bedspread
bedstead
bedstraw
bedtime
Beduin (*or* ~douin)
bee
beech
beef (*pl* beefs, beeves)
beefburger
beefcake
Beefeater (b~)
beefiness

beefsteak
beefy
beehive
beeline
Beelzebub
been (! bean) *past form of* be
beep
beeper
beer
beeriness
Beersheba
beery
beestings
beeswax
beet (! beat) *sugar*
Beethoven
beetle (! Beatle) *insect*
beetroot
befall (befell, ~fallen, ~falling)
befit (~tted, ~tting)
before
beforehand
befriend
befuddle
beg (~gged, ~gging)
began
beggar
beggarliness
beggarly
beggary
begin
beginner
beginning
begone
begonia
begrudge
beguile
beguine (! begin) *dance*
begum (B~)
behalf
behave
behaviour (US ~or)
behavioural (US ~or~)
behaviourism (US ~or~)
behaviourist (US ~or~)
behead
beheld
behemoth

behest
behind
behold (beheld)
beholden
behoves (US ~hooves)
beige
beigel (*or* bag~)
Beijing
being
Beirut
bejewel (~lled, ~lling; US ~led, ~ling)
bel (B~)
belabour (US ~or)
Belarus (*or* Byela~)
Belarusian (*also* ~russian, Byela~)
belated
Belau
Belauan
belay
belch
belcher
Belfast
belfry
Belgian
Belgium
Belial
belie
belief
believability
believe
Belisha (*UK*)
belittle
Belize
bell
belladonna
bellboy (*UK*) *hotels*
bell buoy *sea*
belle
Bellerophon
belles-lettres
bellhop (*US*)
bellicose
bellicosity
belligerence
belligerent
belligerently
Bellingshausen
bellow

belly
bellyache
bellyflop
bellyful
belong
belonging
Belorussia (*or* Byela~)
Belorussian (*or* ~rusian, Bye~)
beloved
below
Belshazzar
belt
Beltane
belting
beluga
belvedere
belying
Bemba
bemire
bemoan
bemuse
bench
bencher
benchmark
bend
bendy
beneath
Benedictine
benediction
Benedictus
benefaction
benefactor
benefice
beneficence
beneficent
beneficial
beneficiary
benefit
Benelux
benevolence
benevolent
benevolently
Bengal
Bengalese
Bengali
benighted
benign
benignant
Benin

bent
benthic
benthos
benumb
benzaldehyde
Benzedrine (*tr*)
benzene
benzine
benzoic
Beowulf
bequeath
bequest
berate
Berber
bereave
bereavement
bereft
beret
bergamot
bergenia
beribboned
beriberi
Bering
Berkshire
Berlin
Berlioz
Bermuda
Berne
Bernese
berry
berserk
berth
beryl
beryllium
beseech
beset (~tting)
beside
besides
besiege
besmirch
besot (~tted, ~tting)
bespoke
Bessemer
best
bestial
bestiality
bestiary
bestir (~rred, ~rring)
bestow
bestrewn

bestride (bestrode)
bet (~tted, ~tting)
beta
beta-blocker
Betamax (*tr*)
bête noire (*pl* bêtes noires)
betel
Betelgeuse
Bethesda
betide
betray
betrothed
better
betterment
betting (*n*)
between
betwixt
bevel (~lled, ~lling; *US* ~led, ~ling)
beverage
bewail
beware
bewilder
bewildered
bewilderment
bewitch
bewitching
bewitchingly
bey (B~; ! bay) *ruler*
beyond
bezel
Bhagavadgita
bhaji (*or* ~jee)
bhakti
bhangra
bhindi
Bhopal
Bhutan
Bhutanese
biannual
Biarritz
bias (~sed, ~sing, *or* ~ssed, ~ssing)
biathlon
bib
bible (B~)
biblical (B~)
bibliographer
bibliography

bibliophile
bibulous
bicameral
bicarbonate
bicentenary
bicentennial
biceps
bicker
bicolour (*US* ~or)
bicultural
bicuspid
bicycle
bid
biddable
bidder
bidding
bidet
biennial
bier
bifid
bifocal
bifurcate
bifurcation
big (~gger, ~ggest)
bigamy
bigeneric
Bigfoot
biggie (*or* biggy)
bighead
big-hearted
bighorn
bight
bigot
bigotry
bigwig
bijou (*pl* ~ux)
bijouterie
bike
biker
Bikini *atoll*
bikini *clothing*
bilabial
bilateral
bilateralism
bilberry
bile
bilet-doux
bilge
bilharzia
biliary

bilinear
bilinearity
bilingual
bilingualism
bilious
biliousness
bilirubin
bilk
bill
billabong
billboard
billet
billfold (*US*)
billhook
billiards
billion
billionaire
billionth
billow
billposter
biltong
bimbo
bimetallic
bimillenary
bimonthly
bin
binary
binaural
bin-bag
bind
binder
binding
bindweed
binge
bingo (B~)
bin-liner
binnacle
binocular
binomial
binturong
bio
bioassay
biochemical
biochemistry
biodegradable
biodiversity
bioengineering
bioethics
biofeedback
bioflavonoid

biofuel
biogas
biographer
biographic
biographical
biographically
biography
biohazard
biological
biologist
biology
bioluminescence
biomass
biome
biometry
biomorphic
bionic
bionics
biophysics
biopic
biopsy
biorhythm
biosphere
biosynthesis
biota
biotechnology
biotin
bipartisan
bipartite
biped
bipedal
bipedalism
bipedality
biplane
bipolar
bipolarity
birch
bird
birdbath
birdcage
birdcall
birder (*US*)
birdie
birdseed
birdsfoot trefoil
birdshot
birdsong
birdwatcher
birdwing
birefringence

biretta
biriani (*or* birya~)
Birmingham
biro (B~ *tr*; *pl* ~os)
birth
birthday
birthing
birthmark
birthplace
birthright
biryani (*or* biria~)
Biscay
Biscayan
biscotti
biscuit
bisect
bisexual
bishop
bishopric
Bismarck
bismuth
bison
bisque
bistort
bistro
bisulphate
bit
bitch
bitchiness
bitchy
bite (*n* ! byte) *mouth*
bite (*v* bit, bitten, biting)
bitesize
bitmap
bitmapping
bitonal
bitstream
bitter
bittern
bittersweet
bittiness
bitty
bitumen
bituminisation (*or* ~iz~)
bituminise (*or* ~ize)
bituminous
bivalent
bivalve
bivouac
biweekly (*or* bi-~)

bizarre
bizarrely
blab (~bbed, ~bbing)
blabber
blabbermouth
black
blackball
blackberry
blackbird
blackcurrant
blacken
blackguard
blackhead
blacking
blackjack
blackleg
blacklist
blackmail
blackout
blackshirt
blacksmith
blackthorn
bladder
blade
blag (~gged, ~gging)
blain
Blairism
blame
blameless
blameworthy
blanch
blancmange
blanco
bland
blandish
blandishment
blank
blanket
blankly
blankness
blanquette
blare
Blarney *castle*
blarney *speech*
blasé
blaspheme
blasphemer
blasphemous
blasphemy
blast

blastula (*pl* ~ae, ~as)
blatancy
blatant
blather
blatherskite
blaxploitation
blaze
blazer
blazered
blazing
blazon
blazonry
bleach
bleacher
bleaching
bleak
bleariness
bleary
bleat
bled
bleed
bleeder
bleeding
bleep
bleeper
blemish
blench
blend *mix*
blende *mineral*
blender
Blenheim
blenny
blent
blesbok
bless (blessed *or* blest)
blew
blight
blighter
Blighty
blimp
blind
blinder
blindfold
blinding
blindly
blindness
blink
blinker
blinkered
blinking

blintze
bliny
blip
bliss
blissful
blister
blistering
blithe
blitheness
blithering
blithesome
blitz
blitzkrieg
blizzard
bloat
bloater
bloatware
blob
bloc (! block) *political group*
block
blockade
blockage
blockbuster
blockbusting
blocker
blockhead
blocking
Bloemfontein
bloke
blonde (*esp female, or* blond *esp male*)
blood
bloodbath
bloodcurdling
blooded
bloodhound
bloodily
bloodiness
bloodless
bloodlessness
bloodletting
bloodlust
bloodshed
bloodshot
bloodstain
bloodstream
bloodsucker
bloodthirstily
bloodthirstiness

bloodthirsty
bloody
bloom
bloomer
bloomers
bloop
blooper (*US*)
blossom
blot
blotch
blotter
blotting
blotto
blouse
blouson
blow (blew, blown)
blowback
blower
blowfish
blowfly
blowhole
blowing
blown
blowout (*or* blow-~)
blowpipe
blowsy (*or* blowzy)
blowtorch
blowy
blub (~bbed, ~bbing)
blubber
bludgeon
blue (*v* blued, bluing *or* blueing)
Bluebeard
bluebell
blueberry
bluebird
bluebottle
blue-chip
blue-collar
bluegrass
bluenose
blueprint
blues
bluescreen
bluestocking
bluesy
bluey
bluff
bluing (*or* blueing)

bluish (*or* blueish)
blunder
blunderbuss
blunt
blur (~rred, ~rring)
blurb
blurt
blush
blusher
bluster
blustery
bo
boa
Boadicea (*or* Boudicca)
boar
board
boarded
boarder
boarding
boardroom
boardwalk
boast
boastful
boat
boater
boathook
boathouse
boatload
boatman
boatswain (*or* bo'sun, bosun)
boatyard
bob (~bbed, ~bbing)
bobber
bobbin
bobble
bobby *policeman*
bobcat
bobsleigh (*US esp* ~sled)
bobtail
bode
bodega
bodge
bodger
bodhisattva (B~)
bodhran *drum*
bodice
bodiliness
bodily
bodkin

body
bodybag
bodyguard
bodywork
Boer
boffin
bog
bogey (*or* bogy, *pl* ~ys *or* ~gies; ! bogie) *evil*
bogey (*pl* ~ys; ! bogie) *golf*
boggart
boggle
bogie (*or* bogey; ! bogey) *wheel assembly*
bogus
bogy *see* bogey
Bohemian *from Bohemia*
bohemian *artist*
bohrium
boil
boiled
boiler
boilermaker
boilersuit
boiling
boisterous
boisterously
boisterousness
bolas
bold
boldface
bole
bolero
Bolivia
bollard
bollock (*occ* ba~, *tab*)
bollocking (*occ* ba~, *tab*)
Bollywood
Bologna
Bolognese
boloney (*or* ba~)
Bolshevik
bolshie (*or* ~shy)
bolster
bolt
bolthole
bolus
bomb
bombard *attack*

bombarde *music*
bombardier (*occ* ~eer)
bombast
bombastic
Bombay (*or* Mumbai)
bombe (! bomb) *food*
bomber
bombshell
bombsight
bon mot
bon vivant
bon voyage
bona fide
bonanza
Bonaparte (*occ* Buon~)
Bonapartist (*occ* Buon~)
bonbon (*or* bon-~)
bond
bondage
bonded
bondholder
bondsman (*pl* ~men)
bone
bonehead
bonemeal
bonfire
bongo
bonhomie
boniness
bonk
Bonn
bonnet
bonniness
bonsai
bontebok
bonus
bony (*occ* ~ney)
boo
boob
booby
boodle
boogie
boogie-woogie
book
bookable
bookbinder
bookcase
bookie
booking
bookish

bookishness
booklet
bookmaker
bookmark
bookseller
bookshop
bookstall
bookstand
bookworm
Boolean
boom
boomer
boomerang
boon
boondocks
boor
boorish
boorishly
boorishness
boost
booster
boot
bootable
bootee (*or* ~ie; ! booty) *footwear*
booth
bootlace
bootleg (~gged, ~gging)
bootlicker
bootstrap
booty (*pl* ~ties; ! bootee) *treasure*
booze
boozy
bop
boracic
borage
borax
Bordeaux
bordello
borderer
borderland
borderline
bore
boreal (B~)
bored
boredom
borehole
borer
boric

boring
born (! borne) *birth*
borne (! born) *carry*
Borneo
boron
borough
borrow
borscht (*or* borsch)
borstal (B~)
borzoi
Bosnia
Bosniak
Bosnian
bosom
boson
Bosphorus (*or* ~por~)
boss
bossiness
bossy
Boston
bosun (*or* boatswain)
bot
botanic
botanise (*or* ~ize)
botanist
botany
botch
botcher
both
bother
botheration
bothersome
Botswana
bottle
bottlebrush
bottleful
bottleneck
bottler
bottom
bottomless
bottommost
botulism
Boudicca (*or* Boadicea)
boudoir
bouffant
bougainvillea (*or* ~llaea)
bough
bought
bouillabaisse
bouillon

boulder
boule
boulevard
boulevardier
Boulogne
bounce
bouncer
bouncing
bouncy
bound
boundary
bounded
boundedness
bounder
boundless
boundlessness
bounteous
bounteousness
bountiful
bountifulness
bounty
bouquet
bourbon (B~)
bourdon
bourgeois
bourgeoisie
bourguignon
bourse (B~)
bout
boutique
bouzouki (*pl* ~is)
bovine
bow
bowdlerise (*or* ~ize)
bowel
bower
bowerbird
bowie (B~)
bowl
bowler
bowlful
bowline
bowling
bowser
bowsprit
bowstring
bow-wow
box
boxcar
boxer

Boxing *Day*
boxing *sport*
boy
boyar
boycott
Boyle
boysenberry
bra
brace
bracelet
bracer
brachial
brachiopod (B~)
brachiosaurus (*pl* ~ri)
bracing
bracken
bracket
brackish
brackishness
bradawl
brag (~gged, ~gging)
braggadocio
braggart
Brahma
Brahman
Brahmin
Brahms
braid
braille (B~)
brain
brainchild
braininess
brainless
brainstem
brainstorm
brainstorming
brainwash
brainwashing
brainy
braise
braised
braising
brake
bramble
Bramley (*pl* ~eys)
bran
branch
brand
brandish
brandy

brash
brass
brasserie
brassica (*pl* ~ae)
brassiere (*or* ~ère)
brassiness
brassy
brat
brattish
bratwurst
bravado
brave
bravery
bravo
bravura
brawl
brawn
brawniness
brawny
bray
brazen
brazenness
brazier
Brazil *country*
brazil *nut*
Brazilian
breach (! breech) *break*
bread
breadboard
breadcrumb
breadfruit
breadline
breadth
break
breakable
breakaway
breakdance
breakdancing
breakdown
breaker
breakfast
break-in
breaking
breakneck
breakthrough
breakwater
bream
breast
breastfeed
breastplate

breaststroke
breath
breathalyse (*or* ~yze;
  ~ysed, ~ysing)
breathalyser (*or* ~yzer;
  B~ *tr*)
breathe
breather
breathiness
breathing
breathless
breathlessness
breathtaking
breathy
bred
breech (! breach) *gun*
breeches
breed (bred)
breeder
breeding
breeze
breezeblock
breeziness
breezy
brethren
Breton
breve
breviary
brevity
brew
brewer
brewery
briar (*or* brier)
bribability
bribable
bribe
briber
bribery
bric-a-brac (*or* ~à~)
brick
brickbat
bricklayer
brickworks
bricolage
bricoleur
bridal
bride
bridegroom
bridesmaid
bridge

bridgehead
bridging
bridle
Brie
brief
briefcase
briefing
briefs
brier (*or* briar)
brig
brigade
brigadier
brigand
brigandine
brigantine
bright
brighten
brilliance
brilliant
brim
brimful
brimstone
brindled
brine
bring (brought)
bringer
brink
brinkmanship (*or*
  brinks~)
briny
brio
brioche
briquet (*or* ~ette)
brisk
brisket
brisling
bristle
bristly
Bristol
Britain
Britannia
Britannic
British
Briton
Britpop
brittle
brittleness
Brittonic (*or* Brytho~)
broach
broad

broadband
broadcast
broad-minded
broadsheet
broadside
broadsword
brocade
broccoli
brochette
brochure
brogue
broil
broiler
broiling
broke
broken
broken-hearted
brokenness
broker
brokerage
broking
brolly (*UK*)
bromeliad
bromide
bromine
bronchiole
bronchitic
bronchitis
bronchus (*pl* ~chi)
bronco
brontosaurus (*pl* ~ri)
Bronx
bronze
brooch
brood
brooding
broody
brook
Brooklyn
Brooklynese
broom
broomrape
broomstick
broth
brothel
brother
brotherhood
brother-in-law
brotherliness
brotherly

brought
brouhaha
brow
browbeat
browbeaten
browbeater
brown
browned
Brownian
Brownie (*UK*) *scouting*
brownie (*esp US*) *cake*
browning
browse
browser
brucellosis
bruise
bruiser
bruit
brulé
brunch
brunette (*US* ~net)
Brunswick
brunt
bruschetta (*pl* ~as, ~tte)
brush
brushwood
brushwork
brusque
brusqueness
Brussels
brut *very dry*
brutal
brutalise (*or* ~ize)
brutalism
brutalist
brutality
brute
brutish
bryony
bryophyte
Brythonic (*or* Britto~)
bubble
bubble-jet
bubbly
bubo (*pl* ~oes)
bubonic
buccal
buccaneer
buccinator
Bucharest

buck
buckaroo
bucket
buckle
buckler
buckminsterfullerene
buckram
buckshee
buckshot
buckskin
buckwheat
bucolic
bud (~dded, ~dding)
Buddha
Buddhism
buddleia
buddy
budge
budgerigar
budget
buff
buffalo (*pl* ~lo, ~los, ~loes)
buffer
buffet
buffeting
buffoon
buffoonery
bug
bugbear
bugger (*tab*)
buggery (*tab*)
buggy
bugle
bugloss
build
builder
building
built
bulb
bulbosity
bulbous
Bulgar
Bulgarian
bulge
bulimia
bulimic
bulk
bulkhead
bulkiness

buzz

bulky
bull
bulldog
bulldoze
bulldozer
bullet
bulletin
bullet-proof
bullfight
bullfinch
bullfrog
bullion
bullish
bullishness
bullock
bull's-eye
bully
bulrush
bulwark
bum (*tab*)
bumble
bumble-bee
bumf (*or* bumph, *UK*)
bump
bumper
bumpiness
bumpkin
bumptious
bumptiousness
bumpy
bun
bunch
bundle
bung
bungalow
bungee (*or* ~gy, ~gie)
bunghole
bungle
bungy *see* bungee
bunion
bunk
bunker
bunkhouse
bunkum (*US also* buncombe)
bunny
Bunsen
bunting
bunyip
Buonapartist (*or* Bona~)

buoy
buoyancy
buoyant
burb
burble
burbot
burden
bureau (*pl* ~ux, ~us)
bureaucracy
bureaucrat
burette (*US* ~ret)
burgee
burgeon
burger
burgess
burgh
burgher
burglar
burglary
burgle
burgomaster
burgonet
Burgundian
Burgundy *place*
burgundy (B~) *wine*
burial
burin
burka (*or* burqa, burkha)
burl
burlap (*US*)
burlesque
burliness
burly
Burma
Burman
Burmese
burn (burnt *or* burned)
burner
burnish
burnous
burnout
burnside
burp
burqa *see* burka
burr
burrito
burrow
bursar
bursary
bursitis

burst
bury
bus (*pl* ~ses, *esp US* ~sses)
busby
bush
bushfire
Bushman (*pl* ~men)
bushwhack
bushy
busily
business (! busyness) *commerce*
businesslike
businessman
businesswoman
busk
bust
bustard
bustle
busy
busybody
busyness (! business) *activity*
but (! butt) *conjunction*
butane
butch
butcher
butchery
butler
butt (! but) *push; smoking; target*
butte
butter
buttercup
butterfingers
butterfly
buttermilk
butterscotch
butterwort
buttery
buttock
button
buttonhole
buttress
buxom
buxomness
buy
buyer
buzz

buzzard
buzzer
bye
bye-bye
bye-law (*or* by~, *UK*)
by-election (*UK*)
Byelorussian (*or* Belo~)
bygone
byline (*or* by-~)
bypass (*or* by-~)
by-product
byroad
bystander
byte (! bite) *computing*
byway
byword
Byzantian
Byzantine

Caaba (*or* K~)
cab (~bbed, ~bbing)
cabal
cabala (C~) *see* Kabbala
caballero (*pl* ~os)
cabaret
cabbage
cabbageworm
cabbagy
cabbala (C~) *see* Kabbala
cabbalist (C~) *see*
  Kabbalist
cabbalistic (C~) *see*
  Kabbalistic
cabby
caber
cabildo
cabin
cabined
cabinet
cabinetmaker

cabinetry
cable
cabled
caboodle (*or* ka~)
caboose
cabotage
cabriole
cabriolet
cacao
cacciatore (*or* ~ra)
cache
cachepot
cachet
cachexia
cachinnate
cachinnation
cachou
cackle
cackling
cacodemon
cacography
cacomistle
cacophonous
cacophony
cactaceous
cactus (*pl* ~ti, ~uses)
cad
cadaver
cadaveric
cadaverous
caddie (*n*; *v or* ~ddy) *golf*
caddis
caddish
caddishly
caddishness
caddy (! caddie) *tea*
cadence
cadenced
cadential
cadenza
cadet
cadetship
cadge
cadger
cadmium
cadre
caducity
caecal (*US* ce~)
caecitis (*US* ce~)
caecum (*US* ce~)

Caen
Caerphilly
Caesar
Caesarean (*c*; *also* ~rian,
  US Ce~) *section*
Caesarian (*or* ~rean)
  Julius Caesar
caesium (*US* ce~)
caesura (*US* ce~)
cafard
cafe (*or* café)
cafeteria
cafetière
caffeinated
caffeine
caftan (*or* kaf~)
cage
cagebird
caged
cagey (*or* ~gy)
cagily
caginess (*or* cagey~)
cagoule (*or* ~goul, ka~)
cahier
cahoots
caiman (*or* cay~)
Cain (! cane)
caique
cairn
cairngorm
Cairo
caisson
cajole
cajolement
cajolery
Cajun
cake
cakewalk
calamander
calamari (*or* ~res, ~ries)
calamine
calamitous
calamitously
calamity
calcaneus (*or* ~eum; *pl*
  ~ei, ~ea)
calcareous
calceolaria
calciferous
calcification

calcify
calcimine (*or* kalsomine)
calcite
calcium
calculability
calculable
calculably
calculate
calculated
calculating
calculation
calculative
calculator
calculus (*pl* ~uli, *med*)
calculus (*pl* ~uses, *math*)
caldera
caldron (*US; UK* caul~)
calendar (! calender)
  dates
calender (! calendar)
  device
calendric
calendrical
calendula
calenture
calf (*pl* calves)
calfskin
calibrate
calibration
calibrator
calibre (*US* ~ber)
calico (*pl* ~oes, *esp US*
  ~os)
California
Californian
Caligula
caliper (*also UK* call~)
caliph (*occ* ka~, ~if)
caliphate
calisthenics (*US; UK*
  call~)
calix (*pl* ~ices; ! calyx)
  chalice
calk *spike*
calk (*US, cf* caulk) *boat*
call
Callanetics (*tr*)
caller
calligraph
calligraphed

calligrapher
calligraphic
calligraphist
calligraphy
calling
Calliope *muse*
calliope *instrument*
calliper (*US* cali~)
callisthenics (*US* cali~)
Callisto
callosity
callous (*or* callus)
calloused (*or* callused)
callously
callousness
callow
calm
calmative
calming
calmly
calmness
caloric
calorie (C~)
calorific
calorifically
calorimeter
calozne (*pl* ~ni, ~nes)
calque
calumniate
calumny
Calvados
Calvary
calve (calved, calving)
calves
Calvin
Calvinism
Calvinist
Calypso *Saturn*
calypso *song*
calyx (*pl* ~yces, ~yxes;
  ! calix) *plants*
cam
camaraderie
camber
cambered
Cambodia
Cambodian
Cambrian
cambric
Cambridge

camcorder
came
camel
camelback
cameleer
camelhair
camelid
camellia
Camelot
Camembert
cameo (*pl* ~os)
camera
cameraman (*pl* ~men)
camerawork
Cameroon
Cameroonian
camiknickers
camisole
camomile (*esp US, phar*
  chamo~)
camouflage
camp
campaign
campaigner
campanile
campanological
campanologist
campanology
campanula
campcraft
camper
campfire
camphor
campily
campiness
campion *plant*
campsite
campus
camshaft
can
Canaan
Canaanite
Canada
Canadian
canal
canalise (*or* ~ize)
canapé (*or* ~pe)
canard
canary
canasta

Canberra
cancan (or can-~)
cancel (~lled, ~lling; US ~led, ~ling)
cancellation (US ~cela~)
canceller (US ~celer)
Cancer *zodiac*
cancer *disease*
cancerous
candela
candelabrum (*pl* ~ra)
candid
candidacy
candidate
candidature
candidly
candidness
candied
candle
candleberry
candleholder
candlelight
candlelit
Candlemas
candlepower
candlestick
candlewick
candour (US ~or)
candy
candyfloss
candyman (*pl* ~men)
cane
caned
caner
canine
caning
canister
canker
cankered
cankerous
cannabis
canned
cannelloni
cannelure
cannery
cannibal
cannibalisation (or ~iz~)
cannibalise (or ~ize)

cannibalism
cannibalistic
cannibalistically
cannily
canniness
cannon (! canon) *gun*
cannonade
cannonball
cannoneer
cannot
cannula (*pl* ~ae, ~as)
cannulate
canny
canoe (~oes, ~oed, ~oeing)
canoeing (*n*)
canola
canon (C~; ! cannon) *music*
canonical
canonically
canonicity
canonise (or ~ize)
canonist
canonry
canoodle
canoodling
canopied
Canopus
canopy
cant
cantabile
cantaloupe (*also* ~loup, ~lope, ~elope)
cantankerous
cantankerously
cantankerousness
cantata
canteen
canter
Canterbury
canthus
canticle
cantilever
cantilevered
cantillate
cantillation
cantina
cantle
canto (*pl* ~os)

Canton *China*
canton *district*
cantonal
Cantonese
cantonment
cantor
cantorial
cantoris
canvas (*n pl* ~ases, ~asses) *fabric*
canvas (*n*, or ~ass) *survey*
canvass (*v* ~assed, ~assing; US *occ* ~as, ~ased, ~asing; ! canvas) *support*
canvasser
canyon
canyoning
canzone (*pl* ~ni)
caoutchouc
cap (~pped, ~pping)
capability
capable
capably
capacious
capaciously
capaciousness
capacitance
capacitate
capacitated
capacitation
capacitative
capacitive
capacitor
capacity
cape
caped
caper
capercaillie (or ~cailzie)
Capetian
capillarity
capillary
capital (! capitol) *city, letter*
capitalisation (or ~iz~)
capitalise (or ~ize)
capitalised (or ~ized)
capitalism
capitalist
capitalistic

capitalistically
capitally
capitation
capitol (C~; *esp US*, *pol*;
! capital)
capitulate
capitulation
capitulator
caplet
capo (*pl* ~os)
capon
capped
cappuccino (*pl* ~os)
capriccio (*pl* ~os)
caprice
capricious
capriciously
capriciousness
Capricorn
caprine
capsicum
capsize
capsized
capstan
capstone
capsular
capsulate
capsule
capsulise (*or* ~ize)
captain
captaincy
caption
captioned
captious
captiously
captiousness
captivate
captivating
captivatingly
captivation
captive
captivity
captor
capture
capturer
Capuchin *monk*
capuchin *monkey*
capybara
car
carabineer (*or* ~ier)

carabiner (*or* ka~)
caracal
Caracas
caracole
caracul (*or* karakul)
carafe
carambola
caramel
caramelisation (*or* ~iz~)
caramelise (*or* ~ize)
caramelised (*or* ~ized)
carapace
carat (*or* ka~)
Caravaggesque
Caravaggio
caravan
caravanette
caravanserai (*occ US*
~sery)
caraway
carbide
carbine
carbohydrate
carbolic
carbon
carbonaceous
carbonado
carbonate
carbonated
carbonic
Carboniferous
carbonisation (*or* ~iz~)
carbonise (*or* ~ize)
carbonised (*or* ~ized)
carbonyl
carborundum
carboxyl
carboxylic
carbuncle
carbuncular
carburation
carburetted (*US* ~eted)
carburettor (*US* ~etor)
carburisation (*or* ~iz~)
carburise (*or* ~ize)
carcajou
carcass (*occ* ~case)
carcinogen
carcinogenesis
carcinogenic

carcinoma (*pl* ~as,
~mata)
carcinomatous
card
cardamom (*occ* ~mum,
~mon)
cardboard
carded
carder
cardholder
cardiac
Cardiff
cardigan
cardinal
cardinalate
cardinally
cardinalship
carding
cardiogram
cardiograph
cardiographer
cardiography
cardioid
cardiological
cardiologist
cardiology
cardiomegaly
cardiomyopathy
cardiopulmonary
cardiorespiratory
cardiovascular
cardphone
care
careen
career
careerism
careerist
carefree
carefreeness
careful
carefully
carefulness
caregiver
careless
carelessness
carer
caress
caressing
caressingly
caretaker

careworn
carful
cargo (*pl* ~oes, ~os)
Carib
Caribbean
caribou
caricatural
caricature
caricatured
caricaturist
caries
carillon
carillonneur
caring
cariogenic
carload
Carlovingian
Carmelite
carminative
carmine
carnage
carnal
carnality
carnally
carnassial
carnation
carnauba
carnelian (*occ* cor~)
carnet
carnival
carnivalesque
carnivore
carnivorous
carnivorously
carnivorousness
carob
carol (~lled, ~lling; *US*
  ~led, ~ling)
caroler
Carolingian
carolling
carotene (*also* ~tin)
carotenoid
carotid
carousal
carouse
carousel (*occ* carr~)
carouser
carousing
carp

carpaccio
carpal (! carpel) *bone*
carpel (! carpal) *part of*
  plant
carpenter
carpentry
carpet
carpetbagger
carpet-bagging
carpeted
carpeting
carpological
carpology
carpool
carpooler
carport
carpus
carrel (*or* ~ell)
carriage
carrier
carrion
carrot
carroty
carrousel (*or* caro~)
carry
carryall
carrycot
carrying
carry-on
carsick
cart
cartage
carte blanche
cartel
cartelise (*or* ~ize)
Carthage
Carthaginian
Carthusian
cartilage
cartilaginoid
cartilaginous
cartload
cartogram
cartographer
cartographic
cartographical
cartographically
cartography
carton
cartoon

cartooned
cartooning
cartoonish
cartoonist
cartoony
cartouche
cartridge
cartwheel
cartwright
carve
carved
carver
carvery
carving
caryatid (*pl* ~ids, ~ides)
Casablanca
casbah (*or* kas~, C~,
  K~)
cascade
case
casebook
case-harden
case-hardened
caseload
casement
casework
caseworker
cash
cashback
cashew
cashier
cashiered
cashless
cashmere
cashpoint
casing
casino (*pl* ~os)
cask
casket
casque
cassava (*UK*)
casserole
cassette
cassia
Cassini
Cassiopeia
cassis
cassock
cassocked
cassowary

cast
castanets
castaway
caste
casteism
castellated
castellation
caster (! castor) *one who casts*
caster (*UK also* ~or) *sugar*
castigate
castigation
castigator
castigatory
Castile
Castilian
casting
castle
castling
Castor *star*
castor (! caster) *hat, oil*
castor (*UK; US* caster) *wheels*
castrate
castration
castrato (*pl* ~ati, ~os)
castrator
casual
casually
casualness
casualty
casuist
casuistic
casuistical
casuistically
casuistry
cat
cataclysm
cataclysmic
cataclysmically
catacomb
Catalan
catalepsy
cataleptic
catalog (*US; UK* ~logue)
catalogue (*UK v* ~logued, ~loguing; *US also* ~loged, ~loging)

cataloguer (*US also* ~loger)
Catalonia
Catalonian
catalyse (*US* ~yze)
catalyser (*US* ~yz~)
catalysis
catalyst
catalytic
catamaran
cataplectic
cataplexy
catapult
cataract
catarrh
catarrhal
catastrophe
catastrophic
catastrophically
catastrophism
catastrophist
catatonia
catatonic
catcall
catch (caught)
catchily
catchiness
catchment
catchpenny
catch-phrase
catchweight
catchword
catchy
catechesis
catechetic
catechetical
catechetics
catechise (*or* ~ize)
catechiser (*or* ~iz~)
catechism
catechist
catechumen
categorial
categoric
categorical
categorically
category
catenary
catenated
catenation

cater
caterer
catering
caterpillar
caterwaul
caterwauling
catfish
catgut
catharsis (*pl* ~rses)
cathartic
cathartically
cathedral
catheter
catheterisation (*or* ~iz~)
catheterise (*or* ~ize)
cathodal
cathode
cathodic
Catholic *religion*
catholic *interests*
Catholicise (*or* ~ize)
Catholicism
catholicity
cation
catkin
catlick
catlike
catmint
catnap (~pped, ~pping)
catnip
catsuit
catsup (*US*)
cattery
cattily
cattiness
cattish
cattishly
cattishness
cattle
cattleya
catty
catwalk
Caucasian
Caucasoid
caucus
caudal
caudally
caudillo (*pl* ~os)
caught
cauldron (*US also* cal~)

cauliflower
caulk (*UK*, *cf* calk) *boat*
caulker
causal
causality
causally
causation
causative
cause
cause célèbre (*pl* causes célèbres)
causeless
causer
causeway
caustic
caustically
causticity
cauterisation (*or* ~iz~)
cauterise (*or* ~ize)
caution
cautionary
cautious
cautiously
cautiousness
cava (*or* ka~)
cavalcade
cavalier
cavalierly
cavalry
cavalryman (*pl* ~men)
cave
caveat
cavefish
cave-in
caveman (*pl* ~men)
caver
cavern
cavernous
cavernously
cavewoman (*pl* ~women)
caviar (*also* ~are)
cavil (~lled, ~lling; *US* ~led, ~ling)
caviller (*US* ~iler)
caving
cavity
cavort
cavy
caw

cay
cayenne
cayman (*occ* cai~)
CD-ROM
ceanothus
cease
ceasefire
ceaseless
ceaselessly
cedar
cede
cedilla
ceilidh
ceiling
celandine
celebrant
celebrate
celebration
celebrator
celebratory
celebrity
celeriac
celerity
celery
celesta
celestial
celestially
celibacy
celibate
cell
cellar
cellarage
cellarer
cellist
cell-like
cello (*pl* ~os)
cellophane
cellotape
cellphone
cellular
cellularity
cellulite
cellulitis
celluloid
cellulose
cellulosic
celosia
Celsius
Celt
Celtic (*occ* K~)

cement
cementation
cementer
cemetery
cenacle
cenobite (*US*; *cf* coen~)
cenotaph
cense
censer (! censor) *one who censes*
censor (! censer) *examiner*
censorial
censorious
censoriously
censoriousness
censorship
censurable
censure
censured
census
cent
centaur
Centaurus
centavo (*pl* ~os)
centenarian
centenary
centennial
centesimal
centigrade
centigram (*occ* ~mme)
centilitre (*US* ~ter)
centime
centimetre (*US* ~ter)
centimo (*pl* ~os)
centipede
central
centralisation (*or* ~iz~)
centralise (*or* ~ize)
centralised (*or* ~ized)
centralism
centralist
centrality
centre (*US* ~ter)
centreboard (*US* ~ter~)
centred (*US* ~ter~)
centredness (*US* ~ter~)
centrefield (*US* ~ter~)
centrefold (*US* ~ter~)
centremost (*US* ~ter~)

centrepiece (*US* ~ter~)
centric
centricity
centrifugal
centrifugally
centrifugation
centrifuge
centring (*US* ~ter~)
centripetal
centrism
centrist
centuple
centurion
century
cephalometric
cephalometry
cephalopod
cephalosporin
Cepheid
ceramic
Cerberus
cere
cereal
cerebellar
cerebellum (*pl* ~ums *or*
~lla)
cerebral
cerebrally
cerebration
cerebrospinal
cerebrovascular
cerebrum (*pl* ~ra)
cerecloth
ceremonial
ceremonialism
ceremonialist
ceremonially
ceremonious
ceremoniously
ceremoniousness
ceremony
cereologist
cereology
ceresin
cerise
cerium
cert
certain
certainly
certainty

certifiable
certificate
certificated
certification
certify
certitude
cerulean
cerumen
cervical
cervicitis
cervix (*pl* ~ices)
Cesarean (*c*; *esp US*; *cf*
Caesarian) *section*
cessation
cession
cesspit
cesspool
Cetacea
cetacean (C~)
cetane
Cetus
Ceylon
Ceylonese
chaat
Chablis
cha-cha-cha
chaconne
Chad
Chadian
Chadic
chador (*occ* ~dar,
chudder)
chafe
chafer
chaff
chaffer
chaffinch
chaffweed
chaffy
chafing
chagrin
chai
chain
chainmail
chainsaw
chain-smoke
chain-smoker
chair
chairlift
chairman (*pl* ~men)

chairperson
chairwoman (*pl*
~women)
chaise longue
chakra
chalcedonic
chalcedony
chalet
chalice
chalk
chalkboard
chalkface
chalkiness
chalky
challenge
challengeable
challenged
challenger
challenging
challengingly
Chamaeleon
constellation
chamber
chambered
chamberlain
chamberlainship
chambray *fabric*
chambré *wine*
chameleon (*or* ~mae~)
animal
chameleonic (*or*
~mae~)
chamfer
chamfering
chamois *animal*
chamois (*or* chammy,
shammy) *cloth*
chamomile (*esp UK, lit*
ca~)
champ
champagne
champignon
champion
championship
champlevé
chance
chancel
chancellery (*occ* ~ory)
chancellor
chancellorship

chancy
chandelier
chandler
chandlery
change
changeability
changeable
changeableness
changeably
changeful
changeless
changelessly
changelessness
changeling
change-over
changer
channel (~lled, ~lling;
  US ~led, ~ling)
chanson
chant
chanter
chanterelle
chanteuse
chanticleer
Chantilly
Chanukkah (*esp UK*; *or*
  Han~)
chaos
chaotic
chaotically
chap (~pped, ~pping)
chaparral
chapati (*or* ~tti, *pl* ~is,
  ~ies)
chapel
chaperonage
chaperone (*also* ~on)
chaplain
chaplaincy
chaplet
chapleted
chapped
chapter
char (~rred, ~rring)
charabanc
character
characterful
characterfully
characterisation (*or*
  ~iz~)

characterise (*or* ~ize)
characteristic
characteristically
characterless
charade
charango
charbroil
charbroiled
charcoal
charcuterie
chard
Chardonnay
charge
chargeable
charged
charger
chargrill
chargrilled
charily
chariot
charioteer
charioteering
charisma
charismatic
charismatically
charitable
charitableness
charitably
charity
charlatan
charlatanism
charlatanry
Charlemagne
Charleston
charlock
charm
charmed
charmer
charmeuse
charming
charmingly
charmless
charmlessly
charmlessness
charnel
Charon
charro (*pl* ~os)
chart
chartbuster
charter

chartered
charterer
chartering
chartreuse (C~)
charwoman (*pl*
  ~women)
chary
Charybdis
chase
chaser
chasm
chasmic
chassé
chasseur
chassis
chaste
chasten
chastened
chastener
chasteness
chastening
chastise
chastisement
chastising
chastity
chasuble
chat (~tted, ~tting)
chateau (*occ* chât~, *pl*
  ~ux, ~us)
chateaubriand (C~)
chatline
chattel
chatter
chatterbox
chatterer
chattering
chattery
chattily
chattiness
chatty
chauffeur
chauffeuse
chauvinism
chauvinist
chauvinistic
chauvinistically
chayote
cheap
cheapen
cheapish

cheaply
cheapness
cheapskate
cheat
cheater
Chechen
Chechnya (*occ* ~nia)
check
checkable
checked
checker (! chequer) *stop, verify*
checkered
check-in
checklist
checkmate
checkout
checkpoint
checkroom
Cheddar
cheek
cheekbone
cheekily
cheekiness
cheekpiece
cheeky
cheep
cheer
cheerful
cheerfully
cheerfulness
cheerily
cheeriness
cheerleader
cheerless
cheerlessly
cheerlessness
cheers
cheery
cheese
cheeseboard
cheeseburger
cheesecake
cheesecloth
cheese-cutter
cheesemonger
cheesewood
cheesily
cheesiness
cheesy

cheetah
chef
chelate
chelation
chelator
Chelmsford
cheloid *see* keloid
Chelsea
chemical
chemically
chemiluminescence
chemiluminescent
chemise
chemisette
chemist
chemistry
chemotherapist
chemotherapy
chenille
cheque (*US* check)
chequebook (*US* check~)
chequer (*US* checker; ! checker) *board*
chequerboard (*US* checker~)
chequered (*US* checker~)
cherish
Chernobyl
Cherokee
cheroot
cherry
chert
cherub (*pl* ~bs, *rel* ~bim)
cherubic
cherubically
chervil
Cheshire
chess
chessboard
chessman (*pl* ~men)
chest
chesterfield
chestily
chestiness
chestnut
chesty
chevalier

Cheviot
chevron
chevrotain
chew
chewable
chewer
chewiness
chewy
Cheyenne
chez
chi *letter*
chi (*or* qi, ki) *life force*
Chianti
chiaroscuro
chiasma
chic
Chicago
Chicagoan
chicane
chicanery
chicha
chichi
chick
chickadee
chicken
chickenpox
chickpea (*or* chick-~)
chickweed
chicle
chicly
chicory
chide (chid *or* chided, chiding)
chider
chidingly
chief
chiefly
chieftain
chieftaincy
chiffon
chiffonade (*also* ~onn~)
chiffonier (*also* ~onn~)
chignon
chihuahua
chilblain
chilblained
child (*pl* children)
childbearing
childbirth
childcare

child-centred (US
~ter~)
childhood
childish
childishly
childishness
childless
childlessness
childlike
childminder
childminding
childproof
Chile
Chilean
chili (*or* chilli; *pl* ~is,
~ies; ! chilly) *pepper*
chill
chilled
chiller
chilliness
chilling
chillingly
chillness
chilly (UK) *cold*
chime
chimer
chimera (*or* ~mae~)
chimerical
chimerically
chimney (*pl* ~eys)
chimpanzee
chin
China
china
chinaberry
Chinaman (*pl* ~men)
Chinatown
chinchilla
chine
Chinese
chink
chinless
chinned
chino (*pl* ~os, ~oes)
chinoiserie
Chinook
chinstrap
chintz
chintzily
chintziness

chintzy
chinwag (~gged,
~gging)
chip (~pped, ~pping)
chipboard
chipmunk
chipolata
Chippendale
chipper
chipping
chirograph
chirographer
chirographic
chirography
chiromancy
Chiron
chiropodist
chiropody
chiropractic
chiropractor
chiropteran
chirp
chirper
chirpily
chirpiness
chirpy
chirrup
chirrupy
chisel (~lled, ~lling; US
~led, ~ling)
chiseller (US ~eler)
chit (~tted, ~tting)
chital
chit-chat
chitin
chitlings
chitterlings
chivalric
chivalrous
chivalrously
chivalry
chives
chivvy (*or* chivy)
chlamydia (*pl* ~iae)
chlamydial
chloasma
chloral
chlorate
chloride
chlorinate

chlorinated
chlorination
chlorinator
chlorine
chlorofluorocarbon
chloroform
chlorophyll (*occ US*
~phyl)
chlorophyllous
chloroplast
choc
chock
chock-a-block
chock-full
chockstone
chocoholic (*also*
~aholic)
chocolate
chocolatey (*or* ~aty)
chocolatier
Choctaw (*pl* ~w, ~ws)
choice
choicely
choiceness
choir
choirboy
choirgirl
choirmaster
choirmistress
choke
choked
choker
chokiness
cholera
cholesterol
chomp
choose (chose, chosen,
choosing)
chooser
choosily
choosiness
choosy
chop (~pped, ~pping)
chophouse
chopper
choppily
choppiness
choppy
chopstick
choral (*adj*)

chorale (*n*)
chorally
chord
chordal
Chordata
chordate
chording
chordophone
chore
chorea
choreograph
choreographer
choreographic
choreographically
choreography
choreologist
choreology
choric
chorionic
chorister
chortle
chorus (*pl* ~uses)
chose
chosen
choucroute
chough
choux
chow
chow mein
chowder
chrism
Christ
Christadelphian
christen
Christendom
christened
christener
Christian
Christianisation (*or* ~iz~)
Christianise (*or* ~ize)
Christianity
Christingle
Christmas (*pl* ~ases)
Christmassy
Christocentric
Christological
Christologically
Christology
chroma

chromakey
chromate
chromatic
chromatically
chromaticism
chromaticity
chromatism
chromatogram
chromatograph
chromatographic
chromatography
chromatopsia
chrome
chromic
chrominance
chromium
chromophore
chromosomal
chromosome
chromosphere
chronic
chronically
chronicity
chronicle
chronicler
Chronicles *bible*
chronobiology
chronological
chronologically
chronologist
chronology
chronometer
chronometric
chronometrical
chronometrically
chronometry
chronoscope
chrysalid (*pl* ~s, ~des)
chrysalis (*pl* ~ises)
chrysanthemum
chrysolite
chrysoprase
chub
chubbily
chubbiness
chubby
chuck
chucker
chuckle
chucklehead

chuckler
chuckwalla
chuff
chuffed
chug (~gged, ~gging)
chukka (*or* ~kker)
chum (~mmed, ~mming)
chummily
chumminess
chummy
chump
chunk
chunkily
chunkiness
chunky
Chunnel
chunter
church
churchgoer
Churchill
Churchillian
churchiness
churchwarden
churchy
churchyard
churl
churlish
churlishly
churlishness
churn
churrascaria
chute
chutney (*pl* ~eys)
chutzpah
ciabatta (*pl* ~tte, ~as)
ciao
cicada
cicatrice (*pl* ~ices)
cicatricial
cicatrisation (*or* ~iz~)
cicatrise (*or* ~ize)
cicatrix (*pl* ~ixes)
cicely
Cicero
Ciceronian
cider (*occ* cyd~)
cigar
cigarette (*US also* ~et)
cigarillo (*pl* ~os)

ciliary
ciliate
cilium (*pl* ~ia)
cimbalom
cinch
cinchona
cincture
cinder
Cinderella
cineaste (*or* ciné~, ~ast)
cinema
cinematheque
cinematic
cinematically
cinematise (*or* ~ize)
cinematograph
cinematographer
cinematographic
cinematographically
cinematography
cinephile
cineplex
cineraria
cinnabar
cinnamon
cinquefoil
cipher (*or* cy~)
circa
circadian
Circe
circle
circlet
circuit
circuit-breaker
circuitous
circuitously
circuitousness
circuitry
circular
circularisation (*or* ~iz~)
circularise (*or* ~ize)
circularity
circularly
circulate
circulating
circulation
circulative
circulatory
circumambulate
circumambulation

circumambulatory
circumcise
circumcision
circumference
circumferential
circumferentially
circumflex
circumlocution
circumlocutory
circumnavigate
circumnavigation
circumnavigator
circumscribe
circumscribed
circumscriber
circumscription
circumspect
circumspection
circumspectly
circumstance
circumstanced
circumstantial
circumstantiality
circumstantially
circumstantiate
circumstantiating
circumvent
circumvention
circus
cire (*or* ciré)
cirque
cirrhosis
cirrhotic
cirrocumulus
cirrostratus
cirrus (*pl* ~rri)
cisalpine
cisatlantic
cislunar
cissy (*also UK* si~; *US* si~)
cist
Cistercian
cistern
citable
citadel
citation
cite
citified (*occ* city~)
citizen

citizenry
citizenship
citrate
citric
citriculture
citrine
citron
citronella
citrous (*adj, or* citrus)
citrus (*n*)
citrusy
cittern
city
cityward
citywards
civet
civic
civically
civics
civil
civilian
civilisable (*or* ~iz~)
civilisation (*or* ~iz~)
civilise (*or* ~ize)
civilised (*or* ~ized)
civiliser (*or* ~iz~)
civility
civilly
civvy
clack
clacker
clad (~dded, ~dding)
cladding (*n*)
cladistics
claim
claimable
claimant
claimer
clairaudience
clairaudient
clairvoyance
clairvoyancy
clairvoyant
clam (~mmed, ~mming)
clamber
clammily
clamminess
clammy
clamorous

clamorously
clamorousness
clamour (US ~or)
clamp
clampdown
clamper
clan
clandestine
clandestinely
clandestinity
clang
clanger
clank
clankingly
clannish
clannishly
clannishness
clanship
clansman (pl ~men)
clap (~pped, ~pping)
clapboard
clapper
clapperboard
claptrap
claque
claqueur
claret
clarification
clarificatory
clarifier
clarify
clarinet
clarinettist (US ~etist)
clarion
clarity
clash
clasher
clasp
class
class-conscious
classic
classical
classicalism
classicality
classically
classicise (or ~ize)
classicism
classicist
Classics *specific literary, racing*

classics *great works*
classifiable
classification
classificatory
classified
classifieds
classifier
classify
classifying
classily
classiness
classless
classlessness
classmate
classroom
classy
clatter
clausal
clause
claustrophobe
claustrophobia
claustrophobic
claustrophobically
clavichord
clavicle
clavicular
clavier
claw
clawback
clawed
clawless
clay
clayey
clayish
clay-like
claymore
clean
cleanable
cleaner
cleanish
cleanliness
cleanly
cleanness
cleanse
cleanser
cleansing
clear
clearance
clearing
clearly

clearway
cleat
cleated
cleavage
cleave (clove, cleft *or* cleaved, cloven, cleaving)
cleaver
clef
cleft
clematis
clemency
clement
clementine
clemently
clench
clenched
clergy
cleric
clerical
clericalism
clericalist
clerically
clerihew
clerk
clerkly
clerkship
clever
cleverly
cleverness
clew (! clue) *carpentry*
clianthus
cliché (or cliche)
clichéd (or clichéed, cliché'd, cliche'd, cliched)
click
clickable
clicker
clicking
client
clientele
cliff
cliffhanger
cliffhanging
climacteric
climactic
climactically
climate
climatic

climatical
climatically
climatological
climatologist
climatology
climax
climb
climbable
climbdown
climber
climbing
clime
clinch
clincher
cling (clung)
clinger
clingfilm
clinginess
clinging (*n*)
clingy
clinic
clinical
clinically
clink
clinker
clinking
clip (~pped, ~pping)
clipboard
clipper
clippers
clipping
clique
cliquey (*occ* ~quy)
cliquish
cliquishness
clitoral
clitoridectomy
clitoris
cloak
cloakroom
clobber
cloche
clock
clocker
clockmaker
clockwise
clockwork
clod
cloddish
clodhopper

clog (~gged, ~gging)
cloggy
cloisonné
cloister
cloistered
cloistral
clonal
clone
clonk
clonky
clop (~pped, ~pping)
close
close-down
close-fisted
close-grained
close-hauled
close-knit
close-lipped
closely
closeness
closer
close-range
close-run
closet
close-up
closing
clostridium
closure
clot (~tted, ~tting)
cloth
clothe
clothes
clothesline
clothier
clothing
cloud
cloudberry
cloudburst
clouded
cloudily
cloudiness
cloudscape
cloudy
clout
clove
cloven
clover
clown
clownery
clownish

cloy
cloyedness
cloyingly
cloyingness
club (~bbed, ~bbing)
clubbability
clubbable (*occ* clubable)
clubber
club-footed
clubhouse
clubland
clubman (*pl* ~men)
clubmoss
clubroot
cluck
clue (*n*, ! clew) *help*
clue (*v* clued, cluing)
clueless
cluelessly
cluelessness
clump
clumpy
clumsily
clumsiness
clumsy
clung
clunk
clunky
cluster
clustered
clutch
clutter
cluttered
Clwyd
Clytemnestra
coach
coachbuilder
coaching
coachload
coachman (*pl* ~men)
coachroof
coachwork
coadjutor (*occ* co-a~)
coagulable
coagulant
coagulase
coagulate
coagulation
coagulative
coagulator

coal
coalesce
coalescence
coalescent
coalface
coalfield
coal-fired
coalhouse
coalition
coalitional
coalitionist
coarse
coarsely
coarsen
coarseness
coast
coastal
coaster
coastguard
coastland
coastline
coastwise
coat
coated
coatee
coat-hanger
coati
coating
coat-tails
coauthor (*or* co-~)
coax
coaxial
coaxingly
cob
cobalt
cobaltic
cobaltous
cobber
cobble
cobbled
cobbler
cobblestone
cobby
Cobol (or COBOL)
cobra
cobweb
cobwebbed
cobwebby
coca
Coca-Cola (*tr*)

cocaine
coccus
coccyx (*pl* ~yges, ~yxes)
cochineal
cochlea (*pl* ~eae, ~eas)
cochlear
cock
cockade
cockatiel (*occ* ~teel)
cockatoo
cockatrice
cockchafer
cockcrow
cocker
cockerel
cock-eye
cockfight
cock-horse
cockily
cockiness
cockle
cockleshell
cockling
cock-loft
cockney (C~)
cockneyism
cockpit
cockroach
cockscomb
cockspur
cocksure
cocksurely
cocksureness
cocktail
cocky
cocoa
coconut
cocoon
cocooned
cocooner
cod
coda
coddle
coddler
coddling
code
codec
coded
codeine
codependence

codependency
codependent
co-determination
co-determine
codex (*pl* ~dices, ~exes)
codfish
codicil
codicillary
codification
codifier
codify
coding
codling
co-edit
co-edition
co-editor
co-education
co-educational
coefficient
coelacanth
coelenterate
coeliac (*or* cel~)
coelom (*or* cel~)
coenobite (*or* cen~)
coenobitic (*or* cen~)
coenobitical (*or* cen~)
coenocyte (*or* cen~)
coenocytic (*or* cen~)
co-enzyme
co-equal
co-equality
co-equally
coerce
coercible
coercion
coercive
coercively
coerciveness
coercivity
coeval
coevality
coevally
co-exist (*occ* coe~)
co-existence (*occ* coe~)
co-existent (*occ* coe~)
co-extend (*occ* coe~)
co-extension (*occ* coe~)
co-extensive (*occ* coe~)
coffee
coffeepot

coffer
cofferdam
coffin
cog
cogency
cogent
cogently
cogged
cogitate
cogitation
cogitative
cogitator
cognac
cognate
cognately
cognateness
cognisable (or ~iz~)
cognisance (or ~iz~)
cognisant (or ~iz~)
cognise (or ~ize)
cognition
cognitional
cognitive
cognitively
cognomen
cognoscenti
cohabit
cohabitant
cohabitation
cohabitee
cohabiter
cohere
coherence
coherency
coherent
coherently
cohesion
cohesive
cohesively
cohesiveness
cohort
coif (~ffed, ~ffing; US
   ~fed, ~fing)
coiffeur
coiffeuse
coiffure
coil
coiler
coin
coinage

coincide
coincidence
coincident
coincidental
coincidentally
coiner
coin-op
Cointreau
coir
coitus
coke
cola (or ko~)
colander
colchicine
cold
cold-blooded
cold-hearted
coldish
Colditz
coldness
Coleoptera
coleopteran
coleopterist
coleopterous
coleslaw
colic
coliseum (occ ~losse~)
   stadium
colitis
collaborate
collaboration
collaborative
collaboratively
collaborator
collage
collagen
collagenic
collagist
collapse
collapsed
collapsibility
collapsible
collar
collared
collarless
collate
collateral
collaterality
collation
collator

colleague
collect
collectability
collectable (esp UK; esp
   US ~tible)
collected
collectedly
collectible (esp US; esp
   UK ~table)
collection
collective
collectively
collectiveness
collectivisation (or
   ~iz~)
collectivise (or ~ize)
collectivism
collectivist
collectivity
collector
colleen
college
collegial
collegiality
collegian
collegiate
collide
collie
collier
colliery
collimator
collinear
collinearity
collision
collisional
colloid
colloidal
colloquial
colloquialism
colloquially
colloquium (pl ~ia)
colloquy
collotype
collude
colluder
collusion
collusive
collusively
colobus
Cologne place

cologne *perfume*
Colombia
Colombian
colon
colonaded
colonel
colonial
colonialism
colonialist
colonially
colonic
colonisation (*or* ~iz~)
colonise (*or* ~ize)
coloniser (*or* ~iz~)
colonist
colonnade
colonoscope
colonoscopy
colony
colophon
colophony
Coloradan
Colorado
colorant (*occ* ~our~)
coloration (*occ* ~our~)
coloratura
colorific (*occ* ~our~)
colorimeter
colorimetry
colossal
colossally
Colosseum (*cf* coliseum)
    Rome
colossus (*pl* ~si)
colostomy
colour (*US* ~or)
colourable (*US* ~or~)
colourant (*or* ~or~)
colouration (*or* ~or~)
coloured (*US* ~or~)
colourful (*US* ~or~)
colourfully (*US* ~or~)
colourific (*or* ~or~)
colouring (*US* ~or~)
colourist (*US* ~or~)
colouristic (*US* ~or~)
colourize (*US* ~or~)
colourless (*US* ~or~)
colourlessly (*US* ~or~)
colt

coltish
coltishly
coltishness
Columbia
Columbian
Columbus
column
columnated
columned
columnist
coma (*bot, astron, pl* ~ae)
coma (*med, pl* ~as)
Comanche
comatose
comb
combat (*US & incr UK* ~ted, ~ting; *also* ~tted, ~tting)
combatable
combatant
combative
combatively
combativeness
comber
combfish
combinable
combination
combinational
combinative
combinatorial
combinatorially
combinatory
combine
combined
combings
combining
combo (*pl* ~os)
combust
combustibility
combustible
combustion
come (came, coming)
comeback
comedian
comedic
comedienne
comedy
comeliness
comely

come-on
comer
comestible
comet
comeuppance (*or* come-~)
comfily
comfiness
comfit
comfort
comfortable
comfortableness
comfortably
comforter
comfortingly
comfortless
comfrey (*pl* ~eys)
comfy
comic
comical
comicality
comically
coming
comity
comma
command
commandant
commandeer
commander
commandership
commanding
commandment
commando (*pl* ~os, ~oes)
commedia
commemorate
commemoration
commemorative
commemorator
commemoratory
commence
commencement
commend
commendable
commendably
commendation
commendatory
commensurability
commensurable
commensurate

commensuration
comment
commentary
commentate
commentating
commentator
commenter
commerce
commercial
commercialisation (*or*
~iz~)
commercialise (*or* ~ize)
commercialism
commercialist
commercialistic
commerciality
commercially
commination
comminatory
commingle
comminute
comminution
commiserate
commiserating
commiseration
commiserative
commissar
commissarial
commissariat
commissary
commission
commissionaire
commissioned
commissioner
commissural
commissure
commit (~tted, ~tting)
commitable
commiter
commitment
committal
committed
committee
commix
commixture
commode
commodious
commodiously
commodiousness
commodity

commodore
common
commonality
commoner
commonly
commonness
commonplace
commonplaceness
commonwealth (C~)
commotion
communal
communalisation (*or*
~iz~)
communalise (*or* ~ize)
communalism
communalist
communalistic
communality
communard
commune
communicability
communicable
communicably
communicant
communicate
communication
communicative
communicativeness
communicator
communicatory
Communion *religion*
communion *group*
communional
communionist
communiqué
communism (C~)
communist (C~)
communistic
community
commutable
commutate
commutation
commutative
commutator
commute
commuter
Comoros
compact
compacter
compactness

companion
companionable
companionship
companionway
company
comparability
comparable
comparableness
comparably
comparative
comparatively
comparator
compare
comparer
comparison
compartment
compartmental
compartmentalisation
(*or* ~iz~)
compartmentalise (*or*
~ize)
compartmentalism
compartmentally
compass
compassion
compassionate
compassionately
compatibility
compatible
compatibly
compatriot
compeer
compel (~lled, ~lling)
compelling (*adj*)
compendious
compendiously
compendiousness
compendium (*pl* ~ia,
~iums)
compensatable
compensate
compensation
compensational
compensative
compensator
compensatory
compere (*or* ~ère)
compete
competence
competency

competent
competently
competing
competition
competitive
competitively
competitiveness
competitor
compilation
compile
compiler
complacence
complacency
complacent
complacently
complain
complainer
complaint
complaisance
complaisant
complement
  (! compliment)
  complete
complemental
complementarily
complementariness
complementarity
complementary
  (! complimentary)
  completing
complementation
complete
completely
completeness
completer
completing
completion
completist
complex
complexed
complexion
complexioned
complexity
complexly
compliance
compliant
compliantly
complicate
complicated
complication

complicity
compliment
  (! complement) *praise*
complimentary
  (! complementary)
  praising
comply
component
componential
comport
comportment
compos mentis
compose
composed
composedly
composer
composite
compositely
compositeness
compositing
composition
compositional
compositionally
compositor
compost
composure
compote
compound
compoundable
compounded
compounder
comprehend
comprehensibility
comprehensible
comprehensibly
comprehension
comprehensive
comprehensively
comprehensiveness
compress
compressed
compressibility
compressible
compression
compressional
compressive
compressor
comprise
compromise
compromiser

compromising
comptroller
compulsion
compulsive
compulsively
compulsiveness
compulsorily
compulsoriness
compulsory
compunction
compunctious
compunctiously
computability
computable
computation
computational
compute
computed
computer
computerate
computerisation (or
  ~iz~)
computerise (or ~ize)
computerised (or ~ized)
computing
comrade
comradely
comradeship
con (~nned, ~nning)
Conakry
conation
conative
concatenate
concatenation
concave
concavely
concavity
conceal
concealer
concealment
concede
conceder
conceit
conceited
conceitedly
conceitedness
conceivable
conceive
conceived
concentrate

concentrated
concentration
concentre (*US* ~ter)
concentric
concentricity
concept
conception
conceptional
conceptual
conceptualisation (*or* ~iz~)
conceptualise (*or*~ize)
conceptualism
conceptualist
concern
concerned
concerning
concernment
concert
concerted
concertina (*v* ~as, ~aed *or* ~a'd, ~aing)
concerto (*pl* ~rti, ~os)
concession
concessionaire
concessional
concessionary
concessive
conch (*pl* ~ches, ~chs)
conchological
conchologist
conchology
concierge
conciliar
conciliate
conciliation
conciliative
conciliator
conciliatoriness
conciliatory
concise
concisely
conciseness
conclave
conclude
conclusion
conclusive
conclusively
conclusiveness
concoct

concoction
concomitance
concomitancy
concomitant
concomitantly
concord
concordance
concordanced
concordant
concordantly
concordat
concourse
concrescence
concrescent
concrete
concreted
concretely
concreteness
concretion
concretionary
concretisation (*or* ~iz~)
concretise (*or* ~ize)
concubinage
concubinary
concubine
concupiscence
concupiscent
concur (~rred, ~rring)
concurrence
concurrent
concurrently
concuss
concussed
concussion
concussive
condemn
condemnable
condemnation
condemnatory
condemned
condensable
condensate
condensation
condense
condensed
condenser
condescend
condescending
condescendingly
condescension

condiment
condition
conditional
conditionality
conditionally
conditioner
condolence
condolent
condom
condominium (*pl* ~ms)
condone
condoner
condor
conduce
conducive
conduct
conductance
conduction
conductive
conductively
conductivity
conductor
conductress
conduit
cone
coned
coneflower
conehead
coney (*pl* ~eys)
confabulate
confabulation
confabulatory
confection
confectioner
confectionery
confederacy
confederate
confederation
confer (~rred, ~rring)
conferee
conference
conferment
conferrable
conferral
confess
confessant
confessedly
confession
confessional
confessionary

confessor
confetti
confidant
confidante
confide
confidence
confident
confidential
confidentiality
confidentially
confidently
confidingly
configurable
configuration
configure
confine
confined
confinement
confirm
confirmation
confirmative
confirmatory
confirmed
confiscate
confiscated
confiscation
confiscator
confiscatory
conflagration
conflate
conflation
conflict
conflictual
confluence
confluent
conflux
conform
conformability
conformable
conformably
conformal
conformally
conformation
conformational
conformer
conformism
conformist
conformity
confound
confounded

confoundedly
confraternity
confrere (*or* ~ère)
confront
confrontation
confrontational
Confucian
Confucianism
Confucianist
Confucius
confusability
confusable
confuse
confused
confusedly
confusingly
confusion
confutation
confute
conga (~gas, ~gaed *or*
 ~ga'd, ~gaing)
congé
congeal
congealable
congealed
congealment
congener
congenial
congeniality
congenially
conger *eel*
congeries *heap*
congest
congested
congestion
congestive
conglobulate
conglomerate
conglomeration
Congo
Congolese
congratulate
congratulation
congratulatory
congregant
congregate
congregation
congregational
Congregationalism
Congregationalist

congress (C~)
congressional
congressman (*pl* ~men)
congresswoman (*pl*
 ~women)
congruence
congruency
congruent
congruently
congruity
congruous
congruously
conic
conical
conically
conifer
coniferous
coniform
conjecturable
conjectural
conjecturally
conjecture
conjoin
conjoint
conjointly
conjugacy
conjugal
conjugality
conjugally
conjugate
conjugated
conjugation
conjugational
conjunct
conjunction
conjunctional
conjunctiva
conjunctival
conjunctive
conjunctively
conjunctivitis
conjuncture
conjuration
conjure
conjurer (*or esp UK* ~or)
conjuring
conjuror (*or esp US* ~er)
conk
conker
connatural

connaturally
connect
connectable (UK also ~ible)
connected
connectedly
connectedness
connecter (or ~or)
connectible (esp UK; US ~able)
Connecticut
connection (occ ~exion)
connectional
connectionism
connective
connectivity
connector (occ ~er)
connexion (or ~ection)
connivance
connive
conniver
conniving
connoisseur
connoisseurship
connotation
connotative
connote
connubial
connubiality
connubially
conquer
conquerable
conquering
conqueror
conquest
conquistador (pl ~res, ~rs)
consanguineous
consanguinity
conscience
conscienceless
conscientious
conscientiously
conscientiousness
conscious
consciously
consciousness
conscript
conscripted
conscription

consecrate
consecrated
consecration
consecrator
consecratory
consecutive
consecutively
consecutiveness
consensual
consensualist
consensually
consensus
consent
consequence
consequent
consequential
consequentiality
consequentially
conservation
conservational
conservatism
Conservative political party
conservative restrained, traditionalist
conservatively
conservativeness
conservatoire
conservator
conservatorium (pl ~ia, ~iums)
conservatory
conserve
conserved
consider
considerable
considerably
considerate
considerately
considerateness
consideration
considering
consign
consignee
consignment
consignor (or ~er)
consist
consistency
consistent
consistently

consistory
consolable
consolation
consolatory
console
consoler
consolidate
consolidation
consolidator
consolingly
consommé
consonance
consonant
consonantal
consonantly
consort
consortium (pl ~ia, ~iums)
conspectus
conspicuity
conspicuous
conspicuously
conspicuousness
conspiracist
conspiracy
conspirator
conspire
constable
constabulary
constancy
constant
Constantinople
constantly
constellate
constellation
consternate
consternated
consternation
constipate
constipated
constipation
constituency
constituent
constitute
constitution
constitutional
constitutionalism
constitutionalist
constitutionality
constitutionally

constitutive
constrain
constrained
constrainedly
constraint
constrict
constricted
constriction
constrictive
constrictor
construable
construal
construct
construction
constructional
constructionally
constructionism
constructionist
constructive
constructively
constructiveness
constructivism
constructivist
constructor
construe
consubstantial
consubstantiality
consubstantiation
consul
consular
consulate
consulship
consult
consultancy
consultant
consultation
consultative
consulting
consumable
consume
consumed
consumer
consumerism
consumerist
consumingly
consummate
consummately
consummation
consummative
consummator

consumption
consumptive
consumptively
contact
contactable
contagion
contagious
contagiously
contagiousness
contain
containable
container
containerisation (or
~iz~)
containerise (or ~ize)
containment
contaminant
contaminate
contaminated
contamination
contaminator
contemplate
contemplation
contemplative
contemplatively
contemplator
contemporaneity
contemporaneous
contemporaneously
contemporaneousness
contemporary
contempt
contemptibility
contemptible
contemptuous
contemptuously
contemptuousness
contemporarily
contemporariness
contend
contender
content
contented
contentedly
contentedness
contention
contentious
contentiously
contentiousness
contentless

contentment
contest
contestable
contestant
contester
context
contextual
contextualise (or ~ize)
contiguity
contiguous
contiguously
continence
continent
continental
continently
contingency
contingent
contingently
continual
continually
continuance
continuant
continuation
continuative
continuator
continue
continuity
continuo (pl ~os)
continuous
continuously
continuum (pl ~uums,
~nua)
contort
contortion
contortionist
contour
contraband
contrabandist
contrabass
contrabassoon
contraception
contraceptive
contract
contractable (med,
! contractible) diseases
contracted
contractible (anat,
! contractable) muscles
contraction
contractor

contractual
contractually
contradict
contradiction
contradictor
contradictorily
contradictoriness
contradictory
contraflow
contraindicate (*or* contra-~)
contraindication (*or* contra-~)
contraindicative (*or* contra-~)
contralto (*pl* ~os)
contraption
contrapuntal
contrapuntally
contrapuntist
contrariety
contrariwise
contrary
contrast
contrastingly
contrastive
contravene
contravener
contravention
contretemps
contribute
contribution
contributive
contributor
contributory
contrite
contritely
contriteness
contrition
contrivable
contrivance
contrive
contrived
control
controller
controversial
controversialist
controversially
controversy
controvert

controvertible
contuse
contused
contusion
conundrum
conurbation
convalesce
convalescence
convalescent
convect
convection
convectional
convective
convector
convenable
convene
convener (*also esp UK* ~or)
convenience
convenient
conveniently
convent
convention
conventional
conventionalisation (*or* ~iz~)
conventionalise (*or* ~ize)
conventionalism
conventionalist
conventionality
conventioneer
converge
convergence
convergent
conversance
conversancy
conversant
conversation
conversational
conversationalist
conversationally
converse
conversely
conversion
convert
converted
converter (*occ* ~or)
convertibility
convertible

convex
convexity
convexly
convey
conveyable
conveyance
conveyancing
conveyer (*occ* ~or) *information*
conveyor *belt*
convict
convicted
conviction
convince
convinced
convincer
convincible
convivial
conviviality
convivially
convocation
convocational
convoke
convolute
convoluted
convolutedly
convolution
convolutional
convolvulus
convoy
convulse
convulsion
convulsive
coo
cook
cooker
cookery
cookhouse
cookie
cooking
cool
coolant
cooled
cooler
coolie
cooling
coolish
coolly
coolness
coop

co-op
cooper
cooperage
cooperate (*UK also* co-~)
cooperation (*UK also* co-~)
cooperative (*UK also* co-~)
cooperatively (*UK also* co-~)
cooperativeness (*UK also* co-~)
co-opt (*US also* coopt)
co-opted (*US also* coopt~)
co-option (*US also* coopt~)
co-optive (*US also* coopt~)
coordinate (*UK also* co-~)
coordination (*UK also* co-~)
coot
cop (~pped, ~pping)
Copacabana
copal
cope (coped, coping)
Copenhagen
Copernican
Copernicus
copestone
copiable
copier
coping (*n*)
copious
copiously
copiousness
copper
copperhead
coppering
copperplate
coppersmith
coppery
coppice
coppiced
copra
co-produce
co-producer
co-production

copse
Copt
Coptic
copulate
copulation
copulatory
copy
copybook
copycat
copyist
copyread
copyreader
copyright
copywriter
copywriting
coq au vin
coquetry
coquette
coquettish
coquettishly
coquettishness
coracle
coral
coralline
coralloid
corbel (~lled, ~lling)
corbelling (*n*)
cord
cordage
corded
cordial
cordiality
cordially
cordillera
cording
cordite
cordless
cordon
cordon bleu
corduroy
core
corer
co-respondent
corgi
coriander
Corinth
Corinthian
Coriolis
cork
corkage

corked
corker
corkscrew
corky
corm
cormorant
corn
cornbread
corn-cob
corncrake
cornea
corneal
cornelian (*or* car~)
corner
cornered
cornerstone
cornet
cornetist (*occ* ~ettist)
cornflakes
cornflour (! cornflower)
   cookery
cornflower (! cornflour)
   plant
cornice
corniced
cornily
corniness
Cornish
cornucopia
Cornwall
corny
corollary
corona (*pl* ~ae, ~as)
coronal
coronary
coronation
coroner
coronet
coroneted
corporal
corporality
corporate
corporation
corporatism
corporatist
corporeal
corporeality
corporeally
corporeity
corps

corps de ballet
corpse
corpulence
corpulency
corpulent
corpus (*pl* ~pora, ~uses)
corpuscle
corpuscular
corral (~lled, ~lling; *occ*
　US ~led, ~ling)
correct
correctable
correction
correctional
corrective
correctively
correctly
correctness
corrector
correlate
correlation
correlational
correlative
correlatively
correlativity
correspond
correspondence
correspondent
corresponding
corrida
corridor
corrigendum (*pl* ~da,
　~ums)
corrigibility
corrigible
corroborate
corroboration
corroborative
corroborator
corrode
corrodible
corrosion
corrosive
corrosively
corrosiveness
corrugate
corrugated
corrupt
corrupted
corrupter (*occ* ~or)

corruptibility
corruptible
corruption
corruptor (*or* ~er)
corsage
corsair
corselet *armour*
corselette *underclothes*
corset
corseted
corsetiere (*or* ~ère)
corsetry
Corsica
Corsican
cortex (*pl* ~tices)
corticosteroid
cortisone
corundum
coruscate
corvette
corybantic
cos
cosecant
cosh
cosily
cosine
cosiness
cosmetic
cosmetically
cosmetician
cosmetics
cosmetological
cosmetologist
cosmetology
cosmic
cosmically
cosmogenesis
cosmogenetic
cosmogenic
cosmogonic
cosmogonical
cosmogonist
cosmogony
cosmographer
cosmographic
cosmographical
cosmography
cosmological
cosmologist
cosmology

cosmonaut
cosmopolitan
cosmopolite
cosmos
Cossack
cosset (~ted, ~ting, *occ*
　~tted, ~tting)
cost
costal
co-star
cost-cutting
cost-effective
cost-effectively
cost-effectiveness
cost-efficient
costing
costive
costively
costiveness
costliness
costly
costume
costumier (*US* ~mer)
cosy (*US* cozy)
cot
cotangent
coterie
cotinga
Cotswold
cottage
cottager
cottagey
cotton
cottonmouth
cotyledon
cotyledonary
cotyledonous
couch
couchette
couching
cougar
cough
could
coulis
coulomb
council
councillor (*US* ~ilor)
counsel (~lled, ~lling;
　US ~led, ~ling)
counselling (*US* ~eling)

counsellor (*US* ~elor)
count
countable
countdown
countenance
counter
counteract
counteraction
counteractive
counterbalance
counterblast
countercharge
counterculture
counterfeit
counterfeiter
counterfoil
countermand
counterpane
counterpart
counterplot
counterpoint
counterpoise
countersign
countersignature
countersink
counterstroke
countersunk
countertop
counterweight
countess
counting
countless
countrified (*occ* ~ry~)
country
countryman (*pl* ~men)
countryside
countrywide
countrywoman (*pl* ~women)
county
coup (! coupe) *takeover*
coup de grace (*or* ~grâce)
coup d'etat (*or* ~état)
coupe (! coup) *dessert*
coupé (*or* coupe) *car*
couple
coupler
couplet
coupling

coupon
courage
courageous
courageously
courageousness
courante
courgette
courier
course
courser
coursework
coursing
court
courteous
courteously
courteousness
courtesan
courtesy
courthouse
courtier
courtliness
courtly
courtroom
courtship
courtyard
couscous
cousin
cousinly
couture
couturier
couturière (*or* ~ere)
cove
coven
covenant
covenantal
covenantor
Coventry
cover
coverage
coverall
covered
covering
coverlet
covert
covertly
covertness
covet
covetous
covetously
covetousness

covey
cow
coward
cowardice
cowardliness
cowardly
cowbell
cowberry
cowboy
cower
cowgirl
cowhide
cowhouse
cowl
cowling
cowman
co-worker
cowpat
cowpox
cowrie (*or* ~ry)
cowshed
cowslip
cox
coxless
coxswain
coxswainship
coy
coyly
coyness
coyote
coypu
cozen
cozenage
cozener
cozy *see* cosy
crab (~bbed, ~bbing)
crabbedly
crabbedness
crabbily
crabbiness
crabby
crack
crackdown
cracked
cracker
crackerjack
crackers
cracking
crackle
crackling

crackly
cracknel
crackpot
cradle
cradling
craft
crafted
craftily
craftiness
craftsman (*pl* ~men)
craftsmanship
craftswoman (*pl*
~women)
craftwork
craftworker
crafty
crag
cragged
craggily
cragginess
craggy
crake
cram (~mmed,
~mming)
crammer
cramp
cramped
crampon
cranberry
crane
cranefly
cranial
cranium (*pl* ~ia, ~iums)
crank
crankily
crankiness
crankshaft
cranky
crannied
cranny
crap (~pped, ~pping,
tab)
crape
crapper (*tab*)
crappy (*tab*)
craps
crapulence
crapulent
crapulous
craquelure

crash
crashing
crash-land
crash-landing
crass
crassly
crassness
crate
crateful
crater
cratered
cravat
cravatted
crave
craven
cravenly
cravenness
crawfish
crawl
crawler
crawling
crawlingly
crawly
crayfish
crayon
craze
crazed
crazily
craziness
crazy
creak
creakily
creakiness
creaky
cream
creamer
creamery
creamily
creaminess
creamy
crease
creased
create
creation
creative
creatively
creativeness
creativity
creator
creature

creaturely
creche (*or* crèche)
credence
credentials
credibility
credible
credibly
credit
creditability
creditable
creditably
creditor
Credo *name of a creed*
credo (*pl* ~os) *belief*
credulity
credulous
credulously
credulousness
creed
creek
creep (crept)
creeper
creeping
cremate
cremation
cremator
crematorium (*pl* ~ia,
~iums)
crematory
crème
crenellate (*US* ~elate)
crenellations
creole (C~)
creosol
creosote
crepe (*or* crêpe)
crepitant
crepitate
crepitation
crept
crescendo (*pl* ~di, ~dos)
crescent
cress
crest
crested
crestfallen
Cretaceous
Cretan
Crete
cretin

crucible

cretinism
cretinous
crevasse
crevice
crew
crewed
crewman (*pl* ~men)
cri de coeur
crib (~bbed, ~bbing)
cribbage
crick
cricked
cricket
cricketer
cricketing
cried
crier
crime
criminal
criminalisation (*or*
~iz~)
criminalise (*or* ~ize)
criminality
criminally
criminological
criminologist
criminology
crimp
crimper
crimple
crimson
cringe
cringer
cringeworthy
cringing
crinkle
crinkled
crinkly
crinoid
crinoline
cripple
crippled
crippledom
crippler
crippling
crise
crisis (*pl* ~ises)
crisp
crisper
crispiness

crisply
crispy
criss-cross
criss-crossed
criterial
criterion (*pl* ~ia)
critic
critical
criticality
critically
criticisable (*or* ~iz~)
criticise (*or* ~ize)
criticiser (*or* ~iz~)
criticism
critique
critter
croak
croaky
Croat
Croatia
Croatian
crochet (! crotchet) *craft*
crocheter
crock
crockery
crocodile
crocodilian
crocus (*pl* ~ci, ~uses)
Croesus
croft
crofter
croissant
cromlech
crone
crony
crook
crooked
crookedly
crookedness
croon
crooner
crop (~pped, ~pping)
croquet *game*
croquette *food*
cross
crossbar
crossbeam
crossbill
crossbow
crosscheck

cross-country
cross-dressing
cross-examination
cross-examine
cross-eyed
cross-fertilisation (*or*
~iz~)
cross-fertilise (*or* ~ize)
crossfire
cross-hair
cross-hatch
crossing
cross-legged
crossover
cross-ply
cross-pollinate
cross-pollination
cross-purposes
cross-question
cross-refer
cross-reference
crossroads
cross-section
cross-stitch
crosswind
crossword
crotch
crotchet (! crochet)
music
crotchety
crotchless
crouch
croup
croupier
croupy
crouton (*occ* croûton)
crow
crowbar (~rred, ~rring)
crowd
crowded
crowdedness
crown
crowned
crowning
crozier
cru (*pl* cru, crus) *wine*
crucial
cruciality
crucially
crucible

crucifer
cruciferous
crucifier
crucifix
crucifixion
cruciform
crucify
crude
crudely
crudeness
crudity
cruel (~ller, ~llest; US
  esp ~ler, ~lest)
cruelly
cruelty
cruet
cruise
cruiser
cruising (n)
crumb
crumble
crumbliness
crumbling
crumbly
crumby (! crummy)
  bread
crumhorn
crummily
crumminess
crummy (! crumby)
  shoddy
crumpet
crumple
crumpled
crumply
crunch
cruncher
crunchily
crunchiness
crunchy
crupper
crusade
crusader
crusading
crush
crushed
crusher
crushing
crust
crustacean

crusted
crustily
crustiness
crusty
crutch
crux (pl cruxes, occ
  cruces)
cry (cries, cried)
crybaby
cryobiological
cryobiologist
cryobiology
cryogen
cryogenics
cryolite
cryonics
cryosurgery
crypt
cryptanalysis
cryptanalyst
cryptanalytic
cryptanalytical
cryptic
cryptically
cryptogram
cryptograph
cryptographic
cryptographically
cryptography
cryptological
cryptologist
cryptology
cryptonym
crystal
crystalline
crystallinity
crystallisation (or ~iz~)
crystallise (or ~ize)
crystallographer
crystallographic
crystallographically
crystallography
crystalloid
ctenophore
cub (~bbed, ~bbing)
Cuba
Cuban
cubbyhole
cube
cubic

cubicle
cubiform
cubism
cubist
cubit
cubital
cuboid
cuboidal
cuckold
cuckoldry
cuckoo
cucumber
cucurbitaceous
cud
cuddle
cuddlesome
cuddly
cudgel (~lled, ~lling; US
  ~led, ~ling)
cue (cued, cueing or
  cuing)
cuff
cuffed
cufflink
cuirass
cuirassier
cuisine
cul-de-sac
culinary
cull
culminate
culmination
culottes
culpability
culpable
culpably
culprit
cult
cultic
cultish
cultishness
cultism
cultist
cultivable
cultivar
cultivate
cultivation
cultivator
cultural
culturally

culture
cultured
culvert
Cumberland
cumbersome
cumbersomely
cumbersomeness
cumin (or cummin)
cummerbund
cumquat (usu kum~)
  fruit
cumulate
cumulation
cumulative
cumulatively
cumulativeness
cumulonimbus (pl ~bi)
cumulus (pl ~li)
cuneiform
cunnilingus
cunning
cunningly
cunningness
cunt (tab)
cup (~pped, ~pping)
cupboard
cupcake
Cupid
cupidity
cupie (or kew~)
cupola
cupping (n)
cupric
cupro-nickel
cuprous
cup-tie
cur
curability
curable
curacao (or ~çao; pl
  ~os)
curacy
curare
curassow
curate
curation
curative
curatively
curator
curatorial

curatorship
curb (US; UK kerb)
  roadside step
curb (v) restrain
curd
curdle
curdler
cure heal
curé priest
curet (or ~ette)
curettage
curfew
curie
curing
curio (pl ~os)
curiosity
curious
curiously
curiousness
curium
curl
curler
curlew
curlicue
curliness
curling
curly
curmudgeon
curmudgeonliness
curmudgeonly
currant (! current) dried
  fruit
currency
current (! currant) water,
  electricity, happening
  now
currently
curricular
curriculum (pl ~la,
  ~lums)
currier
curry
curse
cursed
cursedly
cursedness
cursive
cursively
cursor

cursorily
cursoriness
cursory
curt
curtail
curtailment
curtain
curtained
curtly
curtness
curtsey (or US ~sy; n pl
  ~sies, ~seys; v ~sies,
  ~sied, ~seying or US
  ~sying)
curvaceous
curvaceousness
curvature
curve
curved
curviness
curvy
cushiness
Cushing
cushion
cushioned
cushy
cusp
cusped
cuspid
cuss
cussed
cussedly
cussedness
custard
custodial
custodian
custodianship
custody
custom
customable
customarily
customariness
customary
customer
customise (or ~ize)
customs
cut (cutting)
cutaneous
cutaway
cutback

cute
cuteness
cuticle
cuticular
cutlass
cutler
cutlery
cutlet
cutpurse
cutter
cut-throat
cutting (*adj*)
cuttingly
cuttle
cuttlebone
cuttlefish
cuvee (*or* ~vée)
cyan
cyanic
cyanide
cyanine
cyanocobalamin
cyanogen
cyanosis (*pl* ~oses)
cyanotic
cybercafe (*or* ~café)
cybernaut
cybernetic
cyberneticist
cybernetics
cyberphobe
cyberphobia
cyberphobic
cyberpunk
cyberspace
cyborg
cycad
cyclamen
cycle
cyclic
cyclical
cyclically
cycling
cyclist
cyclo-cross
cycloid
cyclometer
cyclone
cyclonic
cyclonically

Cyclops
cyclorama
cycloramic
cyclotron
cygnet (! signet) *swan*
Cygnus
cylinder
cylindrical
cymbal
cymbalist
cyme
Cymric
cynic
cynical
cynically
cynicism
cynosure
cyotoxic
cypress
Cyprian
Cypriot
Cyprus
Cyrillic
cyst
cystectomy
cystic
cystitis
cystotomy
cytochrome
cytogenetics
cytolitic
cytological
cytologically
cytologist
cytology
cytolysis
cytoplasm
cytoplasmic
cytosol
czar (C~; *UK* tsar, tzar, T~)
Czech
Czechoslovak
Czechoslovakia
Czechoslovakian

D

dab (~bbed, ~bbing)
dabble
dabbler
dabbling
dabchick
dacha
dachshund
dacoit (*or* dak~)
dactyl
dactylic
dad
dada
Dada (*arts*)
daddy
dado (*pl* ~os, ~oes)
Daedalus
daemon (*occ* dai~)
daffiness
daffodil
daffy
daft
daftness
dagger
Daguerre
daguerreotype (*or* ~ro~)
dahlia
Dáil (*or* Dail)
daily
daimon (*or* dae~)
daintily
daintiness
dainty
daiquiri (*pl* ~is)
dairy
dairying
dairymaid
dairyman (*pl* ~men)
dairywoman (*pl* ~women)

dais
daisy
Dakar
dakoit (*or* dac~)
Dakota
Dakotan
dale
Dalek
dalit (D~)
dalliance
dally
Dalmatia
Dalmatian
daltonism (D~)
dam (~mmed, ~mming)
damage
damageability
damageable
damaged
damager
damages
damagingly
Damascene
damascened
Damascus
damask
dame
damming (! damning)
  hold water
damn
damnable
damnably
damnation
damnatory
damned
damnification
damnify
damning (! damning)
  condemn
Damocles
damp
dampen
dampener
damper
damping
dampish
damply
dampness
damsel

damselfish
damselfly
damson
dan *martial arts*
Danakil
dance
dancer
dancing
dandelion
dandify
dandle
dandruff
dandruffy
dandy
dandyish
dandyism
Dane
danger
dangerous
dangerously
dangerousness
dangle
dangler
dangly
Danish
dank
dankness
danseur
danseuse
Dante
Dantean
Dantesque
Danube
Danubian
dap (~pped, ~pping)
daphne
daphnia
dapper
dapperly
dapperness
dapple
dappled
Darby (! Derby) *and Joan*
Dardanelles
dare
daredevil (*or* dare-~)
daredevilry
darer
daring
daringly

Darjeeling
dark
darken
darkened
darkener
darkish
darkly
darkness
darkroom
darling
darn
darned
darner
darning
dart
dartboard
darter
Dartmoor
darts
Darwin
Darwinian
Darwinism
Darwinist
dash
dashboard
dasheen
dasher
dashing
dashingly
dashingness
dashpot
dastardliness
dastardly
data
databank
database
datable (*or* datea~)
date
dateable (*or* data~)
datebook
dated
dateless
dateline
dating
dative
datum (*pl* ~ta)
daub
dauber
daughter
daughterboard

daughterly
daunt
daunted
daunting
dauntingly
dauntless
dauntlessly
dauntlessness
dauphin (D~)
davenport
davit
dawdle
dawdler
dawn
dawning
day
daybed
daybook
daybreak
daydream
daylight
day-old
dayside
daytime
day-tripper
daywear
daywork
dayworker
daze
dazed
dazedly
dazzle
dazzlement
dazzler
dazzling
dazzlingly
D-Day
de facto
de novo
de rigeur
deaccession
deacon
deaconess
deaconship
deactivate
deactivation
deactivator
dead
deadbeat
deaden

deadener
deadening
dead-eye
deadhead
deadheading
deadline
deadliness
deadlock
deadly
deadpan
deaf
deafen
deafened
deafening
deafeningly
deafness
deal
dealer
dealership
dealing
dealings
dealt
dean
deanery
dear
dearly
dearness
dearth
death
deathbed
deathless
deathlessness
deathly
deathtrap
deathwatch
deattribute
deattribution
debacle
debar (~rred, ~rring)
debark
debarkation
debarment
debase
debased
debasement
debaser
debatable (*or* ~tea~)
debatably (*or* ~tea~)
debate
debater

debauch
debauched
debauchee
debaucher
debauchery
debenture
debilitate
debilitated
debilitating
debilitatingly
debilitation
debilitative
debility
debit
debonair
debonaire
debouch
debouchment
debridement
debrief
debriefer
debriefing
debris
debt
debtor
debug (~gged, ~gging)
debugger
debugging
debunk
debunker
debunkery
deburr (*also* ~bur; ~rred, ~rring)
debut (*or* dé~)
debutante (*or* dé~)
decadal
decade
decadence
decadency
decadent
decadently
decaff
decaffeinate
decaffeinated
decaffeination
decagon
decagonal
decahedral
decahedron (*pl* ~ra, ~rons)

decal (*US*)
decalcification
decalcified
decalcifier
Decalogue
decamp
decanal
decant
decanter
decapitate
decapitated
decapitation
decapitator
decapsulate
decapsulation
decarbonisation (*or* ~iz~)
decarbonise (*or* ~ize)
decarbonised (*or* ~ized)
decasyllabic
decathlete
decathlon
decay
decayed
decaying
decease
deceased
deceit
deceitful
deceitfully
deceitfulness
deceivable
deceive
deceiver
decelerate
deceleration
decelerator
December
Decembrist
decency
decennial
decennially
decennium (*pl* ~ia, ~iums)
decent
decently
decentralisation (*or* ~iz~)
decentralise (*or* ~ize)
decentralised (*or* ~ized)

decentralist
decentre (*US* ~ter)
deception
deceptive
deceptively
deceptiveness
decerebrate
decerebration
decertification
decertify
decibel
decidable
decide
decided
decidedly
decidedness
decider
deciduous
deciduously
deciduousness
decimal
decimalisation (*or* ~iz~)
decimalise (*or* ~ize)
decimally
decimate
decimation
decimator
decimetre (*US* ~ter)
decimetric
decipher
decipherable
decipherment
decision
decisive
decisively
decisiveness
deck
deckchair
deckhouse
decking
declaim
declaimer
declamation
declamatory
declarable
declaration
declarative
declaratively
declaratory
declare

declaredly
declarer
declass
declassed
declassifiable
declassification
declassify
declension
declinable
declinate
declination
declinational
declinatory
decline
decliner
declining
declivitous
declivity
declutch
decoct
decoction
decodable
decode
decoder
decoke
decollate
decollation
decollator
décolletage (*or* de~)
décolleté (*or* de, ~tée, ~te, ~tee)
decolonisation (*or* ~iz~)
decolonise (*or* ~ize)
decolorant
decolourisation (*or* ~iz~, *US* ~or~)
decolourise (*or* ~ize~, *US* ~or~)
decommission
decomposable
decompose
decomposed
decomposer
decomposing
decomposition
decompress
decompression
decongest
decongestant
decongestion

deconsecrate
deconsecrated
deconsecration
deconstruct
deconstruction
deconstructionism
deconstructionist
deconstructive
decontaminate
decontamination
decontextualisation (or ~iz~)
decontextualise (or ~ize)
decontrol (~lled, ~lling)
decor (or dé~)
decorate
decoration
decorative
decoratively
decorativeness
decorator
decorous
decorously
decorousness
decorum
decoupage (or dé~)
decouple
decoupling
decoy
decrease
decreasingly
decree
decrement
decrepit
decrepitate
decrepitation
decrepitude
decrescendo (pl ~dos)
decriminalisation (or ~iz~)
decriminalise (or ~ize)
decry
decrypt
decryption
decussate
decussation
dedicate
dedicated
dedicatedly
dedicatee

dedication
dedicator
dedicatory
deduce
deducible
deduct
deductibility
deductible
deduction
deductive
deductively
deed
deejay
deem
de-emphasis (pl ~ases)
de-emphasise (or ~ize)
de-energise (or ~ize)
deep
deepen
deeper
deepest
deep-freeze
deeply
deepness
deer
deerskin
deerstalker
deface
defaceable
defacement
defacer
defamation
defamatory
defame
defamer
defamiliarise (or ~ize)
default
defaulter
defeat
defeated
defeatedly
defeatism
defeatist
defecate (occ ~faec~)
defecation (occ ~faec~)
defect
defection
defective
defectively
defectiveness

defector
defence (US ~nse)
defend
defendable
defendant (occ ~dent)
defender
defending
defenestrate
defenestration
defensibility
defensible
defensibly
defensive
defensively
defensiveness
defer (~rred, ~rring)
deferable
deference
deferential
deferentially
deferment
deferral
deferrer
defiance
defiant
defiantly
defibrillate
defibrillation
defibrillator
deficiency
deficient
deficit
defier
defilade
defile
defilement
defiler
definable
define
definer
definiendum
definiens
defining
definite
definitely
definiteness
definition
definitional
definitionally
definitive

definitively
deflagrate
deflagration
deflagrator
deflate
deflated
deflation
deflationary
deflect
deflection (*occ* ~exion)
deflector
deflocculate
deflocculation
defocus (~used, ~using;
  or ~ussed, ~ussing)
defoliant
defoliate
defoliation
defoliator
deforest
deforestation
deforested
deform
deformable
deformation
deformed
deformity
defragment
defragmentation
defragmenter
defraud
defrauder
defray
defrayable
defrayal
defrayer
defrayment
defrock
defrocked
defrost
defroster
deft
deftly
deftness
defunct
defuse (! diffuse) *remove
  fuse or heat*
defy
degas (~ssed, ~ssing)
degauss

degeneracy
degenerate
degenerately
degeneration
deglamourisation (*or*
  ~iz~, *US* ~or~)
deglamourise (*or* ~ize,
  US ~or~)
deglaze
deglutition
deglutitive
degradability
degradable
degradation
degradative
degrade
degrader
degrading
degreasant
degrease
degreaser
degreasing
degree
degressive
dehiscence
dehiscent
dehorn
dehumanisation (*or*
  ~iz~)
dehumanise (*or* ~ize)
dehumidification
dehumidifier
dehumidify
dehydrate
dehydrated
dehydration
dehydrator
de-ice
de-icer
deicidal
deicide
deific
deification
deify
deign
Deimos
deism
deist
deistic
deistical

deistically
deity
deja vu (*or* déjà~)
deject
dejected
dejectedly
dejectedness
dejection
delaminate
Delaware
Delawarean
delay
delayed
delayer
dele *delete*
delectability
delectable
delectably
delectation
delegable
delegate
delegation
delete
deleterious
deleteriously
deletion
Delftware
Delhi
deli (*pl* ~is)
deliberate
deliberately
deliberateness
deliberation
deliberative
deliberatively
deliberator
delicacy
delicate
delicatessen
delicious
deliciously
deliciousness
delight
delighted
delightedly
delightful
delightfully
delightfulness
Delilah
delimit

delimitation
delimiter
delineate
delineation
delineator
delinquency
delinquent
delinquently
deliquesce
delirious
deliriously
deliriousness
delirium (pl ~ia, ~iums)
deliver
deliverance
deliverer
delivery
dell
delocalisation (or ~iz~)
delocalise (or ~ize)
delouse
Delphi
Delphic
delphinium
delta
deltiologist
deltiology
deltoid
delude
deluded
deludedly
deluder
deluge
delusion
delusional
delusive
delusively
delusiveness
delusory
delustre (US ~ter)
deluxe (or de luxe)
delve
delver
demagnetisation (or
   ~iz~)
demagnetise (or ~ize)
demagnetiser (or ~iz~)
demagogic
demagogue
demagoguery

demagogy
demand
demander
demanding
demanning
demarcate
demarcation (occ ~ka~)
dematerialisation (or
   ~iz~)
dematerialise (or ~ize)
demean
demeaning
demeanour (US ~or)
dement
demented
dementedly
dementedness
dementia
demerara
demerit
demesne
demigod
demigoddess
demijohn
demilitarisation (or
   ~iz~)
demilitarise (or ~ize)
demise
demisemiquaver
demist
demister
demitasse
demiurge
demo (pl ~os)
demob (~bbed, ~bbing)
   demobilise
demobilisation (or ~iz~)
demobilise (or ~ize)
democracy
democrat
democratic
democratically
democratisation (or
   ~iz~)
democratise (or ~ize)
demographic
demographical
demographically
demographics
demography

demolish
demolisher
demolition
demon
demoniac
demoniacal
demoniacally
demonisation (or ~iz~)
demonise (or ~ize)
demonism
demonolater
demonological
demonologist
demonology
demonopolise (or ~ize)
demonstrability
demonstrable
demonstrably
demonstrate
demonstration
demonstrative
demonstratively
demonstrator
demoralise (or ~ize)
demoralising (or ~iz~)
demoralisingly (or ~iz~)
demote
demotic
demotion
demotivate
demotivation
demount
demountable
demulcent
demur (~rred, ~rring)
demure
demurely
demureness
demurral
demurrer
demystification
demystify
demythologise (or ~ize)
den
denationalisation (or
   ~iz~)
denationalise (or ~ize)
denaturalise (or ~ize)
denaturation
denature

dendrite
dendritic
dendrochronological
dendrochronologist
dendrochronology
dendroid
dendrologist
dendrology
denervate
denervated
denervation
dengue
deniability
deniable
deniably
denial
denier
denigrate
denigration
denigrator
denigratory
denim
denizen
denizenship
Denmark
denominal
denominate
denominated
denomination
denominational
denominationalism
denominator
denotation
denotational
denotative
denote
denouement
denounce
denouncement
denouncer
dense
densely
denseness
densify
density
dent
dental
dentally
dentifrice
dentine

dentist
dentistry
denture
denude
denunciation
denunciatory
deny
deodorant
deodorisation (*or* ~iz~)
deodorise (*or* ~ize)
deodoriser (*or* ~iz~)
deontic
deontological
deontologically
deontologist
deontology
deoxygenate
deoxygenation
deoxyribonucleic
depart
departed
department
departmental
departmentalisation (*or* ~iz~)
departmentalise (*or* ~ize)
departmentalism
departmentally
departure
depend
dependability
dependable
dependably
dependant (*UK n, US occ n or adj*; ! dependent)
dependence
dependency
dependent (*UK adj, US n or adj*; ! dependant)
dependently
depersonalisation (*or* ~iz~)
depersonalise (*or* ~ize)
depict
depiction
depilate
depilation
depilatory
deplane

deplete
depleted
depletion
deplorable
deplorably
deplore
deploringly
deploy
deployment
depolarisation (*or* ~iz~)
depolarise (*or* ~ize)
depolymerisation (*or* ~iz~)
depolymerise (*or* ~ize)
deponent
depopulate
depopulation
deport
deportable
deportation
deportee
deportment
depose
deposit
depositary (*or* ~ory; ! depository) *person*
deposition
depositor
depository (! depositary) *place*
depot
depravation
deprave
depraved
depravity
deprecate
deprecating
deprecatingly
deprecation
deprecative
deprecator
deprecatorily
deprecatory
depreciate
depreciation
depreciatory
depredation
depress
depressant
depressible

depressing
depressingly
depression
depressive
depressor
depressurise (*or* ~ize)
deprivation
deprive
deprived
deprogramme (*US* ~am)
depth
depthless
deputation
depute
deputise (*or* ~ize)
deputy
deputyship
deracinate
deracinated
deracination
derail
derailed
derailleur
derailment
derange
deranged
derangement
Derby (! Darby) *city, race*
derby *local race*, (*US*) *hat*
Derbyshire
deregister
deregistration
deregulate
deregulation
deregulatory
derelict
dereliction
derestrict
derestriction
deride
derisible
derision
derisive
derisively
derisiveness
derisory
derivable
derivate
derivation
derivational

derivative
derivatively
derive
derma
dermatitis
dermatological
dermatologically
dermatologist
dermatology
dermatosis (*pl* ~oses)
dermis
derogate
derogation
derogative
derogatorily
derogatory
derrick
derriere (*or* ~ère)
derringer
dervish
desalinate
desalinated
desalination
descant
descend
descendant
descendent (*astron, hera*)
descending
descent
descramble
descrambler
describable
describe
describer
description
descriptive
descriptively
descriptiveness
descriptivism
descriptivist
desecrate
desecrated
desecration
desecrator
desegregate
desegregation
deselect
deselection
desensitisation (*or* ~iz~)
desensitise (*or* ~ize)

desensitised (*or* ~ized)
desensitiser (*or* ~iz~)
desert (! dessert) *arid area*
deserted
deserter
desertification
desertion
deserve
deserved
deservedly
deserving
deservingly
deservingness
desex
desexed
déshabille (*or* des~, dis~)
desiccant
desiccate
desiccation
desiccative
desideratum (*pl* ~ta, ~ums)
design
designable
designate
designated
designation
designed
designedly
designer
designing
designingly
desirability
desirable
desirableness
desirably
desire
desirous
desist
desk
deskilling
desktop
desolate
desolately
desolateness
desolation
despair
despairing

despairingly
despatch (*or* dis~)
desperado (*pl* ~os, ~oes)
desperate
desperately
desperateness
desperation
despicable
despicably
despise
despiser
despite
despiteful
despoil
despoilation
despoiled
despoiler
despoilment
despoliation
despondence
despondency
despondent
despondently
despot
despotic
despotically
despotism
dessert (! desert) *food*
dessertspoon
dessertspoonful
destabilisation (*or* ~iz~)
destabilise (*or* ~ize)
destination
destine
destiny
destitute
destitution
de-stress
destroy
destroyed
destroyer
destruct
destructibility
destructible
destruction
destructive
destructively
destructiveness
desuetude
desultorily

desultoriness
desultory
desynchronisation (*or* ~iz~)
desynchronise (*or* ~ize)
detach
detachability
detachable
detached
detachedly
detachment
detail
detailed
detailing
detain
detainee
detainer
detainment
detangle
detect
detectability
detectable
detectably
detection
detective
detector
detente (*or* dé~)
detention
deter (~rred, ~rring)
deterge
detergence
detergency
detergent
deteriorate
deteriorating
deterioration
deteriorative
determinable
determinacy
determinant
determinate
determinately
determinateness
determination
determinative
determine
determined
determinedly
determinedness
determiner

determinism
determinist
deterministic
deterministically
deterrence
deterrent
detest
detestable
detestably
detestation
detester
dethrone
dethronement
detonate
detonation
detonative
detonator
detour
detox
detoxification
detoxifier
detoxify
detract
detraction
detractive
detractor
detrain
detriment
detrimental
detrimentally
detrition
detritus
Detroit
detumesce
detumescence
detumescent
detune
detuned
deuce
deuterium
deuterocanonical
deuteron
Deuteronomy
Deutschmark
deutzia
devaluation
devalue
devastate
devastated
devastating

devastatingly
devastation
devastator
develop (~pped,
 ~pping)
developable
developed
developer
development
developmental
developmentally
deverbal
deviance
deviancy
deviant
deviate
deviation
deviationism
deviationist
deviator
device
devil
devilfish
devilish
devilishly
devilishness
devilled
devilment
devilry
devious
deviously
deviousness
devisable
devise
devisee
deviser
devisor
devitalisation (*or* ~iz~)
devitalise (*or* ~ize)
devitrification
devitrify
devoid
devolution
devolutionary
devolutionist
devolve
devolved
devolvement
Devon
Devonian

Devonshire
devoted
devotedly
devotedness
devotee
devotion
devotional
devour
devourer
devouringly
devout
devoutly
devoutness
dew
dewar (D~)
dewberry
dewdrop
dewfall
dewily
dewiness
dewlap
dewy
dewy-eyed
dexter
dexterity
dexterous (*occ* ~trous)
dexterously (*occ* ~tro~)
dexterousness (*or*
 ~tro~)
dextral
dextrality
dextrally
dextrin
dextrose
dezincification
Dhaka
dhal
dharma
dhoti
dhow
diabetes
diabetic
diablerie (*occ* ~ery)
diabolic
diabolical
diabolically
diabolise (*or* ~ize)
diabolism
diabolo (*pl* ~os)
diachroneity

diachronic
diachronically
diachronistic
diachrony
diacid
diaconal
diaconate
diacritic
diacritical
diacritically
diadem
diademed
diaeresis (*or* dier~; *pl*
 ~eses)
diagenesis
diagnosable
diagnose
diagnosis (*pl* ~oses)
diagnostic
diagnostically
diagnostician
diagonal
diagonally
diagram (~mmed,
 ~mming; *US* ~med,
 ~ming)
dial (~lled, ~lling; *US*
 ~led, ~ling)
dialect
dialectal
dialectic
dialectical
dialectician
dialectics
dialectological
dialectologist
dialectology
dialler (*US* ~aler)
dialogic
dialogical
dialogism
dialogue (*US* ~log)
dialyse (*US* ~yze)
dialyser (*US* ~yzer)
dialysis (*pl* ~yses)
dialytic
diamanté
diamantiferous
diamantine
diameter

diametric
diametrical
diametrically
diamond
diamorphine
Diana
Dianetics (*tr*)
dianthus
diapason
diaper (*US*)
diaphanous
diaphone
diaphoresis
diaphoretic
diaphragm
diaphragmatic
diapositive
diarchal
diarchic
diarchy (*or* dy~)
diarise (*or* ~ize)
diarist
diarrhoea (*US* ~hea)
diarrhoeal (*US* ~heal)
diarrhoeic (*US* ~heic)
diary
diaspora (D~)
diastole
diastolic
diathermy
diathesis
diatom
diatomic
diatonic
diatribe
diazepam
diazo
dibasic
dibble
dice
dicey (*or* dicy)
dichotic
dichotomise (*or* ~ize)
dichotomous
dichotomously
dichotomy
dichroic
dichroism
dichromatic
dichromatism

dicotyledon
dicotyledonous
dictaphone (D~, *tr*)
dictate
dictation
dictator
dictatorial
dictatorially
dictatorship
diction
dictionary
dictum (*pl* ~ta, ~tums)
dicy (*or* dicey)
didactic
didactically
didacticism
diddle
diddler
diddling
didgeridoo (*occ*
   didjeridu)
didymous
die (*n pl* dice)
die (*v* dies, died, dying)
die-cast
diehard
dielectric
dielectrically
diesel
diet
dietary
dietetic
dietetically
dietetics
diethyl
dietician (*or* ~itian)
dietitian (*or* ~ician)
differ
difference
different
differentia (*pl* ~iae)
differentiability
differentiable
differential
differentiate
differentiation
differentiator
differently
differentness
difficult

difficultness
difficulty
diffidence
diffident
diffidently
diffract
diffraction
diffractive
diffractively
diffuse (! defuse) *spread*
diffusely
diffuseness
diffuser (*occ* ~or)
diffusible
diffusing
diffusion
diffusionism
diffusionist
diffusive
dig (dug, digging)
digest
digestibility
digestible
digestif
digestion
digestive
digestively
digger
diggings
digit
digital
digitalin
digitalis
digitalisation (*or* ~iz~)
digitalise (*or* ~ize)
digitate
digitisation (*or* ~iz~)
digitise (*or* ~ize)
digitiser (*or* ~iz~)
dignified
dignify
dignitary
dignity
digraph
digress
digresser
digression
digressive
digressively
digressiveness

digs
dihedral
dik-dik
dike (*usu* dyke) *ditch*
diktat
dilapidate
dilapidated
dilapidation
dilatable
dilatation
dilate
dilater (*or* ~or)
dilation
dilator (*or* ~er)
dilatorily
dilatoriness
dildo (*occ* ~doe)
dilemma
dilettante (*pl* ~ti, ~tes)
dilettantish
dilettantism
diligence
diligent
diligently
dill
dilly-dally
diluent
dilute
diluted
diluter
dilution
dilutive
diluvial
diluvian
dim (*adj* ~mmer,
    ~mmest; *v* ~mmed,
    ~mming)
dim sum
dime (*US*)
dimension
dimensional
dimensionless
dimerous
dimetric
dimetrodon
diminish
diminishable
diminished
diminuendo (*pl* ~di,
    ~os)

diminution
diminutive
diminutively
diminutiveness
dimity
dimly
dimmer
dimmish
dimness
dimorphism
dimple
dimply
dimwit
dim-witted
dim-wittedly
dim-wittedness
din (~nned, ~nning)
dine
diner
dinero
dinette
dingbat
ding-dong
dinghy
dingily
dinginess
dingle
dingo (*pl* ~os, ~oes)
dingy
dining
dink
dinner
dinosaur
dinosaurian
dint
diocesan
diocese
diode
dioecious
Diogenes
Dionysiac
Dionysian
Dionysus
dioptre (*US* ~ter)
diorama
dioxide
dioxin
dip (~pped, ~pping)
dipeptide
diphenyl

diphtheria
diphtherial
diphthong
diphthongal
diphthongisation (*or*
    ~iz~)
diphthongise (*or* ~ize)
diplegia
diplodocus
diploid
diploma
diplomacy
diplomat
diplomate
diplomatic
diplomatically
diplomatist
dipolar
dipole
dipper
dippy
dipso (*pl* ~os)
dipsomania
dipsomaniac
dipstick
dipswitch
diptera (D~)
dipterist
diptych
dire
direct
direction
directional
directionless
directive
directly
director
directorate
directorial
directorship
directory
direful
direness
dirge
dirham
dirigible
dirk
dirndl
dirt
dirty

disability
disable
disabled
disablement
disabling
disabuse
disaccharide
disaccord
disadvantage
disadvantaged
disadvantageous
disadvantageously
disaffected
disaffection
disaffiliate
disaffiliation
disaffirm
disaffirmation
disafforest
disafforestation
disafforestment
disaggregate
disaggregation
disagree
disagreeable
disagreeableness
disagreeably
disagreement
disallow
disallowance
disallowed
disambiguate
disambiguation
disamenity
disappear
disappearance
disappearing
disapply
disappoint
disappointed
disappointedly
disappointing
disappointingly
disappointment
disapprobation
disapproval
disapprove
disapprover
disapproving
disapprovingly

disarm
disarmament
disarmer
disarming
disarmingly
disarrange
disarranged
disarrangement
disarray
disarticulate
disassemble
disassembled
disassembler
disassembling
disassembly
disassociate
disassociation
disaster
disastrous
disastrously
disattribution
disavow
disavowal
disband
disbanded
disbandment
disbar (~rred, ~rring)
disbarment
disbelief
disbelieve
disbeliever
disbelieving
disbelievingly
disbursal
disburse
disbursed
disbursement
disburser
disc (*or* disk, *esp comp,*
   US)
discalced
discard
discardable
discern
discernable (*usu* ~ible)
discerner
discernible (*occ* ~able)
discernibly
discerning
discerningly

discernment
discharge
dischargeable
discharged
discharger
disciple
discipleship
disciplinable
disciplinal
disciplinarian
disciplinary
discipline
disciplined
disclaim
disclaimer
disclose
discloser
disclosure
disco (*n pl* ~cos; *v*
   ~coes, ~coed,
   ~coing)
discographer
discography
discoid
discoidal
discoloration (*or* ~our~)
discolour (*US* ~or)
discoloured (*US* ~or~)
discombobulate
discombobulated
discomfit
discomfited
discomfiture
discomfort
discomforting
discommode
discommodious
discommodity
disconcert
disconcerted
disconcertedly
disconcerting
disconcertingly
disconcertment
disconfirm
disconfirmation
disconfirmatory
disconnect
disconnected
disconnectedly

disconnectedness
disconnection (*occ UK* ~exion)
disconsolate
disconsolately
disconsolateness
discontent
discontented
discontentedly
discontentedness
discontentment
discontinuance
discontinuation
discontinue
discontinuity
discontinuous
discontinuously
discord
discordance
discordancy
discordant
discordantly
discotheque
discount
discountable
discounted
discountenance
discountenanced
discounter
discourage
discouragement
discouraging
discouragingly
discourse
discourteous
discourteously
discourteousness
discourtesy
discover
discoverable
discoverer
discovery
discredit
discreditable
discreditably
discredited
discreet (! discrete)
circumspect
discreetly
discreetness

discrepancy
discrepant
discrete (! discreet)
distinct
discretely
discreteness
discretion
discretionary
discriminability
discriminable
discriminably
discriminant
discriminate
discriminately
discriminating
discriminatingly
discrimination
discriminative
discriminator
discriminatory
discursive
discursively
discursiveness
discus (*pl* ~uses)
discuss
discussable (*occ* ~ible)
discussant
discusser
discussible (*usu* ~able)
discussion
disdain
disdainful
disdainfully
disdainfulness
disease
diseased
diseconomy
disembark
disembarkation
disembarrass
disembarrassment
disembodied
disembodiment
disembody
disembowel (~lled, ~lling; *US* ~led, ~ling)
disembowelment
disempower
disempowerment

disenchant
disenchanted
disenchantingly
disenchantment
disencumber
disendow
disenfranchise
disenfranchisement
disengage
disengaged
disengagement
disentangle
disentanglement
disenthral (*US* ~all; ~alled, ~alling)
disentitle
disentitled
disentitlement
disentomb
disentombment
disequilibrium
disestablish
disestablished
disestablishment
disesteem
disfavour (*US* ~or)
disfellowship (~pped, ~pping)
disfiguration
disfigure
disfigurement
disfiguring
disfranchise
disgorge
disgorged
disgorgement
disgorger
disgrace
disgraced
disgraceful
disgracefully
disgruntle
disgruntlement
disguise
disguised
disgust
disgusted
disgustedly
disgusting
disgustingly

disgustingness
dish
dishabille *see* déshabille
disharmonious
disharmoniously
disharmony
dishcloth
dishearten
disheartened
disheartening
dished
dishevelled (*US* ~eled)
dishevelment
dishful
dishonest
dishonestly
dishonesty
dishonour (*US* ~or)
dishonourable (*US* ~or~)
dishonourableness (*US* ~or~)
dishonourably (*US* ~or~)
dishrag
dishwasher
dishwashing
dishwater
dishy
disillusion
disillusioned
disillusionment
disincentive
disinclination
disinclined
disincorporate
disinfect
disinfectant
disinfection
disinfest
disinfestation
disinformation
disingenuous
disingenuously
disingenuousness
disinherit
disinheritance
disintegrate
disintegration
disintegrator

disinter (~rred, ~rring)
disinterest
disinterested
disinterestedly
disinterment
disinvent
disinvest
disinvestment
disinvite
disjoin
disjoined
disjoint
disjointed
disjointedly
disjointedness
disjunct
disjunction
disjunctive
disjunctively
disjuncture
disk (*or* disc, *esp comp, US*)
diskette
diskless
dislikable (*or* ~kea~)
dislike
dislocate
dislocation
dislodge
dislodgeable
dislodgement
disloyal
disloyally
disloyalty
dismal
dismally
dismalness
dismantle
dismantlement
dismantler
dismast
dismasted
dismay
dismayed
dismember
dismembered
dismemberment
dismiss
dismissal
dismissible (*or* ~able)

dismissive
dismissively
dismissiveness
dismount
Disney
disobedience
disobedient
disobediently
disobey
disobeyer
disoblige
disobliging
disorder
disordered
disorderliness
disorderly
disorganisation (*or* ~iz~)
disorganised (*or* ~ized)
disorient
disorientate
disorientation
disown
disowner
disownment
disparage
disparagement
disparaging
disparagingly
disparate
disparately
disparateness
disparity
dispassion
dispassionate
dispassionately
dispassionateness
dispatch (*occ* des~)
dispatcher (*occ* des~)
dispel (~lled, ~lling)
dispeller
dispensability
dispensable
dispensary
dispensation
dispensational
dispensationalism
dispensationalist
dispense
dispenser

dispersal
dispersant
disperse
disperser
dispersible
dispersion
dispersive
dispirited
dispiritedly
dispiritedness
dispiriting
dispiritingly
displace
displaced
displacement
display
displayed
displease
displeasing
displeasingly
displeasure
disport
disposability
disposable
disposal
dispose
disposer
disposition
dispossess
dispossessed
dispossession
dispraise
disproof
disproportion
disproportional
disproportionality
disproportionally
disproportionate
disproportionately
disproportionateness
disprovable
disprove
disputable
disputably
disputant
disputation
disputatious
disputatiously
disputatiousness
disputative

dispute
disputer
disqualification
disqualify
disquiet
disquieted
disquieting
disquietingly
disquietude
disquisition
disquisitional
disregard
disrelish
disrepair
disreputable
disreputableness
disreputably
disrepute
disrespect
disrespectful
disrespectfully
disrespectfulness
disrhythmical
disrobe
disrupt
disrupter (*or* ~or)
disruption
disruptive
disruptively
disruptiveness
disruptor (*or* ~er)
dissatisfaction
dissatisfied
dissatisfy
dissect
dissected
dissection
dissector
dissemblance
dissemble
dissembler
disseminate
dissemination
disseminator
dissension
dissent
dissenter
dissentient
dissenting
dissertation

dissertational
disservice
dissever
dissidence
dissident
dissimilar
dissimilarity
dissimilarly
dissimilitude
dissimulate
dissimulation
dissimulator
dissipate
dissipated
dissipation
dissipative
dissipator
dissociable
dissociate
dissociation
dissociative
dissolubility
dissoluble
dissolute
dissolutely
dissoluteness
dissolution
dissolvable
dissolve
dissonance
dissonant
dissonantly
dissuade
dissuader
dissuasion
dissuasive
dissyllabic (*or* disy~)
dissyllable (*or* disy~)
dissymmetric
dissymmetrical
dissymmetry
distaff
distal
distance
distant
distantly
distaste
distasteful
distastefully
distastefulness

distemper
distempered
distend
distended
distensibility
distensible
distension
distich
distil (*US* ~ll; ~lled,
~lling)
distillate
distillation
distillatory
distiller
distillery
distinct
distinction
distinctive
distinctively
distinctiveness
distinctly
distinctness
distingué
distinguée
distinguish
distinguishable
distinguished
distort
distorted
distortedly
distortedness
distortion
distortional
distortionless
distract
distracted
distractedly
distraction
distractor
distrain
distrainer
distrainment
distraint
distrait (*feminine*
distraite, *rare*)
distraught
distress
distressed
distressful
distressfully

distressing
distressingly
distributable
distributary
distribution
distributional
distributive
distributively
distributor
district
distrust
distrustful
distrustfully
disturb
disturbance
disturbed
disturber
disturbing
disturbingly
disunion
disunited
disunity
disuse
disused
disyllabic (*or* diss~)
ditch
ditchwater
ditheism
ditheist
dither
dithered
ditherer
dithery
dithyramb
dithyrambic
ditto (*pl* ~os, ~oes)
dittographic
ditty
diuresis
diuretic
diurnal
diva
divagate
divagation
divan
divaricate
dive (diving, dived *or US*
dove)
diver
diverge

divergence
divergent
diverging
diverse
diversely
diversification
diversify
diversion
diversionary
diversity
divert
diverticulitis
diverticulum
divertimento (*pl* ~ti,
~os)
diverting
divertingly
divertissement
divest
divestiture
divestment
divesture
divide
divided
dividend
divider
dividing
divination
divinatory
divine
divinely
divineness
diving
divining
divinise (*or* ~ize)
divinity
divisibility
divisible
division
divisional
divisionally
divisive
divisively
divisiveness
divorce
divorced
divorcee (*or* ~cée)
divot
divulge
divulgence

divulger
divulging
Diwali (or ~vali)
dixie
dizzily
dizziness
dizzy
Djakarta (or Ja~)
Djibouti
Djiboutian
djinn (or jinn)
do (does, did, done, doing)
doable
dobermann (D~, US ~man)
dobro (pl ~os)
dobsonfly
Docetism
Docetist
docile
docilely
docility
dock
docker
docket
docking
dockland
dockside
dockyard
doctor
doctoral
doctorate
doctrinaire
doctrinal
doctrinally
doctrine
docudrama
document
documentable
documental
documentalist
documentarian
documentarist
documentary
documentation
documentative
docusoap
docutainment
dodder

dodderer
dodderiness
doddering
doddery
doddle
dodecagon
dodecahedron (pl ~ra, ~rons)
dodge
dodgeball (US)
dodgems
dodger
dodginess
dodging
dodgy
dodo (pl ~os, ~oes)
Dodoma
doe
doe-eyed
doer
does see do
doff
dog (~gged, ~gging)
dogberry
doge (D~)
dog-eared
dogfight
dogfighter
dogfighting
dogged
doggedly
doggedness
doggerel
dogginess
doggish
doggy (or ~gie)
doggy-bag
dogma
dogmatic
dogmatically
dogmatics
dogmatise (or ~ize)
dogmatism
dogmatist
do-gooder
dogsbody (UK)
dogskin
dogtrot
dogwood
doh *music*

doily (occ doiley, doyly, doyley)
doing
doings
dojo (pl ~os)
Dolby
dolce
dolce vita
doldrums
dole
doleful
dolefully
dolefulness
doll
dollar
dollarisation (or ~iz~)
dollarise (or ~ize)
dollop
dolly
dolma (pl ~as, ~mades)
dolman (! dolmen) *robe*
dolmen (! dolman) *tomb*
dolomite
dolomitic
dolorous
dolorously
dolour (US ~or)
dolphin
dolphinarium (pl ~ia, ~iums)
dolphinfish
dolt
doltish
doltishly
doltishness
domain *territory*
domaine *vineyard*
dome
domed
Domesday (or Dooms~) *book*
domestic
domesticable
domestically
domesticate
domesticated
domestication
domesticity
domical
domicile (occ ~cil)

domiciliary
dominance
dominancy
dominant
dominantly
dominate
dominated
domination
dominator
domineer
domineering
domineeringly
dominical
Dominican
dominion
domino (*pl* ~oes)
don (~nned, ~nning)
donate
donation
done *see* do
doner kebab
dongle
donjon
donkey (*pl* ~eys)
donor
donut *see* doughnut
doodle
doodlebug
doodler
doom
doomed
doomsday
doomwatch
door
doorbell
doored
doorjamb
doorknob
doorman
doormat
doorpost
doorstep
doorstop
doorstopper
door-to-door
doorway
dooryard (*US*)
dopa
dopamine
dope

dopey (*or* ~py)
dopily
dopiness
doping
doppelganger (*occ* ~gänger)
Doppler
Dorian
Doric
dork
dorm
dormancy
dormant
dormer
dormitory
Dormobile (*tr*)
dormouse (*pl* ~mice)
dorsal
dorsally
dory
dosage
dose
doss
dosser
dosshouse
dossier
Dostoevsky (*or* ~toy~)
dot (~tted, ~tting)
dotage
dotard
dote
doter
doting
dotingly
dotted
dotter
dottiness
dotty
Douay
double
double-barrelled (*US* ~eled)
double-breasted
double-cross
double-dealing
double-decker
double-edged
double-faced
double-glaze
double-glazing

double-jointed
double-jointedness
double-park
doubler
double-sided
doublespeak (D~)
doublet
doubling
doubloon
doubt
doubtable
doubter
doubtful
doubtfully
doubtfulness
doubting
doubtingly
doubtless
douceur
douche
dough
doughboy
doughiness
doughnut (*US also* donut)
doughtily
doughtiness
doughty
doughy
dour
dourness
douse (*or* dowse; ! dowse) *soak*
dove (*n*)
dove (*v*) *see* dive
dovecot (*or* ~te)
dovelike
Dover
dovetail
dovish
dowager
dowdiness
dowdy
dowel (~lled, ~lling; *US* ~led, ~ling)
dowelling (*n*; *US* ~eling)
dower
Dow-Jones
down
downbeat

downcast
downcountry
downdraught (US ~draft)
downer
downfall
downgrade
downgraded
downhearted
downheartedly
downheartedness
downhill
downiness
Downing Street
download
downloadable
downloaded
downmarket
downplay
downpour
downright
downrightness
downriver
Down's (or Downs) syndrome
downs (D~ for a specific area) hills
downscale
downshift
downside
downsize
downslope
downstage
downstairs
downstream
downswing
downtime
down-to-earth
downtown
downtrodden
downturn
downward
downwardly
downwards
downwind
downy
dowry
dowse (! douse) water search
dowse (or douse) soak

dowsing
doxological
doxology
doyen
doyenne
doyley see doily
doze
dozen
dozenth
dozer
dozily
doziness
dozy
drab (~bber, ~bbest)
drably
drabness
drachma (pl ~ae, ~as)
draconian
draconic
draft (UK; ! draught) banking, army, writing
draft (US) all meanings
draftee (US)
draftily see draughtily
draftiness see draughtiness
draftproof see draughtproof
draftsman (UK; ! draughtsman) writer
draftsman (US) all meanings
drafty see draughty
drag (~gged, ~gging)
draggle
draggled
dragnet
dragon
dragonfish
dragonfly
dragoon
dragster
drain
drainage
drainer
drainpipe
drake
dram
drama
dramatherapy

dramatic
dramatically
dramatics
dramatis personae
dramatisation (or ~iz~)
dramatise (or ~ize)
dramatist
dramaturg (or ~ge)
dramaturgic
dramaturgical
dramaturgically
dramaturgy
Drambuie (tr)
drank
drape
draped
drapery
drapes (US) curtains
drastic
drastically
draught (UK; US draft; ! draft) technical drawing, fluids, wind, animals
draughtboard (UK; US checker~)
draughtily (UK; US drafti~)
draughtiness (UK; US drafti~)
draughtproof (UK; US draft~)
draughts (UK; US checkers)
draughtsman (UK; US drafts~; ! draftsman) technical drawing
draughtsmanship (UK; US drafts~)
draughty (UK; occ drafty; US drafty)
Dravidian
draw (drew, drawn)
drawback
drawbridge
drawcard
drawer
drawers
drawing
drawl

drawler
drawly
drawn
draw-sheet
drawstring
dray
drayman (*pl* ~men)
dread
dreaded
dreadful
dreadfully
dreadfulness
dreadlocked
dreadlocks
dreadnought
dream (dreamed *or* dreamt)
dreamboat
dreamcatcher
dreamer
dreamily
dreaminess
dreamland
dreamscape
dreamworld
dreamy
drear
drearily
dreariness
dreary
dredge
dredger
dregs
drench
drenched
drenching
Dresden
dress
dressage
dressed
dresser
dressiness
dressing
dressmaker
dressmaking
dressy
drew
drey
dribble
dribbler

dribbly
driblet
dried
drier *see* dry (! dryer)
driest *see* dry
drift
drifter
drifting
driftwood
drifty
drill
driller
drilling
drily (*UK occ* dryly; *US usu* dryly)
drink (drank, drunk)
drinkable
drinker
drinking
drip (~pped, ~pping)
drippily
drippiness
dripping
drippy
drivability (*or* ~vea~)
drivable (*or* ~vea~)
drive (drove, driven, driving)
driveable (*or* ~va~)
drive-in
drivel (~lled, ~lling; *US* ~led, ~ling)
driveller (*US* ~eler)
driver
driverless
driveshaft
drive-through
driveway
driving
drizzle
drizzling
drizzly
drogue
droid
droll
drollery
drollness
drolly
dromedary
drone

drool
droop
droopily
droopiness
droopy
drop (~pped, ~pping)
drop-in
drop-leaf
droplet
drop-off
dropout
dropper
droppings
drop-shot
dropsical
drop-stitch
dropsy
drosophila (D~)
dross
drossy
drought
droughtiness
droughty
drove
drover
droving
drown
drowse
drowsily
drowsiness
drowsy
drub (~bbed, ~bbing)
drudge
drudgery
drug (~gged, ~gging)
druggist (*US*)
druggy (*or* ~gie)
drugstore (*US*)
druid (D~)
druidic
druidical
druidism (D~)
drum (~mmed, ~mming)
drumfish
drummer
drumming
drumstick
drunk
drunkard

drunken
drunkenly
drunkenness
drupaceous
drupe
dry (*UK* drier *occ* dryer, driest; *US usu* dryer, dryest)
dryad
dry-clean
dryer (*occ* drier; ! dry) *appliance*
dryly *see* drily
dryness
drystone
drysuit
dual
dualism
dualist
dualistic
dualistically
duality
dually
dub (~bbed, ~bbing)
Dubai
dubbin
dubbined
dubbing
dubiety
dubious
dubiously
dubiousness
dubitability
dubitable
dubitation
dubitative
Dublin
Dubliner
ducal
ducat
duchess *duke*
duchesse *satin*
duchy
duck
ducking
duckling
duckweed
duct
ductile
ductility

ducting
ductular
ductule
dud
dude
dudgeon
duds
due
duel (~lled, ~lling; *US* ~led, ~ling)
dueller (*US* ~eler)
duellist (*US* ~elist)
duenna
duet
duettist
duffel (*or* duffle)
dug
dugong
dugout
duiker
duke
dukedom
dulcet
dulcimer
dull
dullard
dullish
dullness (*occ UK* duln~)
dully
dulse
duly
dumb
dumb-bell
dumbfound (*or* dumf~)
dumbfounded (*or* dumf~)
dumbstruck
dumdum
dumfound (*or* dumbf~)
dumfounded (*or* dumbf~)
dummy
dump
dumpbin
dumper
dumpiness
dumping
dumpling
dumps
dumpster

dumpy
dun
dunce
dunderhead
dunderheaded
dune
dung
dungarees
dungeon
dungheap
dunghill
dunk
dunker
dunking
dunlin
dunnock
duo (*pl* ~os)
duodecimal
duodecimally
duodenal
duodenitis
duodenum (*pl* ~ena, ~ums)
duologue
duopolistic
duopoly
dupable
dupe
duper
duplet
duplex
duplicable
duplicate
duplicated
duplication
duplicator
duplicitous
duplicity
durability
durable
durableness
durably
duration
durational
duress
Durham
during
dusk
duskily
duskiness

dusky
dust
dustball
dustbin
dustcart
dustcoat
dusted
duster
dustily
dustiness
dusting
dustman
dustpan
dusty
Dutch
Dutchman (*pl* ~men)
Dutchwoman (*pl* ~women)
duteous
duteously
duteousness
dutiable
dutiful
dutifully
dutifulness
duty
duvet
dwarf (*pl* ~rves)
dwarfish
dwarfism
dwell (dwelt *or* dwelled)
dweller
dwelling
dwindle
dwindling
dyad
dyadic
dyarchy (*or* dia~)
dybbuk (*pl* ~ukim, ~uks)
dye (! die) *colour*
dyed (! died) *colour*
dyer
dying
dyke (*US & occ UK; UK also* dike) *lesbian, ditch*
dynamic
dynamical
dynamically
dynamics

dynamise (*or* ~ize)
dynamism
dynamite
dynamiter
dynamo (*pl* ~os)
dynast
dynastic
dynastically
dynasty
dysarthria
dysarthric
dyscalculia
dysentery
dysfunction (*occ* dis~)
dysfunctional (*occ* dis~)
dysfunctionally (*occ* dis~)
dysgraphia
dysgraphic
dyslalia
dyslalic
dyslexia
dyslexic
dysmenorrhoea (*or* ~hea)
dyspepsia
dyspeptic
dysphagia
dysphagic
dysphasia
dysphasic
dysphemism
dysphonia
dysphonic
dysplasia
dysplastic
dyspnoea (*or* ~nea)
dystopia
dystopian
dystrophic
dystrophy
dzo (*or* dzho, zho; *pl* ~os)

each
eager
eagerly
eagerness
eagle
eaglet
ear
earache
eardrum
earful
earhole
earl
earldom
earliness
earlobe
early
earmark
earmarked
earmuff
earn
earner
earnest
earnestly
earnestness
earnings
earphone
earpiece
ear-piercing
earplug
earring
earshot
ear-splitting
earth
earthbound
earthed
earthen
earthenware
earthily
earthiness

earthliness
earthling
earthly
earthquake
earth-shattering
earth-shatteringly
earthworm
earthy
earwax
earwig
earwigging
ease
easeful
easel
easement
easily
easiness
east
eastbound
Easter
easterlies (*n*)
easterly (*adj*)
eastern
easternmost
eastward
eastwards
easy
easygoing
eat (ate, eaten)
eatable
eaten
eater
eatery
eating
eau de cologne (C~)
eau de toilette
eaves
eavesdrop (~pped,
 ~pping)
eavesdropper
ebb
Ebola
ebony
ebullience
ebullient
ebulliently
ebullition
eccentric
eccentrically
eccentricity

ecclesial
ecclesiastic
ecclesiastical
ecclesiastically
ecclesiasticism
ecclesiological
ecclesiologist
ecclesiology
echelon
echidna (E~)
echinacea
echinoderm
echo (*n pl* ~oes; *v* ~oes,
 ~oed, ~oing)
echoer
echoey
echoic
echolalia
echoless
echolocation
echovirus
echt
eclair (*or* é~)
eclat (*or* é~)
eclectic
eclectically
eclecticism
eclipse
eclipsed
ecliptic
eclogue
eclose
eclosion
eco-friendly
eco-labelling
ecological
ecologically
ecologist
ecology
economic
economical
economically
economics
economisation (*or* ~iz~)
economise (*or* ~ize)
economist
economy
ecoside
ecosphere
ecossaise (*or* é~)

ecosystem
ecotourism
ecotourist
ecotype
Ecstasy *drug*
ecstasy *rapture*
ecstatic
ecstatically
ectoderm
ectodermal
ectomorph
ectomorphic
ectomorphy
ectopic
ectoplasm
ectoplasmic
ecu (*or* ECU, Ecu)
Ecuador
Ecuadorian
ecumenical
ecumenically
ecumenism
eczema
eczematous
edacious
edacity
Edam
Edda
eddy
edelweiss
Eden
edge
edged
edgeless
edgeways
edgewise
edgily
edginess
edging
edgy
edibility
edible
edict
edictal
edification
edifice
edify
edifying
edifyingly
Edinburgh

edit
editable
edited
editing
edition
editor
editorial
editorialise (*or* ~ize)
editorialist
editorially
editorship
educability
educable
educate
educated
education
educational
educationalist
educationally
educationist
educe
educible
eduction
edutainment
Edwardian
Edwardiana
eek
eel
eerie (*adj* ~ier, ~iest; *occ* eery)
eerily
eeriness
efface
effacement
effect (! affect) (*v*) *make happen*; (*n*) *result*
effective
effectively
effectiveness
effectivity
effects
effectual
effectuality
effectually
effectualness
effectuate
effectuation
effeminacy
effeminate
efferent

effervesce
effervescence
effervescent
effete
effeteness
efficacious
efficaciously
efficaciousness
efficacy
efficiency
efficient
efficiently
effigy
effloresce
efflorescence
efflorescent
effluence
effluent
effluvium (*pl* ~ia)
efflux
effort
effortful
effortfully
effortless
effortlessly
effortlessness
effrontery
effulgence
effulgent
effulgently
effuse
effusion
effusive
effusively
effusiveness
egalitarian
egalitarianism
egg
eggbeater
eggbox
egghead
eggless
eggnog
eggplant
eggshell
eggwhisk
eggy
eglantine
ego
egocentric

egocentrically
egocentricity
egocentrism
egoism
egoist
egoistic
egoistical
egoistically
egoless
egomania
egomaniac
egomaniacal
egotism
egotist
egotistic
egotistical
egotistically
egregious
egregiously
egregiousness
egress
egret
Egypt
Egyptian
Egyptological
Egyptologist
Egyptology
eider
eiderdown
eidetic
eidetically
eidos
eigenvalue
eight
eighteen
eighteenth
eightfold
eighth
eightieth
eighty
eightyfold
Einstein
Einsteinian
eisteddfod (*pl* ~odau, ~ods)
either
ejaculate
ejaculation
ejaculator
ejaculatory

eject
ejected
ejection
ejective
ejector
eke
elaborate
elaborately
elaborateness
elaboration
elaborative
elaborator
elan (or é~)
eland
elapse
elastase
elastic
elastically
elasticated
elasticise (or ~ize)
elasticity
elastin
elate
elated
elatedly
elatedness
elation
Elba
Elbe
elbow
elder
elderberry
elderflower
elderliness
elderly
eldership
eldest
elect
electable
elected
election
electioneer
electioneering
elective
electively
elector
electoral
electorate
electorship
Electra (or ~k~)

electric
electrical
electrician
electricity
electrics
electrification
electrified
electrifier
electrify
electro-acoustic
electrocardiogram
electrocardiograph
electrocardiographic
electrocardiography
electrochemical
electrochemically
electrochemist
electrochemistry
electroconvulsive
electrocorticogram
electrocute
electrocuted
electrocution
electrode
electrodynamics
electroencephalogram
electroencephalograph
electroencephalography
electroluminescence
electroluminescent
electrolyse (US ~yze)
electrolysis
electrolytic
electrolytical
electrolytically
electromagnet
electromagnetic
electromagnetically
electromagnetism
electrometer
electromotive
electron
electronic
electronically
electronics
electroplate
electroplated
electroplating
electroshock
electrostatic

electrosurgery
electrosurgical
electrotechnic
electrotechnical
electrotechnics
electrotechnology
electrovalency
electrovalent
elegance
elegant
elegantly
elegiacally
elegise (or ~ize)
elegist
elegy
element
elemental
elementalism
elementarily
elementariness
elementary
elements
elephant
elephantiasis
elephantine
elephantoid
elevate
elevated
elevation
elevational
elevator (esp US)
elevatory
eleven
elevenfold
elevenses
eleventh
elf (pl elves)
elfin
elfish
elicit
elicitation
elicitor
elide
elided
eligibility
eligible
eligibly
Elijah
eliminable
eliminate

elimination
eliminator
eliminatory
Elisha
elision
elite (*or* é~)
elitism (*or* é~)
elitist (*or* é~)
elixir
Elizabethan
elk
ell
ellipse
ellipsis (*pl* ~pses)
ellipsoid
ellipsoidal
elliptic
elliptical
elliptically
ellipticity
elm
elocution
elocutionary
elocutionist
Elohim
elongate
elongated
elongation
elope
elopement
eloquence
eloquent
eloquently
else
elsewhere
elucidate
elucidation
elucidative
elucidator
elude
elusive (! allusive)
   difficult
elusively (! allusively)
elusiveness
   (! allusiveness)
elven
elver
elves
elvish
Elysian

Elysium
emaciated
emaciation
email (*or* e-mail)
emailer (*or* e-mailer)
emailing (*or* e-mailing)
emanate
emanation
emancipate
emancipation
emancipator
emancipatory
emasculate
emasculated
emasculation
emasculator
emasculatory
embalm
embalmer
embalming
embalmment (*occ*
   ~lment)
embank
embankment
embargo (*n pl* ~oes; *v*
   ~oes, ~oed, ~oing)
embark
embarkation
embarrass
embarrassed
embarrassedly
embarrassing
embarrassingly
embarrassment
embassy
embattle
embattled
embed (*occ* imbed; *v*
   ~dded, ~dding)
embellish
embellisher
embellishment
ember
embezzle
embezzlement
embezzler
embitter
embittered
embitterment
emblazon

emblazoned
emblazonment
emblem
emblematic
emblematical
emblematically
emblematise (*or* ~ize)
emblematist
embodiment
embody
embolden
emboldened
embolism
embolus (*pl* ~oli)
emboss
embossed
embosser
embouchure
embrace
embraceable
embracement
embracer
embrocation
embroider
embroidered
embroiderer
embroidery
embroil
embroiled
embroilment
embryo
embryogenesis
embryogenetic
embryogeny
embryologic
embryological
embryologically
embryologist
embryology
embryonal
embryonic
embryonically
emcee (~ceed, ~ceeing)
emend (! amend) *edit*
   text
emendation
emerald
emerge
emergence
emergency

emergent
emeritus
emersion
emery
emesis
emetic
emigrant
emigrate
emigration
emigre (*or* émigré)
eminence
eminent
eminently
emir (E~; *or* a~)
emirate (E~; *or* a~)
emissary
emission
emit (~tted, ~tting)
emitter
Emmental (*also* ~thal)
Emmy (*pl* ~mys, ~mies)
emollient
emolument
emote
emoter
emoticon
emotion
emotional
emotionalism
emotionally
emotionless
emotive
emotively
emotiveness
emotivity
empanel (*UK* ~lled,
 ~lling; *US* ~led,
 ~ling)
empathetic
empathetically
empathic
empathically
empathise (*or* ~ize)
empathy
emperor
emphasis (*pl* ~ases)
emphasise (*or* ~ize)
emphatic
emphatically
emphysema

empire
empiric
empirical
empirically
empiricism
emplacement
employ
employability
employable
employee
employer
employment
emporium (*pl* ~ia,
 ~iums)
empower
empowerment
empress
emptily
emptiness
empty
empyema
empyreal
empyrean
emu (*pl* emus)
emulate
emulation
emulative
emulator
emulous
emulously
emulsifiable
emulsification
emulsifier
emulsify
emulsifying
emulsion
enable
enablement
enabler
enabling
enact
enactable
enacted
enaction
enactment
enactor
enamel (~lled, ~lling;
 US ~led, ~ling)
enameller
enamelware

enamelwork
enamour (*US* ~or)
encage
encamp
encampment
encapsulate
encapsulation
encase
encasement
encash
encashment
encaustic
enceinte
encephalic
encephalitic
encephalitis
encephalogram
encephalograph
encephalography
encephalomyelitis
encephalon
enchain
enchainment
enchant
enchantedly
enchanter
enchanting
enchantingly
enchantment
enchantress
enchilada
encipher
encipherment
encircle
encirclement
enclave
enclitic
enclose (*occ* in~)
enclosed (*occ* in~)
enclosure (*occ* in~)
encode
encoder
encomiast
encomiastic
encomiastically
encomium (*pl* ~ia,
 ~iums)
encompass
encompassment
encore

encounter
encourage
encouraged
encouragement
encourager
encouraging
encouragingly
encroach
encroacher
encroachment
encrust (*occ* in~)
encrustation (*also* in~)
encrypt
encryption
encumber
encumbrance
encyclopedia (*or*
~paed~)
encyclopedic (*or*
~paed~)
encyclopedism (*or*
~paed~)
encyclopedist (*or*
~paed~)
encyst
encystation
encystment
end
endanger
endangerment
endear
endearment
endeavour (*US* ~or)
endemic
endemically
endemicity
endgame
ending
endive
endless
endlessly
endlessness
endmost
endnote
endocarditis
endocarp
endocrine
endocrinological
endocrinologist
endocrinology

endoderm
endogamous
endogamy
endogenic
endogenous
endomorph
endomorphic
endoplasm
endorphin
endorsable
endorse
endorsed
endorsee
endorsement
endoscope
endoscopic
endoscopically
endoscopist
endoscopy
endoskeletal
endoskeleton
endosperm
endospermic
endow
endower
endowment
endpaper
endue (*or* in~)
endurable
endurance
endure
enduringly
endways
endwise
enema
enemy
energetic
energetically
energise (*or* ~ize)
energiser (*or* ~iz~)
energy
enervate
enervating
enervation
en famille
enfant terrible
enfeeble
enfeebled
enfeeblement
enfilade

enfold (*occ* in~)
enforce
enforceability
enforceable
enforced
enforcedly
enforcement
enforcer
enfranchise
enfranchisement
engage
engaged
engagement
engaging
engagingly
engagingness
en garde
engender
engine
engined
engineer
engineered
engineering
engineless
England
English
Englishman (*pl* ~men)
Englishness
Englishwoman (*pl*
~women)
engorge
engorgement
engraft (*occ* in~)
engrained (*usu* in~)
engram
engrammatic
engrave
engraved
engraver
engraving
engross
engrossed
engrossment
engulf
engulfed
engulfment
enhance
enhancement
enhancer
enharmonic

enharmonically
enigma
enigmatic
enigmatical
enigmatically
enjambed
enjambement (*or* ~bm~)
enjoin
enjoinment
enjoy
enjoyability
enjoyable
enjoyableness
enjoyably
enjoyment
enkephalin
enkindle
enlace
enlarge
enlarged
enlargement
enlarger
enlighten
enlightened
enlightener
enlightenment
enlist
enlister
enlistment
enliven
enlivener
enlivenment
enmesh
enmeshed
enmeshment
enmity
enneagram
ennoble
ennoblement
ennui
enormity
enormous
enormously
enormousness
enough
en passant (*chess*)
enprint
enquire (*or* in~)
enquirer (*or* in~)

enquiry (*or* in~)
enrage
enraged
en rapport
enrapt
enrapture
enraptured
enrich
enriched
enrichment
enrobe
enrol (*US* ~ll; *v* ~lled, ~lling)
enrollee
enrolment (*US* ~oll~)
en route
ensconce
ensemble
ensheath
enshrine
enshrined
enshrinement
enshroud
ensign
enslave
enslavement
enslaver
ensnare
ensnarement
ensnarl
ensue
en suite
ensure (! insure) *make certain*
entablature
entail
entailment
entangle
entangled
entanglement
entente
enter
enterable
enterer
enteric
enteritis
enterotoxin
enterovirus
enterprise
enterpriser

enterprising
enterprisingly
entertain
entertainer
entertaining
entertainingly
entertainment
enthral (*US* ~ll; ~lled, ~lling)
enthralment (*US* ~all~)
enthrone
enthroned
enthronement
enthuse
enthusiasm
enthusiast
enthusiastic
enthusiastically
entice
enticement
enticer
enticingly
entire
entirely
entirety
entitle
entitlement
entity
entomb
entombment
entomological
entomologist
entomology
entourage
entr'acte
entrails
entrance
entranced
entrancement
entrancingly
entrant
entrap (~pped, ~pping)
entrapment
entreat
entreaty
entrechat
entrecote (*or* ~côte)
entree (*or* ~rée)
entrench (*occ* in~)
entrenched (*occ* in~)

entrepot (*or* ~pôt)
entrepreneur
entrepreneurial
entrepreneurialism
entrepreneurially
entrepreneurism
entrepreneurship
entresol
entropic
entropically
entropy
entrust
entry
entryphone (E~, *tr*)
entwine
entwined
entwinement
e-number (E~)
enumerable
enumerate
enumeration
enumerative
enumerator
enunciate
enunciation
enunciative
enunciator
enuresis
enuretic
envelop (~oped,
  ~oping; ! envelope)
  cover
envelope (! envelop)
  packet
envelopment
envenom
enviable
enviably
envier
envious
enviously
environ
environment
environmental
environmentalism
environmentalist
environmentally
environs
envisage
envision

envoi (*or* ~oy) *writing*
envoy *messenger*
envy
enzymatic
enzyme
enzymologist
enzymology
Eocene
eolian (*US; UK* ae~)
  harp
Eolithic
eon (*US & tech; also* ae~)
Eos
eparch
eparchy
epaulette (*US* ~et)
epee (*or* épée)
epeeist (*or* épée~)
ephedrine
ephemera
ephemeral
ephemerality
ephemerally
ephemeralness
ephemeris (*pl* ~rides)
Ephesian
Ephesus
epic
epical
epically
epicalyx
epicene
epicentral
epicentre (*US* ~ter)
epicure
epicurean (E~)
epicureanism (E~)
epicurism
epidemic
epidemiological
epidemiologist
epidemiology
epidermal
epidermic
epidermis
epidermoid
epidural
epiglottal
epiglottis
epigram

epigrammatic
epigrammatically
epigrammatise (*or* ~ize)
epigrammatist
epigraph
epigrapher
epigraphic
epigraphical
epigraphically
epigraphist
epigraphy
epilepsy
epileptic
epilogue (*US* ~og)
epiphanic
Epiphany *Christian feast*
epiphany *revelation*
epiphenomenon (*pl*
  ~ena)
epiphysis (*pl* ~yses)
epiphyte
episcopacy
episcopal
episcopalian
episcopalism
episcopally
episcopate
episode
episodic
episodically
epistemic
epistemically
epistemological
epistemologically
epistemologist
epistemology
Epistle (*rel*)
epistle (*lit*)
epistolary
epitaph
epithet
epithetic
epithetical
epithetically
epitome
epitomisation (*or* ~iz~)
epitomise (*or* ~ize)
epitomist
epizoan
epizoic

epizoon (*pl* ~zoa)
epizootic
epoch
epochal
eponym
eponymous
epoxy
epsilon
Epsom
equability
equable
equably
equal (~lled, ~lling; *US* ~led, ~ling)
equalisation (*or* ~iz~)
equalise (*or* ~ize)
equalitarian
equalitarianism
equality
equally
equanimity
equatable
equate
equation
equational
equative
equatively
Equator *Earth*
equator *celestial*
equatorial
equatorially
equerry
equestrian
equestrianism
equiangular
equidistance
equidistant
equidistantly
equilateral
equilibrate
equilibration
equilibrist
equilibrium (*pl* ~ria)
equine
equinoctial
equinox
equip (~pped, ~pping)
equipage
equipe (*or* é~)
equipment

equipoise
equipollence
equipollency
equipollent
equipotent
equipotential
equipper
equiprobability
equiprobable
equitability
equitable
equitably
equitation
equity
equivalence
equivalency
equivalent
equivalently
equivocal
equivocality
equivocally
equivocalness
equivocate
equivocation
equivocatory
era
eradicable
eradicant
eradicate
eradicated
eradication
eradicator
erasable
erase
erased
eraser
erasure
erbium
ere *before*
erect
erectable
erectile
erection
erectly
erectness
erector (*occ* ~er)
eremite
eremitic
eremitical
ergo

ergonomic
ergonomics
ergonomist
ergot
ergotism
erica (E~)
Eritrea
Eritrean
ermine
ermined
erode
eroded
erodible
erogenic
erogenous
Eros
erosion
erosional
erosive
erotic
erotica
erotically
eroticise (*or* ~ize)
eroticism
erotology
erotomania
erotomaniac
err
errancy
errand
errant
errantry
erratic
erratically
erraticism
erratum (*pl* ~ta)
erroneous
erroneously
erroneousness
error
errorless
ersatz
Erse
erst
erstwhile
erubescent
eructation
erudite
eruditely
erudition

erupt
eruption
eruptive
erysipelas
erythema
erythemal
erythematous
erythrocyte
erythromycin
escalade
escalate
escalating
escalation
escalator
escalope
escapable
escapade
escape
escaped
escapee
escapement
escaper
escapism
escapist
escapologist
escapology
escargot
escarpment
eschatological
eschatologist
eschatology
escherichia (E~)
eschew
eschewal
escort
escritoire
escrow
escudo
esculent
escutcheon
escutcheoned
Eskimo (*pl* ~o, ~os)
esophagus (*or* oe~)
esoteric
esoterica
esoterically
esotericism
esotericist
espadrille
espalier

especial
especially
Esperantist
Esperanto
espial
espionage
esplanade
espousal
espouse
espouser
espresso (*or* ex~; *pl* ~os)
esprit
esprit de corps
espy
esquire
essay
essayist
essence
Essene
essential
essentialism
essentialist
essentiality
essentially
essentialness
establish
established
establisher
establishment (E~)
estate
esteem
ester
esthete (*or* ae~)
esthetic (*or* ae~)
esthetician (*or* ae~)
estimable
estimableness
estimate
estimation
estimator
estival (*or* ae~)
estivate (*or* ae~)
estivation (*or* ae~)
Estonia
Estonian
estrange
estrangement
estranger
estrogen (*or* oe~)
Estuary *accent*

estuary *river*
etalon
etch
etching
eternal
eternalisation (*or* ~iz~)
eternalise (*or* ~ize)
eternally
eternity
ethane
ethanol
ether (*or* ae~)
ethereal
ethereality
Ethernet
ethic
ethical
ethicality
ethically
ethics
Ethiopia
Ethiopian
Ethiopic
ethnic
ethnically
ethnicity
ethnoarchaeological (*or* ~che~)
ethnoarchaeologist (*or* ~che~)
ethnoarchaeology (*or* ~che~)
ethnobotanic
ethnobotanical
ethnobotanist
ethnobotany
ethnocentric
ethnocentrically
ethnocentricity
ethnocentrism
ethnocide
ethnocultural
ethnographer
ethnographic
ethnographical
ethnographically
ethnography
ethnologic
ethnological
ethnologically

ethnologist
ethnology
ethnomusicologic
ethnomusicological
ethnomusicologist
ethnomusicology
ethnoscience
ethnoscientist
ethological
ethologically
ethologist
ethology
ethos
ethyl
ethylene
etiology (*or* ae~)
etiquette
Etna
Eton
Etonian
Etruscan
etymological
etymologically
etymologise (*or* ~ize)
etymologised (*or* ~ized)
etymologist
etymology
eucalyptus (*pl* ~ti,
 ~uses)
Eucharist
Eucharistic
Eucharistical
euchre (*US*)
Euclid
Euclidian (*or* ~dean)
eugenic
eugenically
eugenicist
eugenics
euglena
eukaryote (*occ* euc~)
eukaryotic (*occ* euc~)
eulogise (*or* ~ize)
eulogist
eulogistic
eulogistically
eulogy
eunuch
eunuchoid
eunuchoidism

euphemise (*or* ~ize)
euphemism
euphemistic
euphemistically
euphonic
euphonious
euphoniously
euphonise (*or* ~ize)
euphonium
euphony
euphoria
euphoric
euphorically
Euphrates
euphuism
Eurasia
Eurasian
eureka
eurhythmic (*US* eury~)
eurhythmics (*US* eury~)
eurhythmy (E~, *US*
 eury~)
euro (E~)
Eurocentric
Eurocentricity
Eurocentrism
Eurocracy
Eurocrat
Eurocurrency
Eurodollar
Euroland
Europa
European
Europeanism
europium
Eurosceptic
Eurostar
Eurotrash
Eurovision
eustachian (E~)
eustasy
euthanasia
evacuate
evacuated
evacuation
evacuee
evadable
evade
evader
evaluate

evaluation
evaluator
evanesce
evanescence
evanescent
evanescently
evangelic
evangelical
evangelicalism
evangelically
evangelisation (*or* ~iz~)
evangelise (*or* ~ize)
evangelism
evangelist
evangelistic
evaporability
evaporable
evaporate
evaporated
evaporating
evaporation
evaporative
evaporator
evasion
evasive
evasively
evasiveness
Eve *bible*
eve *evening*
even
even-handed
evening
evenly
evenness
evensong (E~)
event
even-tempered
eventer
eventful
eventfully
eventfulness
eventide
eventing
eventless
eventlessness
eventual
eventuality
eventually
eventuate
ever

Everest
Everglades
evergreen
everlasting
everlastingly
everlastingness
every
everybody
everyday
everyman (E~)
everyone
everything
everywhere
evict
eviction
evictor
evidence
evident
evidential
evidentiality
evidentially
evidently
evil
evilly
evil-minded
evilness
evince
evincible
eviscerate
evisceration
evocation
evocative
evocatively
evocativeness
evoke
evoker
evolution
evolutional
evolutionally
evolutionarily
evolutionary
evolutionism
evolutionist
evolvable
evolve
evolved
evolvement
ewe
ewer
exacerbate

exacerbation
exact
exactable
exacting
exactingly
exactingness
exaction
exactitude
exactly
exactness
exaggerate
exaggerated
exaggeratedly
exaggeration
exaggerative
exaggerator
exalt
exaltation
exalted
exaltedly
exaltedness
exam
examinable
examination
examine
examinee
examiner
example
exasperate
exasperated
exasperatedly
exasperating
exasperatingly
exasperation
Excalibur
ex cathedra
excavate
excavation
excavator
exceed
exceeding
exceedingly
excel (~lled, ~lling)
excellence
excellency (E~)
excellent
excellently
except
excepted
excepting

exception
exceptionable
exceptional
exceptionality
exceptionally
excerpt
excerptible
excerption
excess
excessive
excessively
excessiveness
exchange
exchangeability
exchangeable
exchanger
exchequer (E~)
excise
excised
excision
excitability
excitable
excitably
excitant
excitation
excitatory
excite
excited
excitedly
excitement
exciter (! excitor)
 apparatus
exciting
excitingly
excitingness
excitor (! exciter) *nerve*
exclaim
exclamation
exclamatory
excludability
excludable
exclude
excluded
excluder
excluding
exclusion
exclusionary
exclusionist
exclusive
exclusively

exclusiveness
exclusivism
exclusivist
exclusivity
excommunicant
excommunicate
excommunication
excommunicative
excommunicator
excommunicatory
excoriate
excoriation
excrement
excremental
excrescence
excrescent
excreta
excrete
excreter
excretion
excretive
excretory
excruciate
excruciating
excruciatingly
excruciation
exculpate
exculpation
exculpatory
excursion
excursive
excursively
excursiveness
excusable
excusableness
excusably
excusatory
excuse
execrable
execrableness
execrate
execration
execrative
execratory
executant
execute
executed
execution
executioner
executive

executively
executor
executorial
executorship
executory
executrix
exegesis (*pl* ~eses)
exegete
exegetic
exegetical
exemplar
exemplarily
exemplariness
exemplary
exemplification
exemplify
exemplum (*pl* ~pla)
exempt
exemption
exequy
exercisable
exercise
exerciser
exert
exertion
Exeter
exeunt
exfoliant
exfoliate
exfoliating
exfoliation
exfoliative
exfoliator
ex gratia
exhalable
exhalation
exhale
exhaust
exhausted
exhaustedly
exhauster
exhaustibility
exhaustible
exhausting
exhaustingly
exhaustion
exhaustive
exhaustively
exhaustiveness
exhibit

exhibited
exhibition
exhibitioner
exhibitionism
exhibitionist
exhibitionistic
exhibitionistically
exhibitor
exhilarate
exhilarating
exhilaratingly
exhilaration
exhort
exhortation
exhortative
exhortatory
exhorter
exhumation
exhume
exhumed
exigence
exigency
exigent
exigible
exiguity
exiguous
exiguously
exiguousness
exile
exiled
exilic
exist
existence
existent
existential
existentialism
existentialist
existentially
existing
exit
Exmoor
exobiological
exobiologist
exobiology
Exodus *biblical*
exodus *departure*
ex officio
exogamous
exogamy
exogenous

exogenously
exonerate
exoneration
exonerative
exorbitance
exorbitant
exorbitantly
exorcise (*or* ~ize)
exorcism
exorcist
exoskeletal
exoskeleton
exosphere
exothermic
exotic
exotica
exotically
exoticism
expand
expandable
expanded
expander
expanse
expansibility
expansible
expansion
expansionary
expansionism
expansionist
expansive
expansively
expansiveness
expansivity
expatiate
expatiation
expatriate
expatriation
expect
expectable
expectancy
expectant
expectantly
expectation
expectorant
expectorate
expectoration
expedience
expediency
expedient
expediently

expedite
expediter
expedition
expeditionary
expeditious
expeditiously
expeditiousness
expeditor
expel (~lled, ~lling)
expellable
expeller
expend
expendability
expendable
expendably
expenditure
expense
expensive
expensively
expensiveness
experience
experienceable
experienced
experiencer
experiential
experientially
experiment
experimental
experimentalism
experimentalist
experimentally
experimentation
experimenter
expert
expertise
expertly
expertness
expiable
expiate
expiation
expiator
expiatory
expiration
expiratory
expire
expirer
expiry
explain
explainable
explainer

explanation
explanatorily
explanatory
expletive
explicable
explicate
explication
explicative
explicator
explicatory
explicit
explicitly
explicitness
explode
exploded
exploder
exploit
exploitable
exploitation
exploitative
exploiter
exploitive
exploration
explorational
explorative
exploratory
explore
explorer
explosion
explosive
explosively
explosiveness
exponent
exponential
exponentially
export
exportability
exportable
exportation
exporter
expose
exposé
exposed
exposer
exposition
expositional
expositor
expository
exposure
expound

expounder
express
expressed
expresser
expressible
expression
expressional
expressionism (E~)
expressionist (E~)
expressionistic
expressionistically
expressionless
expressionlessly
expressionlessness
expressive
expressively
expressiveness
expressivity
expressly
expresso (*or* es~)
expressway
expropriate
expropriation
expropriator
expulsion
expulsive
expunction
expunge
expungement
expunger
expurgate
expurgated
expurgation
expurgator
expurgatorial
expurgatory
exquisite
exquisitely
exquisiteness
extant
extemporaneous
extemporaneously
extemporaneousness
extemporarily
extemporariness
extemporary
extempore
extemporisation (*or* ~iz~)
extemporise (*or* ~ize)

extend
extendability (*or* ~ibil~)
extendable (*or* ~ible)
extended
extender
extendibility (*or* ~abil~)
extendible (*or* ~able)
extensibility
extensible
extension
extensional
extensionality
extensive
extensively
extensiveness
extensor
extent
extenuate
extenuating
extenuation
extenuatory
exterior
exteriorise (*or* ~ize)
exteriority
exteriorly
exterminate
exterminated
extermination
exterminator
exterminatory
external
externalisation (*or* ~iz~)
externalise (*or* ~ize)
externalised (*or* ~ized)
externalism
externalist
externally
extinct
extinction
extinguish
extinguishable
extinguished
extinguisher
extinguishment
extirpate
extirpation
extirpator
extol (~lled, ~lling)
extoller
extolment

extort
extorter
extortion
extortionate
extortionately
extortioner
extortionist
extortive
extra
extract
extractability
extractable
extracted
extraction
extractive
extractor
extraditable
extradite
extradition
extrafamilial
extragalactic
extramarital
extramaritally
extramural
extraneous
extraneously
extraneousness
extraordinarily
extraordinariness
extraordinary
extrapolate
extrapolated
extrapolation
extrapolative
extrapolator
extrasensory
extraterrestrial
extravagance
extravagancy
extravagant
extravagantly
extravaganza
extraversion *see*
  extroversion
extravert *see* extrovert
extraverted *see*
  extroverted
extreme
extremely
extremeness

extremism
extremist
extremity
extricable
extricate
extrication
extrinsic
extrinsically
extroversion (*or* extra~)
extrovert (*occ* extra~)
extroverted (*occ* extra~)
extrudable
extrude
extruded
extrusion
extrusive
exuberance
exuberant
exuberantly
exudation
exudative
exude
exult
exultancy
exultant
exultantly
exultation
exultingly
eye (eyed, eyeing *occ* eying)
eyeball
eyebath
eyeblack
eyebright
eyebrow
eyecatcher
eyecatching
eyecatchingly
eyeful
eyeglass
eyehole
eyelash
eyelet
eyelid
eyeline
eyeliner
eye-opener
eyepatch
eyepiece
eyeshade

eyeshadow
eyeshot
eyesight
eyesore
eyespot
eyestrain
eyewash
eyewear
eyewitness
eyrie (*UK; US* aerie)

Ff

Fabian
Fabianism
fable
fabled
fabler
fabliau (*pl* ~ux)
fabric
fabricate
fabrication
fabricator
fabulist
fabulosity
fabulous
fabulously
fabulousness
facade (*or* ~ç~)
face
facecloth
faced
faceless
facelessness
facelift
face-off
facer
facet
faceted
facetious
facetiously
facetiousness

facial
facially
facile
facilely
facileness
facilitate
facilitation
facilitative
facilitator
facilitatory
facility
facing
facsimile
facsimiled
fact
facticity
faction
factional
factionalise (*or* ~ize)
factionalism
factionally
factious
factiously
factiousness
factitious
factitiously
factitiousness
factitive
factoid
factor
factorable
factorial
factorially
factorisation (*or* ~iz~)
factorise (*or* ~ize)
factory
factotum (*pl* ~tums)
factual
factualism
factuality
factually
factualness
facture
facultative
facultatively
faculty
fad
faddily
faddiness
faddish

faddishly
faddishness
faddism
faddist
fade
fade-in
fadeless
fade-out
fader
faecal (*US* fe~)
faeces (*US* fe~)
faerie (*or* ~ry)
Faeroe (*or* Far~) *islands*
Faeroese (*or* Far~)
faery (*or* ~rie)
fag
faggot (*US also* fagot)
fah (*or* fa) *note*
Fahrenheit
faience
fail
failed
failing
failsafe
failure
faint (! feint) *collapse*
faint-hearted
faint-heartedly
faint-heartedness
faintly
faintness
fair
Fair Isle
fair-haired
fairing
fairish
fairly
fair-minded
fair-mindedly
fair-mindedness
fairness
fairway
fairy
fairylike
fait accompli (*pl* ~s ~lis)
faith
faithful
faithfully
faithfulness
faithless

faithlessly
faithlessness
fajitas
fake
faker
fakery
fakir (*occ* faquir)
falafel (*occ* fe~)
falcate
falciform
falcon
falconer
falconry
faldstool
Falklander
Falklands
fall (fell, fallen)
fallacious
fallaciously
fallaciousness
fallacy
fallback (*or* fall-~)
fallen
fallenness
faller
fallibilism
fallibilist
fallibility
fallible
fallibly
falling
falling-out
fall-off
fallopian (F~)
fallout
fallow
fallowness
false
falsehood
falsely
falseness
falsetto (*pl* ~os)
falsifiability
falsifiable
falsification
falsify
falsity
falter
falterer
faltering

falteringly
fame
famed
familia (*pl* ~iae)
familial
familiar
familiarisation (*or* ~iz~)
familiarise (*or* ~ize)
familiarity
familiarly
familist
familistic
family
famine
famished
famishing
famous
famously
famousness
fan (~nned, ~nning)
fanatic
fanatical
fanatically
fanaticise (*or* ~ize)
fanaticism
fanaticist
fanciable
fancier
fanciful
fancifully
fancifulness
fancily
fanciness
fancy
fancywork
fandangle
fandango (*pl* ~os)
fanfare
fang
fanged
fangless
fanny (*tab*)
fantail
fantasia
fantasise (*or* ~ize)
fantasist
fantastic
fantastical
fantastically
fantasy

fanzine
faquir (*usu* fakir)
far (*adj* further *occ*
  farther, furthest *or*
  farthest)
farad
Faraday
faradic
faraway
farce
farceur
farceuse
farcical
farcicality
farcically
fare
farewell
far-fetched
far-flung
farina
farinaceous
faring
farkleberry
farm
farmable
farmer
farmhand
farmhouse
farming
farmland
farmost
farmstead
farmyard
farness
Faroe (*or* Faer~)
Faroese (*or* Faer~)
farouche
farrago (*pl* ~os, ~oes)
farrier
farriery
farrow
far-seeing
Farsi
far-sighted
far-sightedly
far-sightedness
fart
farther *see* far
farthest *see* far
farthing

fascia (*occ* facia; *pl* ~ae,
  ~as)
fascicle (*usu* ~icule)
fascicule (*or* ~icle)
fascinate
fascinated
fascinating
fascinatingly
fascination
fascinator
fascism (F~)
fascist (F~)
fascistic
fashion
fashionability
fashionable
fashionably
fast
fasten
fastener
fastening
fastidious
fastidiously
fastidiousness
fasting
fastness
fat (*adj* ~tter, ~ttest; *v*
  ~tted, ~tting)
fatal
fatalism
fatalist
fatalistic
fatalistically
fatality
fatally
fate
fateful
fathead
father
fatherhood
fathering
fatherland
fatherless
fatherlessness
fatherlike
fatherliness
fatherly
fathom
fathomable
fathomless

fatiguability (*or* ~ga~)
fatiguable (*or* ~ga~)
fatigue
fatigued
fatiguing
fatten
fattening
fattiness
fattism
fattist
fatty
fatuity
fatuous
fatuously
fatuousness
fatwa
fauces (*pl* ~ces)
faucet (*esp US*)
faucial
fault
faulted
faultily
faultiness
faulting
faultless
faultlessly
faultlessness
faulty
faun
fauna (*pl* ~as, ~ae)
faunal
faute de mieux
Fauvism
Fauvist
faux pas
favour (*US* ~or)
favourable (*US* ~or~)
favourableness (*US*
  ~or~)
favourably (*US* ~or~)
favoured (*US* ~or~)
favourer (*US* ~or~)
favourite (*US* ~or~)
favouritism (*US* ~or~)
fawn
fawningly
fax
fayre (*archaic* fair *n*)
faze
fazed

fealty
fear
fearful
fearfully
fearfulness
fearless
fearlessly
fearlessness
fearsome
fearsomely
fearsomeness
feasibility
feasible
feasibly
feast
feaster
feat
feather
featherbrained
featheriness
feathering
featherless
featherweight
feathery
feature
featured
featureless
febrile
febrility
February
fecal (*US*; *UK* fae~)
feces (*US*; *UK* fae~)
feckless
fecklessly
fecklessness
feculence
feculent
fecund
fecundate
fecundity
fed
fedayeen (F~)
federal
federalisation (*or* ~iz~)
federalise (*or* ~ize)
federalism
federalist
federally
federate
federated

federation
federationist
federative
fedora
fee
feeble
feeble-minded
feeble-mindedly
feeble-mindedness
feebleness
feebly
feed (fed)
feedback
feeder
feeding
feedstock
feedstuff
feel
feeler
feeling
feelingless
feelingly
feet
feign
feint (! faint) *pretend*
feistily
feistiness
feisty
felafel (*usu* fa~)
feldspar (*or* fels~)
felicitate
felicitating
felicitations
felicitatious
felicitatiously
felicitatiousness
felicitous
felicitously
felicitousness
felicity
feline
felinity
fell
fellate
fellatio
fellator
felled
fellow
fellowship
fell-walker

fell-walking
felon
felonious
feloniously
felony
felspar (*or* felds~)
felt
felted
felting
female
femaleness
feminine
femininely
feminineness
femininity
feminisation (*or* ~iz~)
feminise (*or* ~ize)
feminism
feminist
femme fatale
femoral
femur (*pl* ~urs, ~mora)
fen
fence
fenceless
fencer
fencing
fend
fender
feng shui
Fenian
Fenianism
fennel
fenny
Fens *England location*
fens *waterlogged area*
fenugreek
feoff
fer-de-lance
ferment (! foment) *brew*
fermentable
fermentation
fermentative
fermenter (*also esp US* ~or)
fermi
fermion
fermium
fern
fernbrake

fernery
ferny
ferocious
ferociously
ferociousness
ferocity
ferret
ferreter
ferreting
ferric
ferrite
ferromagnetism
ferrous
ferruginous
ferrule
ferry
ferryman (*pl* ~men)
fertile
fertilisable (*or* ~iz~)
fertilisation (*or* ~iz~)
fertilise (*or* ~ize)
fertiliser (*or* ~iz~)
fertility
fervency
fervent
fervently
fervid
fervidly
fervour (*US* ~or)
fescue
fesse (*or* fess, *hera*)
fester
festering
festival
festive
festively
festiveness
festivity
festoon
festooned
feta (*or* fetta)
fetal (*or* foe~)
fetch
fetcher
fetching
fetchingly
fete (*or* fête)
fetid (*or* foe~)
fetidly (*or* foe~)
fetidness (*or* foe~)

fetish
fetishisation (*or* ~iz~)
fetishise (*or* ~ize)
fetishism
fetishist
fetishistic
fetlock
fetter
fettered
fettle
fettuccine (*or* ~ucine)
fetus (*or* foe~)
feud
feudal
feudalisation (*or* ~iz~)
feudalise (*or* ~ize)
feudalism
feudalist
feudalistic
feudality
feudally
feudatory
feudist
fever
fevered
feverfew
feverish
feverishly
feverishness
few
fey
feyly
feyness
fez (*pl* fezzes)
fiacre
fiance (*or* ~cé)
fiancee (*or* ~cée)
fiasco (*pl* os, ~oes)
fiat
fib (~bbed, ~bbing)
fibber
Fibonacci
fibre (*US* ~ber)
fibreboard (*US* ~ber~)
fibred (*US* ~ber~)
fibreglass (*US* ~ber~)
fibreless (*US* ~ber~)
fibre-optic (*US* ~ber~)
fibril
fibrillar

fibrillary
fibrillate
fibrillation
fibrin
fibrinogen
fibroid
fibrosis
fibrositic
fibrositis
fibrous
fibrously
fibrousness
fibula (*pl* ~ae, ~as)
fibular
fiche
fickle
fickleness
fiction
fictional
fictionalisation (*or* ~iz~)
fictionalise (*or* ~ize)
fictionality
fictionally
fictitious
fictitiously
fictitiousness
fictive
fictiveness
fiddle
fiddle-faddle
fiddler
fiddlestick
fiddling
fideism
fideist
fideistic
fidelity
fidget
fidgeter
fidgetiness
fidgety
fiducial
fiduciary
fief
fiefdom
field
fielder
fieldfare
fieldmouse (*pl* ~mice)
fieldwork

fieldworker
fiend
fiendish
fiendishly
fiendishness
fiendlike
fierce
fiercely
fierceness
fierily
fieriness
fiery
fiesta
fife
fifteen
fifteenth
fifth
fiftieth
fifty
fiftyfold
fig
fight
fighter
fighting
figment
figuration
figurative
figuratively
figurativeness
figure
figured
figurehead
figureless
figure-skater
figure-skating
figurine
figwort
Fiji
Fijian
filagree (*usu* filig~)
filagreed (*usu* filig~)
filament
filamentary
filamented
filamentous
filaria (F~)
filariasis
filbert
filch
filcher

file
filefish
filename
filer
fileserver
filet (! fillet) *lace*
filet (*or* fillet) *meat, fish;*
  (US) *strip of material*
filet mignon
filial
filially
filibuster
filibustering
filicidal
filicide
filigree (*occ* filag~)
filigreed (*occ* filag~)
filing
fill
filler
fillet (*as n, US also* filet)
  meat, fish
filleter
filleting
filling
fillip
filly
film
filmable
filmgoer
filmic
filmily
filminess
film-maker
film-making
film noir
filmography
filmstar
filmy
filo (*or* phyllo)
filofax (F~, *tr*)
filter
filterable (*occ* ~trable)
filtered
filth
filthily
filthiness
filthy
filtrate
filtration

fin
fin de siecle (*or* ~ècle)
finagle
final (*adj; as n* ! finale)
  last
finale (*n* ! final) *music,*
  stage
finalise (*or* ~ize)
finality
finance
financial
financially
financier
finch
find (found)
finder
finding
fine
fineable
finely
fineness
finery
finesse
finger
fingerbowl
fingered
fingering
fingerless
fingermark
fingernail
fingerprint
fingerstall
fingertip
finickety
finickiness
finicky
finish
finished
finisher
finishing
finite
finitely
finiteness
finitude
Finland
Finn
finned
Finnish
finnless
Finno-Ugric

fiord (*or* fjo~)
fipple
fir
fire
firearm
fire-ball
firebomb
firebox
firebrand
firebreak
firebrick
firecracker
firedamp
firefight
firefighter
firefighting
firefly
fireguard
fireless
firelight
firelighter
fireman (*pl* ~men)
fireplace
firepower
fireproof
firescreen
fireship
fireside
firestorm
firetrap
firewall
firewater
fireweed
firewoman (*pl* ~women)
firewood
firework
firing
firkin
firm
firmament
firmamental
firmly
firmness
first
first-hand
firstly
first-rate
fiscal
fiscally
fish

fishbowl
fishcake
fisher
fisherman (*pl* ~men)
fisherwoman (*pl*
  ~women)
fishery
fish-eye
fishily
fishiness
fishing
fishlike
fishmonger
fishnet
fishplate
fishtail
fishwife (*pl* ~wives)
fishy
fissile
fissility
fission
fissionable
fissiparity
fissiparous
fissiparousness
fissure
fissured
fist
fisted
fistful
fisticuffs
fistula (*pl* ~as, ~ae)
fit (*adj* ~tter, ~ttest; *v*
  ~tted *or esp US* fit,
  ~tting)
fitful
fitfully
fitfulness
fitness
fitted
fitter
fitting
fittingly
five
fivefold
fives
fix
fixable
fixate
fixated

fixation
fixative
fixed
fixedly
fixedness
fixed-wing
fixer
fixing
fixity
fixture
fizgig
fizz
fizzer
fizzily
fizziness
fizzle
fizzy
fjord (*or* fio~)
flab
flabbergasted
flabbergasting
flabbily
flabbiness
flabby
flaccid
flaccidity
flaccidly
flaccidness
flack (*usu* flak)
flacon
flag (~gged, ~gging)
flagellant
flagellar
flagellate
flagellation
flagellator
flagellatory
flagellum (*pl* ~lla)
flageolet
flagged
flagger
flagging
flagon
flagpole
flagrancy
flagrant
flagrantly
flagship
flagstaff
flagstone

flagstoned
flag-waver
flag-waving
flail
flair
flak (*occ* flack)
flake
flaked
flakily
flakiness
flaky
flambé (~bés, ~béed,
~béing; *also* ~be,
~beed, ~being)
flambeau (*pl* ~ux, ~us)
flamboyance
flamboyancy
flamboyant
flamboyantly
flame
flameless
flamenco (*pl* ~os)
flameout
flameproof
flamer
flame-thrower
flaming
flamingo (*pl* ~os, ~oes)
flammability
flammable
flan
Flanders
flange
flanged
flangeless
flanger
flanging
flank
flanked
flanker
flanking
flannel (~lled, ~lling;
US ~led, ~ling)
flannelette
flannelling (*n*)
flap (~pped, ~pping)
flapdragon
flapjack
flapper
flapping (*n*)

flare
flash
flashback
flashbulb
flashcard
flashcube
flasher
flashgun
flashily
flashiness
flashing
flashlight
flashpoint
flashy
flask
flat (*adj* ~tter, ~ttest)
flatbed
flatboat
flatfish
flat-footed
flat-footedly
flat-footedness
flatlet
flatline
flatly
flatmate
flatness
flatten
flattened
flattener
flatter
flattered
flattering
flatteringly
flattery
flatulence
flatulency
flatulent
flatulently
flatus
flatworm
flaunt
flaunter
flaunting
flauntingly
flautist (*US* flutist)
flavescent
flavonoid
flavoprotein
flavorous (*occ* ~our~)

flavour (*US* ~or)
flavoured (*US* ~or~)
flavourful (*US* ~or~)
flavouring (*US* ~or~)
flavourless (*US* ~or~)
flavoursome (*US* ~or~)
flaw
flawed
flawless
flawlessly
flawlessness
flax
flaxen
flaxseed
flay
flayed
flayer
flea
fleabane
fleabite
flea-bitten
fleapit
fleck
flecked
flection (*usu* ~exion)
fled
fledge
fledged
fledgling (*occ* ~gel~)
flee (fled)
fleece
fleeced
fleecily
fleeciness
fleecy
fleet
fleeting
fleetingly
fleetly
fleetness
Fleming
Flemish
flesh
fleshiness
fleshing
fleshly
fleshpots
fleshy
fleur-de-lis (*or* ~lys; *pl*
fleurs~)

flew
flews
flex
flexibility
flexible
flexibly
flexile
flexility
flexion (*occ* ~ection)
flexitime (*US* flextime)
flexor
flextime (*UK* flexitime)
flexuosity
flexuous
flexuously
flexural
flexure
flibbertigibbet
flick
flicker
flickering
flier (*usu* flyer)
flight
flightily
flightiness
flightless
flightlessness
flighty
flimflam
flimsily
flimsiness
flimsy
flinch
flincher
flinchingly
fling (flung)
flinger
flint
flintily
flintiness
flinty
flip (~pped, ~pping)
flipchart
flip-flop
flippancy
flippant
flippantly
flipper
fliptop (also flip-~)
flirt

flirtation
flirtatious
flirtatiously
flirtatiousness
flirty
flit (~tted, ~tting)
flitch
flitter
float
floatable
floatation (*usu* flot~)
floater
floating
floccose
flocculence
flocculent
floccus (*pl* ~cci)
flock
flockmaster
floe
flog (~gged, ~gging)
flood
floodgate
flooding
floodlight
floodtide
floor
floorboard
floorcloth
floored
flooring
flop
floppily
floppiness
floppy
flor
flora (*pl* ~ae, ~as)
floral
Florentine *from Florence*
florentine (F~) *food*
florescence
floret
floriated (*occ* ~reat~)
florid
Florida
Floridian
floridity
floridly
floridness
florin

florist
floristic
floristically
floristry
floss
flossy
flotage (*occ* float~)
flotation (*occ* float~)
flotilla
flotsam
flounce
flounced
flouncy
flounder
flounderer
flour
flouriness
flourish
flourisher
floury
flout
flow
flower
flowered
flowerer
floweriness
flowering
flowerless
flowerpot (*or* flower-~)
flowery
flowing
flowingly
flown
flu
fluctuate
fluctuating
fluctuation
flue
fluency
fluent
fluently
fluff
fluffily
fluffiness
fluffy
flugelhorn (*occ* flü~)
fluid
fluidics
fluidisation (*or* ~iz~)
fluidise (*or* ~ize)

fluidity
fluidly
fluke
flukily
flukiness
fluky (or ~ey)
flume
flummery
flummox
flummoxed
flump
flung cf fling
flunk (US)
flunky (or ~ey, pl ~kies, ~keys)
fluoresce
fluorescence
fluorescent
fluoridate
fluoridated
fluoridation
fluoride
fluorine
fluorite
fluorocarbon
fluoroscope
fluoroscopic
fluoroscopy
fluorspar
flurry
flush
flushed
fluster
flustered
flute
fluted
fluting
flutist (UK flaut~)
flutter
flutterer
flutteringly
fluttery
fluty (or ~ey)
fluvial
flux
fly (flew, flown)
flyblown
fly-by (pl ~bys)
fly-by-night
flycatcher

flyer (or flier)
fly-fishing
flying
flyleaf (pl ~leaves)
flyover
flypaper
flypast
flyposting
flysheet
flyspray
flyweight
flywheel
foal
foam
foamily
foaminess
foamless
foamy
fob (~bbed, ~bbing)
focaccia
focal
focalise (or ~ize)
focally
focus (n pl ~uses, occ foci; v ~used, ~using, also ~ussed, ~ussing)
fodder
foe
foetal see fetal
foetid see fetid
foetidly see fetidly
foetidness see fetidness
foetus see fetus
fog (~gged, ~gging)
fogbound
fogey (or ~gy, pl ~geys, ~gies)
fogginess
foggy
foghorn
foglamp
foglight
fohn (or föhn, F~; also foehn, F~)
foible
foie gras
foil
foist
fold
foldable

folded
folder
folding
foldout
foliaceous
foliage
foliate
foliated
folic
folio (pl ~os)
folk
folkish
folklife
folklore
folkloric
folklorist
folkloristic
folksiness
folksy
follicle
follicular
folliculate
folliculated
follow
follower
following
follow-on
follow-through
follow-up
folly
foment (! ferment) foster
fomentation
fomenter
fond
fondant
fondle
fondler
fondling
fondly
fondness
fondue
font (! fount) baptism
font (or fount) printing
food
fool
foolery
foolhardily
foolhardiness
foolhardy
foolish

foolishly
foolishness
foolproof
foot (*pl* feet)
footage
football
footballer
footballing
footbath
footboard
footbrake
footbridge
footed
footer
footfall
footgear
foothill
foothold
footing
footless
footlights
footloose
footman (*pl* ~men)
footmark
footnote
footpath
footprint
footpump
footrest
footsore
footstep
footstool
footwear
footwork
fop
foppery
foppish
foppishly
foppishness
fora *see* forum
forage
forager
foramen
foraminal
foraminous
foray
forayer
forbad *see* forbid
forbade *see* forbid
forbear (forbore)

forbearance
forbearing
forbid (forbade *occ*
   forbad, forbidden,
   forbidding)
forbiddingly
force
forceable
forced
forceful
forcefully
forcefulness
forcemeat
forceps
forcer
forcible
forcibly
forcing
ford
fordable
fordless
fore
forearm
forearmed
forebear (*or* forb~)
forebode
foreboding
forebodingly
forebrain
forecast
forecasting
forecastle
foreclose
foreclosure
forecourt
foredate
forefather
forefinger
forefoot
forefront
foregather (*UK*, *cf*
   forgather)
forego (foregoes,
   forewent, foregone;
   also forgo)
foregoing
foregone (*or* forgone,
   adj)
foreground
forehand

forehead
foreign
foreigner
foreignness
forejudge
foreknow (foreknown)
foreknowledge
foreland
foreleg
forelimb
forelock
foreman (*pl* ~men)
forementioned
foremost
forename
forensic
forensically
foreordain
forepart
forepayment
foreplay
forequarters
forerun (foreran,
   forerunning)
forerunner
foresaid
foresail
foresee (foresaw,
   foreseen)
foreseeable
foreseeably
foreshadow
foreshore
foreshorten
foreshortened
foreshortening
foresight
foresighted
foresightedly
foresightedness
foreskin
forest
forested
forester
forestry
foretaste
foretell (foretold)
foreteller
forethought
forever (*occ* for ever)

forewarn
forewarned
forewarner
forewoman (*pl* ~women)
foreword (! forward)
 book
forfeit
forfeiture
forgather (*US & occ UK;*
 cf foregather)
forgave
forge
forgery
forget (forgot, forgotten,
 forgetting)
forgetful
forgetfully
forgetfulness
forget-me-not
forgettable
forgivable
forgivably
forgive (forgave,
 forgiven, forgiving)
forgiveness
forgiver
forgiving (*n*)
forgo (*usu* forego; *v*
 forgoes, forwent,
 forgone, forgoing)
forgone (*usu* foregone,
 adj)
forgot
forgotten
fork
forked
forkful
forlorn
forlornly
forlornness
form
formable
formal
formaldehyde
formalisation (*or* ~iz~)
formalise (*or* ~ize)
formalism
formalist
formalistic
formality

formally
formant
format (~tted, ~tting)
formation
formative
formatively
forme (*US* form) *printing*
former
formerly
formica (F~, *tr*)
formidable
formidableness
formidably
formless
formlessly
formlessness
formula (*pl* ~ae, ~as)
formulable
formulaic
formulaically
formulary
formulate
formulation
fornicate
fornication
fornicator
forsake (forsook,
 forsaken, forsaking)
forsakenness
forsaker
forsythia
fort
forte
forth
forthcoming
forthcomingness
forthright
forthrightly
forthrightness
forthwith
fortieth
fortifiable
fortification
fortifier
fortify
fortissimo (*pl* ~os, ~imi)
fortitude
fortnight
fortnightly
FORTRAN (*or* Fortran)

fortress
fortuitous
fortuitously
fortuitousness
fortuity
fortunate
fortunately
fortune
forty
fortyfold
forum (*pl* ~ums, fora)
forward (! foreword)
 direction
forwarding
forwardly
forwardness
forwards
forwent
fosse (*or* foss) *ditch*
fossil
fossiliferous
fossilisation (*or* ~iz~)
fossilise (*or* ~ize)
fossilised (*or* ~ized)
foster
fosterer
fostering
Foucault
fought
foul
foulard
foully
foul-mouthed
foulness
found
foundation
foundational
founder
founding
foundling
foundry
fount (! font) *source*
fount (*usu* font) *printing*
fountain
four
fourfold
fourscore
foursome
four-square
four-stroke

fourteen
fourteenth
fourth
fourthly
fourth-rate
fowl
fowler
fowling
fox
foxed
foxglove
foxhole
foxhound
fox-hunting
foxily
foxiness
foxing
foxtail
foxtrot (~tted, ~tting)
foxy
foyer
fracas
fractal
fraction
fractional
fractionalisation (or ~iz~)
fractionalise (or ~ize)
fractious
fractiously
fractiousness
fracture
fractured
fragile
fragilely
fragility
fragment
fragmental
fragmentary
fragmentation
fragrance
fragranced
fragrancy
fragrant
fragrantly
frail
frailness
frailty
frame
framework

franc
franchise
franchisee
franchisor (or ~er)
Franciscan
francolin
francophile (F~)
francophone (F~)
frangipane *pastry*
frangipani (occ ~ane) *tree*
franglais (F~)
frank
franked
Frankenstein
frankfurter
frankincense
franking
franklin
frankly
frankness
frantic
frantically
frap
frappé *cooled*
frascati (F~)
fraternal
fraternalism
fraternally
fraternise (or ~ize)
fraternity
fratricidal
fraud
fraudulence
fraudulency
fraudulent
fraudulently
fraught
Fraunhofer
fray
frayed
frazzle
frazzled
freak
freakily
freakiness
freakish
freaky
freckle
freckled

freckly
free (*adj* freer, freest; *v* freed)
freebase
freebooter
freeborn
freedom
free-floating
free-for-all
freehand *drawing*
free-handed *generous*
free-handedness
freehold
freeholder
freelance
freelancer
freelancing
freeload
freeloader
freely
freemason (F~)
freemasonry (F~)
freeness
freephone (*occ* freefone)
freepost (F~, *tr*)
free-range
freesia
free-standing
freestyle
freethinker
freethinking
freeware
freeway
freewheel
freewheeling
freezable
freeze (froze, frozen, freezing)
freeze-dried
freeze-dry
freeze-frame
freezer
freezing
freight
freighter
freightliner
French
Frenchify
Frenchman (*pl* ~men)
Frenchness

Frenchwoman (*pl* ~women)
frenetic
frenetically
freneticism
frenum (*pl* ~ums, frena)
frenzied
frenzy
freon (F~, *tr*)
frequency
frequent
frequented
frequenter
frequently
fresco (*pl* ~os, ~oes)
frescoed
fresh
freshen
fresher
freshman (*pl* ~men)
freshness
freshwater
fret (~tted, ~tting)
fretboard
fretful
fretfully
fretfulness
fretsaw
fretted (*adj*)
fretwork
Freud
Freudian
Freudianism
friability
friable
friableness
friar
friarbird
friary
fricassee (~seed)
fricative
friction
frictional
frictionless
Friday
fridge
fridge-freezer
fried
friend
friendless

friendlessness
friendliness
friendly
friendship
Friesian (! Fris~) *cattle*
frieze
frigate
fright
frighten
frightened
frightener
frightful
frightfully
frightfulness
frigid
frigidity
frigidly
frigidness
frill
frilled
frilliness
frilly
fringe
frippery
frisbee (F~, *tr*)
Frisian (*occ* Fries~)
    islands
frisk
friskily
friskiness
frisky
frisson
fritillary
fritter
frivolity
frivolous
frivolously
frivolousness
frizz
frizziness
frizzle
frizzy
frock
frocked
frog
frogging
froggy
frogman (*pl* ~men)
frogmarch
frogspawn

frolic
frolicsome
fromage frais
frond
front
frontage
frontal
frontally
frontier
frontiers
frontiersman (*pl* ~men)
frontierswoman (*pl*
    ~women)
frontispiece
frontless
frontline
frontside
frontward
frontwards
frost
frostbite
frostbitten
frosted
frostily
frostiness
frostless
frosty
froth
frothiness
frothing
frothy
frottage
frown
frowner
frowningly
frowstiness
frowsty
frowziness
frowzy
froze
frozen
fructiferous
fructification
fructify
fructose
fructuous
frugal
frugality
frugally
frugalness

fruit
fruitarian
fruitcake
fruited
fruiter
fruiterer
fruitful
fruitfully
fruitfulness
fruitily
fruitiness
fruition
fruitless
fruitlessly
fruitlessness
fruity
frump
frumpily
frumpiness
frumpish
frumpishly
frumpy
frustrate
frustrated
frustrating
frustratingly
frustration
fry
fryer (*occ* frier)
fu yung (*or* ~yong, ~young)
fuchsia
fuck (*tab*)
fuckable (*tab*)
fucked (*tab*)
fucker (*tab*)
fucking (*tab*)
fuddle
fuddled
fuddy-duddy
fudge
fuel (~lled, ~lling, *US* ~led, ~ling)
fug
fuggy
fugitive
fugue
fulcrum (*pl* ~ums, ~ra)
fulfil (*US* ~fill; *v* ~lled, ~lling)

fulfilled (*adj*)
fulfilling (*adj*)
fulfilment (*US* ~fill~)
fulgent
full
fullback
full-blooded
full-blown
full-bodied
fuller
fullerene
fullness (*occ* fuln~)
full-time
fully
fullyfashioned
fully-fledged
fulmar
fulminant
fulminate
fulmination
fulminatory
fulsome
fulsomely
fulsomeness
fumble
fumbler
fumbling
fume
fumigate
fumigation
fumigator
fun
funambulist
function
functional
functionalism
functionalist
functionality
functionally
functionary
fund
fundamental
fundamentalism
fundamentalist
fundamentality
fundamentally
funded
funding
fundraiser

fundraising
funeral
funerary
funereal
funereally
funfair
fungal
fungi *see* fungus
fungicide
fungous (*adj*)
fungus (*n pl* fungi, ~uses)
funicular
funk
funkily
funkiness
funky
funnel (~lled, ~lling, *US* ~led, ~ling)
funnily
funniness
funny
fur (~rred, ~rring)
furbish
furbished
furbisher
furbishment
furcate
furcation
furious
furiously
furiousness
furl
furled
furless
furlong
furlough
furnace
furnish
furnished
furnishing
furniture
furore (*US* ~ror)
furrier
furriery
furriness
furring
furrow
furrowed
furry

further (*occ* farther; *cf* far)
furtherance
furthermore
furthermost (*occ* far~)
furthest (*or* far~; *cf* far)
furtive
furtively
furtiveness
fury
fuse (*n US also* fuze)
fuselage
fusibility
fusible
fusilier (*occ* ~eer)
fusillade
fusilli
fusion
fusional
fuss
fussed
fussily
fussiness
fusspot
fussy
fustian
fustic
fustily
fustiness
fusty
futhark (F~; *or* ~ork)
futile
futilely
futility
futon
futtock
future
futureless
futurism
futurist
futuristic
futuristically
futurity
futurological
futurologist
futurology
fuzz
fuzzily
fuzziness
fuzzy

gab (~bed, ~bbing)
gabardine (! gaberdine)
   cloth
gabbily
gabbiness
gabble
gabbler
gabbro
gabby
gaberdine (! gabardine)
   garment
gable
gabled
Gabon
Gabonese
gad (~dded, ~dding)
gadabout
Gadarene
gadfly
gadget
gadgetry
gadgety
gadoid
gadolinium
gadroon
gadrooned
gadwall
Gaea (*or* Gaia)
Gael
Gaelic
Gaeltacht
gaff
gaffe
gaffer
gag (~gged, ~gging)
gaga
gage
gaggle
gagster

Gaia (*or* Gaea)
gaiety (*US* gayety)
gaijin (*pl* ~jin)
gaily
gain
gainable
gainer
gainful
gainfully
gainfulness
gaining
gainsay
gainsayer
Gainsborough
gait
gaiter
gaitered
gal
gala
galactic
galactose
galah
Galahad
Galapagos
galaxy
gale
Galen
galena
galenic
galenical
galette
Galicia
Galician
Galilean
Galilee *Palestine*
galilee *church porch*
Galileo
gall
gallant
gallantry
gallberry
Galle
galleon
galleria
galleried
gallery
galley (*pl* ~eys)
gallfly
Galliano
galliard

galliass (*or* ~llea~)
Gallic *French*
gallic *acid*
Gallicise (*or* ~ize)
Gallicism
gallimimus
gallinaceous
galling
gallingly
galliot
Gallipoli
gallipot
gallium
gallivant
gallnut
gallon
gallonage
galloon
gallop (~lloped,
   ~lloping; ! gallup,
   galop) *horse*
galloper
gallophile (G~)
gallophilia (G~)
gallophobe (G~)
gallophobia (G~)
galloway (G~)
gallows
gallstone
gallup (G~; ! gallop) *poll*
galop (! gallop) *dance*
galore
galoshes (*or* gol~)
galumph
galumphing
galvanic
galvanically
galvanisation (*or* ~iz~)
galvanise (*or* ~ize)
galvanised (*or* ~ized)
galvaniser (*or* ~iz~)
galvanism
galvanometer
galvanometric
galvanoscope
galvanoscopic
Galway
Gamay
Gambia
Gambian

gambier (*or* ~bir)
gambit
gamble (! gambol) *bet*
gambler
gambling
gamboge
gambol (~lled, ~lling;
   US ~led, ~ling;
   ! gamble) *playfully*
gambrel
game
gamecock
gamefowl
gamekeeper
gamekeeping
gamelan
gamely
gameness
gameplay
gamer
gamesman (*pl* ~men)
gamesmanship
gamesome
gamesomely
gamesomeness
gamester
gamete
gametic
gametocyte
gametogenesis
gametogenetic
gametogeny
gaminess (*or* gamey~)
gaming
gamma
gammon
gammy
gamopetalous
gamut
gamy (*or* ~ey)
ganache
Ganapati
gander
Gandhi
Ganesh
gang
gangboard
gangbuster
ganger
gangland

gangling
ganglion (*pl* ~lia,
   ~lions)
gangly
gangplank
gangrene
gangrenous
gangsta (! gangster) *rap
   music*
gangster (! gangsta)
   criminal
gangsterism
gangue (*or* gang)
gangway
ganister (*or* gann~)
ganja
gannet
gannetry
ganoid
gantlet (*UK* gaun~)
gantry
Ganymede
gaol (*or* jail; *US* jail)
gaoler (*or* jailer; *US*
   jailer)
gap
gape
gaper
gaping
gapingly
gapped
gappy
gap-toothed
garage
garb
garbage
garbed
garble
garbled
garbler
garçon
garda (G~)
garden
gardener
gardenia
gardening
garderobe
garfish
garganey (*pl* ~eys)
gargantuan

gargle
gargler
gargoyle
gargoyled
garial (*or* gha~, gavi~)
Garibaldi *patriot*
garibaldi (*UK*) *biscuit*
garish
garishly
garishness
garland
garlic
garlicky
garment
garner
garnet
garni
garnish
garnishment
garniture
garotte (*or* garr~)
garret
garrison
garrotte (*or* garo~)
garrulity
garrulous
garrulously
garrulousness
garryowen
garter
gartered
garth
gas (*n pl* gases, *US* ~sses;
  v ~ssed, ~ssing)
gasbag
Gascon
gasconade
Gascony
gaseous
gaseousness
gash
gasification
gasify
gasket
gaslight
gasman (*pl* ~men)
gasohol
gasoline (*or* ~lene; *US*)
gasometer
gasp

gaspacho
gasper
gasping
gasser
gassily
gassiness
gassy
gastarbeiter
gastrectomy
gastric
gastrin
gastritis
gastrocolic
gastroenteritis
gastroenterological
gastroenterologist
gastroenterology
gastrolith
gastrology
gastronome
gastronomer
gastronomic
gastronomical
gastronomically
gastronomist
gastronomy
gastroscope
gastrula (*pl* ~ae)
gastrulation
gasworks
gate
gateau (*pl* ~us, ~ux,
  gâ~)
gatecrash
gatecrasher
gated
gatehouse
gatekeeper
gateleg
gatepost
gateway
gather
gatherer
gathering
gatling (G~)
Gatwick
gauche
gauchely
gaucheness
gaucherie

gaucho (*pl* ~os)
gaud
gaudily
gaudiness
gaudy
gauge (*US* gage)
gaugeable (*US* ~gab~)
Gaul
Gaulish
Gaullism
Gaullist
gaunt
gauntlet (*US* gant~)
gaur
gauss
gauze
gauzily
gauziness
gauzy
gavel (~lled, ~lling; *US*
  ~led, ~ling)
gavial (*or* gari~, ghari~)
gavotte (*or* ~ot)
Gawain
gawk
gawker
gawkily
gawkiness
gawkish
gawky
gawp
gawper
gay
gayness
gazar (! gazer) *silk*
gaze
gazebo (*pl* ~os, ~oes)
gazelle
gazer
gazette
gazetted
gazetteer
gazillion
gazillionth
gazpacho (*pl* ~os)
gazump
gazumped
gazumper
gean
gear

gearbox
geared
gearing
gears
gearshift
gearwheel
gecko (pl ~os, ~oes)
geek
geeky
geese
geezer (! geyser) old man
gefilte (or gefüllte)
Gehenna
geiger (G~)
geisha
Geist
gel (~lled, ~lling)
gelada
gelatin (or ~ine)
gelatinisation (or ~iz~)
gelatinise (or ~ize)
gelatinous
gelatinously
gelatinousness
gelation
geld
gelding
gelignite
gelly (! jelly) explosive
gem
Gemara
gematria (G~)
gemetophyte
geminate
gemination
Gemini
Geminian
gemma (pl ~ae)
gemmation
gemmological
gemmologist
gemmology
gemsbok
gemstone
gemütlich
gendarme
gendarmerie (G~)
gender
gendered
gene

genealogical
genealogically
genealogise (or ~ize)
genealogist
genealogy
generable
general
generalise (or ~ize)
generalissimo (pl ~os)
generalist
generality
generalship
generate
generating
generation
generational
generative
generator
generic
generically
generosity
generous
generously
generousness
Genesis bible
genesis origin
genet (or ~ette)
genetic
genetical
genetically
geneticist
genetics
Geneva
Genevan
genever
Genevese
genial
geniality
genially
genic
genie (pl ~nii)
genital
genitalia
genitals
genitival
genitivally
genitive
genitor
geniture
genius (pl ~nii, ~uses)

genlock
Genoa Italy
genoa cake, jib
genocidal
genocide
Genoese
genome
genomic
genotype
genotypic
genotypical
genotypically
Genovese
genre
gent
genteel
genteelism
genteelly
genteelness
gentian
gentile (G)
gentility
gentle
gentlefolk
gentleman (pl ~men)
gentlemanliness
gentlemanly
gentlewoman (pl
  ~women)
gentoo
gentrify
gentry
gents (G~)
genuflect
genuflection (or ~exion)
genuflector
genuine
genuinely
genuineness
genus (pl ~nera)
geocentric
geocentrically
geocentrism
geochemical
geochemist
geochemistry
geochronological
geochronologist
geochronology
geode

geodesic
geodesist
geodesy
geodetic
geodic
geographer
geographic
geographical
geographically
geography
geologic
geological
geologically
geologise (*or* ~ize)
geologist
geology
geomagnetic
geomagnetically
geomagnetism
geometer
geometric
geometrical
geometrically
geometrician
geometry
geomorphic
geomorphological
geomorphologically
geomorphologist
geomorphology
geophagy
geophysical
geophysicist
geophysics
geopolitical
geopolitically
geopolitician
geopolitics
Geordie
George
georgette
Georgia
Georgian
geoscience
geoscientist
geosphere
geostationary
geostrophic
geosynchronous
geosyncline

geothermal
geotropism
geraniol
geranium
gerbera
gerbil
gerfalcon (gyr~)
geriatric
geriatrician
geriatrics
germ
German *Germany*
german *same parents*
germane
germanely
germaneness
Germanic
Germanisation (*or*
~iz~)
Germanise (*or* ~ize)
Germanist
germanium
Germanophile
Germanophilia
Germanophobe
Germanophobia
Germany
germicidal
germicide
germinal
germinally
germinate
germination
germinative
germinator
germy
Geronimo
gerontic
gerontocracy
gerontocrat
gerontocratic
gerontological
gerontologist
gerontology
gerrymander
gerrymandering
gerund
gerundial
gerundive
gesso (*pl* ~oes)

gestalt (G~; *pl* ~ts,
~ten)
gestaltism
gestaltist
Gestapo
gestate
gestation
gestational
gestative
gesticulate
gesticulation
gesticulational
gesticulative
gesticulator
gesticulatory
gestural
gesture
gesturer
gesundheit (G~)
get (got *or US* gotten,
getting)
getable (*or* gett~)
get-at-able
getaway
Gethsemane
get-out
getter
Gettysburg
get-up-and-go
gewgaw
geyser
Ghana
Ghanaian
gharial (*or* gari~, gavi~)
ghastliness
ghastly
ghat
ghee (*or* ghi)
gherkin
ghetto (*n pl* ~os, ~oes; *v*
~oes, ~oed, ~oing)
ghettoisation (*or* ~iz~)
ghettoise (*or* ~ize)
Ghibelline
ghibli
ghost
ghostbuster
ghosting
ghostlike
ghostliness

ghostly
ghostwrite
ghostwriter
ghoul
ghoulish
ghoulishly
ghoulishness
ghyll (*or* gill)
giant
giantess
giantism
giantlike
giardiasis
gibber
gibberellin
gibbering
gibberish
gibbet
gibbon
gibbosity
gibbous
gibbously
gibbousness
gibe (*or* gybe) *sail*
gibe (*or* jibe) *jeer*
giber (*or* ji~)
gibing (*or* ji~)
gibingly (*or* ji~)
giblets
Gibraltar
giddily
giddiness
giddy
Gideon
gift
gifted
giftedness
gift-wrap
gig (~gged, ~gging)
gigabyte
gigaflop
gigantesque
gigantic
gigantically
gigantism
gigantomachy
giggle
giggler
giggling
giggly

gigolo (*pl* ~os)
gigot
gigue
gila
gild
gilded
gilding
gilet
Gilgamesh
gill
gilled
gillyflower (*or* gilli~)
gilt
gilt-edged
gimbals
gimcrack
gimcrackery
gimlet
gimmick
gimmickry
gimmicky
gimp
gin (~nned, ~nning)
ginger
gingerbread
gingered
gingerliness
gingerly
gingham
gingiva (*pl* ~ae)
gingival
gingivitis
gingko (*or* ginkgo, *pl* ~oes)
ginormous
ginseng
giocoso
gipsy (G~; *or* gyp~)
giraffe
girandole
gird (girded *or* girt)
girder
girdle
girl
girlfriend
girlhood
girlie (*or* ~ly)
girlish
girlishly
girlishness

girner
giro (G~; *pl* ~os)
girth
gismo (*or* giz~; *pl* ~os)
gist
gittern
give (gave, given, giving)
give-and-take
giveaway
given
giver
giving
Giza
gizmo (*or* gis~, *pl* ~os)
gizzard
glabrous
glabrousness
glacé
glacial
glacially
glaciate
glaciation
glacier
glaciological
glaciologist
glaciology
glad (~dder, ~ddest)
gladden
gladdon (! gladden) *flower*
glade
gladiator
gladiatorial
gladiolus (*pl* ~oli, ~uses)
gladly
gladness
gladsome
Gladstone
Glagolitic
glair
glairy
glam
glamorisation (*or* ~iz~)
glamorise (*or* ~our~, ~ize)
glamorous (*or* ~our~)
glamorously (*or* ~our~)
glamour (*US* ~or)

glance
glancing
glancingly
gland
glanders
glandular
glans
glare
glareshield
glaring
glaringly
glaringness
glary
Glasgow
glasnost
glass
glass-blower
glass-blowing
glasses *spectacles*
glassful (*pl* ~fuls)
glassily
glassiness
glassless
glass-maker
glass-making
glasspaper
glassware
glassy
Glastonbury
Glaswegian
Glauber
glaucoma
glaucomatous
glaucous
glaze
glazed
glazier
glazing
gleam
gleaming
gleamingly
glean
gleanings
glebe
glee
gleeful
gleefully
gleefulness
gleeman (*pl* ~men)
gleesome

glen
glengarry
glib (~bber, ~bbest)
glibly
glibness
glide
glider
gliding
glimmer
glimmering
glimmeringly
glimpse
glint
glioma (*pl* ~mata, ~as)
gliomablastoma (*pl*
   ~mata, ~as)
gliomatosis
gliomatous
gliosis
glissade
glissando (*pl* ~di, ~os)
glissé
glisten
glistening
glisteningly
glister
glitch
glitchy
glitter
glitterati
glittering
glitteringly
glittery
glitz
glitzily
glitziness
glitzy
gloaming
gloat
gloater
gloatingly
glob
global
globalisation (*or* ~iz~)
globalise (*or* ~ize)
globalist
globally
globe
globeflower
globetrotter

globigerina
globin
globoid
globose
globular
globularity
globule
globulous
glockenspiel
glomerate
glomerule
glomerulus (*pl* ~li)
gloom
gloomily
gloominess
gloomy
Gloria
glorifiable
glorification
glorified
glorifier
glorify
glorious
gloriously
gloriousness
glory
gloss
glossa (*pl* ~ae, ~as)
glossal
glossarial
glossarist
glossary
glossily
glossiness
glossitis
glossolalia
glossolalic
glossy
glottal
glottic
glottidean
glottis (*pl* ~ises, ~ides)
Gloucester
glove
gloved
gloveless
glover
glow
glower
gloweringly

glowing
glow-worm
gloxinia
gloze
glucagon
glucose
glucoside
glue (glues, glued, glueing *or* gluing)
gluey (gluier, gluiest)
glug (~gged, ~gging)
glum (~mmer, ~mmest)
glume
glumly
glumness
gluon
glut (~tted, ~tting)
glutamate
glutamatic
gluteal (*or* ~taeal)
gluten
gluteus (*or* ~taeus, *pl* ~tei, ~taei)
glutinosity
glutinous
glutinously
glutinousness
glutton
gluttonous
gluttonously
gluttony
glyceride
glycerine (*US* ~rin)
glycerol
glycogen
glycol
glycolysis
glycoside
glyph
glyptic
glyptics
glyptography
gnarl
gnarled
gnarly
gnash
gnat
gnathal
gnathic
gnaw

gnawingly
gneiss
gnocchi
gnome
gnomic
gnomish
gnomon
gnomonic
gnosis
gnostic (G~)
Gnosticism
gnu
go (goes, went, gone, going)
Goa
goad
go-ahead
goal
goalie
goalkeeper
goalkeeping
goalless
goalmouth
goalpost
goaltender
goaltending
Goanese
goat
goatee (! goaty) *beard*
goateed
goatherd
goatish
goatishly
goatskin
goaty (! goatee) *goat-like*
gob (~bbed, ~bbing)
gobbet
gobble
gobbledegook (*or* ~dy~)
gobbler
go-between
Gobi
goblet
goblin
gobo (*pl* ~os, ~oes)
gobsmacked (*UK*)
gobsmacking (*UK*)
gobstopper
goby (*pl* ~by, ~bies)
go-cart (*or* ~ka~)

go-carting (*or* ~ka~)
god (G~)
godchild
god-daughter
goddess
godetia
godfather
God-fearing
godforsaken (G~)
God-given
godhead
godhood
godless
godlessness
godlike
godlikeness
godliness
godly
godmother
godparent
godsend
god-son
godwit
goer
goes
go-getter
go-getting
goggle
goggle-eyed
goggles
gohst (! ghost) *Indian food*
Goidelic
going
goitre (*US* ~ter)
goitred (*US* ~ter~)
goitrous
go-kart (~cart)
gold
goldcrest
golden
goldenrod
goldfield
goldfinch
goldfish
Goldilocks *fairy tale*
goldilocks *golden hair*
goldsmith
goldwork
golem

golf
golfer
golfing
Golgotha
Goliath
golliwog (*tab*)
golly
goloshes (*or* gal~)
gonad
gonadal
gonadotrophic
gonadotrophin
gondola
gondolier
Gondwana
Gondwanaland
gone
goner
gonfalon
gong
goniometer
gonococcal
gonococcus
gonorrhoea (*US* ~hea)
gonorrhoeal (*US* ~heal)
good
goodbye (*US* goodby)
good-for-nothing
good-hearted
good-heartedness
good-humoured
good-humouredly
goodies
goodish
goodliness
goodly
goodness
goodnight
goods
good-temperedly
goodwill
goody (*or* ~die)
gooey
goofy
Google (! googol) *search engine*
googly (pl ~lies)
googol (! Google) *large number*
googolplex

goosander
goose (*pl* geese)
gooseberry
gooseflesh
goosegrass
gooseneck
gooseskin
goosey (*or* ~sy)
gopher (*US* gofer)
gordian (G~)
gore
gorge
gorged
gorgeous
gorgeously
gorgeousness
gorger
gorget
gorgon (G~)
gorgonzola (G~)
gorilla
gorily
goriness
gormandise (~ize)
gormandiser (~iz~)
gormandising (~iz~)
gormless
gormlessly
gormlessness
gorse
gory
goshawk
gosling
gospel (G~)
gossamer
gossamery
gossip (~pped, ~pping)
got
Goth
Gothic *people*
gothic (G~) *style*
gotten
gouache
Gouda
gouge
gouger
goujons
goulash
gourd
gourdful

gourmand
gourmandise (*or* gor~, ~ize)
gourmandism
gourmet
gout
goutiness
gouty
govern
governability
governable
governance
governess
governessy
government (G~ *for a specified government*)
governmental
governmentally
governor
governorship
gown
Graafian
grab (~bbed, ~bbing)
grabber
grace
graceful
gracefully
gracefulness
graceless
gracelessly
gracelessness
gracious
graciously
graciousness
gradability
gradable
gradate
gradated
gradation
gradational
gradationally
grade
graded
grader
gradient
gradiometer
gradual
gradualism
gradualist
gradualistic

graduality
gradually
gradualness
graduand
graduate
graduation
Graecism (or Grec~)
graffitist
graffito (pl ~ti)
graft
grafter
grafting
Grail
grain
graininess
grainy
gram (UK ~mme)
graminaceous
gramineous
graminivorous
grammar
grammarian
grammaticality
grammatically
grammaticalness
grammatologist
grammatology
Grammy (pl ~mies,
    ~meys)
gramophone
granadilla (or gren~)
granary
grand
grand mal
grandad (or granddad)
grandaddy
grandchild (pl ~dren)
granddaughter
grandee
grandeur
grandfather
grandiloquence
grandiloquent
grandiloquently
grandiose
grandiosely
grandiosity
grandly
grandma
grandmamma

grandmaster
grandmother
grandmotherly
grandness
grandpa
grandpapa
grandparent
grandson
grandstand
grandstanding *seeking to*
    attract attention
grange
granger
graniferous *seed*
    producing
granite
graniteware
granitic
granitoid
granivorous *feeding on*
    grain
granny (pl ~nies)
grant
granted
grantee
Granth
grantor
granular
granularity
granulate
granulated
granulation
granule
granulocyte
granuloma
grape
grapefruit
grapeseed
grapeshot
grapevine
graph
grapheme
graphemic
graphemically
graphemics
graphic
graphical
graphically
graphics
graphite

graphological
graphologist
graphology
grapnel
grappa
grapple
grappler
grappling
graptolite
grasp
grasping
graspingly
graspingness
grass
grasshopper
grassiness
grassland
grassless
grassy
grate
grateful
gratefully
gratefulness
grater
graticulate
graticulation
gratification
gratifier
gratify
gratifying
gratifyingly
gratin
gratiné (or ~née)
gratinéed
grating
gratingly
gratis
gratitude
gratuitous
gratuitously
gratuitousness
gratuity
gravadlax (or gravlax)
gravamen (pl ~mina)
grave
gravel
gravelly
gravely
graven
graveness

graver
Graves *wine*
graveside
gravestone
graveyard
gravid
gravimeter
gravimetric
gravitas
gravitate
gravitation
gravitational
gravitationally
gravity
gravlax (*or* ~vadl~)
gravure
gravy
gray *radiation*
gray (*UK* grey) *colour*
grayling
graze
grazer
grazing
grease
greasepaint
greaseproof
greaser
greasily
greasiness
greasy
great
greatcoat
greatly
greatness
greaves
grebe
Grecian
Greece
greed
greedily
greediness
greedy
Greek
Greekness
green
greenback (*US*)
greenbottle
greenery
greenfield
greenfinch

greenfly
greengage
greengrocer
greenhorn (*US*)
greenhouse
greening
greenkeeper
greenkeeping
Greenland
Greenlander
Greenlandic
Greenpeace
greenroom
greenstick
Greenwich
greet
greeter
greeting
gregarious
gregariously
gregariousness
Gregorian
gremlin
grenade
grenadier
grenadine
grew
grey (*US* gray; ! gray)
   colour
greybeard (*US* gray~)
greyhound (*US* gray~)
greying (*US* gray~)
greyish (*US* gray~)
greylag (*US* gray~)
greyly (*US* gray~)
greyness (*US* gray~)
greyscale (*US* gray~)
grid
gridded
griddle
gridiron
gridlock
gridlocked
grief
grievance
grieve
griever
grieving
grievous
grievously

grievousness
griffin (*or* gryphon,
   gryfon)
grill *cook, interrogate*
grille (*or* grill) *window*
griller
grim (~mmer, ~mmest)
grimace
grimacer
grime
grimily
griminess
grimly
grimness
grimy
grin (~nned, ~nning)
grind
grinder
grinding
grindstone
gringo (*pl* ~os, *tab*)
grinner
grinningly
grip (~pped, ~pping)
gripe
griper
grisaille
grisliness
grisly
grissini
grist
gristle
gristly
grit (~tted, ~tting)
grits (*US*)
gritter
grittily
grittiness
gritty
grizzle
grizzled
grizzly
groan
groaner
groaningly
groats
grocer
grocery
grog
groggily

grogginess
groggy
grogram
groin
grommet (*or* grum~)
groom
groomsman (*pl* ~men)
groove
grooved
groovily
grooviness
groovy
grope
groper
groping
gropingly
grosbeak
grosgrain
gros point
gross
grossly
grossness
grotesque
grotesquely
grotesqueness
grotesquery (*or* ~erie)
grotto (*pl* ~oes, ~os)
grotty
grouch
grouchily
grouchiness
grouchy
ground
groundbreaking
grounded
groundedness
groundhog
groundhopper
grounding
groundless
groundlessly
groundlessness
groundling
groundnut
groundsel
groundsheet
groundsman (*pl* ~men)
groundstroke
groundswell
group

grouper
groupie
grouping
groupware
grouse
grouser
grout
grouter
grouting
grove
grovel (~lled, ~lling; *US* ~led, ~ling)
grow (grew, grown)
growable
grower
growing
growl
growler
grown
grown-up
growth
groyne
grub (~bbed, ~bbing)
grubber
grubbily
grubbiness
grubby
grudge
grudger
grudging
grudgingly
grudgingness
gruel
gruelling (*US* ~eling)
gruellingly
gruesome
gruesomely
gruesomeness
gruff
gruffly
gruffness
grumble
grumbler
grumblingly
grumbly
grummet (*or* grom~)
grump
grumpily
grumpiness
grumpy

grunge
grungily
grunginess
grungy
grunt
grunter
Gruyère
gryphon (*or* griffin, griffon)
g-spot (G~)
G-string (*or* gee-~)
g-suit (G~)
guacamole
Guadeloupe
Guam
guano (*pl* ~os)
guarantee
guaranteed
guarantor
guaranty
guard
guardant
guarded
guardedly
guardedness
guardhouse
guardian
guardianship
guardrail
guardroom
guardsman (*pl* ~men)
Guatemala
Guatemalan
guava
gubbins (*UK*)
gubernatorial
gudgeon
guelder
guenon
guerdon
Guernsey *cattle, island*
guernsey *pullover*
guerrilla (*or* ~eri~)
guess
guessable
guesser
guessing
guesstimate
guesswork
guest

guesthouse
guffaw
Guiana
guidable
guidance
guide
guidebook
guided
guideline
guidepost
guider
guiding
guidon
guild (*or* gild)
guilder (*or* gil~)
guildhall (G~)
guile
guileful
guilefully
guilefulness
guileless
guilelessly
guilelessness
guillemot
guillotine
guilt
guiltily
guiltiness
guiltless
guiltlessly
guiltlessness
guilty
Guinea *country*
guinea *coin*
guineafowl
Guinean
guinea-pig
Guinevere
Guinness
guipure
guise
guitar
guitarist
gulag (G~)
gulch
gules
Gulf *Stream, States, Persian*
gulf *inlet*
gull

gullery
gullet
gulley (*pl* ~eys)
gullibility
gullible
gullibly
gully
gulp
gulper
gum (~mmed, ~mming)
gumbo (*pl* ~os)
gumboil
gumboot
gumdrop
gumminess
gummy
gumption
gumshield
gumshoe (*US*)
gun (~nned, ~nning)
gunboat
gunfire
gunge (~ged, ~geing, *UK*)
gung-ho
gungy
gunk
gunmaker
gunman (*pl* ~men)
gunmetal
gunnel
gunner
gunnery
gunning
gunny
gunplay
gunpoint
gunpowder
gunroom
gunrunner
gunrunning
gunship
gunshot
gun-shy
gunsight
gunslinger
gunslinging
gunsmith
gunstock

gunwale
guppie
guppy
gurdwara
gurgle
gurgling
gurglingly
Gurkha
Gurmukhi
gurn (*UK*)
gurner (*UK*)
gurney
gurning (*UK*)
guru
gush
gusher
gushiness
gushing
gushingly
gushy
gust
gustation
gustative
gustatory
gustily
gustiness
gusto (*pl* ~os, ~oes)
gusty
gut (~tted, ~tting)
gutless
gutlessly
gutlessness
guts
gutsily
gutsiness
gutsy
gutta-percha
gutted
gutter
guttering
guttersnipe
gutting
guttural
gutturally
guy
Guyana
Guyanan
Guyanese
guyot
guzzle

guzzler
Gwent
Gwynedd
gybe (*or* gibe, jibe)
gybing
gym
gymkhana
gymnasial
gymnasium (*pl* ~ia,
  ~iums)
gymnast

gymnastic
gymnastically
gymnastics
gymnosperm
gynaecium (*or* ~nes~)
gynaecologic (*or* ~nec~)
gynaecological (*or*
  ~nec~)
gynaecologically (*or*
  ~nec~)
gynaecologist (*or*
  ~nec~)
gynaecology (*or* ~nec~)
gynophobia
gynophobic
gyp (~pped, ~pping)
gypsum
gypsy (G; *or* gip~)
gyrate
gyration
gyrator
gyratory
gyre
gyrfalcon (*or* ger~)
gyrocompass
gyromagnetic
gyroscope
gyroscopic
gyroscopics
gyrostabiliser (*or* ~iz~)
gyrostatic
gyrostatics
gyrus (*pl* ~ri)

Habakkuk
habanera
habeas corpus
haberdasher
haberdashery
habiliment
habilitate
habilitation
habit
habitability
habitable
habitableness
habitant
habitat
habitation
habitative
habitual
habitually
habitualness
habituate
habituation
habitude
habitué
hachure
hachured
hacienda
hack
hackamore
hackberry (*or* hagb~)
hacker
hackery
hacking
hackle
Hackney *London*
hackney *carriage, horse*
hackneyed
hacksaw (~sawn *or*
  ~sawed)
had

hadal
haddock
Hades
Hadith (*pl* ~th, ~ths)
hadj (*or* hajj)
hadji (*or* haji, hajji)
hadrosaur
haem (*US* heme)
haemal (*US* hem~)
haematemesis (*US*
  hem~)
haematic (*US* hem~)
haematin (*US* hem~)
haematite (*US* hem~)
haematocele (*US* hem~)
haematoglobulin (*US*
  hem~)
haematologic (*US*
  hem~)
haematological (*US*
  hem~)
haematologist (*US*
  hem~)
haematology (*US* hem~)
haematolysis (*US* hem~)
haematoma (*pl* ~as,
  ~mata; *US* hem~)
haematophagous (*US*
  hem~)
haematuria (*US* hem~)
haemocyte (*US* hem~)
haemodialysis (*pl* ~yses;
  US hem~)
haemoglobin (*US*
  hem~)
haemolysis (*pl* ~yses; *US*
  hem~)
haemolytic (*US* hem~)
haemophilia (*US* hem~)
haemophiliac (*US*
  hem~)
haemophilic (*US* hem~)
haemopoiesis (*US*
  hem~)
haemopoietic (*US*
  hem~)
haemoptysis (*US*
  hem~)
haemorrhage (*US*
  hem~)

haemorrhagic (*US* hem~)
haemorrhoid (*US* hem~)
haemostasis (*US* hem~)
haemostat (*US* hem~)
haemostatic (*US* hem~)
hafiz
hafnium
haft
hag
Hagar
hagberry (*or* hackb~)
Haggadah (*pl* ~doth, ~dot; Ag~)
Haggadic
Haggadist
Haggai
haggard
haggardly
haggardness
haggis
haggish
haggishly
haggle
haggler
Hagiographa
hagiographer
hagiographic
hagiographical
hagiography
hagiolatry
hagiological
hagiologist
hagiology
Hague
ha-ha (*or* haw-haw)
hahnium
haiku (*pl* ~ku, ~kus)
hail
hailed
hailer
hailing
hailstone
hailstorm
hair
hairband
hairbrained
hairbrush
haircare

haircloth
haircut
hairdo (*pl* ~dos)
hairdresser
hairdressing
hairdryer (*or* ~drier)
haired
hairgrip
hairily
hairiness
hairless
hairline
hairnet
hairpiece
hairpin
hair-raising
hairslide
hair-splitter
hair-splitting
hairspray
hairspring
hairstyle
hairstyling
hairstylist
hairy
Haiti
Haitian
haji (*pl* ~is; *or* hajji, hadji)
hajj (*or* haj, hadj)
haka
hake
Halacha (*or* ~lakah)
Halachic (*or* ~lakic)
halal
halation
halberd (*or* ~rt)
halberdier
halcyon
hale
haleness
haler
half (*pl* halves)
halfback
half-baked
half-breed
half-brother
half-caste
half-cock
half-cocked

half-day
half-hearted
half-heartedly
half-heartedness
half-hour (*adj*)
half-hourly
half-life
half-marathon
half-moon
half-nelson
halfpenny (*pl* ~nnies, ~pence; *or* ha'penny)
half-price
half-size
half-term
half-time
half-track
half-truth
halfway
halfwit
halfwitted
halfwittedly
halfwittedness
half-yearly
halibut
halide
Halifax
halitosis
hall
hallelujah (*or* ~iah, alleluia)
halliard (*or* halyard)
hallmark
hallo (*or* hello, hullo)
halloo (*or* hallo, halloa)
halloumi
hallow
hallowed
Halloween (*or* ~e'en)
hallstand
Hallstatt
hallucinant
hallucinate
hallucination
hallucinator
hallucinatory
hallucinogen
hallucinogenic
hallway
halm (*or* haulm)

haphazard

halma
halo (*n pl* ~os, ~oes)
haloed
haloform
halogen
halogenate
halogenated
halogenation
halogenic
halogenous
halon
halt
halter
halting
haltingly
halva (*or* ~vah)
halve
halving
halyard (*or* halliard)
ham (~mmed, ~mming)
hamadryad
hamadryas
Hamas
Hamburg
hamburger
Hamite
Hamitic
Hamlet *Shakespeare*
hamlet *village*
hammer
hammerhead
hammering
hammerless
hammerlock
hammily
hamminess
hammock
hammy
hamper
hampered
Hampshire
hamster
hamstring (~strung)
hamza
Han
hand
handbag
handball
handbasin

handbell
handbill
handbook
handbrake
handbreadth
handcart
handclap
handcraft
handcrafted
handcuff
handcuffs
hander
handful
handgun
hand-held
handhold
handicap (~pped, ~capping)
handicapped
handicapper
handicraft
handicrafts
handicraftsman (*pl* ~men)
handicraftswoman (*pl* ~women)
handily
handiness
handiwork
handkerchief (*pl* ~iefs, ~ieves)
handle
handleability
handleable
handlebar
handlebars
handled
handleless
handler
handmade (! handmaid)
handmaid (! handmade)
handmaiden
hand-me-down
handout
handover
hand-pick
hand-picked
handprint
handpump
handrail

handsaw
handset
handshake
handshaking
handsome (*adj* ~somer, ~somest)
handsomely
handsomeness
hands-on
handspring
handstand
hand-to-hand
hand-to-mouth
handwriting
handwritten
handy
handyman (*pl* ~men)
hang (hung *or* hanged)
hangar (! hanger) *aircraft building*
hangarage
hangdog
hanger (! hangar) *clothes frame*
hanger-on (*pl* ~rs~)
hang-glide
hang-glider
hang-gliding
hanging
hangman (*pl* ~men)
hangnail
hang-out
hangover
hang-up
hank
hanker
hankerer
hankering
hanky (*or* ~kie)
hanky-panky
Hannibal
Hanoi
Hanoverian
Hansard
Hanseatic
hansom
Hanukkah (*or* Cha~)
Hanuman
ha'penny (*or* halfpenny)
haphazard

haphazardly
haphazardness
hapless
haplography
haploid
haploidy
happen
happening
happenstance
happily
happiness
happy
happy-go-lucky
hapten
haptic
haptics
hara-kiri
harangue
haranguer
harass
harassed
harasser
harassingly
harassment
harbinger
harbour (*US* ~or)
harbourage (*US* ~or~)
hard
hardback
hardball
hardbitten
hardboard
hard-boiled
hardcore
hardcover
hard-earned
harden
hardened
hardener
harder
hard-head
hard-headed
hard-headedly
hard-headedness
hard-hearted
hard-heartedly
hard-heartedness
hard-hit
hard-hitting
hardihood

hardily
hardiness
hardish
hardliner
hardly
hardness
hardpad
hard-pressed
hardship
hardtop
hardware
hard-wearing
hard-wire
hard-wired
hardwood
hard-working
hardy
hare
harebell
hare-brained
hare-lip
harem (*or* ~reem)
harewood
haricot
hark
harken (*usu* hearken)
Harlem
harlequin (H~)
harlequinade (H~)
harlot
harlotry
harm
harmful
harmfully
harmfulness
harmless
harmlessly
harmlessness
harmonic
harmonica
harmonically
harmonious
harmoniously
harmoniousness
harmonisation (*or* ~iz~)
harmonise (*or* ~ize)
harmonist
harmonium
harmony
harness

harnesser
harp
harper
harpist
harpoon
harpooner
harpsichord
harpsichordist
harpy
harquebus (*or* ar~)
harridan
harrier
Harrovian
Harrow *place*
harrow *machine, vex*
harrower
harrowing
harrowingly
harry
harsh
harshen
harshly
harshness
hart
hartbeest (*or* harte~)
hartshorn
harum-scarum
Harvard
harvest
harvestable
harvester
harvesting
harvestman
has-been
hash
Hashemite
hashish (*or* ~sheesh)
Hasidism (*or* Cha~,
  ~assi~)
Hasmonean
hasp
hassle
hassock
haste
hasten
hastily
hastiness
hasty
hat
hatband

hatbox
hatch
hatchback
hatchery
hatchet
hatchetfish
hatching
hatchment
hatchway
hate
hateful
hatefully
hatefulness
hatful
hatpin
hatred
hatstand
hatter
hat-trick
hauberk
haughtily
haughtiness
haughty
haul
haulage
haulier (US ~ler)
haulm (or halm)
haunch
haunt
haunted
haunter
haunting
hauntingly
haustellum (pl ~lla)
haute couture
haute cuisine
hauteur
Havana
have
haven
haversack
havoc
haw
Hawaii
Hawaiian
hawfinch
hawk
hawker
hawk-eyed
hawkish

hawkishly
hawkishness
hawkmoth
hawk-nosed
hawksbill
hawkweed
hawse
hawser
hawthorn
hay
haycock
hayfork
haying
hayloft
haymaker
haymaking
haymow
hayrick
hayseed
haystack
haywire
hazard
hazardous
hazardously
hazardousness
haze
hazel
hazelnut
hazily
haziness
hazy
head
headache
headachy
headband
headbang
headbanger
headbanging
headboard
head-butt
headcount
headdress
headed
header
headgear
headhunt
headhunted
headhunter
headhunting
headily

headiness
heading
headlamp
headland
headless
headlight
headline
headlock
headlong
headman (pl ~men)
headmaster
headmasterly
headmistress
headmistressy
headnote
head-on
headphones
headpiece
headquarter
headquarters
headrest
headroom
headscarf (pl ~rves)
headset
headship
headsman (pl ~men)
headstone
headstrong
head-to-head
head-turning
headwater
headway
headwind
headword
headwork
heady
heal
healable
healer
healing
health
healthful
healthily
healthiness
healthy
heap
hear (heard)
hearer
hearing
hearken (or harken)

hearsay
hearse
heart
heartache
heartbeat
heartbreak
heartbreaker
heartbreaking
heartbreakingly
heartbroken
heartburn
hearten
heartened
heartening
hearteningly
heartfelt
hearth
hearthrug
hearthstone
heartily
heartiness
heartland
heartless
heartlessly
heartlessness
heart-rending
heart-rendingly
heart-searching
heartsease (*or* heart's~)
heartsick
heartsore
heart-stopper
heart-stopping
heart-stoppingly
heartstrings
heart-throb
heart-to-heart
heart-warming
heartwood
hearty
heat
heated
heatedly
heater
heath
heathen
heather
heathery
heathland
Heath-Robinson

Heathrow
heating
heatproof
heat-resistant
heat-seeking
heatstroke
heatwave
heave (heaved, heaving)
heaven (H~)
heavenliness
heavenly
heaven-sent
heaver
heavily
heaviness
heaving
Heaviside
heavy
heavy-duty
heavy-footed
heavy-handed
heavy-handedly
heavy-handedness
heavy-hearted
heavyish
heavyweight
hebdomadal
hebdomadally
Hebraic
Hebraically
Hebraise (*or* ~ize)
Hebraism
Hebraist
Hebraistic
Hebrew
Hebridean
Hebrides
Hecate
hecatomb
heck
heckle
heckler
hectarage
hectare
hectic
hectically
hectogram (*or* ~mme)
hectolitre (*US* ~ter)
hectometre (*US* ~ter)
Hector *Greek*

hector *bully*
hectoring
hectoringly
Hecuba
hedge
hedged
hedgehog
hedge-hop
hedge-hopper
hedgerow
hedge-trimmer
hedging
hedonic
hedonism
hedonist
hedonistic
hedonistically
heebie-jeebies
heed
heedful
heedfully
heedfulness
heedless
heedlessly
heedlessness
hee-haw
heel
heeled
heeler
heelless
heft
heftily
heftiness
hefty
Hegelian
hegemonic
hegemony
Hegira (*or* Heji~, Hijra)
heifer
heigh-ho
height
heighten
heinous
heinously
heinousness
heir
heirdom
heiress
heirless
heirloom

heirship (! airship)
inheritance
Heisenberg
heist
held
heliacal
helianthus
helical
helicity
helicoid
helicoidal
helicon
helicopter
helictite
helideck
heliocentric
heliocentrically
heliogram
heliograph
heliographic
heliographical
heliographically
heliography
heliometer
Heliopolis
heliosphere
heliospheric
heliostat
heliotherapy
heliotrope
heliotropic
heliotropical
heliotropically
heliotropism
helipad
heliport
helium
helix (*pl* ~lices)
hell (H~)
Helladic
hellbender
hellbent
hellcat
hellebore
Hellene
Hellenic
Hellenisation (*or* ~iz~)
Hellenise (*or* ~ize)
Helleniser (*or* ~iz~)
Hellenism

Hellenist
Hellenistic
Hellenistical
hellfire
hellhole
hellhound
hellish
hellishly
hellishness
hello (*or* hallo, hullo; *n*
  pl ~los)
hellraiser
hellraising
helm
helmet
helmeted
helminth
helminthiasis
helminthological
helminthologist
helminthology
helmsman
help
helper
helpful
helpfully
helpfulness
helping
helpless
helplessly
helplessness
helpline
helpmate (*or* ~meet)
Helsinki
helter-skelter
helve
Helvetian
Helvetic
hem (~mmed,
  ~mming)
hemal- *see* haemal-
he-man (~men)
hemat- *see* haemat-
heme *see* haem
hemicycle
hemicylindrical
hemidemisemiquaver
hemiplegia
hemiplegic
hemipterous

hemisphere
hemispheric
hemispherical
hemispherically
hemistich
hemline
hemlock
hemming
hemo- *see* haemo-
hemor- *see* haemor-
hemp
hempen
hemp-nettle
hempseed
hemstitch
hen
henbane
hence
henceforth
henceforward
henchman (*pl* ~men)
hendecagon
hendecagonal
hendecasyllabic
hendecasyllable
hendiadys
henequen (*or* ~quin,
  heni~)
henge
henna
henotheism
henotheist
henotheistic
henpeck
henpecked
henry *electricity*
heparin
hepatic
hepatitis
hepatocyte
hepatologist
hepatoma (*pl* ~as,
  ~mata)
hepatomegaly
hepatotoxic
hepatotoxicity
hepatotoxin
hepcat
Hephaestus
heptagon

heptagonal
heptahedral
heptahedron (pl ~ra,
  ~rons)
heptameter
heptane
heptarchy
heptathlete
heptathlon
Hera
Heracles
herald
heralded
heraldic
heraldically
heraldist
heraldry
herb
herbaceous
herbage
herbal
herbalism
herbalist
herbarium (pl ~ia,
  ~iums)
herbicidal
herbicide
herbist
herbivore
herbivorous
Hercegovina (or Herz~)
Herculean
Hercules
herd
herder
herdsman (pl ~men)
here
hereabout
hereabouts
hereafter
hereat
hereby
hereditable
hereditament
hereditarily
hereditariness
hereditary
heredity
Hereford
herein

hereinafter
hereinbefore
hereof
hereon
heresiarch
heresy
heretic
heretical
heretically
hereto
heretofore
hereunder
hereunto
hereupon
herewith
heritability
heritable
heritably
heritage
hermaphrodite
hermaphroditic
hermaphroditical
hermaphroditically
hermaphroditism
hermeneutic
hermeneutical
hermeneutically
hermeneutics
Hermes
hermetic
hermetically
hermeticism
hermeticity
hermetics
hermit
hermitage
hermitic
hernia (pl ~ae, ~as)
hernial
herniate
herniated
hero (pl ~oes)
Herod
heroic
heroically
heroics
heroin (! heroine) *drug*
heroine *hero*
heroism
heron

heronry
hero-worship
herpes
herpesvirus
herpetic
herpetological
herpetologist
herpetology
herring
herringbone (or ~-bone)
herself
hertz (H~)
Herzegovina (or Herc~)
hesitance
hesitancy
hesitant
hesitantly
hesitate
hesitater
hesitatingly
hesitation
Hesperides
hesperidium (pl ~ia)
Hesperus
hessian
heterodox
heterodoxy
heterodyne
heterogamous
heterogamy
heterogeneity
heterogeneous
heterogeneously
heterogeneousness
heterogenesis
heterologous
heterology
heteromerous
heteromorphic
heteromorphism
heteromorphy
heteronomous
heteronomy
heteronym
heteronymic
heteronymous
heteroplasia
heteroplastic
heteroplasty
heteropolar

heteropteran
heteropterous
heterosexism
heterosexist
heterosexual
heterosexuality
heterosexually
heterotroph
heterotrophic
heterotrophically
heterozygosity
heterozygote
heterozygous
heuristic
heuristically
heuristics
hew (hewn *or* hewed)
hewer
hex
hexachlorophene
hexachord
hexad
hexadecimal
hexadecimally
hexagon
hexagonal
hexagram
hexahedral
hexahedron (*pl* ~ra, ~rons)
hexameter
hexane
hexose
hey
heyday
Hezbollah (*or* Hizbullah)
hiatus (*pl* ~uses)
Hiawatha
hibachi (*pl* ~chis)
hibernal
hibernate
hibernation
hibernator
Hibernian
Hibernianism
Hibernicism
hibiscus
hic
hiccup (*or* hiccough; *v* ~pped, ~pping)

hiccupy
hick (*US*)
hickory
hid
hidalgo (*pl* ~gos)
hidden
hiddenness
hide (hid *or* hidden, hiding)
hide-and-seek
hideaway
hidebound
hideous
hideously
hideousness
hideout
hiding
hidrosis
hidrotic
hierarch
hierarchic
hierarchical
hierarchically
hierarchisation (*or* ~iz~)
hierarchise (*or* ~ize)
hierarchism
hierarchy
hieratic
hieratically
hierocracy
hierocratic
hieroglyph
hieroglyphical
hieroglyphically
hieroglyphics
hierogram
hierolatry
hierology
hierophant
hierophantic
hi-fi
higgledy-piggledy
high
highball
high-born
highbrow
high-chair
high-class
higher

high-flier (or ~flyer)
high-flown
high-flyer (or ~flier)
high-flying
high-handed
high-handedly
high-handedness
high-hat (*or* hi-hat; ~tted, ~tting)
highjack (*usu* hijack)
Highland *Scotland*
highland *mountains*
high-level
highlight
highlighter
highly
high-minded
high-mindedly
highmindedness
Highness
high-octane
high-pitched
high-powered
high-pressure (*adj*)
high-rise
high-risk
high-sounding
high-speed
high-spirited
hightail
high-tech (*or* hi-~, ~-tec)
high-tensile
high-toned
high-top
highway
highwayman (*pl* ~men)
hi-hat (*or* high)
hijack (*occ* high~)
hijacker (*occ* high~)
hijacking (*occ* high~)
hike
hiker
hiking
hilarious
hilariously
hilariousness
hilarity
hill
hillbilly

hilliness
hillock
hillside
hilltop
hillwalker
hillwalking
hilly
hilt
hilted
Himalayan
Himalayas
himself
Hinayana
hind
hindbrain
hinder
Hindi
hindmost
hindquarters
hindrance
hindsight
Hindu (*pl* ~us)
Hinduise (*or* ~ize)
Hinduism
Hindustan
Hindustani
hindwing
hinge (~ged, ~geing *or* ~ging)
hinny
hint
hinterland
hip (*adj* ~pper, ~ppest)
hip-hop
hipped
hippie (*or* ~ppy)
hippiedom
hippiness (*or* ~ien~)
hippocampus (*pl* ~pi)
Hippocrates
Hippocratic
hippodrome
hippogriff (*or* ~gryph)
hippopotamus (*pl* ~mi , ~uses)
hippy (*or* ~ppie)
hippyish
hipster
hiragana
hircine

hire
hireable (*or US* hira~)
hireling
hirer
Hiroshima
hirsute
hirsuteness
hirsutism
Hispanic
hispid
hiss
hist
histamine
histidine
histogram
histological
histologically
histologist
histology
histolysis
histolytic
histopathological
histopathologist
histopathology
historian
historiated
historic
historical
historically
historicisation (*or* ~iz~)
historicise (*or* ~ize)
historicism
historicist
historicity
historiographer
historiographic
historiographical
historiographically
historiography
history
histrionic
histrionically
histrionics
hit (hitting)
hitch
hitchhike (*or* hitch-~)
hitchhiker (*or* hitch-~)
hi-tec (*or* high~, ~tech)
hither
hithermost

hitherto
hitherward
Hitler
Hitlerian
Hitlerism
Hittite
hive
hives
Hizbollah (*or* Hezbullah)
hoactzin (*or* ~atz~)
hoar
hoard
hoarded
hoarder
hoarding
hoarfrost
hoarhound (*or* hore~)
hoarily
hoariness
hoarse
hoarsely
hoarsen
hoarseness
hoary
hoatzin (*or* ~actz~)
hoax
hoaxer
hob
Hobart
hobbit
hobble
hobbled
hobbledehoy
hobbler
hobby
hobby-horse
hobbyist
hobgoblin
hobnail
hobnailed
hobnob (~bbed, ~bbing)
hobo (*US*; *pl* ~os, ~oes)
hock
hockey
hocus-pocus
hod
hodgepodge (*US*; *UK* hotchpotch)
hodiernal

hoe
hoedown
hoer
hog
hogback (or hog's-~)
hogfish
hogger
hoggery
hoggin
hoggish
hoggishly
Hogmanay
hogshead
hog-tie
hogwash
hogweed
hoi polloi
hoist
hoister
hoity-toity
hokey-cokey
hokum (US)
hold (held)
holdable
holdall
holder
holdfast
holding
holdings
hold-up
hole
hole-in-the-wall (UK)
holey (! holy) with holes
Holi
holiday
holily
Holiness religious leader
holiness holy state
holism
holist
holistic
holistically
Holland country
holland fabric
hollandaise
Hollander
holler
hollow
hollowly
hollowness

holly
hollyhock
Hollywood
holmium
Holocaust World
   War 2
holocaust slaughter
Holocene
hologram
holographic
holographical
holographically
holography
holohedral
holohedralism
holohedron
holophrase
holophrasis
holophrastic
holster
holt
holy (! holey) sacred
Holyhead
homage
homburg (H~)
home
home-brew
homebuyer
homecoming
home-grown
homeland
homeless
homelessness
homeliness
homely
home-made
homemaker
home-making
homeopath (or
   ~moeo~)
homeopathic (or
   ~moeo~)
homeopathically (or
   ~moeo~)
homeopathist (or
   ~moeo~)
homeopathy (or
   ~moeo~)
homeostasis (pl ~ases; or
   ~moeo~)

homeostatic (or
   ~moeo~)
home-owner
Homer Greek, Simpson
homer baseball
Homeric
homesick
homesickness
homespun
homestead
homesteader
homesteading
homeward
homewards
homework
homicidal
homicidally
homicide
homiletic
homiletical
homiletics
homilist
homily
homing
hominid
hominoid
homo (H~)
homoeo- see homeo-
homogamous
homogamy
homogeneity
homogeneous
homogeneously
homogeneousness
homogenisation (or
   ~iz~)
homogenise (or ~ize)
homogeniser (or ~iz~)
homogeny
homograph
homographic
homologate
homologation
homologise (or ~ize)
homologous
homologous (US ~log)
homology
homomorphic
homomorphically
homomorphism

homomorphous
homonym
homonymic
homonymous
homonymy
homophobe
homophobia
homophobic
homophone
homophonic
homophonically
homophonous
homophony
homoptera (H~)
homopteran
homopterous
homosexual
homosexuality
homosexually
homozygosity
homozygote
homozygous
homuncular
homunculus (or ~ule; pl ~uli, ~ules)
honcho (US; pl ~os)
Honduran
Honduras
hone
honed
honest
honestly
honesty
honey (pl ~eys)
honeybee
honeycomb
honeydew
honeyed (also honied)
honeymoon
honeymooner
honey-pot
honeysuckle
honk
honker
honky-tonk
Honolulu
honor see honour
honorand
honorarium (pl ~ia, ~iums)

honorary
honorific
honorifically
Honour (US ~or) title
honour (US ~or) esteem
honourable (US ~or~)
honourably (US ~or~)
honoured (US ~or~)
hooch (also hootch, US)
hood
hooded
hoodless
hoodlum
hoodoo (pl ~oos)
hoodwink
hoof (pl hoofs, hooves)
hoo-ha (or ~hah)
hook
hookah
hooked
hooker
hookey (or US ~ky)
hook-up
hookworm
hooligan
hooliganism
hoop
hooped
hoop-la
hoopoe
hooray (or ~rah, hurray, hurrah)
hoot
hootch (usu hooch, US)
hootenanny (or hootnanny, US)
hooter
hoover (H~, tr)
hop (~pped, ~pping)
hope
hopeful
hopefully
hopefulness
hopeless
hopelessly
hopelessness
hopper
hopping
hoppy
hopscotch

horary
Horatian
horde
horehound (or hoar~)
horizon
horizontal
horizontality
horizontally
Horlicks (tr)
hormonal
hormone
horn
hornbeam
hornbill
hornblende
horned
hornet
hornily
horniness
hornpipe
horn-rimmed
horntail
horny
horologe
horologer
horologic
horological
horologist
horology
horoscope
horoscopic
horoscopy
horrendous
horrendously
horrent
horrible
horribleness
horribly
horrid
horridly
horridness
horrific
horrifically
horrify
horrifying
horrifyingly
horripilant
horripilate
horripilation
horror

horror-struck (or
~stricken)
hors de combat
hors d'oeuvre
horse
horseback
horsebox
horseflesh
horsefly
horsehair
horseleech
horseless
horseman (pl ~men)
horsemanship
horsemint
horseplay
horseplayer
horsepower
horse-race
horseradish
horseshoe
horse-shoeing
horsetail
horsewhip
horsewoman (pl
~women)
horsey (or ~sy)
horsily
horsiness
horst
hortation
hortative
hortatory
hortensia
horticultural
horticulturalist
horticulture
horticulturist
Horus
hosanna (H~; or ~nah)
hose
hosier
hosiery
hospice
hospitable
hospitableness
hospitably
hospital
hospitalisation (or ~iz~)
hospitalise (or ~ize)

hospitality
hospitaller (US ~aler)
host
hostage
hostel
hosteller (US ~eler)
hostelling (US ~eling)
hostelry
hostess
hostile
hostilely
hostility
hot (adj ~tter, ~ttest)
hotbed
hot-blooded
hotchpotch (US
hodgepodge)
hot-desking
hotel
hotelier
hothead
hotheaded
hotheadedly
hotheadedness
hothouse
hotline
hotly
hotplate
hotpot
hotshot
hot-tempered
hot-wire
Houdini
hoummos (or houmus,
hummus)
hound
hour
hourglass
hourly
house
houseboat
housebound
houseboy
housebreaking
housecoat
housefly
household
householder
house-hunt
house-hunter

housekeeper
housekeeping
housemaid
housemaster
house-mistress
houseplant
house-proud
house-top
house-train
house-warming
housewife (pl ~wives)
housewifely
housewifery
housework
housey-housey
housing
hove
hovel
hover
hovercraft
hoverfly
how
howbeit
howdah (or houdah)
however
howitzer
howl
howler
howling
howsoever
hoyden
hoydenish
hub
hubbub
hubby
hubris
hubristic
huckleberry
huckster
hucksterism
huddle
hue
hued
hueless
huff
huffer
huffily
huffiness
huffish
huffy

hug (~gged, ~gging)
huge
hugely
hugeness
huggable
hugger
Huguenot
huh
hula
hulk
hulking
hull
hullabaloo
hulled
hullo (or hallo, hello)
hum (~mmed, ~mming)
human
humane
humanely
humaneness
humanisation (or ~iz~)
humanise (or ~ize)
humanism
humanist
humanistic
humanistically
humanitarian
humanitarianism
humanities
humanity
humankind
humanly
humanness
humanoid
humble
humbleness
humbling
humbly
humbug (~gged, ~gging)
humdinger
humdrum
humectant
humeral
humerus (pl ~ri)
humid
humidification
humidifier
humidify

humidity
humidly
humidor
humification
humify
humiliate
humiliating
humiliatingly
humiliation
humiliator
humility
hummable
hummer
hummingbird
hummock
hummocky
hummus (or hoummos, humous)
humongous (or ~mun~)
humoral
humoresque
humorist
humorous
humorously
humorousness
humour (US ~or)
humourless (US ~or~)
humourlessly (US ~or~)
humourlessness (US ~or~)
hump
humpback
humped
humph
humpless
humpy
humungous (or ~mon~)
humus
Hun
hunch
hunchback
hunchbacked
hundred
hundredfold
hundredth
hundredweight
Hungarian
Hungary

hunger
hung-over
hungrily
hungriness
hungry
hunk
hunky
Hunnish
hunt
hunted
hunter
hunting
huntress
huntsman (pl ~men)
huntswoman (pl ~women)
hurdle
hurdler
hurdles
hurdy-gurdy
hurl
hurler
hurley
hurling
hurly-burly
Huron
hurrah (or hooray, hoorah, hurray)
hurricane
hurried
hurry
hurt
hurtful
hurtfully
hurtfulness
hurtle
husband
husbandly
husbandry
hush
hushed
husk
huskily
huskiness
husky
hussar
hussy
hustings
hustle
hustler

hut
hutch
hyacinth
hyaline
hyalite
hyaloid
hybrid
hybridisable (*or* ~iz~)
hybridisation (*or* ~iz~)
hybridise (*or* ~ize)
hybridism
hybridity
hydatid
Hydra *mythology,*
  constellation
hydra *polyp*
hydrangea
hydrant
hydratable
hydrate
hydration
hydrator
hydraulic
hydraulically
hydraulics
hydric
hydride
hydro
hydrocarbon
hydrocele
hydrocephalic
hydrocephalus
hydrocephaly
hydrochloric
hydrochloride
hydrochlorofluorocarbon
hydrocolloid
hydrocortisone
hydrodynamic
hydrodynamical
hydrodynamicist
hydrodynamics
hydroelectric
hydroelectricity
hydrofluoric
hydrofoil
hydrogel
hydrogen
hydrogenate
hydrogenated

hydrogenation
hydrogenise (*or* ~ize)
hydrogenous
hydrographer
hydrographic
hydrographical
hydrographically
hydrography
hydroid
hydrologic
hydrological
hydrologically
hydrologist
hydrology
hydrolyse
hydrolysis
hydromassage
hydromechanical
hydromechanics
hydromel
hydrometer
hydrometric
hydrometry
hydropathic
hydropathically
hydropathist
hydropathy
hydrophile
hydrophilicity
hydrophobia
hydrophobic
hydrophobicity
hydrophone
hydrophyte
hydrophytic
hydroplane
hydroponic
hydroponically
hydroponics
hydropower
hydroquinone
hydrospeed
hydrosphere
hydrostatic
hydrostatical
hydrostatically
hydrostatics
hydrotherapist
hydrotherapy
hydrothermal

hydrothermally
hydrotropism
hydrous
hydroxide
hydroxil
hydrozoa (H~)
hydrozoan
hyena (*or* ~aena)
hygiene
hygienic
hygienically
hygienist
hygrology
hygrometer
hygrometric
hygrometrically
hygrometry
hygrophilous
hygrophyte
hygrophytic
hygroscope
hygroscopic
hygroscopical
hygroscopically
hymen
hymenal
hymeneal
hymenoptera (H~)
hymenopteran
hymenopterous
hymn
hymnal
hymnic
hymnodist
hymnody
hymnographer
hymnography
hymnological
hymnologist
hymnology
hyoid
hypaesthesia (*or* ~pes~)
hypaesthetic (*or* ~pes~)
hypallage
hype
hyped
hyper
hyperactive
hyperactivity
hyperaemia (*or* ~rem~)

hyperaemic (or ~rem~)
hyperaesthesia (or
 ~res~)
hyperaesthetic (or
 ~res~)
hyperalgesia
hyperalgesic
hyperbola (pl ~ae, ~as)
hyperbole
hyperbolic
hyperbolical
hyperbolically
hyperbolise (or ~ize)
hyperbolism
hyperborean (H~)
hypercritical
hypercritically
hyperglycaemia (or
 ~cem~)
hyperglycaemic (or
 ~cem~)
hypericum
hyperinflation
Hyperion
hyperkinesia
hyperkinesis
hyperkinetic
hyperlink
hypermarket
hypermedia
hypermetropia
hypermetropic
hypernym
hyperon
hyperopia
hyperopic
hyperphysical
hyperphysically
hyperplasia
hyperrealism
hyperrealist
hyperrealistic
hyperreality
hypersensitive
hypersensitiveness
hypersensitivity
hypersonic
hypersonically
hyperspace
hyperspatial

hypertension
hypertensive
hypertext
hypertextual
hyperthermal
hyperthermia
hyperthermic
hyperthyroid
hyperthyroidic
hyperthyroidism
hypertonia
hypertonic
hypertonicity
hypertrophic
hypertrophied
hypertrophy
hyperventilate
hyperventilated
hyperventilation
hyphen
hyphenate
hyphenated
hyphenation
hypnosis
hypnotherapist
hypnotherapy
hypnotic
hypnotically
hypnotisable (or ~iz~)
hypnotise (or ~ize)
hypnotism
hypnotist
hypo
hypoblast
hypochondria
hypochondriac
hypochondriacal
hypochondriasis
hypocorism
hypocoristic
hypocoristical
hypocoristically
hypocrisy
hypocrite
hypocritical
hypocritically
hypoderma
hypodermic
hypodermically
hypodermis

hypogeal
hypogean
hypogene
hypogenic
hypogeous
hypogeum (pl ~gea)
hypoglycaemia (or
 ~cem~)
hypoglycaemic (or
 ~cem~)
hypogonadal
hypogonadic
hypogonadism
hypomania
hypomanic
hyponym
hyponymy
hypophysial (or ~yseal)
hypophysis (pl ~yses)
hypospray
hypostasis (pl ~ases)
hypostasise (or ~ize; US
 ~statize)
hypostatic
hypostatical
hypostatically
hypotaxis
hypotension
hypotensive
hypotenuse
hypothalamic
hypothalamus (pl ~ami)
hypothecate
hypothermia
hypothesis (pl ~ises)
hypothesise (or ~ize)
hypothetic
hypothetical
hypothetically
hypothyroid
hypothyroidism
hypotonia
hypotonic
hypotonicity
hypoventilation
hypoxia
hypoxic
hypsography
hypsometer
hypsometric

hypsometry
hyrax
hyssop
hysterectomise (*or* ~ize)
hysterectomy
hysteresis
hysteretic
hysteria
hysteric
hysterical
hysterically

iamb
iambic
iambics
iambus
Iapetus
iatrochemical
iatrochemist
iatrochemistry
iatrogenesis
iatrogenic
Iberia
Iberian
ibex (*pl* ibexes, ibices)
ibid
ibidem
ibis
Ibiza
ibuprofen
Icarus
ice
iceberg
iceblink
iceblock
iceboat
ice-bound
icebox
ice-breaker
icecap

ice-cold
iced
icefall
Iceland
Icelander
Icelandic
iceman (*pl* ~men)
ichneumon
ichnography
ichthyological
ichthyologist
ichthyology
ichthyophagous
ichthyosaur
ichthyosaurus (*pl* ~ri,
  ~uses)
ichthyosis
icicle
icily
iciness
icing
icon (*or* ikon)
iconic
iconically
iconicity
iconify
iconoclasm
iconoclast
iconoclastic
iconoclastically
iconodule
iconodulist
iconographer
iconographic
iconographical
iconographically
iconography
iconolatry
iconological
iconology
iconostasis (*pl* ~ases)
icosahedral
icosahedron (*pl* ~ra,
  ~rons)
ictus
icy
id
Idaho
Idahoan
Id-al-Adha

Id-al-Fitr
idea
ideal
idealisation (*or* ~iz~)
idealise (*or* ~ize)
idealiser (*or* ~izer)
idealism
idealist
idealistic
idealistically
ideally
ideate
ideation
ideational
ideationally
idée fixe (*pl* idées fixes)
idem
ident
identical
identically
identicalness
identifiable
identifiably
identification
identifier
identify
identikit (I~, *tr*)
identity
ideogram
ideograph
ideographic
ideographically
ideography
ideological
ideologically
ideologist
ideologue
ideology
idiocy
idiolect
idiom
idiomatic
idiomatically
idiosyncrasy
idiosyncratic
idiosyncratically
idiot
idiotic
idiotically
idiotype

idle
idleness
idler
idly
idol
idolater
idolatress
idolatrous
idolatrously
idolatry
idolisation (or ~iz~)
idolise (or ~ize)
idoliser (or ~iz~)
idyll (also idyl)
idyllic
idyllically
iffy
igloo (pl ~oos)
igneous
ignis fatuus
ignitability
ignitable (or ~ible)
ignite
igniter
ignition
ignobility
ignoble
ignobleness
ignobly
ignominious
ignominiously
ignominiousness
ignominy
ignorable
ignoramus (pl ~uses)
ignorance
ignorant
ignorantly
ignore
ignorer
iguana
iguanodon
ikat
ikebana
ilang-ilang (or ylang-ylang)
ileac
ileal
ileitis
ileostomy

ileum (pl ilea)
ileus
ilex
iliac
Iliad
ilium (pl ilia)
ilk
ill
ill-advised
ill-advisedly
ill-affected
ill-assorted
ill-bred
ill-breeding
ill-conceived
ill-considered
ill-defined
ill-disposed
illegal
illegality
illegally
illegibility
illegible
illegibly
illegitimacy
illegitimate
illegitimately
ill-equipped
ill-fated
ill-favoured (US ~or~)
ill-founded
ill-gotten
ill-humoured
ill-humouredly
illiberal
illiberalism
illiberality
illiberally
illicit
illicitly
illicitness
illimitability
illimitable
illimitably
ill-informed
Illinois
illiteracy
illiterate
illiterately
illiterateness

ill-judged
ill-mannered
ill-natured
ill-naturedly
illness
illocution
illocutionary
illogic
illogical
illogicality
illogically
ill-omened
ill-starred
ill-tempered
ill-timed
ill-treat
ill-treatment
illuminance
illuminant
illuminate
illuminated
illuminati
illuminatingly
illumination
illuminative
illuminator
illumine
ill-use
ill-used
illusion
illusional
illusionism
illusionist
illusionistic
illusive
illusively
illusiveness
illusorily
illusoriness
illusory
illustrate
illustrated
illustration
illustrational
illustrative
illustrator
illustrious
illustriously
illustriousness
illuvial

illuviated
illuviation
Illyria
Illyrian
ilmenite
image
imageless
image-maker
imager
imagery
imaginable
imaginably
imaginarily
imaginary
imagination
imaginative
imaginatively
imaginativeness
imagine
imagined
imagineer
imagineering
imaginer
imaging
imaginings
imago (*pl* ~os, ~gines)
imam (I~)
imamate
IMAX (Imax, *tr*)
imbalance
imbecile
imbecilic
imbecility
imbed (*usu* em~)
imbibe
imbiber
imbibition
imbricate
imbrication
imbroglio (*pl* ~ios)
imbue
imitability
imitable
imitate
imitation
imitative
imitatively
imitativeness
imitator
immaculacy

immaculate
immaculately
immaculateness
immanence
immanency
immanent
immanentism
immanentist
immaterial
immaterialism
immateriality
immaterially
immature
immaturely
immaturity
immeasurability
immeasurable
immeasurably
immediacy
immediate
immediateness
immemorial
immemorially
immense
immensely
immenseness
immensity
immerse
immersed
immersibility
immersible
immersion
immersive
immigrant
immigrate
immigration
imminence
imminent
imminently
immiscibility
immiscible
immiscibly
immitigable
immitigably
immobile
immobilisation (*or*
  ~iz~)
immobilise (*or* ~ize)
immobilism
immobility

immobiliser (*or* ~iz~)
immoderacy
immoderate
immoderately
immoderateness
immoderation
immodest
immodestly
immodesty
immolate
immolation
immolator
immoral
immorality
immorally
immortal
immortalisation (*or*
  ~iz~)
immortalise (*or* ~ize)
immortality
immortally
immotile
immovability
immovable (*or* ~vea~)
immovably
immune
immunise (*or* ~ize)
immunity
immunoassay
immunochemistry
immunocompetent
immunocompromised
immunodeficiency
immunogenic
immunogenicity
immunoglobulin
immunological
immunologically
immunologist
immunology
immunosuppressant
immunosuppressed
immunosuppression
immunotherapy
immure
immured
immurement
immutability
immutable
immutably

imp
impact
impacted
impaction
impactive
impair
impaired
impairment
impala
impale
impaled
impalement
impaler
impalpability
impalpable
impalpably
impanel (or em~)
impart
impartation
impartial
impartiality
impartially
impartment
impassability
impassable (! impassable)
  obstruction
impassableness
impassably
impasse
impassibility
impassible (! impassable)
  no pain
impassibly
impassion
impassioned
impassionedly
impassionedness
impassive
impassively
impassiveness
impassivity
impasto (~toed, ~to'd)
impatience
impatiens
impatient
impatiently
impeach
impeachable
impeachment
impeccability

impeccable
impeccably
impecuniosity
impecunious
impecuniousness
impedance
impede
impediment
impedimenta
impedimental
impeding
impedingly
impel (~lled ~lling)
impellant
impeller (or ~or)
impend
impending
impenetrability
impenetrable
impenetrably
impenitence
impenitency
impenitent
impenitently
imperatival
imperative
imperatively
imperativeness
imperator
imperatorial
imperceptibility
imperceptible
imperceptibly
imperceptive
imperceptiveness
impercipience
impercipient
impercipiently
imperfect
imperfection
imperfective
imperfectly
imperial
imperialise (or ~ize)
imperialised (or ~ized)
imperialism
imperialist
imperialistic
imperialistically
imperially

imperil (~lled, ~lling)
imperilment
imperious
imperiously
imperiousness
imperishability
imperishable
imperishableness
imperishably
imperium
impermanence
impermanency
impermanent
impermanently
impermeability
impermeable
impermeably
impermissibility
impermissible
impermissibly
impersonal
impersonalisation (or
  ~iz~)
impersonalise (or ~ize)
impersonalised (or
  ~ized)
impersonality
impersonally
impersonate
impersonation
impersonator
impertinence
impertinency
impertinent
impertinently
imperturbability
imperturbable
imperturbably
impervious
imperviously
imperviousness
impetigo
impetration
impetuosity
impetuous
impetuously
impetuousness
impetus
impiety
impinge

impingement
impinger
impious
impiously
impiousness
impish
impishly
impishness
implacability
implacable
implacableness
implacably
implant
implantation
implausibility
implausible
implausibly
implement
implemental
implementation
implementer
implicate
implication
implicational
implicative
implicatively
implicit
implicitly
implicitness
implied
impliedly
implode
imploration
imploratory
implore
imploring
imploringly
implosion
implosive
imply
impolite
impolitely
impoliteness
impolitic
impoliticly
imponderability
imponderable
imponderably
import
importable

importance
important
importantly
importation
importer
imports
importunate
importunately
importune
importunely
importuner
importuning
importunity
impose
imposing
imposingly
imposition
impossibilism
impossibilist
impossibility
impossible
impossibly
imposter (*or* ~or)
imposture
impotence
impotency
impotent
impotently
impound
impoundable
impoundage
impounder
impoundment
impoverish
impoverished
impoverishment
impracticability
impracticable
impracticably
impractical
impracticality
impractically
imprecate
imprecation
imprecatory
imprecise
imprecisely
impreciseness
imprecision
impregnability

impregnable
impregnably
impregnate
impregnated
impregnation
impresario (*pl* ~os)
impress
impressible
impression
impressionability
impressionable
impressionably
impressional
impressionism (I~)
impressionist (I~)
impressionistic
impressionistically
impressive
impressively
impressiveness
imprest
imprimatur
imprint
imprinted
imprinting
imprison
imprisoned
imprisonment
improbability
improbable
improbably
improbity
impromptu (*pl* ~us)
improper
improperly
impropriety
improvability
improvable
improve
improvement
improver
improvidence
improvident
improvidently
improving
improvingly
improvisation
improvisational
improvisatorial
improvisatory

improvise
improviser
imprudence
imprudent
imprudently
impudence
impudent
impudently
impugn
impugnable
impugnment
impulse
impulsion
impulsive
impulsively
impulsiveness
impulsivity
impunity
impure
impurely
impureness
impurity
imputable
imputation
impute
imputed
in
inability
in absentia
inaccessibility
inaccessible
inaccessibly
inaccuracy
inaccurate
inaccurately
inaction
inactivate
inactivated
inactivation
inactive
inactively
inactivity
inadequacy
inadequate
inadequately
inadmissibility
inadmissible
inadmissibly
inadvertence
inadvertency

inadvertent
inadvertently
inadvisability
inadvisable
inalienability
inalienable
inalienably
inalterability
inalterable
inalterableness
inalterably
inamorata
inane
inanely
inaneness
inanimate
inanimately
inanimation
inanition
inanity
inapplicability
inapplicable
inapplicably
inapposite
inappositely
inappositeness
inappreciable
inappreciably
inappreciative
inappropriate
inappropriately
inappropriateness
inapt
inaptitude
inaptly
inaptness
inarticulacy
inarticulate
inarticulately
inarticulateness
inartistic
inartistically
inasmuch
inattention
inattentive
inattentively
inattentiveness
inaudibility
inaudible
inaudibly

inaugural
inaugurate
inauguration
inaugurator
inauguratory
inauspicious
inauspiciously
inauspiciousness
inauthentic
inauthentically
inauthenticity
in-between
inboard
inborn
inbound
inbred
inbreed (inbred)
inbreeding
inbuilt
Inca
incalculability
incalculable
incalculably
Incan
incandesce
incandescence
incandescent
incandescently
incantation
incantatory
incapability
incapable
incapably
incapacitant
incapacitate
incapacitation
incapacity
incapsulate (*usu* en~)
incarcerate
incarcerated
incarceration
incarcerator
incarnate
Incarnation *Christianity*
incarnation *embodiment*
incaution
incautious
incautiously
incautiousness
incendiarism

incendiary
incensation
incense
incensed
incentive
incentivise (*or* ~ize)
inception
inceptive
inceptor
incertitude
incessancy
incessant
incessantly
incessantness
incest
incestuous
incestuously
incestuousness
inch
inchoate
inchoately
inchoateness
inchworm
incidence
incident
incidental
incidentally
incinerate
incinerated
incineration
incinerator
incipience
incipiency
incipient
incipiently
incipit
incise
incised
incision
incisional
incisive
incisively
incisiveness
incisor
incitation
incite
incitement
inciter
incitingly
incivility

inclemency
inclement
inclemently
inclinable
inclination
incline
inclined
incliner
inclose (*usu* en~)
inclosure (*usu* en~)
includable (*or* ~ible)
include
included
includible (*or* ~able)
including
inclusion
inclusive
inclusively
inclusiveness
inclusivism
inclusivist
incognisance (*or* ~iz~)
incognisant (*or* ~iz~)
incognito
incoherence
incoherency
incoherent
incoherently
incohesion
incombustibility
incombustible
income
incomer
incoming
incommensurability
incommensurable
incommensurably
incommensurate
incommensurately
incommensurateness
incommode
incommodious
incommodiously
incommodiousness
incommunicability
incommunicable
incommunicableness
incommunicably
incommunicado
incomparability

incomparable
incomparableness
incomparably
incompatibility
incompatible
incompatibly
incompetence
incompetency
incompetent
incompetently
incomplete
incompletely
incompleteness
incompletion
incomprehensibility
incomprehensible
incomprehensibleness
incomprehensibly
incomprehension
inconceivability
inconceivable
inconceivableness
inconceivably
inconclusive
inconclusively
inconclusiveness
incongruence
incongruent
incongruently
incongruity
incongruous
incongruously
incongruousness
inconnu
inconsecutive
inconsecutively
inconsequence
inconsequent
inconsequential
inconsequentiality
inconsequently
inconsiderable
inconsiderably
inconsiderate
inconsiderately
inconsiderateness
inconsideration
inconsistency
inconsistent
inconsistently

inconsolability
inconsolable
inconsolably
inconspicuous
inconspicuously
inconspicuousness
inconstancy
inconstant
inconstantly
incontestability
incontestable
incontestably
incontinence
incontinent
incontinently
incontrovertibility
incontrovertible
incontrovertibly
inconvenience
inconvenient
inconveniently
inconvertibility
inconvertible
inconvertibly
incorporate
incorporated
incorporation
incorporative
incorporator
incorporeal
incorporeality
incorporeally
incorporeity
incorrect
incorrectly
incorrectness
incorrigibility
incorrigible
incorrigibly
incorrupt
incorruptibility
incorruptible
incorruptibly
in-country
increasable
increase
increasing
increasingly
incredibility
incredible

incredibleness
incredibly
incredulity
incredulous
incredulously
incredulousness
increment
incremental
incrementally
incriminate
incriminating
incrimination
incriminatory
incrust (*or* en~)
incrustation (*or* en~)
incubate
incubating
incubation
incubative
incubator
incubus (*pl* ~bi)
inculcate
inculcation
inculcator
inculpate
inculpation
inculpatory
incumbency
incumbent
incumbrance (*usu* en~)
incunabulum (*pl* ~la)
incur (~rred, ~rring)
incurability
incurable
incurably
incuriosity
incurious
incuriously
incuriousness
incurrable
incursion
incursive
incurvate
incurvated
incurvation
incus (*pl* ~uses, ~cudes)
indebted
indebtedness
indecency
indecent

indecently
indecipherability
indecipherable
indecipherably
indecision
indecisive
indecisively
indecisiveness
indeclinable
indecorous
indecorously
indecorousness
indecorum
indeed
indefatigability
indefatigable
indefatigably
indefeasibility
indefeasible
indefeasibly
indefensibility
indefensible
indefensibly
indefinable
indefinably
indefinite
indefinitely
indefiniteness
indehiscence
indehiscent
indelibility
indelible
indelibly
indelicacy
indelicate
indelicately
indemnification
indemnifier
indemnify
indemnity
indemonstrable
indent
indentation
indented
indenter
indenture
independence
independency
independent
independently

in-depth
indescribability
indescribable
indescribably
indestructibility
indestructible
indestructibly
indeterminable
indeterminably
indeterminacy
indeterminate
indeterminately
indeterminateness
indetermination
indeterminism
indeterminist
indeterministic
index (*pl* ~dices,
  ~dexes)
indexable
indexation
indexer
indexible
indexical
indexing
India
Indian
Indianisation (*or* ~iz~)
Indianise (*or* ~ize)
Indianness
Indic
indicant
indicate
indication
indicative
indicatively
indicator
indicatory
indices
indict
indictable
indictee
indicter
indiction
indictment
indie
indifference
indifferent
indifferently
indigence

indigene
indigenisation (*or* ~iz~)
indigenise (*or* ~ize)
indigenous
indigenously
indigenousness
indigent
indigently
indigestibility
indigestible
indigestibly
indigestion
indigestive
indignant
indignantly
indignation
indignity
indigo (*pl* ~os, ~oes)
indirect
indirection
indirectly
indirectness
indiscernible
indiscernibly
indiscipline
indiscreet (! indiscrete)
  injudicious
indiscreetly
indiscrete (! indiscreet)
  indivisible
indiscretion
indiscriminate
indiscriminately
indiscriminateness
indiscriminating
indiscrimination
indispensability
indispensable
indispensableness
indispensably
indispose
indisposed
indisposition
indisputability
indisputable
indisputableness
indisputably
indissolubility
indissoluble
indissolubly

indistinct
indistinctly
indistinctness
indistinguishable
indistinguishably
indium
individual
individualisation (*or*
  ~iz~)
individualise (*or* ~ize)
individualism
individualist
individualistic
individualistically
individuality
individually
individuate
individuation
indivisibility
indivisible
indivisibly
indoctrinate
indoctrination
indoctrinator
indoctrinatory
Indo-European
indolence
indolent
indolently
Indology
indomitability
indomitable
indomitableness
indomitably
Indonesia
Indonesian
indoor
indoors
indorse (*usu* en~)
indorsement (*usu* en~)
indrawn
indri (*pl* ~is)
indubitability
indubitable
indubitableness
indubitably
induce
induced
inducement
inducer

inducible
induct
inductance
inductee
induction
inductive
inductively
inductiveness
inductivism
inductivist
inductivity
inductor
indue (*usu* en~)
indulge
indulgence
indulgent
indulgently
indulger
indurate
induration
indurative
Indus
industrial
industrialisation (*or* ~iz~)
industrialise (*or* ~ize)
industrialism
industrialist
industrially
industrious
industriously
industriousness
industry
indwell (indwelt)
indweller
inebriate
inebriated
inebriation
inebriety
inedibility
inedible
ineducable
ineffability
ineffable
ineffableness
ineffably
ineffective
ineffectively
ineffectiveness
ineffectual

ineffectuality
ineffectually
ineffectualness
inefficaceous
inefficaceously
inefficacy
inefficiency
inefficient
inefficiently
inelegance
inelegant
inelegantly
ineligibility
ineligible
ineligibly
ineluctability
ineluctable
ineluctably
inept
ineptitude
ineptly
ineptness
inequable
inequality
inequitable
inequitably
inequity
inerrability
inerradicable
inerradicably
inerrancy
inerrant
inerrantly
inert
inertia
inertial
inertialess
inertly
inertness
inescapability
inescapable
inescapably
inessential
inestimable
inestimably
inevitability
inevitable
inevitably
inexact
inexactitude

inexactly
inexactness
inexcusable
inexcusably
inexhaustibility
inexhaustible
inexhaustibly
inexorability
inexorable
inexorably
inexpedience
inexpediency
inexpedient
inexpediently
inexpensive
inexpensively
inexpensiveness
inexperience
inexperienced
inexpert
inexpertly
inexplicability
inexplicable
inexplicably
inexplicit
inexplicitly
inexpressible
inexpressibly
inexpressive
inexpressively
inexpressiveness
inextinguishable
inextricability
inextricable
inextricably
infallibility
infallible
infallibly
infamous
infamously
infamy
infancy
infant
infanticidal
infanticide
infantile
infantilism
infantility
infantry
infantryman (*pl* ~men)

infarction
infatuate
infatuation
infeasibility
infeasible
infect
infection
infectious
infectiously
infectiousness
infective
infectiveness
infector
infelicitous
infer (~rred, ~rring)
inferable (or ~ferra~)
inference
inferential
inferentially
inferior
inferiority
infernal
infernally
inferno
inferrable (or ~fera~)
infertile
infertility
infest
infestation
infested
infidel
infidelity
infield
infielder
infighter (or in-~)
infighting (or in-~)
infill
infilling
infiltrate
infiltration
infiltrator
infinite
infinitely
infiniteness
infinitesimal
infinitesimally
infinitival
infinitivally
infinitive
infinitude

infinity
infirm
infirmary
infirmity
infirmly
infix
infixation
inflame
inflamed
inflamer
inflammability
inflammable
inflammably
inflammation
inflammatory
inflatable
inflate
inflated
inflatedly
inflater (or ~or)
inflation
inflect
inflected
inflection (or ~exion)
inflectional
inflective
inflexibility
inflexible
inflexibleness
inflexibly
inflexion (or ~ection)
inflict
inflictable
inflictably
inflicter (or ~or)
infliction
inflictor (or ~er)
in-flight
inflorescence
inflow
inflowing
influence
influenceable
influencer
influential
influentially
influenza
influenzal
influx
info

infold (*usu* en~)
infolded (*usu* en~)
infomercial
inform
informal
informality
informally
informant
informatics
information
informational
informationally
informative
informatively
informativeness
informatory
informed
informedly
informedness
informer
infotainment
infra
infra dig
infraction
infractor
infrangibility
infrangible
infrangibly
infrared (or infra-~)
infrasonic
infrasound
infrastructural
infrastructure
infrequency
infrequent
infrequently
infringe
infringement
infringer
infuriate
infuriating
infuriatingly
infuse
infusible
infusion
infusive
ingeniosity
ingenious (! ingenuous)
 clever
ingeniously

ingeniousness
ingénue (*or* ~gen~)
ingenuity
ingenuous (! ingenious)
  naive
ingenuously
ingenuousness
ingest
ingestible
ingestion
ingestive
ingle
inglorious
ingloriously
ingloriousness
ingoing
ingot
ingraft (*or* en~)
ingrain
ingrained (*or* en~)
ingrainedly (*or* en~)
ingrainedness (*or* en~)
ingrate
ingratiate
ingratiating
ingratiatingly
ingratiation
ingratitude
ingravescence
ingravescent
ingredient
ingress
ingression
ingressive
ingrowing
ingrown
ingrowth
inguinal
inhabit (~tted, ~tting)
inhabitability
inhabitable
inhabitance
inhabitancy
inhabitant
inhabitation
inhalant
inhalation
inhale
inhaler
inharmonic

inharmonicity
inharmonious
inharmoniously
inharmoniousness
inhere
inherence
inherent
inherently
inherit
inheritability
inheritable
inheritance
inheritor
inhesion
inhibit
inhibited
inhibition
inhibitive
inhibitor
inhibitory
inhospitable
inhospitableness
inhospitably
inhospitality
in-house
inhuman
inhumane
inhumanely
inhumanity
inhumanly
inhumation
inhume
inimical
inimically
inimitability
inimitable
inimitableness
inimitably
iniquitous
iniquitously
iniquitousness
iniquity
initial (~lled, ~lling; *US*
  ~led, ~ling)
initialisation (*or* ~iz~)
initialise (*or* ~ize)
initialism
initially
initiate
initiated

initiation
initiative
initiator
initiatory
inject
injectable
injection
injector
in-joke
injudicious
injudiciously
injudiciousness
injunction
injunctive
injure
injured
injurer
injurious
injuriously
injuriousness
injury
injustice
ink
inkblot
inkhorn
inkiness
inkjet
inkling
ink-pad
inkstand
inkwell
inky
inlaid
inland
in-law
inlay
inlaying
inlet
inly
inlying
inmate
in memoriam
inmost
inn
innards
innate
innately
innateness
inner
innerly

innermost
innerness
innervate
innervation
inning (*US*)
innings (*UK*)
innkeeper
innocence
innocent
innocently
innocuous
innocuously
innocuousness
innovate
innovation
innovational
innovationist
innovative
innovator
innovatory
innuendo
innumerability
innumerable
innumerableness
innumerably
innumeracy
innumerate
inoculable
inoculant
inoculate
inoculation
inoculative
inoculator
inoffensive
inoffensively
inoffensiveness
inoperability
inoperable
inoperableness
inoperably
inoperative
inopportune
inopportunely
inopportuneness
inordinacy
inordinate
inordinately
inorganic
inorganically
in-patient

inpouring
input (~tted, ~tting)
inquest
inquietude
inquire (*UK usu* en~; *US
   also* en~)
inquirer (*UK usu* en~;
   US also en~)
inquiring (*UK usu* en~;
   US also en~)
inquiry (*UK or* en~; *US*)
Inquisition *Spain*
inquisition *inquiry*
inquisitional
inquisitive
inquisitively
inquisitiveness
inquisitor
inquisitorial
inquisitorially
inroad
inrush
inrushing
insalubrious
insalubriously
insalubrity
insane
insanely
insanitariness
insanitary
insanity
insatiability
insatiable
insatiably
insatiate
insatiety
inscape
inscribe
inscribed
inscriber
inscription
inscriptional
inscriptionally
inscriptive
inscrutability
inscrutable
inscrutably
insect
insectarium (*pl* ~ia,
   ~iums)

insecticidal
insecticide
insectivora (I~)
insectivore
insectivorous
insecure
insecurely
insecurity
inselberg (*pl* ~ge)
inseminate
insemination
inseminator
insensate
insensately
insensateness
insensibility
insensible
insensibly
insensitive
insensitively
insensitiveness
insensitivity
insentience
insentient
inseparability
inseparable
inseparably
insert
insertable
inserted
inserter
insertion
insertional
in-service
inset (~tted, ~tting)
inshore
inside
insider
insides
insidious
insidiously
insidiousness
insight
insightful
insightfully
insignia (*pl* ~ia, ~ias)
insignificance
insignificant
insignificantly
insincere

insincerely
insincerity
insinuate
insinuating
insinuatingly
insinuation
insinuative
insinuator
insinuatory
insipid
insipidity
insipidly
insipidness
insist
insistence
insistent
insistently
in situ
insofar as (or insofaras)
insolation
insole
insolence
insolent
insolently
insolubility
insoluble
insolubly
insolvency
insolvent
insomnia
insomniac
insomuch
insouciance
insouciant
insouciantly
inspect
inspection
inspector
inspectorate
inspectorial
inspectorship
inspiration
inspirational
inspirationally
inspiratory
inspire
inspired
inspirer
inspiring
inspiringly

instability
install (~lled, ~lling)
installation
instalment (or US ~all~)
instance
instant
instantaneity
instantaneous
instantaneously
instantaneousness
instantiate
instantiation
instantly
instate
instatement
instauration
instead
instep
instigate
instigation
instigative
instigator
instil (~lled, ~lling)
instillation
instiller
instilment
instinct
instinctive
instinctively
instinctual
instinctually
institute
instituter (or ~or)
institution
institutional
institutionalisation (or
    ~iz~)
institutionalise (or ~ize)
institutionalised (or
    ~ized)
institutionalism
institutionalist
institutionally
in-store
instruct
instruction
instructional
instructive
instructively
instructiveness

instructor
instructress
instrument
instrumental
instrumentalism
instrumentalist
instrumentality
instrumentally
instrumentation
insubordinate
insubordinately
insubordination
insubstantial
insubstantiality
insubstantially
insufferable
insufferableness
insufferably
insufficiency
insufficient
insufficiently
insular
insularity
insularly
insulate
insulated
insulation
insulator
insulin
insulitis
insult
insulter
insulting
insultingly
insuperability
insuperable
insuperably
insupportable
insupportably
insurability
insurable
insurance
insure (! ensure)
    safeguard
insured
insurer
insurgence
insurgency
insurgent
insurmountability

insurmountable
insurmountably
insurrection
insurrectionary
insurrectionist
insusceptibility
insusceptible
intact
intactness
intaglio (*pl* ~os)
intake
intangibility
intangible
intangibly
intarsia
integer
integrability
integrable
integrably
integral
integrality
integrally
integrant
integrate
integration
integrationist
integrative
integrator
integrity
integument
integumental
integumentary
intellect
intellection
intellective
intellectual
intellectualise (*or* ~ize)
intellectualism
intellectualist
intelligence
intelligent
intelligently
intelligentsia
intelligibility
intelligible
intelligibly
intemperance
intemperate
intemperately
intemperateness

intend
intendancy
intendant
intended
intendedly
intense
intensification
intensifier
intensify
intension
intensional
intensionally
intensity
intensive
intensively
intensiveness
intent
intention
intentional
intentionalism
intentionality
intentionally
intentioned
intently
intentness
inter (~rred, ~rring)
inter alia
interact
interactant
interaction
interactional
interactionism
interactionist
interactive
interactively
interactivity
inter-agency
interbreed (interbred)
intercalary
intercalate
intercalated
intercalation
intercede
interceder
inter-cellular
intercept
interception
interceptive
interceptor
intercession

intercessional
intercessor
intercessorial
intercessory
interchange
interchangeability
interchangeable
interchangeableness
interchangeably
intercity
intercollegiate
intercom
intercommunicate
intercommunication
intercommunity
interconnect
interconnection
intercontinental
intercontinentally
intercostal
intercostally
intercourse
intercrop (~pped, ~pping)
intercut (~tting)
interdenominational
interdenominationally
interdepartmental
interdepartmentally
interdepend
interdependence
interdependency
interdependent
interdependently
interdict
interdiction
interdictor
interdictory
interdigital
interdigitate
interdisciplinary
interest
interested
interestedly
interestedness
interesting
interestingly
interestingness
interface
interfacial

interfacing
interfaith
interfere
interference
interferential
interferer
interfering
interferingly
interferometer
interferon
interflow
interfold
interfuse
interfusion
intergalactic
intergovernmental
intergovernmentally
interim
interior
interiorise (or ~ize)
interiority
interiorly
interject
interjection
interjectional
interjectory
interlace
interlaced
interlacement
interlacing
interlay (interlaid)
interleaf (pl ~leaves)
interline
interlinear
interlineate
interlineation
interlingua
interlingual
interlining
interlink
interlinkage
interlock
interlocker
interlocking
interlocution
interlocutor
interloper
interlude
intermarriage
intermarry

intermediacy
intermediary
intermediate
intermediately
intermediateness
intermediation
intermediator
interment
intermesh
intermezzo (pl ~zzi,
　~os)
interminable
interminableness
interminably
intermingle
intermission
intermit (~tted, ~tting)
intermittence
intermittency
intermittent
intermittently
intermix
intermixable
intermixture
intermodal
intern
internal
internalisation (or ~iz~)
internalise (or ~ize)
internality
internally
international
internationalisation (or
　~iz~)
internationalise (or ~ize)
internationalised (or
　~ized)
internationalism
internationalist
internationally
interne
internecine
internee
internet (I~)
internment
internship
interpellate
interpellation
interpellator
interpenetrate

interpenetration
interpenetrative
interpersonal
interpersonally
interplanetary
interplay
Interpol
interpolate
interpolation
interpolative
interpolator
interpose
interposition
interpret
interpretability
interpretable
interpretation
interpretational
interpretative
interpretatively
interpreter
interpretive
interpretively
interprovincial
interracial
interracially
interregnum (pl ~na,
　~ums)
interrelate
interrelated
interrelatedness
interrelation
interrelationship
interrogate
interrogation
interrogative
interrogatively
interrogator
interrogatory
interrupt
interrupted
interrupter (or ~or)
interruptible
interruption
interruptive
interruptor (or ~er)
intersect
intersection
intersectional
intersegmental

intersegmentally
intersex
intersexual
intersexuality
interspace
interspaced
intersperse
interspersed
interspersion
interstate (*US*)
interstellar
interstice
interstitial
interstitially
intertextual
intertextuality
intertidal
intertribal
intertrigo (*pl* ~os)
intertwine
intertwinement
interurban
interval
intervene
intervener
intervening
intervenor
intervention
interventional
interventionism
interventionist
intervertebral
interview
interviewee
interviewer
intervocalic
intervocalically
interweave (interwove,
  interwoven,
  interweaving)
interwoven
intestacy
intestate
intestinal
intestine
intifada (I~)
intimacy
intimate
intimately
intimation

intimidate
intimidating
intimidatingly
intimidation
intimidator
intimidatory
intimism (*or* ~isme)
intimist
into
intolerability
intolerable
intolerableness
intolerably
intolerance
intolerant
intolerantly
intonate
intonation
intonational
intonationally
intone
intoner
in toto
intoxicant
intoxicate
intoxicated
intoxicating
intoxicatingly
intoxication
intracellular
intracellularly
intracranial
intracranially
intractability
intractable
intractableness
intractably
intramolecular
intramolecularly
intramural
intramurally
intramuscular
intramuscularly
intranet (I~)
intransigence
intransigency
intransigent
intransigently
intransitive
intransitively

intransitivity
intrauterine
intravascular
intravascularly
intravenous
intravenously
in-tray
intrench (*usu* en~)
intrepid
intrepidity
intrepidly
intricacy
intricate
intricately
intrigue
intriguer
intriguing
intriguingly
intrinsic
intrinsically
intro
introduce
introduced
introducer
introductible
introduction
introductorily
introductory
intromission
intron
introspect
introspection
introspective
introspectiveness
introversion
introversive
introvert
introverted
intrude
intruded
intruder
intrusion
intrusive
intrusively
intrusiveness
intrust (*or* en~)
intubate
intubation
intuit
intuitable

intuition
intuitional
intuitionalism
intuitionism
intuitionist
intuitive
intuitively
intuitiveness
intumesce
intumescence
intumescent
Inuit
inundate
inundated
inundation
inure
inurement
invade
invader
invaginate
invaginated
invagination
invalid
invalidate
invalidation
invalidity
invalidly
invaluable
invaluableness
invaluably
invariability
invariable
invariably
invariance
invariant
invasion
invasive
invected
invective
inveigh
inveigle
inveiglement
invent
invention
inventive
inventively
inventiveness
inventor
inventory
inventress

inverse
inversely
inversion
inversive
invert
invertebral
invertebrate
inverted
inverter
invertibility
invertible
invest
investigable
investigate
investigation
investigational
investigative
investigator
investigatory
investiture
investment
investor
inveteracy
inveterate
inveterately
inviability
inviable
invidious
invidiously
invidiousness
invigilate
invigilation
invigilator
invigorate
invigorating
invigoratingly
invigoration
invigorator
invincibility
invincible
invincibly
inviolability
inviolable
inviolably
inviolacy
inviolate
inviolately
invisibility
invisible
invisibly

invitation
invitational
invitatory
invite
invitee
inviter
inviting
invitingly
in vitro
invocation
invocatory
invoice
invoke
invoker
involuntarily
involuntariness
involuntary
involute
involuted
involution
involve
involved
involvement
invulnerability
invulnerable
invulnerably
inward
inwardly
inwardness
inwards
Io
iode
iodine
iodism
ion
Ionic *column*
ionic *compound*
ionisable (*or* ~iz~)
ionisation (*or* ~iz~)
ionise (*or* ~ize*)
ionised (*or* ~ized*)
ioniser (*or* ~iz~)
ionosphere
iota
Iowa
ipecacuanha
ipsilateral
ipso facto
Iran
Irangate

Iranian
Iraq
Iraqi (*pl* ~is)
irascibility
irascible
irascibly
irate
irately
irateness
ire
ireful
Ireland
Irenaeus
irenic (*or* eir~)
irenical (*or* eir~)
iridescence
iridescent
iridescently
iridium
iridological
iridologist
iridology
iris (*pl* irises, irides)
Irish
Irishman (*pl* ~men)
Irishness
Irishwoman (*pl* ~women)
irk
irksome
irksomely
irksomeness
iron
ironclad
ironic
ironical
ironically
ironing
ironise (*or* ~ize)
ironist
ironmonger
ironmongery
iron-on
ironstone
ironware
ironwork
irony
Iroquoian
Iroquois
irradiance
irradiant

irradiate
irradiated
irradiation
irrational
irrationalise (*or* ~ize)
irrationalism
irrationalist
irrationality
irrationally
irreclaimable
irreclaimably
irreconcilability
irreconcilable
irreconcilably
irredeemable
irredeemably
irreducibility
irreducible
irreducibly
irrefragability
irrefragable
irrefragableness
irrefragably
irrefutability
irrefutable
irrefutably
irregular
irregularity
irregularly
irrelevance
irrelevancy
irrelevant
irrelevantly
irreligion
irreligious
irreligiously
irreligiousness
irremediable
irremediably
irremissibility
irremissible
irremissibleness
irremissibly
irremovability
irremovable
irremovably
irreparability
irreparable
irreparably
irreplaceability

irreplaceable
irreplaceably
irrepressibility
irrepressible
irrepressibly
irreproachability
irreproachable
irreproachably
irresistibility
irresistible
irresistibleness
irresistibly
irresoluble
irresolute
irresolutely
irresoluteness
irresolution
irresolvable
irrespective
irrespectively
irresponsibility
irresponsible
irresponsibly
irresponsive
irresponsiveness
irretrievability
irretrievable
irretrievably
irreverence
irreverent
irreverential
irreverently
irreversibility
irreversible
irreversibleness
irreversibly
irrevocability
irrevocable
irrevocably
irrigable
irrigate
irrigation
irrigator
irritability
irritable
irritableness
irritably
irritancy
irritant
irritate

irritatedly
irritating
irritatingly
irritation
irritative
irritator
irrupt
irruption
irruptive
Isaiah
ischaemia (*or* ~hem~)
ischaemic (*or* ~hem~)
isinglass
Isis
Islam
Islamic
Islamicisation (*or* ~iz~)
Islamicise (*or* ~ize)
Islamicist
Islamisation (*or* ~iz~)
Islamise (*or* ~ize)
Islamist
island
islander
isle
islet
isobar
isobaric
isochromatic
isochronal
isochronous
isochronously
isoclinal
isocline
isocracy
isodiametric
isodiametrical
isodynamic
isoelectric
isoelectronic
isogamete
isogamous
isogamy
isogenic
isogloss
isohel
isohyet
isokinetic
isolable
isolatable

isolate
isolated
isolating
isolation
isolationism
isolationist
isolator
isomer
isomeric
isomerise (*or* ~ize)
isomerism
isometric
isometrically
isometrics
isometry
isomorph
isomorphic
isomorphism
isomorphous
isoprene
isopropanol
isopteran
isosceles
isoseismal
isoseismic
isospin
isostasy
isostatic
isotherm
isothermal
isothermally
isotonic
isotonically
isotonicity
isotope
isotopic
isotopically
isotopy
isotropic
isotropically
isotropy
Israel
Israeli
Israelite
issuant
issue
Istanbul
isthmian
isthmus (*pl* ~uses)
ital

Italian
Italianate
Italianise (*or* ~ize)
Italianism
Italianist
Italic *languages*
italic *typeface*
italicisation (*or* ~iz~)
italicise (*or* ~ize)
italics
Italy
itch
itchiness
itching
itchy
item
itemisation (*or* ~iz~)
itemise (*or* ~ize)
itemiser (*or* ~iz~)
iterate
iteration
iterative
iteratively
itineracy
itinerancy
itinerant
itinerantly
itinerary
itinerate
itineration
itself
ivoried
ivory
ivy

jab (~bbed, ~bbing)
jabber
jabberer
jabberwocky (J~)

jabiru
jacaranda
jacinth
jack
jackal
jackanapes
jackass
jackboot
jackdaw
jacket
jackfish
jackfruit
jackhammer
Jack-in-the-box
jackknife (pl ~knives)
jack-o'-lantern (J~)
jackpot
jackrabbit
jackstaff
jackstay
jack-up
Jacobean James I
Jacobian function
Jacobin club
Jacobinism
Jacobite
jaconet
jacquard
jactitation
jacuzzi (pl ~is)
jade
jaded
jadedly
jadedness
jadeite
Jaffa
jag (~gged, ~gging)
jagged
jaggedly
jaggedness
jaggy
Jaguar (tr) car
jaguar animal
jaguarundi (pl ~is)
Jah
jail (or gaol)
jailbird (or gaol~)
jailbreak (or gaol~)
jailed (or gaol~)
jailer (or gaol~)

jailhouse (or gaol~)
Jain
Jainism
Jainist
Jakarta (or Dja~)
jalap
jalapeño (or ~no; pl
  ~os)
jaleo
jalopy
jalousie
jam (~mmed, ~mming)
Jamaica
Jamaican
jamb
jambalaya
jambeau (pl ~ux, ~us)
jamboree
jammer
jammy
jangle
jangly
janissary
janitor (US)
janitorial (US)
Jansen
Jansenism
Jansenist
January
Japan country
japan (v ~nned,
  ~nning) varnish
Japanese
jape
japery
Japheth
japonica
jar (v ~rred, ~rring)
jardinière (or ~ere)
jargon
jargonise (or ~ize)
jargonistic
Jarlsberg
jarrah
jasmine
jaspé
jasper
jaundice
jaunt
jauntily

jauntiness
jaunty
Java
Javanese
javelin
jaw
jawbone
jawbreaker
jawed
jawfish
jawless
jawline
jay
jaywalk
jaywalker
jaywalking
jazz
jazzercise (J~)
jazzily
jazziness
jazzy
jealous
jealously
jealousy
jeans
jeep (J~, tr)
jeer
jeering
jehad (or ji~)
Jehoshaphat (or ~sa~)
Jehovah
Jehovist
jejune
jejunely
jejuneness
jejunum
Jekyll
jell (or gel)
jellied
jellification
jellify
jello (US)
jelly
jellyfish
jemmy
jennet
jenny
jeopardise (or ~ize)
jeopardy
Jephthah

jerboa
jeremiad
Jeremiah
Jerez
jerfalcon (*or* gyr~)
Jericho
jerk
jerked
jerker
jerkily
jerkin
jerkiness
jerky
jeroboam (J~)
jerry
jerry-build
jerry-builder
jerry-building
jerry-built
jerrycan (*or* ~ric~)
Jersey (*pl* ~eys) *cattle*
jersey (*pl* ~eys) *garment*
Jerusalem
jess
jessamine
jest
jester
Jesuit
jesuitical
jesuitically
Jesus
jet (*v* ~tted, ~tting)
jeté
jetfoil
jetliner
jetsam (*occ* ~som)
jettison
jetty
Jew
jewel
jewelled (*US* ~eled)
jeweller (*US* ~eler)
jewellery (*US* ~elry)
Jewess
Jewish
Jewishly
Jewishness
Jewry
jezebel (J~)
jib (*v* ~bbed, ~bbing)

jibber
jibe (*or* gibe)
Jiffy (*tr*) *bag*
jiffy *moment*
jig (~gged, ~gging)
jigger
jiggery-pokery
jiggle
jiggly
jigsaw
jihad (*occ* je~)
jilt
jilted
Jimmu
jingle
jingler
jingly
jingo (*pl* ~oes)
jingoism
jingoist
jingoistic
jingoistically
jinn (*or* djinn)
jinricksha (*or* ~rik~)
jinx
jinxed
jitterbug (~gged,
  ~gging)
jitteriness
jitters
jittery
jiu-jitsu (*usu* ju~)
jive
jiver
Job *biblical*
job *work*
jobbed
jobber
jobbing
jobless
joblessness
jobseeker
jobseeking
jobsworth
jockey (*n pl* ~eys)
jockstrap
jocose
jocosely
jocoseness
jocosity

jocular
jocund
jocundity
jocundly
jodhpurs
joey
jog (~gged, ~gging)
jogger
joggle
jog-trot
join
joinable
joiner
joinery
joint
jointed
jointer
jointing
jointless
jointly
jointure
joist
jojoba
joke
joker
jokey (*or* ~ky)
jokily
jokiness
jokingly
joky (*or* ~key)
jollification
jollify
jolliness
jollity
jolly
jolt
Jonah
jongleur
jonquil
Jordan
Jordanian
Jordanite
joss-stick
jostle
jot (~tted, ~tting)
jotter
jotting
joule
jounce
journal

journalese
journalise (or ~ize)
journalism
journalist
journalistically
journalistic
journey
journeyman (pl ~men)
joust
jouster
jousting
Jove
jovial
joviality
jovially
jowl
joy
joyful
joyfully
joyfulness
joyless
joylessly
joyous
joyously
joyousness
joyride (~ride, ~rode,
   ~ridden, ~riding)
joystick
jubilance
jubilant
jubilantly
jubilation
jubilee
Judaea (or ~dea)
Judaean (or ~dean)
Judah
Judaic
Judaisation (or ~za~)
Judaise (or ~ize)
Judaiser (or ~iz~)
Judaism
Judaist
Judas
judder
juddery
judge
judgement (UK, also
   ~gm~; US ~gm~, occ
   ~gem~)
judgemental (or ~gm~)

judgementally (or
   ~gm~)
judgment see judgement
judicatory
judicature
judicial
judicially
judiciary
judicious
judiciously
judiciousness
judo
judogi
judoist
judoka
jug
jugful
jugged
Juggernaut Hindu chariot
juggernaut heavy lorry
jugging
juggle
juggler
jugglery
juggling
jugular
jugulate
juice
juiced
juiceless
juicer
juicily
juiciness
juicy
ju-jitsu (or jiu~, ~jutsu)
juju (or ju-~)
jujube
jukebox
julep
Julian
julienne
July
jumble
jumbo
jump
jumper
jumpily
jumpiness
jumping
jumpsuit

jumpy
junction
juncture
June
Jung
Jungian
jungle
jungled
jungly
junior
juniority
juniper
junk
junket
junkie (or ~ky) addict
junky little value
junkyard
junta
Jupiter
Jurassic
juridical
juridically
jurisdiction
jurisdictional
jurisdictionally
jurisprudence
jurisprudent
jurisprudential
jurisprudentially
jurist
juristic
juror
jury
just
justice
justiciable
justiciar
justiciary
justifiability
justifiable
justifiableness
justifiably
justification
justifier
justify
jut (~tted, ~tting)
jute
juvenescence
juvenescent
juvenile

juvenilia
juxtapose
juxtaposition
juxtapositional

Kaaba (*occ* C~)
Kabbala (k~; *or* Kaba~,
  ~lah, Qab~, Qabba~,
  Cab~, Cabba~)
Kabbalist (k~; *see*
  Kabbala *for other*
  spellings)
Kabbalistic (k~; *see*
  Kabbala *for other*
  spellings)
kabob (*or* ke~)
kaboodle (*or* ca~)
kabuki
Kabul
Kaddish (*occ* Qa~)
kaffir (*occ* kafir, K~)
kaffiyeh (*or* ke~)
Kafkaesque
kaftan (*or* ca~)
kagoule (*or* ca~)
kahuna (K~)
kaiser (K~)
kakemono (*pl* ~nos)
kakiemon (K~)
kala-azar
Kalahari
kalashnikov (K~)
kale (*occ* kail)
kaleidoscope
kaleidoscopic
kaleidoscopically
Kali *goddess*
kali *plant*
kaliph (*or* khalif, *usu*
  caliph)

kalong
kalsomine (*or* calci~)
Kama Sutra (*or*
  Kamasutra)
kame
kamikaze
Kampala
kampong
Kampuchea
kana
Kanchenjunga (*or*
  Kang~, *occ* Kinchin~)
Kandahar
kangaroo
kangha
kanji
Kansas
Kant
Kantian
Kantianism
kanuka
kanzu
kaolin
kaolinise (*or* ~ize)
kaolinite
kapellmeister (K~)
kapok
kappa
kaput
karabiner (*or* ca~)
Karachi
karahi (*pl* ~is)
Karakorum
karakul (*occ* K~, caracul)
karanga
karaoke
karat (*usu* ca~)
karate
karateka
karma (K~)
karmic
karmically
karst
kart
karting
karyology
kasbah (*or* ca~, *occ* K~,
  C~)
Kashmir
Kashmiri

kata
katabatic
katakana
katana
Kathmandu
katydid
katzenjammer
Kauai
kaumatua
kauri
kava (*or* ca~)
Kawasaki
kayak
Kazakh
Kazakhstan
kazoo
kea
Keats
Keatsian
kebab (*US occ* ka~)
kedge
kedgeree
keel
keelboat
keeled
keelhaul
keelless
keema
Keemun (*or* Kee-~, K~
  M~)
keen
keenly
keenness
keep (*kept*)
keepable
keeper
keepership
keep-fit
keepsake
keeshond
keffiyeh (*or* ka~)
keftedes
keg
kelim (*or* ki~)
Kells
keloid (*occ* che~)
kelp
kelpfish
kelpie
kelvin (K~)

kemp
kempt
kendo
kendoist
kennel (~lled, ~lling; US ~led, ~ling)
keno (K~)
Kent
Kentuckian
Kentucky
Kenya
Kenyan
kepi (pl ~is)
keratin
keratinisation (or ~iz~)
keratinise (or ~ize)
keratinocyte
keratinous
keratitis
keratosis (pl ~oses)
kerb (UK; ! curb v) roadside step
kerbside (US curb~)
kerbstone (US curb~)
kerchief
kerf
kerfuffle
Kerguelen
Kermadec
kermes
kernel
kerosene (occ ~sine)
kersey
kerseymere
kestrel
Keswick
ketch
ketchup (US catsup)
ketone
ketosis
kettle
kettledrum
kettledrummer
kettleful
Kevlar (tr; also k~)
kewpie (also cupie) doll
key (pl keys)
keyboard
keyboarder
keyboardist

keyholder
keyhole
Keynesian
keynote
keypad
keypunch
keypuncher
keystone
keystroke
keyword
khadi (or khaddar)
khaki (pl ~is)
khalif (or kaliph, usu caliph)
khan (K~)
khanate
Khartoum
khat (or qat)
Khedive
khir
Khmer
Khoisan
Khomeini
Khrushchev
Khyber
ki see chi
kibble
kibbutz (pl ~zim)
kibbutznik
kibe
kiblah (or ~la, keb~, qib~)
kibosh (occ ky~)
kick
kickback
kick-boxer
kick-boxing
kicked
kicker
kicking
kick-off
kickstand
kick-start
kid (~dded, ~dding)
kidder
Kidderminster
kiddush (K~)
kiddy (or ~die)
kidnap (~pped, ~pping; US also ~ped, ~ping)

kidnapper (US occ ~aper)
kidney (pl ~eys)
kidult
Kiel
Kierkegaardian
Kiev
Kigali
kilim (occ ke~)
kill
killer
killick
killing
killingly
killjoy
kiln
kilo
kilobit
kilobyte
kilocalorie
kilogram (occ ~mme)
kilohertz
kilojoule
kilolitre (US ~ter)
kilometre (US ~ter)
kiloton (occ ~nne)
kilovolt
kilovoltage
kilowatt
kilowattage
kilt
kilted
kimono (pl ~os)
kimonoed
kin
kinaesthesia (or nes~)
kinaesthetic (or ~nes~)
kind
kindergarten
kindergartener
kind-hearted
kind-heartedly
kind-heartedness
kindle
kindler
kindliness
kindling
kindly
kindness
kindred

kine
kinematics
kinesics
kinesiological
kinesiologist
kinesiology
kinesis (*pl* ~eses)
kinetic
kinetically
kinetics
kinetoscope
kinfolk (*or* kins~)
king (K~)
kingcup (*UK*)
kingdom
kingfisher
kingless
kinglike
kingliness
kingly
kingpin
kingship
king-size
king-sized
kingsnake
Kingston
kink
kinkajou
kinkily
kinkiness
kinky
kinless
kino
kinsfolk (*or* kinf~)
Kinshasa
kinship
kinsman (*pl* ~men)
kinswoman (*pl*
~women)
kiosk
kip (~pped, ~pping)
kippah (*or* kipa, ~ppa)
kipper
Kir
Kiribati
kirk
kirkyard
kirpan
kirsch
kirtle

Kislev (*occ* ~ew)
kismet
kiss (~ssed, ~ssing)
kissable
kiss-curl
kisser
kissogram (*occ* kissa~)
kit (~tted, ~tting)
kitbag
kitchen
kitchenette
kitchenware
kite
kite-flying
kith
kitsch
kitschiness
kitschy
kitten
kittenish
kittenishly
kittenishness
kittiwake
kitty
Kiwanian (*US*)
Kiwanis (*US*)
Kiwi *New Zealander*
kiwi (*pl* ~is) *bird*
Klansman
klaxon
Kleenex (*tr*)
kleptomania
kleptomaniac
kleptoparasite
klezmer (*pl* ~morim)
klipspringer
Klondike
klutz (*US*)
klutziness
klutzy
klystron
knack
knacker
knackered
knackwurst (*or* knock~)
knaidel (*or* knei~, *pl*
knaidlach)
knapsack
knapweed
knave

knavery
knavish
knavishly
knavishness
knead
kneadable
kneader
knee (kneed)
kneeboard
kneeboarder
kneeboarding
kneecap (~pped,
~pping)
knee-deep
knee-high
kneehole
knee-jerk
kneel (knelt *or*
kneeled)
kneeler
kneepad
knees-up
knell
knelt
Knesset
knickerbockers
knickered
knickerless
knickers
knick-knack
knife (*pl* knives; *v*
knifed, knifing)
knifepoint
knife-thrower
knife-throwing
knight
knighthood
knightliness
knightly
knish
knit (knitted *or* knit,
knitting)
knitter
knitwear
knob
knobble
knobbly
knobkerrie
knock
knockabout

knock-back
knock-down
knocker
knock-on
knockout
knoll
knot (~tted, ~tting)
knothole
knottily
knottiness
knotty
knotwork
know (knew, known)
knowable
know-all
know-how
knowingly
knowingness
know-it-all
knowledge
knowledgeability (*occ* ~dga~)
knowledgeable (*occ* ~dga~)
knowledgeably (*occ* ~dga~)
known
knuckle
knuckle-bone
knuckleduster
knucklehead
koala
koan
kobold
Kodiak
koel
Koh-i-noor
kohl
koi
koine (*or* ~né)
kola (*usu* co~)
kolo (*pl* ~os)
Komodo
Komondor
kookaburra
kookily
kookiness
kooky
kopek (*or* ~peck, copeck)

kopje (*South Africa* koppie)
Koran (*or* Qu~, Qu'~)
Koranic (*or* Qu~)
Korea
Korean
korfball
korma
kosher
Kosovo
koto
Kowloon
kowtow
kowtower
kraal
krait
Krakatoa
kraken
Kremlin
Kremlinologist
Kremlinology
krill (*occ* kril)
kris (*occ* creese)
Krishna
Krishnaism
krugerrand (K~)
krypton
kudos
kudzu
kugel
kukri (*pl* ~is)
kumite
kumquat (*also* cu~)
Kurd
Kurdish
Kurdistan
kurgan
kurta (*or* ~tha)
Kuwait
Kuwaiti
kybosh (*usu* ki~)
Kyrgyz (*or* Kirghiz)
Kyrgyzstan (*also* Kirgizstan, Kirghizia)
Kyrie

L

la (*or* lah) *note*
lab
labefaction
label (~lled, ~lling; *US* ~led, ~ling)
labial
labialise (*or* ~ize)
labially
labile
lability
labium (*pl* ~ia)
laboratory
laborious
laboriously
laboriousness
labour (*US* ~or)
laboured (*US* ~or~)
labourer (*US* ~or~)
labouring (*US* ~or~)
Labrador *territory*
labrador *dog*
laburnum
labyrinth
labyrinthian
labyrinthine
labyrinthitis
lac
laccolith
laccolithic
lace
laced
lacemaker
lacemaking
lacerate
lacerated
lacerating
laceration
lacewing
lacework

laches
lachrymal (*or* lacr~)
lachrymose
lachrymosely
lachrymosity
lacily
laciness
lacing
lack
lackadaisical
lackadaisically
lackey (*pl* ~eys)
lacking
lacklustre (*US* ~ter)
laconic
laconically
laconicism
lacquer
lacquered
lacquerer
lacquerware
lacquerwork
lacrimal (*or* lachr~)
lacrosse
lactarium (*pl* ~ia)
lactase
lactate
lactation
lactational
lacteal
lactescent
lactic
lactiferous
lactometer
lactoprotein
lactose
lacuna (*pl* ~ae, ~as)
lacustrine
lacy
lad
ladder
laddered
laddish
laddishness
lade
laden
la-di-da (*or* lah-di-dah)
lading
ladle
lady

ladybird (*UK*)
ladybug (*US*)
ladyhood
lady-in-waiting (*pl*
    ladies~)
lady-killer
ladylike
ladyship (L~)
lag (~gged, ~gging)
lagan
lager
laggard
laggardly
laggardness
lagged
lagger
lagging
lagomorph
lagoon
lah (*or* la)
laical
laically
laicisation (*or* ~iz~)
laicise (*or* ~ize)
laicism
laicity
laid
lain
lair
laird
lairdship
laisser-faireism
laissez-faire
laissez-passer
laity
lake
lakeside
Lakshmi
Lalique
lallation
lam (~mmed, ~mming)
lama
Lamaism
Lamaist
lamb
lambada
lambaste (*or* ~st)
lambda
lambency
lambent

lambently
lambert
lambing
lambskin
lambswool
lame
lamé
lamella (*pl* ~ae)
lamellate
lamellibranch (*pl* ~chs)
lamelliform
lamely
lameness
lament
lamentable
lamentably
lamentation
lamented
lamia (*pl* ~ae, ~as)
lamina (*pl* ~inae)
laminal
laminar
laminate
laminated
lamination
laminator
laminectomy
laminitis
laminose
Lammas
lammergeier (*or* ~eyer)
lamp
lampblack
lampless
lamplight
lamplighter
lampoon
lampooner
lampoonery
lampoonist
lamprey
lampshade
Lancashire
Lancastrian
lance
lancelet
Lancelot (*or* Laun~)
lanceolate
lancer
lancet

lateralise

lanceted
land
landau
landed
lander
landfall
landfill
landform
landholder
landholding
landing
landlady
landless
landlessness
landline
landlocked
landlord
landlordism
landlubber
landmark
landmass
landmine
landowner
landownership
landowning
Landrover (*tr*)
landscape
landscaped
landscaping
landscapist
landslide
landward
landwards
lane
langosta
langouste
langoustine
language
languid
languidly
languidness
languish
languisher
languishing
languishingly
languishment
languor
languorous
languorously
langur

lank
lankily
lankiness
lankly
lankness
lanky
lanner
lanolin
lantern
lanternfish
lanthanide
lanthanum
lanugo
lanyard
Laodicean
Laos
lap (~pped, ~pping)
laparoscope
laparoscopic
laparoscopically
laparoscopy
laparotomy
lapdog
lapel
lapelled
lapful
lapidary
Lapland
Lapp
lappet
lapse
lapsed
laptop
lapwing
larboard
larcenist
larcenous
larceny
larch
lard
larded
larder
lardon (*or* ~doon)
large
largely
largeness
large-scale
largesse (*or* ~ess)
larghetto
largish

largo
lariat
lark
larkiness
larkspur
larva (*pl* ~ae)
larval
larvicide
laryngeal
laryngectomy
laryngitic
laryngitis
laryngologist
laryngology
laryngoscope
laryngoscopy
laryngotomy
larynx (*pl* ~xes, ~nges)
lasagne (*or* ~na)
lascivious
lasciviously
lasciviousness
laser
lash
lashed
lasher
lashes
lashing
lass
lassitude
lasso (*pl* ~oes, ~os)
last
lasting
lastingly
lastingness
lastly
latch
latchkey
late
latecomer
lateen
lately
latency
lateness
latent
latently
later
lateral
lateralisation (*or* ~iz~)
lateralise (*or* ~ize)

laterality
laterally
latest
latex (*pl* ~ices, ~xes)
lath
lathe
lather
lathery
lathyrism
Latin
Latinate
Latinisation (*or* ~iz~)
Latinise (*or* ~ize)
Latinism
Latinist
Latinity
latish
latitude
latitudinal
latitudinally
latitudinarian
latitudinarianism
latrine
latte
latter
latterly
lattice
latticed
latticework
Latvia
laud
laudability
laudable
laudably
laudanum
laudatory
lauds
laugh
laughable
laughably
laugher
laughing
laughingly
laughter
launch
launcher
launder
laundered
launderette (*or* ~drette)
laundress

laundromat
laundry
Laurasia
laureate
laureateship
laurel (~lled, ~lling; *US* ~led, ~ling)
laurels
lava
lavabo (*pl* ~os)
lavage
lavatorial
lavatory
lave
lavender
laver
lavish
lavishly
lavishness
law
law-abiding
lawbreaker
lawbreaking
lawcourt
lawful
lawfully
lawfulness
lawgiver
lawless
lawlessly
lawlessness
lawmaker
lawman (*pl* ~men)
lawn
lawnmower
lawrencium
lawsuit
lawyer
lax
laxative
laxity
laxly
laxness
lay (laid)
layabout
lay-by (*pl* ~bys)
layer
layered
layering
layette

layman (*pl* ~men)
lay-off
layout
lay-up
laywoman (*pl* ~women)
laze
lazily
laziness
lazurite
lazy
lazybones
lea
leach
lead (led)
leaded
leaden
leadenly
leadenness
leader
leadership
lead-in
leading
lead-off
lead-up
leaf (*pl* leaves)
leafage
leafed
leafiness
leafless
leafy
league
leak
leakage
leakiness
leaky
lean
leaning
leant
lean-to
leap (leaped *or* lept)
leaper
leap-frog
leaping
learn (learned *or* learnt)
learnèd (*or* ~ed)
    scholarly
learner
learning
lease
leaseback

leasehold
leaseholder
leash
least
leastways
leastwise
leather
leatheriness
leathery
leave
leaven
leaving
Lebanon
lebensraum (L~)
lech
lecher
lecherous
lecherously
lecherousness
lechery
lecithin
lectern
lectin
lectionary
lector
lecture
lecturer
lectureship
ledge
ledger
lee
leech
leek
leer
leering
leeringly
leeward
leeway
left
left-handed
left-handedly
left-handedness
left-hander
leftover
leg
legacy
legal
legalese
legalisation (or ~iz~)
legalise (or ~ize)

legalism
legalist
legality
legally
legate
legatee
legation
legato
legend
legendary
legerdemain
leggings
leggy
leghorn
legibility
legible
legibly
legion
legionary
legionnaire (L~)
legislate
legislation
legislative
legislator
legislatorial
legislature
legit
legitimacy
legitimate
legitimateness
legitimisation (or ~iz~)
legitimise (or ~ize)
legless
leglessly
leglessness
Lego (tr)
legroom
legume
leguminous
Leicester
leishmaniasis
leisure
leisureliness
leisurely
leitmotif (or ~tiv)
lemma (pl ~as, ~mata)
lemmatise (or ~ize)
lemming
lemon
lemonade

lemur
lend (lent)
lender
lending
length
lengthen
lengthiness
lengthways
lengthwise
lengthy
lenience
leniency
lenient
Leninism
Leninist
lenity
lens
Lent
Lenten
lenticle
lenticular
lenticularly
lentil
lento
Leo
leonine
leopard
leopardess
leotard
leper
lepidoptera (L~)
lepidopterist
lepidopterous
leprechaun
leprosy
leprous
lepton
leptosomatic
leptosome
leptosomic
lesbian
lesbianism
lese-majesty
lesion
Lesotho
less
lessee
lessen (! lesson) reduce
lesser
lesson (! lessen) teaching

lest
let
lethal
lethally
lethargic
lethargically
lethargy
Lethe
letter
lettered
letterhead
lettering
letterpress
lettuce
let-up
leucine
leucoblast (or ~ko~)
leucocyte (or ~ko~)
leucoma (US ~ko~)
leucorrhoea (US ~rhea)
leucotomy (or ~ko~)
leukaemia (or ~kem~)
levee
level
leveller (US ~eler)
levelling (US ~eling)
lever
leverage
leveret
leviathan (L~)
levirate
Levis (tr)
levitate
levitation
levity
levy
lewd
lewdly
lewdness
lewisia
lewisite
lexeme
lexical
lexicographer
lexicographic
lexicographical
lexicography
lexicological
lexicology
lexicon

lexis
ley
liability
liable
liaise
liaison
liana
liar
libation
libel (~lled, ~lling; US
   ~led, ~ling)
libeller (US ~eler)
libellous (US ~elous)
libellously (US ~elously)
liberal
liberalisation (or ~iz~)
liberalise (or ~ize)
liberaliser (or ~iz~)
liberalising (or ~iz~)
liberalism
liberalist
liberalistic
liberality
liberate
liberated
liberation
liberator
Liberia
libertarian
libertarianism
libertine
libertinism
liberty
libidinal
libidinous
libidinously
libidinousness
libido
Libra
librarian
librarianship
library
librettist
libretto (pl ~tti, ~os)
Libya
Libyan
lice
licence (UK n; US ~nse)
license (UK v)
licensed

licensee
licentiate
licentious
licentiously
licentiousness
lichee (or litch~, ly~)
lichen
lichenology
lich-gate (or ly~)
licit
lick
licking
licorice (UK liquo~)
lid
lido
lie (lay, laid, lain, lying)
   position
lie (lied, lying) false
Liechtenstein
lied (L~; pl ~er)
lie-in
lien
lieu
lieutenancy
lieutenant
life (pl lives)
lifebelt
lifeblood
lifeboat
lifebuoy
lifeguard
lifeless
lifelessly
lifelessness
lifelike
lifelikeness
lifeline
lifelong
lifer
lifesaver
lifesaving
life-size
life-sized
lifestyle
lifetime
lift
lifter
lifting
lift-off
ligament

ligand
ligase
ligation
ligature
lige
liger
light
lighted
lighten
lightening
lighter
lighthouse
lighthousekeeper
lighting
lightless
lightly
lightness
lightning
lightproof
lightship
lightweight
light-year
ligneous
lignification
lignify
lignite
lignocaine
lignum
likable (*or* likea~)
likableness (*or* likea~)
like
likeable (*or* lika~)
likeableness (*or* lika~)
likelihood
likely
like-minded
liken
likeness
likewise
liking
lilac
lilliputian (L~)
lilt
lily
limber
limbic
limbless
limbo (L~)
lime
limeade

limekiln
limelight
limerick
limestone
limit
limitation
limited
limitedly
limitedness
limiter
limitless
limitlessly
limitlessness
limnological
limnologist
limnology
limo (*pl* ~os)
limousine
limp
limpet
limpid
limpidity
limpidly
limpidness
limping
limpingly
limpness
limy
linchpin
Lincoln
lincomycin
linctus
linden
line
lineage
lineal
lineament
linear
linearity
lineation
lined
linen
line-out
liner
linesman (*pl* ~men)
line-up
lingam
linger
lingerer
lingerie

lingering
lingeringly
lingo
lingual
lingually
linguini
linguist
linguistic
linguistically
linguistician
linguistics
liniment
lining
link
linkage
linked
linkman (*pl* ~men)
links
link-up
Linnaean
linnet
lino
linocut
linoleum
Linotype (*tr*)
linseed
lint
lintel
lion
lioness
lionise (*or* ~ize)
lip
lipid
lipliner
lipogram
lipoid
lipoprotein
liposome
liposuction
lipped
lipsalve
lip-service
lipstick
lip-synch (*or* ~sync)
liquefaction
liquefactive
liquefied
liquefier
liquefy (*or* ~uify)
liqueur

liquid
liquidate
liquidation
liquidator
liquidise (or ~ize)
liquidity
liquify (or ~uefy)
liquor
liquorice (US lico~)
lisle
lisp
lisping
lispingly
lissom
lissomness
list
listed
listen
listener
listening
listeria
listeriosis
listing
listless
listlessly
listlessness
Liszt
lit
litany
litchee (or lichee, lychee)
liter (US; UK ~tre)
literacy
literal
literalise (or ~ize)
literalism
literalist
literalistic
literality
literally
literariness
literary
literate
literati
literature
lithe
lithely
litheness
lithium
lithograph
lithographer

lithographic
lithographically
lithography
lithological
lithologist
lithology
lithophyte
lithophytic
lithosphere
lithotomy
lithotripsy
lithotripter (or ~or)
lithotrity
Lithuania
litigant
litigate
litigation
litigator
litigious
litigiousness
litmus
litotes
litre (UK; US ~ter)
litter
littering
little
littleness
littoral
liturgical
liturgically
liturgiology
liturgy
live
liveability (or liva~)
liveable (or liva~)
live-in
livelihood
liveliness
livelong
lively
liven
liver
liverish
liverishness
Liverpool
Liverpudlian
liverwort
livery
livestock
livid

lividity
lividly
lividness
living
lizard
llama
loach
load
loaded
loader
loading
loadstar (or lode~)
loadstone (or lode~)
loaf (pl loaves)
loafer
loam
loaminess
loamy
loan
loanword
loath (adj; or loth)
loathe (v)
loather
loathing
loathsome
loathsomeness
lob
lobate
lobby
lobbyer
lobbying
lobbyist
lobe
lobectomy
lobed
lobelia
lobotomise (or ~ize)
lobotomy
lobster
lobule
local
locale
localisation (or ~iz~)
localise (or ~ize)
localism
locality
locate
location
locative
locator

loch (*Scotland*; L~ *in titles*; *Irish* lough)
lock
lockable
lockage
locker
locket
locking
lockjaw
lockout
locksmith
lock-up
locomotion
locomotive
locomotor
loculus (*pl* ~li)
locum
locus (*pl* ~ci)
locust
locution
locutor
locutory
lode
lodestar (*or* load~)
lodestone (*or* load~)
lodge
lodgement
lodger
lodging
loess
loft
loftiness
lofty
log
loganberry
logarithm
logarithmic
logarithmically
logbook
logged
logger
loggerhead
loggia
logging
logic
logical
logicality
logically
logician
logistic

logistical
logistically
logistics
logo (*pl* ~os)
logocentric
logocentrism
logogram
logograph
logorrhoea (*US* ~hea)
logos (L~)
loincloth
loins
loiter
loiterer
loll
Lollard
lolling
lollingly
lollipop
lolly
London
lone
loneliness
lonely
lonelyhearts
loner
lonesome
long
longboat
longbow
long-distance
longevity
long-haired
longhand
longhorn
longing
longish
longitude
longitudinal
long-lasting
long-legged
long-lived
long-playing
long-range
long-running
longshore
long-sighted
long-standing
long-suffering
long-term

longtime
longueur
long-winded
long-windedness
Lonsdale
loo
look
lookalike
look-in
looking
looking-glass
lookout
loom
looming
loon
loop
looper
loophole
loose
loose-leaf
loosely
loosen
looseness
loosestrife
loot
looter
looting
lop (~pped, ~pping)
lope
lop-eared
lopsided
lopsidedness
loquacious
loquaciously
loquaciousness
loquacity
loquat
loran (L~)
lord (L~)
lordliness
lordly
lordosis
lordotic
lordship (L~)
lore
Lorelei
lorgnette
lorikeet
loris
lorry

lose
loser
losing
loss
lost
lot
loth (*or* loath)
Lothario
lotion
lottery
lotto
lotus
loud
loudish
loudly
loudness
loudspeaker
lough (*Ireland; Scotland* loch)
lounge
loupe
lour
louring
louse (*pl* lice)
lousily
lousiness
lousy
lout
loutishly
loutishness
louvre (*US* ~ver)
lovable (*or* lovea~)
lovableness (*or* lovea~)
lovage
love
loveable (*or* lova~)
loveableness (*or* lova~)
lovebird
loveless
lovelessness
loveliness
lovelorn
lovely
lover
lovesick
lovesickness
lovey-dovey
loving
low
lowbrow

lowdown
lower
low-key
lowland
low-life
lowliness
lowly
lowness
loyal
loyalist
loyalty
lozenge
lubber
lubberly
lubricant
lubricate
lubrication
lubricator
lucent
lucid
lucidity
lucidly
lucidness
Lucifer
luckiness
luckless
lucky
lucrative
lucre
Luddite
ludic
ludicrous
ludicrously
ludicrousness
ludo (L~)
luff
lug (~gged, ~gging)
luge (luged, luging *or* lugeing)
luggage
lugger
lugubriosity
lugubrious
lugubriously
lugubriousness
lugworm
lukewarm
lukewarmly
lull
lullaby

lumbago
lumbar
lumber
lumbering
lumberjack
lumberjacket
lumen
luminance
luminary
luminescence
luminescent
luminosity
luminous
luminously
luminousness
lummox
lump
lumpectomy
lumpily
lumpiness
lumpish
lumpishness
lumpy
lunacy
lunar
lunate
lunatic
lunch
luncheon
lunchtime
lunette
lung
lunge
lungfish
lungwort
lupin
lupine
lupus (*pl* ~uses, ~pi)
lurch
lurcher
lure
lurgi (*or* ~gy)
lurid
luridly
luridness
lurk
luscious
lush
lushly
lushness

lust
lustful
lustfully
lustfulness
lustiness
lustration
lustre (*US* ~ter)
lustrous
lustrously
lute
lutein
Lutheran
Lutheranism
luvvy (*or* ~vie)
Luxembourg (*or* ~burg)
luxuriance
luxuriant
luxuriantly
luxurious
luxuriously
luxury
lycanthrope
lycanthropy
lyceum (L~)
lychee (*or* li~, litch~)
lychgate
lycra (L~, *tr*)
lye
lying
lymph
lymphatic
lymphoblast
lymphocyte
lymphoma (*pl* ~as,
  ~mata)
lymphomatosis
lynch
lynx
lyophilic
lyophobic
lyre
lyrebird
lyric
lyrical
lyrically
lyricise (*or* ~ize)
lyricism
lyricist
lysergic
lysine

lysis
lysosome
lysozyme

ma'am
macabre
macadam
macadamed
macadamia
macadamise (*or* ~ize)
macadamised (*or* ~ized)
Macao (*or* ~cau)
macaque
macaroni
macaronic
macaronics
macaroon
macaw
mace
Macedonia
macerate
maceration
macerator
mach (M~) *number*
machete
Machiavelli
Machiavellian
machicolate
machicolated
machicolation
machinability
machinable
machinate
machination
machinator
machine
machined
machine-gun (~nned,
  ~nning)
machinery

machinist
machismo
macho (*pl* ~os)
mackerel
mackintosh (*or* maci~)
macramé
macro (*pl* ~os)
macrobiotic
macrobiotics
macrocephalic
macrocephalous
macrocephaly
macrocosm
macrocosmic
macrocosmically
macrocyclic
macroeconomic
macroeconomics
macroeconomy
macroevolution
macroevolutionary
macromolecular
macromolecule
macron
macronutrient
macrophage
macrophotography
macrophyte
macropod
macroscopic
macroscopically
macula (*pl* ~ae)
macular
maculate
maculation
mad (~dder, ~ddest)
Madagascar
madam (M~)
madcap
madden
maddened
maddening
maddeningly
madder
madding
made
Madeira
madeleine
mademoiselle (M~)
made-up

madhouse
madison (M~)
madly
madman (pl ~men)
madness
madonna (M~)
madras
Madrid
madrigal
madrigalian
madrigalist
madwoman (pl ~women)
maelstrom
maenad
maenadic
maestoso
maestro (pl ~ri, ~os)
mafia (M~)
mafioso (M~; pl ~si, ~sos)
magazine
Magdalenian
Magellanic
magenta
maggot
maggoty
Maghrib (or ~reb)
magi (M~)
magic (~cked, ~cking)
magical
magicality
magically
magician
Maginot
magisterial
magisterially
magisterium
magistracy
magistral
magistrate (M~)
magistrature
maglev
magma
magmatic
magmatism
magnanimity
magnanimous
magnanimously
magnanimousness

magnate
magnesia
magnesian
magnesite
magnesium
magnet
magnetic
magnetically
magnetisable (or ~iz~)
magnetisation (or ~iz~)
magnetise (or ~ize)
magnetism
magnetite
magneto (pl ~os)
magnetograph
magnetometer
magnetometry
magnetomotive
magnetosphere
magnetospheric
magnetron
magnifiable
Magnificat
magnification
magnificence
magnificent
magnificently
magnifier
magnify
magnifying
magniloquence
magniloquent
magniloquently
magnitude
magnolia
magnox (M~)
magnum
magpie
magus (M~; pl ~gi)
Magyar
Mahabharata
maharaja (or ~jah)
maharani (or ~nee)
maharishi (M~)
mahatma (M~)
Mahayana
Mahdi
mah-jong (or ~ngg)
mahlstick (or maul~)
mahogany

mahout
maid
maiden
maidenhair
maidenhead
maidenhood
maidenly
maidservant
mail
mailable
mailbag
mailboat
mailbomb
mailbox
mailer
mailing
mailmerge (MailMerge, tr)
mailshot
maim
maimed
maiming
main
mainbrace
Maine USA
mainframe
mainland
mainlander
mainline
mainliner
mainly
mainmast
mainsail
mainsheet
mainspring
mainstay
mainstream
maintain
maintainability
maintainable
maintained
maintainer
maintenance
maiolica (or majo~)
maisonette (or ~onne~)
maize
majestic
majestically
majesty (M~)
major (! mayor) *great*

Majorca
major-domo (*pl* ~os)
majorette
major-general
majority
majorly
majuscular
majuscule
makable (*or* make~)
make
makeable (*or* maka~)
make-believe
make-or-break
makeover
maker
makeshift
make-up
makeweight
making
mako (*pl* ~os)
malabsorption
malachite
malacological
malacologist
malacology
maladaptation
maladapted
maladaptive
maladjusted
maladjustment
maladminister
maladministration
maladroit
maladroitly
maladroitness
malady
Malagasy
malaise
malapert
malapropism
malapropos
malaria
malarial
malariological
malariologist
malariology
malarious
malarkey (*or* ~ky)
Malawi
Malawian

Malay
Malayan
Malaysia
Malaysian
malcontent
malcontented
maldevelopment
maldistributed
maldistribution
Maldives
Maldivian
male
malediction
maledictive
maledictory
malefaction
malefactor
malefic
malefically
maleficence
maleficent
maleic
maleness
malevolence
malevolent
malevolently
malfeasance
malfeasant
malformation
malfunction
Mali
malic
malice
malicious
maliciously
maliciousness
malign
malignancy
malignant
malignantly
maligner
malignity
malignly
malinger
malingerer
mall
mallard
malleability
malleable
malleableness

malleably
mallet
malleus (*pl* ~ei)
mallow
malm
malnourished
malnourishment
malnutrition
malocclusion
malodorous
malodour (*US* ~or)
malperformance
malpractice (*US* ~ise)
malt
Malta
maltase
malted
Maltese
Malthusian
maltiness
malting
maltodextrin
maltose
maltreat
maltreated
maltreater
maltreatment
maltster
malty
Malvern
malversation
mamba
mambo
mamilla (*or* mamm~)
mamillary (*or*
  mamm~)
mamillated (*or*
  mamm~)
mammal
mammalian
mammalogist
mammalogy
mammary
mammogram
mammograph
mammography
mammon (M~)
mammonish
mammonism
mammoth

man (*n pl* ~men; *v*
  ~nned, ~nning)
manacle
manage
manageability
manageable
manageableness
manageably
managed
management
manager
manageress
managerial
managerially
managership
managing
mañana (*or* manana)
man-at-arms (*pl* men~)
manatee
Manchester
Manchu
Manchuria
manciple
mandala
Mandalay
mandamus
Mandarin *China*
mandarin *fruit*
mandate
mandated
mandatorily
mandatory
Mandela
Mandelbrot
mandible
mandolin (*or* ~ine)
mandolinist
mandragora
mandrake
mandrel (*or* ~ril)
mandrill
mane
man-eater
man-eating
maned
manège (*or* ~ege)
maneless
manes
maneuver (*US; UK*
  manoeuvre)

manful
manfully
manfulness
manganate
manganese
mange
mangel-wurzel
manger
mangetout
mangey (*or* ~gy)
manginess
mangle
mangled
mango (*pl* ~oes, ~os)
mangosteen
mangrove
mangy (*or* ~gey)
manhandle
manhandling
Manhattan
manhole
manhood
man-hour
manhunt
mania
maniac
maniacal
maniacally
Manichaean (*or* ~che~)
Manichaeanism (*or*
  ~che~)
Manichaeism (*or*
  ~che~)
manicure
manicured
manicurist
manifest
manifestable
manifestation
manifestly
manifesto (*pl* ~os, ~oes)
manifold
manifoldly
manifoldness
manikin (*or* manni~;
  ! mannequin) *teaching
  model*
Manila *city*
manila (*or* ~lla) *paper*
manioc

manipulability
manipulable
manipulatable
manipulate
manipulation
manipulative
manipulatively
manipulativeness
manipulator
manipulatory
mankind
manliness
manly
man-made
manna
manned
mannequin
  (! manniquin) *fashion
  model*
manner
mannered
mannerism (M~)
mannerist (M~)
manneristic
manneristically
mannerless
mannerliness
mannerly
mannikin (*or* mani~;
  ! mannequin) *teaching
  model*
manning
mannish
mannishly
mannishness
manoeuvrability (*US*
  ~neuv~)
manoeuvrable (*US*
  ~neuv~)
manoeuvre (*US*
  ~neuver*)
manoeuvrer (*US*
  ~neuv~)
man-of-war (*or* ~o'-war;
  pl men~)
manometer
manometric
manometry
manor
manorial

manpower
manqué
mansard
manse
manservant (*pl*
  menservants)
mansion
mansize (*or* ~zed)
manslaughter
mansuetude
manta
manteau
mantel (! mantle)
  mantelpiece
mantelpiece
mantelshelf (*pl*
  ~shelves)
mantilla
mantis
mantissa
mantle (! mantel) *cloak*
mantra
mantrap
mantric
manual
manufacturability
manufacturable
manufacturably
manufacture
manufactured
manufacturer
manufacturing
manumission
manumit (~itted,
  ~itting)
manumitter
manure
manured
manuscript
Manx
Manxman (*pl* ~men)
Manxwoman (*pl*
  ~women)
many
Maoism
Maoist
Maori
map (~pped, ~pping)
maple
mapless

map-maker
map-making
mappable
mapper
mapping
map-read
map-reader
map-reading
maquette
maquillage
maquis (M~)
mar (~rred, ~rring)
marabou (*or* ~out)
maraca
maraschino (*pl* ~os)
marathon
maraud
marauder
marauding
marble
marbled
marbling
marbly
marc
marcasite
marcato
march
March
marcher
marching
marchioness
mare
margarine
margarita
margin
marginal
marginalia
marginalisation (*or*
  ~iz~)
marginalise (*or* ~ize)
marginalised (*or* ~ized)
marginality
marginally
marginate
margination
margined
marguerite
Marian
Marianas
mariculture

marigold
marijuana (*or* ~ihu~)
marimba
marina
marinade
marinate
marination
marine
mariner
Mariolatry
Mariological
Mariology
marionette
marital
maritally
maritime
marjoram
mark
marked
markedly
markedness
marker
market
marketability
marketable
marketeer
marketer
marketing
marketisation (*or* ~iz~)
marketize (*or* ~ize)
marketplace (*or* ~-place)
marking
markka
marksman (*pl* ~men)
marksmanship
markswoman (*pl*
  ~women)
mark-up
marl
marlin
marlinspike (*or* ~line~)
marly
marmalade
Marmite (*tr*) *spread*
marmite *cooking pot*
marmoreal
marmoreally
marmoset
marmot
maroon

marque
marquee
marquess (M~; *esp in Europe* ~quis)
marquessate (*occ* ~quisa~)
marquetry
marquis (M~; *usu in UK* ~quess)
marquisate (*usu* ~quessa~)
marquise (M~)
marram
marriage
marriageability
marriageable
marriageableness
married
marrow
marrowbone
marrowfat
marrowless
marrowy
marry
marrying
Mars
Marseillaise
Marseilles
marsh
marshal (~lled, ~lling; *US* ~led, ~ling)
marshaller (*US* ~aler)
marshalling (*US* ~aling)
marshalship
marshiness
marshland
marshmallow
marshy
marsupial
mart
martello (*pl* ~os)
marten
martial
martialism
martially
Martian
martin
martinet
martingale
martini (M~, *tr*)

Martinique
Martinmas
martlet
martyr
martyrdom
martyred
martyrolatry
martyrological
martyrologist
martyrology
marvel (~lled, ~lling; *US* ~led, ~ling)
marvellous (*US* ~elo~)
marvellously (*US* ~elo~)
marvellousness (*US* ~elo~)
Marxism
Marxist
marzipan
marzipanned
masala
mascara
mascaraed
mascarpone
mascot
masculine
masculinely
masculinisation (*or* ~iz~)
masculinise (*or* ~ize)
masculinised (*or* ~ized)
masculinist
masculinity
maser
mash
mashed
masher
mask
masked
masker
masking
masochism
masochist
masochistic
masochistically
mason
Masonic
masonry
masque

masquer
masquerade
masquerader
Mass *church service*
mass *amount*
Massachusetts
massacre
massage
massager
masseur
masseuse
massif
massive
massively
massiveness
mast
mastaba
mastectomy
masted
master
masterclass
masterdom
masterful
masterfully
masterfulness
masterless
masterliness
masterly
mastermind
masterpiece
mastership
masterstroke
masterwork
mastery
masthead
mastic
masticate
mastication
masticator
masticatory
mastiff
mastitis
mastodon
mastoid
mastoiditis
masturbate
masturbation
masturbator
masturbatory
mat (~tted, ~tting)

matador
match
matchable
matchbox
matching
matchless
matchlessly
matchlessness
matchmaker
matchmaking
matchstick
matchwood
mate *partner*
maté *tea*
material
materialisation (*or* ~iz~)
materialise (*or* ~ize)
materialism
materialist
materialistic
materialistically
materiality
materially
materialness
matériel (! material)
  army supplies
maternal
maternalism
maternalist
maternalistic
maternalistically
maternally
maternity
mateship
matey (*or* maty)
mateyness (*or* ~tin~)
math (*US; UK* maths)
mathematical
mathematically
mathematician
mathematics
mathematisation (*or*
  ~iz~)
mathematise (*or* ~ize)
maths (*US* math)
matily
matinee (*or* ~née)
mating
matins (M~)
matriarch

matriarchal
matriarchate
matriarchy
matrices
matricidal
matricide
matriculate
matriculation
matrifocal
matrilineal
matrilineality
matrilineally
matrilocal
matrilocality
matrimonial
matrimonially
matrimony
matrix (*pl* ~rices,
  ~rixes)
matron
matronhood
matronly
matronymic (*or* met~)
matt (*occ* mat; ! mat,
  matte) *paint*
matte (! matt) *cinema*
matted
matter
Matterhorn
matting
mattock
mattress
maturate
maturation
maturational
maturative
mature
maturely
maturity
matutinal
maty (*or* ~tey)
matzo (*or* ~oh; *pl* ~os,
  ~ohs, ~oth)
maud
maudlin
maul
maulstick (*or* mahl~)
maunder
maundering
Maundy

Mauritania
Mauritius
mausoleum (*pl* ~ea,
  ~eums)
mauve
mauvish
maven (*US*)
maverick
maw
mawkish
mawkishly
mawkishness
maxi (*pl* ~is)
maxilla (*pl* ~ae)
maxillary
maxillofacial
maxim
maximal
maximalist
maximally
maximisation (*or* ~iz~)
maximise (*or* ~ize)
maximiser (*or* ~iz~)
maximum (*pl* ~ma,
  ~mums)
maxwell
May
maybe
mayday (M~)
mayflower
mayfly
mayhem
mayonnaise
mayor (M~; ! major)
  councillor
mayoral
mayoralty
mayoress
mayorship
Mayotte
maypole
mayweed
maze
mazurka
mazy
McCarthyism
McCoy
McGuffin
McKinley
mea culpa

mead
meadow
meadowland
meadowlark
meadowsweet
meadowy
meagre (US ~ger)
meagrely (US ~ger~)
meagreness (US ~ger~)
meal
mealiness
mealtime
mealworm
mealy
mealy-mouthed
mean (meant)
meander
meanie (or ~ny)
meaning
meaningful
meaningfully
meaningfulness
meaningless
meaninglessly
meaninglessness
meanly
meanness
means
meantime
meanwhile
meany (or ~nie)
measles
measly
measurability
measurable
measure
measureably
measured
measuredly
measureless
measurement
measurer
measuring
meat
meatball
meatily
meatiness
meatless
meatus
meaty

Mecca *Islam*
mecca *goal*
mechanic
mechanical
mechanically
mechanicalness
mechanician
mechanics
mechanisation (or ~iz~)
mechanise (or ~ize)
mechaniser (or ~iz~)
mechanism
mechanist
mechanistic
meconium
mecopteran
medal
medalled
medallion
medallist (US ~alist)
meddle
meddler
meddlesome
meddlesomely
meddlesomeness
meddling
media
mediacy
mediaeval (or ~ie~)
mediaevalise (or ~ie~,
    ~ize)
mediaevalism (or ~ie~)
mediaevalist (or ~ie~)
mediaevally (or ~ie~)
mediagenic
medial
medially
median
mediant
mediastinum
mediate
mediately
mediation
mediator
mediatory
medic
medicable
Medicaid (US)
medical
medically

medicament
Medicare (US)
medicate
medicated
medication
medicative
medicinal
medicinally
medicine
medieval (or ~iae~)
medievalise (or ~iae~,
    ~ize)
medievalism (or ~iae~)
medievalist (or ~iae~)
medievally (or ~iae~)
mediocracy
mediocre
mediocrely
mediocrity
meditate
meditation
meditative
meditatively
meditativeness
Mediterranean
medium (*pl* ~ia, ~ums)
mediumistic
mediumship
medlar
medley (*n pl* ~eys; *v*
    ~leyed *or* ~lied,
    ~leying)
medulla (*pl* ~ae, ~as)
medullary
medusa (*pl* ~ae, ~as)
medusoid
meek
meekly
meekness
meerkat
meerschaum
meet (met)
meeting
megabit
megabucks (US)
megabyte
megadeath
megaflop
megahertz
megalith

megalithic
megaloblast
megaloblastic
megalomania
megalomaniac
megalomaniacal
megalopolis
megalopolitan
megalosaurus
megaphone
megastar
megastardom
megastore
megatherium (*pl* ~ia,
~ums)
megaton (*or* ~nne)
megavolt
megawatt
megohm
meiosis (*pl* ~oses)
meiotic
meiotically
meitnerium
melamine
melancholia
melancholic
melancholically
melancholy
Melanesia
melange (*or* mél~)
melanin
melanism
melanite
melanocyte
melanoid
melanoma
melanosis
melanotic
melatonin
Melbourne
meld
melee (*or* melée)
meliorate
melioration
meliorative
mellifluence
mellifluent
mellifluently
mellifluous
mellifluously

mellifluousness
mellow
mellowly
mellowness
melodic
melodically
melodious
melodiousness
melodist
melodrama
melodramatic
melodramatically
melodramatics
melodramatise (*or* ~ize)
melodramatist
melody
melon
melt
meltable
meltdown
melted
melter
melting
meltingly
meltwater
member
membered
membership
membranaceous
membrane
membraneous
membranous
meme
memento (*pl* ~os, ~oes)
memo (*pl* ~os)
memoir
memoirist
memorabilia
memorability
memorable
memorably
memorandum (*pl* ~da,
~ums)
memorial
memorialise (*or* ~ize)
memorialising (*or* ~iz~)
memorialist
memorisable (*or* ~iz~)
memorisation (*or* ~iz~)
memorise (*or* ~ize)

memoriser (*or* ~iz~)
memory
men
menace
menaced
menacer
menacing
menacingly
ménage
ménage à trois
menagerie
menaquinone
menarche
mend
mendable
mendacious
mendaciously
mendacity
mendelevium
Mendelian
mendicancy
mendicant
mendicity
mending
menfolk
menhir
menial
menially
meningeal
meninges (*sg* meninx)
meningioma (*pl* ~mata,
~as)
meningitic
meningitis
meningococcal
meningococcic
meningococcus (*pl* ~cci)
meninx (*pl* ~ninges)
meniscus (*pl* ~ci)
Mennonite
menopausal
menopause
menorah
menorrhagia
menorrhoea (*US* ~hea)
Mensa
menses
menstrual
menstruate
menstruation

menstruous
mensurability
mensurable
mensural
mensuration
menswear
mental
mentalism
mentalist
mentalistic
mentality
mentally
mentation
menthol
mentholated
mention
mentionable
mentioned
mentor
mentoring
mentorship
menu
meow (or miaow)
Mephistophelean (or ~ian)
Mephistopheles
mercantile
mercantilism
mercantilist
Mercator
mercenary
mercer
mercerise (or ~ize)
merchandisable (US ~iz~)
merchandise (US ~ize)
merchandiser (US ~iz~)
merchandising (US ~iz~)
merchant
merchantable
merchantman (pl ~men)
merciful
mercifully
mercifulness
merciless
mercilessly
mercilessness
mercurial

mercuriality
mercurially
mercuric
mercurous
Mercury element
mercury planet, pod
mercy
mere
merely
merengue (or ~rin~)
meretricious
meretriciously
meretriciousness
merganser
merge
merger
meridian
meridional
meringue (or ~ren~)
merino (pl ~os)
meristem
merit
meritless
meritocracy
meritorious
meritoriously
meritoriousness
Merlin wizard
merlin bird
merlon
mermaid
merman (pl ~men)
meronym
meronymy
merrily
merriment
merriness
merry
merry-go-round
merrymaker
merrymaking
mesa
mésalliance
mescal
mescaline (or ~in)
mesembryanthemum
mesencephalon
mesenteric
mesentery
mesh

meshed
mesial
mesially
mesmeric
mesmerically
mesmerisation (or ~iz~)
mesmerise (or ~ize)
mesmeriser (or ~iz~)
mesmerising (or ~iz~)
mesmerism
mesmerist
Mesoamerica
Mesoamerican
mesocarp
mesoderm
mesogastric
mesogastrium (pl ~ia)
Mesolithic
mesomorph
mesomorphic
mesomorphous
meson
mesopause
mesopelagic
Mesopotamia
mesosaur
mesosphere
mesospheric
mesozoan
Mesozoic
mesquite
mess
message
messenger
messiah (M~)
messianic
messianism (M~)
messily
messiness
messy
mestiza
mestizo
met
metabolic
metabolically
metabolisable (or ~iz~)
metabolise (or ~ize)
metaboliser (or ~iz~)
metabolism
metabolite

metacarpal
metacarpus (*pl* ~pi)
metacognition
metacognitive
metal (~lled, ~lling; *US* ~led, ~ling)
metalanguage
metalicity
metalinguistic
metalinguistically
metalinguistics
metallic
metallically
metalliferous
metallisation (*or* ~iz~)
metallise (*or* ~ize)
metallographic
metallographical
metallographically
metallography
metalloid
metallurgic
metallurgical
metallurgically
metallurgist
metallurgy
metalwork
metalworker
metamorphic
metamorphism
metamorphose
metamorphosis (*pl* ~oses)
metanoia
metaphase
metaphor
metaphoric
metaphorical
metaphorically
metaphrase
metaphrastic
metaphysical
metaphysically
metaphysician
metaphysics
metaplasia
metaplastic
metastability
metastable
metastasis (*pl* ~ases)

metastasise (*or* ~ize)
metastatic
metatarsal
metatarsus (*pl* ~arsi)
metatheoretical
metatheoretically
metatheory
metathesis
metazoan
mete
meteor
meteoric
meteorically
meteorite
meteoritic
meteorograph
meteoroid
meteorological
meteorologically
meteorologist
meteorology
meter
metered
metering
methacrylic
methadone
methamphetamine
methanal
methane
methanogen
methanogenesis
methanol
method
methodic
methodical
methodically
Methodism
Methodist
methodological
methodologically
methodologist
methodology
Methuselah *bible*
methuselah *wine bottle*
methyl
methylate
methylated
methylene
meticulous
meticulously

meticulousness
métier
metonym
metonymic
metonymical
metonymically
metonymy
metre (*US* meter)
metric
metrical
metrically
metricate
metrication
metro (*pl* ~os)
metronome
metronomic
metronomically
metronymic (*or* mat~)
metroplex
metropole
metropolis
metropolitan
metropolitanate
metropolitanism
metropolitical
metrorrhagia
mettle
mettlesome
meunière
mew
mewing
mewl
mewling
mews
Mexican
Mexico
meze
mezzanine
mezzo
mezzo-soprano
miaow (*or* meow)
miasma
miasmal
miasmatic
miasmic
miasmically
mica
micaceous
mice
Michaelmas

Michelangelo
Michigan
mickey
micro
microanalyser
microanalysis
microanalytical
microbe
microbial
microbic
microbiological
microbiologically
microbiologist
microbiology
microburst
microcapsule
microcar
microcellular
microchemical
microchemist
microchemistry
microchip
microchiropteran
microcircuit
microcircuitry
microclimate
microclimatic
microclimatically
microclimatology
microcode
microcomputer
microcosm
microcosmic
microcosmically
microcrystalline
microcyte
microdot
microeconomic
microeconomics
microelectronic
microelectronics
microenvironment
microevolution
microevolutionary
microfauna
microfibre (*US* ~er)
microfiche
microfilm
microflora
microform

micrograph
micrographic
micrographically
micrographics
micrography
microgravity
microhabitat
microlight
micromesh
micrometer *instrument*
micrometre (*US* ~er)
    length unit
micrometry
microminiaturisation (*or*
    ~iz~)
microminiaturise (*or*
    ~ize)
micron
Micronesia
Micronesian
micronutrient
micro-organism
microphage
microphagic
microphagous
microphone
microphonic
microphotograph
microphotography
microphyll
microphysical
microphysicist
microphysics
microporosity
microporous
microprocessor
micropsia
micropyle
microreader
microscope
microscopic
microscopical
microscopically
microscopist
microscopy
microsecond
microspecies
microspore
microsurgeon
microsurgery

microsurgical
microtechnological
microtechnologist
microtechnology
microtome
microwatt
microwave
microwaveable (*or*
    ~va~)
micrurgical
micrurgy
micturate
micturition
mid
Midas
midbrain
midday
middle
middlebrow
middleman (*pl* ~men)
middleweight
middling
middlingly
midfield
midge
midget
midi (*pl* ~is)
midiron
midland (M~)
midlander
midlife
midline
midmost
midnight
mid-off
mid-on
Midrash (*pl* ~shim)
midrib
midriff
midshipman (*pl* ~men)
midships
midst
midstream
midsummer
midterm
midway
midweek
Midwest (*US*)
mid-wicket
midwife (*pl* ~wives)

midwifery
midwinter
midyear
mien
miff
might
mightily
mightiness
mighty
migmatite
migraine
migrainous
migrant
migrate
migration
migrational
migrator
migratory
milch
mild
mildew
mildewed
mildewy
mildish
mildly
mildness
mile
mileage (or milage)
mileometer (or milo~)
milestone
miliaria
milieu (pl ~ux, ~us)
militancy
militant
militantly
militaria
militarily
militarisation (or ~iz~)
militarise (or ~ize)
militarised (or ~ized)
militarism
militarist
militaristic
militaristically
military
militate
militia
milk
milker
milkiness

milking
milkmaid
milkman (pl ~men)
milkshake
milksop
milkweed
milkwort
milky
mill
millable
milled
millefeuille
millenarian
millenarianism
millenarianist
millenary
millennial
millennialism
millennialist
millennium (pl ~ia,
    ~iums)
millepede (or millip~)
miller
millesimal
millet
milliampere
millibar
milligram (or ~mme)
millilitre (US ~ter)
millimetre (US ~ter)
milliner
millinery
milling
million
millionaire
millionairess
millionfold
millionth
millipede (or millep~)
millisecond
millivolt
millpond
millstone
millstream
millwheel
millworker
millwright
milo
milometer (or mileo~)
milt

mime
mimeograph
mimer
mimesis
mimetic
mimetically
mimic (~icked, ~icking)
mimicker
mimicry
mimosa
minaret
minareted
minatory
mince
minced
mincemeat
mincer
mincing
mind
minded
minder
mindful
mindfully
mindfulness
mindless
mindlessly
mindlessness
mindreader
mindreading
mindset
mine
minefield
minehunter
minehunting
minelayer
minelaying
miner
mineral
mineralisation (or ~iz~)
mineralise (or ~ize)
mineralogical
mineralogically
mineralogist
mineralogy
mineshaft
minestrone
minesweeper
minesweeping
Ming
mingler

mingling
mini (*pl* ~is)
miniature
miniaturisation (*or* ~iz~)
miniaturise (*or* ~ize)
miniaturist
minibar
minibreak
minibus
minicab
minicam
minicomputer
minidisk (*or* ~disc)
minigolf
minim
minimal
minimalism
minimalist
minimally
minimart
minimisation (*or* ~iz~)
minimise (*or* ~ize)
minimiser (*or* ~iz~)
minimum (*pl* ~ums, ~ma)
mining
minion
minipill
miniseries
miniskirt
minister
ministerial
ministerially
ministering
ministership
ministrant
ministration
ministrative
ministry
minivan
miniver
mink
Minneapolis
minneola
Minnesota
minnow
Minoan
minor
Minorca

minority
minster
minstrel
minstrelsy
mint
mintage
minted
minter
minty
minuend
minuet
minus
minuscular
minuscule
minute
minutely
minuteness
minutest
minutia (*pl* ~iae)
minx
Miocene
miosis
miracle
miraculous
miraculously
miraculousness
mirage
mire
mired
mirin
mirror
mirrorball
mirth
mirthful
mirthfully
mirthless
mirthlessly
mirthlessness
miry
misadventure
misadvised
misadvisedly
misalign
misaligned
misalignment
misalliance
misanthrope
misanthropic
misanthropical
misanthropically

misanthropist
misanthropy
misapplication
misapplied
misapply
misapprehend
misapprehension
misapprehensive
misappropriate
misappropriation
misbegotten
misbehave
misbehaviour (*US* ~or)
miscalculate
miscalculation
miscall
miscarriage
miscarry
miscast
miscegenation
miscellanea
miscellaneous
miscellaneously
miscellaneousness
miscellanist
miscellany
mischance
mischief
mischievous
mischievously
mischievousness
miscibility
miscible
miscommunication
misconceive
misconceived
misconceiver
misconception
misconduct
misconstruct
misconstruction
misconstrue
miscount
miscreant
miscue (~cueing *or* ~cuing)
misdate
misdeal
misdeed
misdemeanour (*US* ~or)

misdiagnose
misdiagnosis
misdial (~lled, ~lling;
  US ~led, ~ling)
misdirect
misdirected
misdirection
mise-en-scène
misemploy
misemployment
miser
miserable
miserableness
miserably
misericord
miserliness
miserly
misery
misfeasance
misfire
misfit
misfortune
misgive (~gave, ~given,
  ~giving)
misgivings
misgovern
misgovernment
misguide
misguided
misguidedly
misguidedness
mishandle
mishap
mishear (misheard)
mishit (~tting)
mishmash
Mishnah
Mishnaic
misidentification
misidentify
misinform
misinformation
misinformed
misinterpret
misinterpretation
misinterpreter
misjudge
misjudgement (or
  ~dgm~)
miskey

miskeyed
miskick
mislay (mislaid)
mislead (misled)
misleading
misleadingly
misleadingness
mismanage
mismanagement
mismatch
mismatched
misname
misnomer
misogamist
misogamy
misogynist
misogynistic
misogynous
misogyny
misperceive
misperception
misplace
misplaced
misplacement
misprint
mispronounce
mispronunciation
misquotation
misquote
misread
misremember
misreport
misrepresent
misrepresentation
misrepresentative
misroute
misrule
miss
missal
misshapen
misshapenly
misshapenness
missile
missing
mission
missionary
missioner
Mississippi
missive
Missouri

misspell (misspelled *or*
  misspelt)
misspend (misspent)
misstate
misstatement
misstep
mist
mistake (mistaken,
  mistook, mistaking)
mistakeable (*or* ~aka~)
mistakeably (*or* ~aka~)
mistaken
mistakenly
mistakenness
misteach (mistaught)
mister
mistily
mistime
mistiness
mistitle
mistletoe
mistook
mistral
mistranslate
mistranslation
mistreat
mistreatment
mistress
mistrial
mistrust
mistrustful
mistrustfully
mistrustfulness
misty
mistype
misunderstand
  (misunderstood)
misunderstanding
misusage
misuse
misuser
mite
mitigable
mitigatable
mitigate
mitigating
mitigation
mitigator
mitigatory
mitochondrial

mitochondrion (*pl* ~ia)
mitogen
mitogenic
mitosis (*pl* ~oses)
mitotic
mitre (*US* ~ter)
mitred (*US* ~ter~)
mitt
mitten
mittened
mitzvah (*pl* ~ahs, ~voth)
mix
mixable
mixed
mixer
mixing
mixture
mix-up
mizzen
mizzle
mizzly
mnemonic
mnemonically
mnemonics
moa
moan
moaner
moanful
moat
moated
mob (~bbed, ~bbing)
mobber
mobile
mobilisable (*or* ~iz~)
mobilisation (*or* ~iz~)
mobilise (*or* ~ize)
mobiliser (*or* ~iz~)
mobility
Möbius
mobocracy
mobster
moccasin
mocha
mock
mockable
mocker
mockery
mock-heroic
mocking

mockingbird
mockingly
mock-up
mod
modal
modalism
modalist
modality
modally
mode
model (~lled, ~lling; *US* ~led, ~ling)
modella
modeller (*US* ~eler)
modelling (*US* ~eling)
modem
moderate
moderately
moderateness
moderating
moderation
moderatism
moderatist
moderato
moderator
moderatorship
modern
modernisation (*or* ~iz~)
modernise (*or* ~ize)
moderniser (*or* ~iz~)
modernism (M~)
modernist (M~)
modernistic
modernity
modernly
modernness
modest
modestly
modesty
modicum
modifiability
modifiable
modification
modificatory
modifier
modify
modish
modishly
modishness
modular

modularisation (*or* ~iz~)
modularise (*or* ~ize)
modularity
modulate
modulation
modulator
module
modulus
modus (*pl* ~di)
mogul (M~)
mohair
Mohammed (*or* Muh~, ~hamed)
Mohammedan (*or* Muh~)
Mohammedanism (*or* Muh~)
mohel
Mohican *people*
mohican *hairstyle*
moiety
moil
moire (*or* ~ré)
moist
moisten
moistly
moistness
moisture
moistureless
moisturise (*or* ~ize)
moisturiser (*or* ~iz~)
molar
molarity
molasses
mold (*US; see entries at UK* mould)
Moldova
mole
molecular
molecularity
molecularly
molecule
molehill
moleskin
molest
molestation
molester
mollification
mollifier

mollify
mollusc (*US* ~sk)
mollycoddle
moloch
Molotov
molten
molto
molybdenum
moment
momentarily
momentariness
momentary
momentous
momentousness
momentum (*pl* ~ums, ~ta)
Monaco
monad
monadic
monadism
monandrous
monandry
monarch
monarchal
monarchial
monarchic
monarchical
monarchically
monarchism
monarchist
monarchistic
monarchy
monastery
monastic
monastically
monasticism
monatomic
monaural
monaurally
Monday
monetarily
monetarism
monetarist
monetary
monetisation (*or* ~iz~)
monetise (*or* ~ize)
money
moneybox
moneychanger
moneyed

moneylender
moneylending
moneyless
moneymaker
moneymaking
mongol
Mongolia
mongolism
mongoloid (M~)
mongoose (*pl* ~gooses)
mongrel
monism
monist
monistic
monitor
monitorial
monitoring
monitorship
monitory
monk
monkey (*pl* ~keys)
monkeyish
monkish
monkishly
monkishness
monkshood
mono
monocarpic
monocarpous
monochromatic
monochromatically
monochromatism
monochrome
monochromic
monochromy
monocle
monocled
monoclinal
monocline
monoclonal
monocotyledon
monocotyledonous
monocracy
monocrat
monocratic
monocrystalline
monocular
monocularly
monocultural
monoculture

monocycle
monocyte
monodactyl
monodactyly
monoecious
monogamist
monogamous
monogamously
monogamy
monoglot
monogram
monogrammatic
monograph
monographer
monographic
monographical
monographist
monohull
monolingual
monolingualism
monolith
monolithic
monologic
monological
monologise (*or* ~ize)
monologist (*or* ~guist)
monologue
monomania
monomaniac
monomaniacal
monomer
monomeric
monomolecular
monomorphic
monomorphism
monomorphous
mononuclear
mononucleosis
monophagous
monophonic
monophonically
monophony
monoplane
monoplegia
monoplegic
monopod
monopole
monopolisation (*or* ~iz~)
monopolise (*or* ~ize)

monopoliser (or ~iz~)
monopolist
monopolistic
monopolistically
Monopoly (tr) game
monopoly exclusiveness
monorail
monosaccharide
monosemous
monosemy
monoski
monosodium
monosyllabic
monosyllabically
monosyllabicity
monosyllabism
monosyllable
monotheism
monotheist
monotheistic
monotheistically
monotone
monotonic
monotonically
monotonicity
monotonous
monotonously
monotony
monotreme
monotype
monotypic
monounsaturated
monovalent
monoxide
monozygosity
monozygotic
monozygous
Mons
monsoon
monsoonal
monster
monstera
monstrance
monstrosity
monstrous
monstrously
monstrousness
montage
Montana
montane

montbretia
monte (or monty)
    everything
Montenegro
month
monthly
Montserrat
Montserratian
monty (or monte)
    everything
monument
monumental
monumentality
monumentally
moo
mooch
moocher
mood
moodily
moodiness
moody
Moog
moon
moonbeam
moon-faced
Moonies
moonless
moonlight
moonlighter
moonlighting
moonlit
moonrise
moonscape
moon-shaped
moonshine
moonstone
moonstruck
moonwalk
moonwalker
moonwalking
moony
Moor Africa
moor countryside
moorage
moorfowl
moorhen
mooring
Moorish
moorland
moose (! mousse) animal

moot
mooted
mop (~pped, ~pping)
mope
moped cycle
moper
mopey (or ~py)
mopily
mopiness
mopish
moppet
mopy (or ~pey)
moquette
morainal
moraine
morainic
moral (! morale) lesson
morale (! moral) spirits
moralise (or ~ize)
moraliser (or ~iz~)
moralising (or ~iz~)
moralist
moralistic
moralistically
morality
morally
morass
moratorium (pl ~ia,
    ~ums)
Moravian
moray
morbid
morbidity
morbidly
morbidness
morbific
mordacious
mordancy
mordant
mordantly
mordent
more
moreish (or morish)
morel
morello (pl ~os)
moreover
mores
morganatic
morganatically
morgue

moribund
moribundity
morish (*or* moreish)
Mormon
Mormonism
mornay (M~)
morning
Morocco *country*
morocco *leather*
moron
moronic
moronically
morose
morosely
moroseness
morph
morpheme
morphemic
morphemically
morphemics
Morpheus
morphine
morphing
morphogenesis
morphogenetic
morphogenic
morphological
morphologically
morphologist
morphology
morphometric
morphometrically
morphometrics
morrow
Morse
morsel
mortal
mortality
mortally
mortar
mortarboard
mortgage
mortgageable
mortgaged
mortgagee
mortgagor
mortice (*or* ~ise)
mortician
mortification
mortified

mortify
mortifyingly
mortise (*or* ~tice)
mortised
mortiser
mortuary
Mosaic *Moses*
mosaic (~cked, ~cking)
   design
mosaicist
moschatel
Moscow
Moses
Moslem (*or* Muslim)
mosque
mosquito (*pl* ~os, ~oes)
moss
mossed
mossiness
mossy
most
mostly
mote
motel
motet
moth
mothball
moth-eaten
mother
motherboard
motherhood
mothering
mother-in-law
motherland
motherless
motherlessness
motherliness
motherly
mothproof
mothy
motif
motion
motional
motionless
motionlessly
motivate
motivation
motivational
motivationally
motivator

motive
motiveless
motivelessly
motivelessness
mot juste
motley
motocross
motocrosser
motor
motorable
motorcade
motorcycle
motorcycling
motorcyclist
motorhome
motoring
motorisation (*or* ~iz~)
motorise (*or* ~ize)
motorised (*or* ~ized)
motorist
motormouth
motorway
Motown
motte
mottle
mottled
motto (*pl* ~oes, ~os)
moue
mouillé
mould (*US* mold)
moulder (*US* mold~)
mouldering (*US* mold~)
mouldiness (*US* mold~)
moulding (*US* mold~)
mouldy (*US* moldy)
moult (*US* molt)
mound
mount
mountable
mountain
mountaineer
mountaineering
mountainous
mountainside
mounted
mounter
Mountie (*or* ~ty)
mounting
mourn
mourner

mournful
mournfully
mournfulness
mourning
mouse (*pl* mice)
mouser
mousetrap
mousey (*or* ~sy)
mousiness
moussaka
mousse (! moose) *dessert, hair*
mousseline
mousseux
moustache (*or US* mus~)
mousy (*or* ~sey)
mouth
mouthed
mouther
mouthful
mouthiness
mouthless
mouthparts
mouthpiece
mouth-to-mouth
mouthwash
mouth-watering
mouthy
movability (*or* ~vea~)
movable (*or* ~vea~)
movably (*or* ~vea~)
move
movement
mover
movie
moviegoer
moving
movingly
mow (mown)
mower
mowing
moxa
moxibustion
Mozambican
Mozambique
Mozartian (*or* ~ean)
mozzarella
much
muchness
mucilage

mucilaginous
mucin
mucinous
muck
muckheap
muckiness
muckrake
muckraker
muckraking
mucky
mucoid
mucosa (*pl* ~ae)
mucosal
mucosity
mucous (*adj*)
mucus (*n*)
mud
mudbank
mudbath
muddily
muddiness
muddle
muddled
muddler
muddlingly
muddy
mudflap
mudguard
mudhopper
mudlark
mudpack
mudskipper
mudslide
muesli (*pl* ~is)
muezzin
muff
muffin
muffle
muffled
muffler
muffling
mufti
mug (~gged, ~gging)
mugful
mugger
mugginess
mugging
muggins
muggy
Muhammad (*or* Moh~)

Muhammadan (*or* Moh~)
Muhammadenism (*or* Moh~)
mujahedin (M~; *or* ~heddin, ~hidin, ~hideen, ~hadeen)
mulatto (*pl* ~oes, ~os)
mulberry
mulch
mulct
mule
muleteer
mulish
mulishly
mulishness
mull
mullah (M~)
mulled
mullein
mullet
mulligatawny
mullion
mullioned
multicultural
multiculturalism
multiculturalist
multiculturally
multifarious
multifariously
multifariousness
multiform
multiformity
multilateral
multilateralism
multilateralist
multilaterally
multilingual
multilingualism
multilingually
multimedia
multinomial
multiparous
multipartite
multiple
multiplex
multiplexer
multipliable
multiplicable
multiplicand

multiplication
multiplicative
multiplicity
multiplier
multiply
multiracial
multiracialism
multiracialist
multiracially
multitude
multitudinous
multitudinously
multitudinousness
mumble
mumbler
mumbling
mumblingly
mumbo-jumbo
mummer
mummification
mummify
mumming
mummy
mumpish
mumps
munch
Munchausen
muncher
mundane
mundanely
mundaneness
mundanity
municipal
municipalisation (or ~iz~)
municipalise (or ~ize)
municipality
municipally
munificence
munificent
munificently
muniment
munition
munitioner
muntjac (or ~ak)
muon
mural
muralist
murder
murderer

murderess
murderous
murderously
murderousness
murine
murk (occ mirk)
murkily
murkiness
murky (occ mirky)
murmur
murmuration
murmurer
murmuring
murmuringly
murmurous
murrain
muscat
muscatel (or ~adel)
muscle
muscle-bound
muscled
muscleless
muscly
muscovado
Muscovite Moscow
muscovite mineral
muscular
muscularity
muscularly
musculature
muse (M~)
museum
mush
mushed
mushily
mushiness
mushroom
mushy
music
musical
musicalise (or ~ize)
musicality
musically
musician
musicianly
musicianship
musicological
musicologist
musicology
musk

musket
musketeer
musketry
muskiness
muskrat
musky
Muslim (or Moslem)
muslin
muslined
muss
mussel
Mussolini
mussy
must
mustache (US; UK mous~)
mustachioed
mustachios
mustang
mustard
mustardy
mustelid
muster
musterer
mustily
mustiness
musty
mutability
mutable
mutably
mutagen
mutagenesis
mutagenic
mutant
mutate
mutation
mutational
mutationally
mutative
mute
muted
mutely
muteness
mutilate
mutilated
mutilation
mutilator
mutineer
mutinous
mutinously

mutiny
mutism
mutt
mutter
mutterer
muttering
mutteringly
mutton
mutual
mutualism
mutualist
mutualistic
mutualistically
mutuality
mutually
muzzily
muzziness
muzzle
muzzy
mwah
myalgia
myalgic
myasthenia
mycelial
mycelium (*pl* ~ia)
Mycenae
Mycenaean (*or* ~nean)
mycetoma
mycological
mycologically
mycologist
mycology
mycoplasma (*pl* ~mata, ~as)
mycoprotein
mycosis (*pl* ~oses)
mycotoxin
mycotrophic
mycotrophy
mydriasis
myeloid
myeloma (*pl* ~mata, ~as)
myelopathy
myenteric
Mylar (*tr*)
mylodon
mynah
myocardial
myocarditis

myocardium
myogenic
myological
myologist
myology
myomatous
myomorph
myopathic
myopathy
myope
myopia
myopic
myopically
myositis
myotonia
myotonic
myriad
myringotomy
myrmecological
myrmecologist
myrmecology
myrmecophile
myrmecophilous
myrmecophily
myrmidon
myrrh
myrtaceous
myrtle
myself
mysterious
mysteriously
mysteriousness
mystery
mystic
mystical
mysticality
mysticete
mysticism
mystification
mystifier
mystify
mystifying
mystifyingly
mystique
myth
mythic
mythical
mythically
mythicise (*or* ~ize)
mythographer

mythography
mythologer
mythologic
mythological
mythologically
mythologise (*or* ~ize)
mythologiser (*or* ~iz~)
mythologist
mythology
mythomania
mythomaniac
mythopoeia
mythopoeic
mythopoetic
mythos (*pl* mythoi)
mythus (*pl* mythi)
myxoedema (*US* ~xed~)
myxoma (*pl* ~mata, ~as)
myxomatosis

naan (*or* nan)
nab (~bbed, ~bbing)
nabob
nacelle
nacho (*pl* ~os)
nacre
nacreous
nadir
naevus (*US* nev~; *pl* ~vi)
nag (~gged, ~gging)
nagger
nagging
naggingly
naggy
naiad (*pl* ~ads, ~ades)
naif (*or* naïf)
nail

nail-biting
nailbrush
nailed
nailer
nailless
nailscissors (*or* nail-~)
naive (*or* ~ïve)
naively (*or* ~ïve~)
naiveness (*or* ~ïve~)
naivety (*or* ~ïv~)
naked
nakedly
nakedness
namby-pamby
name
name-calling
namecheck
name-drop
name-dropper
name-dropping
nameless
namelessly
namelessness
namely
nameplate
namesake
nametape
Namibia
naming
nan (*or* naan)
nankeen
nanny
nannying
nannyish
nanometre (*US* ~ter)
nanoplankton
nanosecond
nanotechnological
nanotechnologist
nanotechnology
nanotube
nap (~pped, ~pping)
napa (*or* ~ppa)
napalm
nape
naphtha
naphthalene
naphthalic
naphthene
naphthenic

naphthol
napkin
napless
Napoleon
Napoleonic
nappa (*or* napa)
nappe
napped
napping
nappy
naproxene
narcissism
narcissist
narcissistic
narcissistically
Narcissus *mythology*
narcissus (*pl* ~ssi, ~uses)
flower
narcolepsy
narcoleptic
narcosis (*pl* ~oses)
narcoterrorism
narcoterrorist
narcotic
narcotically
narcotisation (*or* ~iz~)
narcotise (*or* ~ize)
narcotism
nard
nares
nark
narked
narratable
narrate
narrated
narration
narrative
narratively
narrativise (*or* ~ize)
narrativity
narratological
narratologist
narratology
narrator
narratorial
narrow
narrowband
narrowcast
narrowcaster
narrowcasting

narrow-gauge
narrowish
narrowly
narrow-minded
narrow-mindedly
narrow-mindedness
narrowness
narthex
narwhal
NASA
nasal
nasalisation (*or* ~iz~)
nasalise (*or* ~ize)
nasalised (*or* ~ized)
nasality
nasally
nascency
nascent
naseberry
Nashville
nasogastric
nasopharyngeal
nasopharynx
Nassau
nastic
nastily
nastiness
nasturtium
nasty
natal
natality
natant
natation
natatorial
natatorium
natatory
nates
nation
national
nationalisation (*or*
~iz~)
nationalise (*or* ~ize)
nationalised (*or* ~ized)
nationaliser (*or* ~iz~)
nationalism
nationalist
nationalistic
nationalistically
nationality
nationally

nationhood
nationwide
native
natively
nativeness
nativism
nativist
nativistic
Nativity *Christ*
nativity *birth*
NATO (*or* Nato)
natter
natterer
natterjack
nattily
nattiness
natty
natural
natural-born
naturalisation (*or* ~iz~)
naturalise (*or* ~ize)
naturalised (*or* ~ized)
naturalism
naturalist
naturalistic
naturalistically
naturally
naturalness
nature
natured
naturism
naturist
naturopath
naturopathic
naturopathy
naught
naughtily
naughtiness
naughty
Nauru
Nauruan
nausea
nauseate
nauseating
nauseatingly
nauseous
nauseously
nauseousness
nautical
nautically

nautiloid
nautilus (*pl* ~li, ~uses)
navaid (N~)
Navajo (*or* ~aho)
naval
navarin
nave
navel
navicular
navigability
navigable
navigate
navigation
navigational
navigator
navvy
navy
nay
naysay
naysayer
Nazarene
Nazareth
Nazi (*pl* ~is)
Nazidom
Nazify
Naziism (*or* ~zism)
neanderthal (N~)
neap
Neapolitan
near
nearby
nearish
nearly
nearness
nearside
near-sighted
near-sightedly
near-sightedness
neat
neaten
neatly
neatness
neb
Nebraska
Nebuchadnezzar
nebula (*pl* ~ae, ~as)
nebular
nebulise (*or* ~ize)
nebuliser (*or* ~iz~)
nebulosity

nebulous
nebulously
nebulousness
necessarily
necessary
necessitarian
necessitarianism
necessitate
necessitous
necessity
neck
neckband
neckcloth
necked
necker
neckerchief
necking
necklace
neckless
necklet
neckline
necktie
neckwear
necrobiosis
necrobiotic
necrological
necrologist
necrology
necromancer
necromancy
necromantic
necromantically
necrophile
necrophilia
necrophiliac
necrophilic
necrophilism
necrophilist
necrophobia
necropolis
necropsy
necroscopic
necrosis (*pl* ~oses)
necrotic
necrotising (*or* ~iz~)
nectar
nectarean
nectareous
nectariferous
nectarine

nectarivorous
nectarous
nectary
née (*or* nee)
need
needful
needfully
needfulness
needle
needlecraft
needlepoint
needless
needlessly
needlessness
needlewoman (*pl* ~women)
needlework
needleworker
needs
needy
ne'er-do-well
nefarious
nefariously
nefariousness
negate
negation
negative
negatively
negativeness
negativism
negativist
negativistic
negativity
negator
neglect
neglected
neglectful
neglectfully
neglectfulness
negligée (*or* ~gee)
negligence
negligent
negligently
negligibility
negligible
negligibly
negotiability
negotiable
negotiant
negotiate

negotiation
negotiator
negress (N~; *tab*)
negrification
negro (N~; *tab*)
negroid (N~)
negus
neigh
neighbour (*US* ~or)
neighbourhood (*US* ~or~)
neighbouring (*US* ~or~)
neighbourless (*US* ~or~)
neighbourliness (*US* ~or~)
neighbourly (*US* ~or~)
neither
nekton
nektonic
nelson
nematic
nematocidal
nematocide
nematocyst
nematode
nematologist
nematology
nematomorph
Nembutal (*tr*)
nemertean
nemertine
nemesia
nemesis (*pl* ~eses)
neoclassical
neoclassicism
neoclassicist
neocolonial
neocolonialism
neocolonialist
neo-Confucian
neo-Confucianism
neoconservative
neoconservativism
neocortex (*pl* ~tices)
neocortical
neo-Darwinian
neo-Darwinism
neo-Darwinist
neodymium

neo-fascism (N~)
neo-fascist (N~)
neo-Georgian
neo-Gothic
neo-impressionism (N~)
neo-impressionist (N~)
neo-liberal
neo-liberalism
neolithic (N~)
neologic
neological
neologise (*or* ~ize)
neologism
neologist
neology
neo-Marxism
neo-Marxist
neomycin
neon
neonatal
neonate
neonatologist
neonatology
neo-Nazi
neo-Nazism
neopagan
neopaganism
neophobia
neophobic
neophyte
neoplasia
neoplasm
neoplastic
neoplasticism
neoplatonic (N~)
neoplatonism (N~)
neoplatonist (N~)
neoprene
neo-realism
neo-realist
neo-realistic
neotenic
neotenous
neoteny
neoteric
neoterically
neotropical
Neozoic
Nepal
nephew

nephologic
nephological
nephologist
nephology
nephrectomy
nephrite
nephritic
nephritis
nephrological
nephrologist
nephrology
nephron
nephrosis
nephrotic
nephrotoxic
nephrotoxicity
nephrotoxin
nepotism
nepotist
nepotistic
Neptune
neptunium
nerd
nerdish
nerdishness
nerdy
nereid (N~)
Nereus
neroli
nervation
nerve
nerved
nerveless
nervelessly
nervelessness
nerve-wracking (or
  ~rack~)
nervily
nerviness
nervous
nervously
nervousness
nervy
nescience
nescient
nest
nested
nester
nestful
nestle

nestled
nestling
Nestorian
Nestorianism
net (~tted, ~tting)
netball
netful
nether
Netherlander
Netherlandic
Netherlands
nethermost
netherworld
netiquette
netizen
netter
netting
nettle
nettlerash
network
networked
networker
networking
neum (or neume)
neural
neuralgia
neuralgic
neurally
neurasthenia
neurasthenic
neuritic
neuritis
neuroanatomical
neuroanatomist
neuroanatomy
neurobiological
neurobiologist
neurobiology
neuroblast
neuroblastoma
neurofibroma (pl ~mata,
  ~as)
neurofibromatosis
neurogenesis
neurogenic
neurohormone
neuroleptic
neurolinguistic
neurolinguistics
neurological

neurologically
neurologist
neurology
neuroma (pl ~mata,
  ~as)
neuromuscular
neuron (or ~one)
neuronal
neuronic
neuropath
neuropathic
neuropathological
neuropathologist
neuropathology
neuropathy
neuropeptide
neuropharmacologic
neuropharmacological
neuropharmacologist
neuropharmacology
neurophysiological
neurophysiologist
neurophysiology
neuropsychiatric
neuropsychiatrist
neuropsychiatry
neuropsychological
neuropsychologist
neuropsychology
neuropteran
neuropterous
neuroscience
neuroscientist
neurosis (pl ~oses)
neurosurgeon
neurosurgery
neurosurgical
neurotic
neurotically
neuroticism
neurotomy
neurotoxic
neurotoxicity
neurotoxicology
neurotoxin
neurotransmission
neurotransmitter
neurotrophic
neurotropic
neurotropism

neuter
neutered
neutral
neutralisation (*or* ~iz~)
neutralise (*or* ~ize)
neutralism
neutralist
neutrality
neutrally
neutrino (*pl* ~os)
neutron
neutrophil
neutrophilic
Nevada
never
nevermore
nevertheless
Nevis
new
newbie
newborn
Newcastle
newcomer
newel
newfangled
new-fashioned
Newfoundland
newly
newly-weds
newness
news
newsagent
newsboy
newscast
newscaster
newscasting
newsflash
newsgirl
newsgroup
newsletter
newspaper
newspeak
newsprint
newsreader
newsreel
newsroom
news-sheet
news-stand
newsvendor
newsworthiness

newsworthy
newsy
newt
newton
Newtonian
next
nexus (*pl* ~xus, ~uses)
niacin
Niagara
nib
nibbed
nibble
nibbler
nibbling
nibblingly
niblick
nibs
Nicam (*or* NICAM)
Nicaragua
Nice *France*
nice *pleasant*
nicely
Nicene
niceness
nicety
niche
nick
nickel (~lled, ~lling; *US* ~led, ~ling)
nickelodeon
nickname
Nicobar
nicotiana
nicotinamide
nicotinate
nicotine
nicotinic
nictate
nictating
nictation
nictitate
nidiculous
nidification
niece
Nietzsche
Nietzschean
niffy
niftily
niftiness
nifty

nigella
Niger
Nigeria
Nigerian
niggard
niggardliness
niggardly
nigger (*tab*)
niggle
niggler
niggling
nigglingly
nigglingness
nigh
night
nightcap
nightclass
nightclothes
nightclub
nightclubber
nightclubbing
nightdress
nightfall
nightgown
nighthawk
nightie (*or* ~ty)
nightingale
nightjar
nightless
nightlife
nightlong
nightly
nightmare
nightmarish
nightmarishly
nightshade
nightshirt
nightspot
night-time
nightwatchman (*pl* ~men)
nightwear
nighty (*or* ~tie)
nigrescence
nigrescent
nigritude
nihilism
nihilist
nihilistic
nihility

Nike (*tr*)
Nikkei
nil
Nile
nilgai (*or* ~gau)
Nilotic
nilpotent
nim
nimble
nimbleness
nimbly
nimbostratus
nimbus (*pl* ~bi, ~uses)
nimby (N~)
nimbyism (N~)
nincompoop
nine
ninefold
ninepins
nineteen
nineteenth
ninetieth
ninety
ninetyfold
ninja
ninjutsu (*or* ~jit~)
ninny
ninon
ninth
ninthly
nip (~pped, ~pping)
nipper
nippily
nippiness
nipple
nipplewort
nippy
nirvana (N~)
nit
nitinol
nit-pick
nit-picker
nit-picking
nitrate
nitration
nitrazepam
nitre (*US* ~ter)
nitric
nitride
nitrification

nitrify
nitrite
nitro
nitrobenzene
nitrocellulose
nitrochalk
nitrogen
nitrogenous
nitroglycerine (*US* ~rin)
nitromethane
nitrophilous
nitrosamine
nitrous
nitty-gritty
nitwit
nitwitted
nitwittedness
Niue
no (*pl* noes)
Noah
nob
no-ball
nobble
nobbler
Nobel
Nobelist
nobelium
nobiliary
nobility
noble
nobleman (*pl* ~men)
nobleness
noblesse
noblewoman (*pl* ~women)
nobly
nobody
no-brainer
nociceptive
nociceptor
nock (! knock) *notch*
no-claims
noctambulation
noctambulism
noctambulist
noctilucence
noctilucent
nocturnal
nocturnally
nocturne

nod (~dded, ~dding)
nodal
noddy
node
nodosity
nodular
nodulated
nodulation
nodule
nodulose
nodulous
Noel (*or* ~ël)
noesis
noetic
no-frills
nog
noggin
no-go
no-good
Noh (*or* No; *also* noh, no) *theatre*
noise
noiseless
noiselessly
noiselessness
noisemaker
noisette
noisily
noisiness
noisome
noisomeness
noisy
nom de guerre (*pl* noms~)
nom de plume (*pl* noms~; *also* noms-de-~)
nomad
nomadic
nomadically
nomadism
no-man's-land
nombril
nomen
nomenclature
nominal
nominalisation (*or* ~iz~)
nominalise (*or* ~ize)
nominalism

nominalist
nominalistic
nominally
nominate
nomination
nominative
nominator
nominee
nomogram
nomograph
nomographic
nomographical
nomography
nomological
nomologically
nomothetic
nonagenarian
nonagon
nonagonal
no-name
nonane
nonary
nonce
nonchalance
nonchalant
nonchalantly
nonconformism (N~)
nonconformist (N~)
nonconformity
nondescript
nondescriptly
nondescriptness
none
nonentity
no-no
no-nonsense
nonpareil
nonplus
nonplussed
nonsense
nonsensical
nonsensicality
nonsensically
nonsensicalness
nontheless
noodles
nook
noon
noose
nootropic

nor
noradrenaline (*or* ~in)
Nordic
Norfolk
nori
norm
normal
normalcy
normalisation (*or* ~iz~)
normalise (*or* ~ize)
normaliser (*or* ~iz~)
normality
normally
normalness
Norman
Normandy
Normanesque
normative
normatively
normativeness
normoglycaemia (*or*
    ~cem~)
normoglycaemic (*or*
    ~cem~)
normotensive
Norse
Norseman (*pl* ~men)
Norsewoman (*pl*
    ~women)
north
north-east
north-easter
north-easterly
north-eastern
northerly
northern
northerner
northernmost
northing
Northumberland
Northumbria
Northumbrian
northward
northwardly
northwards
northwest
northwester
northwesterly
northwestern
Norway

Norwegian
Norwich
nose
nosebag
noseband
nosebleed
nose-cone
nosedive
nosegay
nosepiece
nosey (*or* nosy)
no-show
nosily
nosiness
nosing
nosographer
nosographic
nosography
nosological
nosologist
nosology
nostalgia
nostalgic
nostalgically
Nostradamus
nostril
nostrum (*pl* ~ums, ~ra)
nosy (*or* ~sey)
notability
notable
notableness
notably
notaphilic
notaphilist
notaphily
notarise (*or* ~ize)
notary
notate
notation
notational
notator
notch
notched
notcher
notchy
note
notebook
notecase
noted
notelet

notepad
notepaper
noteworthiness
noteworthy
nothing
nothingness
nothosaur
notice
noticeable
noticeably
noticeboard (or ~board)
notification
notify
notion
notional
notionally
notochord
notoriety
notorious
notoriously
Nottingham
notwithstanding
Nouakchott
nougat
nougatine
nought
noumenal
noumenon (*pl* ~ena)
noun
nourish
nourisher
nourishing
nourishingly
nourishment
nous
nouveau (*pl* ~ux)
nouvelle
nova (*pl* ~ae, ~as)
novate
novation
novel
novelese
novelette
novelettish
novelisation (or ~iz~)
novelise (or ~ize)
novelist
novelistic
novella

novelly
novelty
November
novice
novitiate (*or* ~ici~)
novocaine (N~, *tr*)
now
nowadays
Nowell (*or* ~el)
nowhere
no-win
nowise
noxious
noxiously
noxiousness
nozzle
nth
nuance
nub
nubile
nubility
nucellar
nucellus (*pl* ~lli)
nuciferous
nucivorous
nuclear
nuclease
nucleate
nucleated
nucleation
nucleic
nucleoid
nucleolus (*pl* ~oli)
nucleon
nucleonics
nucleophile
nucleophilic
nucleoplasm
nucleoside
nucleosomal
nucleosome
nucleosynthesis
nucleosynthetic
nucleotide
nucleus (*pl* ~ei)
nuclide
nuclidic
nude
nudge
nudger

nudibranch (*pl* ~chs)
nudism
nudist
nudity
nugacity
nugatoriness
nugatory
nugget
nuggety
nuisance
nuke
null
nullification
nullifier
nullify
nullity
nullness
numb
numbat
numbed
number
numberless
numberplate (or ~-plate)
numbly
numbness
numbskull (*or* nums~)
numen (*pl* ~mina)
numerability
numerable
numerably
numeracy
numeral
numerate
numeration
numerator
numeric
numerical
numerically
numerological
numerologist
numerology
numerous
numerously
numerousness
numinous
numismatic
numismatically
numismatics
numismatist
numismatologist

numismatology
numskull (*or* numbs~)
nun
nunciature
nuncio (*pl* ~os)
nunnery
nunnish
nuptial
nuptiality
nuptially
Nuremberg
nurse
nurseling
nursemaid
nursery
nurserymaid
nurseryman
nursing
nurturance
nurture
nut (~tted, ~tting)
nutcase
nutcrackers
nutgall
nuthatch
nutlet
nutmeg
nutria
nutrient
nutriment
nutrimental
nutrition
nutritional
nutritionalist
nutritionally
nutritionist
nutritious
nutritiously
nutritiousness
nutritive
nutritively
nuts
nutshell
nutter
nuttiness
nutty
nuzzle
nyala
Nyasaland
nylon

nymph
nymphal
nymphean
nymphet (*or* ~ette)
nympholepsy
nympholept
nympholeptic
nymphomania
nymphomaniac
nymphomaniacal
nystagmic
nystagmoid
nystagmus

oaf
oafish
oafishly
oafishness
oak
oaken
oar
oarlock
oarsman (*pl* ~men)
oarswoman (*pl*
  ~women)
oasis (*pl* ~ses)
oat
oaten
oath
oatmeal
obbligato (*or* obl~; *pl*
  ~os, ~ati)
obduracy
obdurate
obdurately
obdurateness
obedience
obedient
obeisance
obeisant

obelisk
obelus
obese
obeseness
obesity
obey
obfuscate
obfuscation
obfuscatory
obituarial
obituarist
obituary
object
objectifiable
objectifiably
objectification
objectify
objection
objective
objectively
objectiveness
objectivisation (*or* ~iz~)
objectivise (*or* ~ize)
objectivism
objectivist
objectivistic
objectivity
objet d'art (*pl* objets~)
objuration
objure
oblate
oblation
obligate
obligation
obligato (*or* obb~; *pl*
  ~os, ~ati)
obligatoriness
obligatory
oblige
obliging
obligingly
obligingness
oblique
obliquely
obliqueness
obliquity
obliterate
obliteration
obliterative
oblivion

oblivious
obliviously
obliviousness
oblong
obloquy
obnoxiously
obnoxiousness
oboe
obscene
obscenely
obsceneness
obscenity
obscurant
obscurantism
obscurantist
obscure
obscurely
obscurity
obsequious
obsequiously
obsequiousness
observable
observably
observance
observant
observantly
observation
observational
observationally
observatory
observe
observer
obsess
obsession
obsessional
obsessionally
obsessionist
obsessive
obsessively
obsessiveness
obsidian
obsolesce
obsolescence
obsolescent
obsolete
obsoletely
obsoleteness
obstacle
obstetrical
obstetrically

obstetrician
obstetrics
obstinacy
obstinance
obstinancy
obstinate
obstinately
obstreperous
obstreperousness
obstruct
obstruction
obstructionism
obstructionist
obstructive
obstructively
obstructiveness
obstructivism
obstructivist
obstructor
obtain
obtainable
obtainer
obtainment
obtrude
obtrusion
obtrusive
obtrusively
obtrusiveness
obtuse
obtusely
obtuseness
obverse
obversely
obviate
obviation
obvious
obviously
obviousness
ocarina
occasion
occasional
occasionalism
occasionalist
occasionally
occident (O~)
occidental
occidentally
occipital
occiput
occlude

occlusion
occlusive
occult
occultation
occultism
occultist
occultly
occultness
occupancy
occupant
occupation
occupational
occupationally
occupy
occur (~rred, ~rring)
occurrence
occurrent
ocean
oceanarium (*pl* ~iums,
~ia)
oceanic
oceanicity
oceanographer
oceanographic
oceanographical
oceanography
oceanological
oceanologist
oceanology
ocellated
ocellus
ocelot
oche
ochre (*UK*; *US* ocher)
o'clock
octagon
octagonal
octagonally
octahedral (*or* octo~)
octahedron (*or* octo~)
octal
octane
octant
octave
octavo (*pl* ~os)
octet (*or* ~ette)
October
octogenarian
octohedral (*or* octa~)
octohedron (*or* octa~)

octopus (*pl* ~pi, ~uses)
octopush
octuple
ocular
ocularist
oculist
oculomotor
odd
oddish
oddity
oddly
oddment
oddness
odds
ode
odious
odiously
odiousness
odium
odometer
odometry
odontalgia
odontalgic
odontological
odontologist
odontology
odor (*US*; *UK* ~our)
odorant
odoriferous
odoriferousness
odorise (*or* ~ize)
odorosity
odorous
odorously
odorousness
odour (*US* odor)
odyssey
oecumenical (*or* ec~)
oecumenist (*or* ec~)
oedema (*or* ed~)
oedematose (*or* ed~)
oedematous (*or* ed~)
Oedipus
oenological
oenologist
oenology
oersted
oesophagus (*or* es~; *pl* ~guses, ~gi)
oestrogen (*or* es~)

oestrous (*adj*; *or* es~)
oestrus (*n*; *or* es~)
off
offal
offbeat
offcut
offence (*US* ~nse)
offend
offender
offense (*US*; *UK* ~nce)
offensive
offensively
offensiveness
offer (~ered, ~ering)
offered
offerer
offering
offertory
offhand
offhanded
offhandedly
offhandedness
office
officer
official
officialdom
officialese
officialism
officiant
officiate
officiation
officiator
officinal
officious
officiously
officiousness
offing
offish
offishly
offishness
off-key
off-licence
off-limits
offline (*or* off-~)
off-load
off-peak
off-putting
off-season
offset
offshoot

offshore
offside
offspring
often
ogam (O~; *or* ogham)
ogee
ogham (O~; *or* ogam)
ogle
ogre
ogress
Ohio
ohm
ohmmeter
oil
oilbird
oilcloth
oiler
oilfield
oilily
oiliness
oilman
oilseed
oilskin
oilstone
oily
oink
ointment
OK (*or* okay)
okapi (*pl* ~pi, ~pis)
okay (*or* OK)
Oklahoma
okra
old
olden
old-fashioned
oldie
old-time
old-timer
old-world
oleaceous
oleaginous
oleaginousness
oleander
oleomargarine
olfactory
oligarch
oligarchic
oligarchical
oligarchy
Oligocene

oligopolist
oligopolistic
oligopoly
olivaceous
olive
olivine
olm
Olympiad
Olympian
Olympic
ombudsman (O~; *pl* ~men)
omega
omelette (*US* ~let)
omen
omicron
ominous
ominously
ominousness
omissible
omission
omit (~tted, ~tting)
omnibus
omnidirectional
omnidirectionality
omnidirectionally
omnifarious
omnifariously
omnifariousness
omnipotence
omnipotent
omnipotently
omnipresence
omnipresent
omniscience
omniscient
omnisciently
omnivore
omnivorous
omnivorously
omnivorousness
onanism
onanist
onanistic
once
once-over
oncogene
oncogenesis
oncogenic
oncologist

oncology
oncoming
one
oneiric (*or* onir~)
oneness
one-off
onerous
onerously
onerousness
oneself
one-sided
one-sidedly
one-sidedness
one-stop
one-to-one
one-track
one-upmanship
one-way
ongoing
onion
online
onlooker
only
onomastics
onomatopoeia
onomatopoeic
onomatopoeically
onrush
onscreen
onset
onshore
onside
onslaught
onstage
onstream
onto
ontogenesis
ontogenetic
ontogenetically
ontogenic
ontogenically
ontogeny
ontologic
ontological
ontologically
ontology
onus
onward
onwards
onyx

oocyte
oodles
oogamous
oogamy
oogenesis
oolite
oolith
oolitic
oological
oologist
oology
oomph
oospore
ooze
oozily
ooziness
oozy
opacity
opal
opalescence
opalescent
opaque
opaquely
opaqueness
open
open-cast
open-ended
open-endedly
open-endedness
opener
open-handed
open-handedly
open-handedness
open-hearted
open-heartedly
open-heartedness
opening
open-minded
open-mindedly
open-mindedness
openness
opera
operability
operable
operant
operate
operatic
operatically
operating
operation

operational
operationalism
operationalist
operationality
operationally
operative
operatively
operativeness
operator
operetta
ophthalmia
ophthalmic
ophthalmological
ophthalmologist
ophthalmology
ophthalmoscope
ophthalmoscopic
ophthalmoscopy
ophthalmy
opiate
opine
opinion
opinionated
opinionatedness
opium
opossum
opponency
opponent
opportune
opportunely
opportuneness
opportunism
opportunist
opportunistic
opportunity
opposability
opposable
oppose
opposed
opposedness
opposer
opposing
opposite
oppositely
oppositeness
opposition
oppress
oppression
oppressional
oppressive

oppressively
oppressiveness
oppressor
opprobrious
opprobriously
opprobrium
oppugn
oppugner
opt
optic
optical
optically
optician
optics
optimal
optimalisation (or ~iz~)
optimalise (or ~ize)
optimality
optimisation (or ~iz~)
optimise (or ~ize)
optimism
optimist
optimistic
optimistically
optimum (pl ~ums,
   ~tima)
option
optional
optionally
optometer
optometric
optometrist
optometry
opt-out
opulence
opulency
opulent
opulently
opuntia
opus (pl ~ses, opera)
oracle
oracular
oracularity
oracy
oral
Orange phones, order
orange fruit
orangeade
orangery
orang-utan

orate
oration
orator
oratorial
oratorical
oratorically
oratorio
oratory
orb
orbicular
orbiculate
orbit (~tted, ~tting)
orbital
orc
orchard
orchestra
orchestral
orchestrally
orchestrate
orchestration
orchestrator
orchid
ordain
ordainer
ordainment
ordeal
order (~ered, ~ering)
ordered
orderedness
orderly
ordinal
ordinance
ordinarily
ordinariness
ordinary
ordinate
ordination
ordnance
Ordovician
ordure
ore
oregano (pl ~os)
Oregon
organ
organellar
organelle
organic
organically
organisation (or ~iz~)
organisational (or ~iz~)

organisationally (or
  ~iz~)
organise (or ~ize)
organiser (or ~iz~)
organism
organismal
organismic
organismically
organist
organza
orgasm
orgasmic
orgasmically
orgastic
orgastically
orgiastic
orgy
oribi (pl ~bi, ~bis)
oriel
Orient countries
orient position
oriental (O~)
Orientalist
orientate
orientation
oriented
orienteer
orienteering
orifice
origami
origanum
origin
original
originality
originally
originate
origination
originative
originator
oriole
Orion
orison
Orkney
ormer
ormolu (or ~mu~)
ornament
ornamental
ornamentally
ornamentation
ornamenter

ornamentist
ornate
ornately
ornateness
ornithischian
ornithological
ornithologically
ornithologist
ornithology
orogen
orogenesis
orogenetic
orogenic
orogeny
orographic
orographical
orographically
orography
orological
orologist
orology
oropharyngeal
oropharynx
orotund
orotundity
orphan
orphanage
Orphean
Orphic
Orphism
orris
orthoclase
orthodontic
orthodontics
orthodontist
Orthodox Church
orthodox accepted
orthodoxy
orthogenesis
orthogenetic
orthogenetically
orthogonal
orthographer
orthographic
orthographically
orthographist
orthography
orthopaedic (or ~ped~)
orthopaedically (or
  ~ped~)

orthopaedics (or ~ped~)
orthopaedist (or ~ped~)
orthopteran
oscillate
oscillating
oscillation
oscillator
oscillatory
oscillograph
oscillographic
oscillographically
oscilloscope
oscine
oscular
osculate
osculation
osculatory
osier
osmiridium
osmium
osmose
osmosis
osmotic
osmotically
osprey (pl ~eys)
osseous
ossicle
ossification
ossify
ossuarium (pl ~ria)
ossuary
ostensibility
ostensible
ostensibly
ostensive
ostensively
ostensiveness
ostentation
ostentatious
ostentatiousness
osteoarthritic
osteoarthritis
osteological
osteologically
osteologist
osteology
osteomalacia
osteomalacial
osteomalactic
osteomyelitis

osteopath
osteopathic
osteopathically
osteopathy
osteoporosis
osteoporotic
ostracise (*or* ~ize)
ostracism
ostrich
otalgia
other
otherwise
otherworldliness
otherworldly
otiose
otioseness
otiosity
otitis
otolaryngological
otolaryngologist
otolaryngology
otological
otologist
otology
otorhinolaryngology
otoscope
otter
Ottoman *Empire*
ottoman *seat*
ought
ouija (O~)
ounce
ourselves
oust
out
outage
out-and-out
outback
outbid (~dding)
outboard
outbreak
outbuilding
outburst
outcast
outclass
outcome
outcrop
outcry
outdate
outdated

outdatedness
outdistance
outdo (outdid, outdone)
outdoor
outer
outermost
outface
outfield
outfielder
outfit
outflank
outflow
outfox
outgoing
outgrow (outgrew,
     outgrown)
outgrowing
outgrowth
outgun
outhouse
outing
outlandish
outlandishly
outlandishness
outlast
outlaw
outlay
outlet
outlier
outline
outlive
outlook
outmode
outmoded
outmost
outpatient
outperform
outpost
outpouring
output
outrage
outrageous
outrageously
outrageousness
outran
outrank
outreach
outrider
outrigger
outright

outrightness
outrun
outrun (outran,
     outrunning)
outsell (outsold)
outset
outshine (outshone)
outshoot
outside
outsider
outsize
outskirts
outsmart
outsource
outsourcing
outspoken
outspokenly
outspokenness
outstanding
outstay
outstretch
outstretched
outstrip
out-take
outvote
outward
outweigh
outwit (~tted, ~tting)
outworn
ouzel (*or* ~sel)
ouzo
oval
ovarian
ovariectomy
ovary
ovation
ovational
oven
ovenproof
ovenware
over
overall
overarching
overcast
overcoat
overcome
overdo (overdid,
     overdone)
overdose
overdraft

overdrive
overdue
overestimate
overflow
overgrown
overhaul
overhead
overhear (overheard)
overkill
overlap
overlay
overliness
overload
overlook
overly
overlying
overmuch
overnight
overpaid
overpower
overrate
override
overrule
overrun
overseas
oversee (oversaw,
  overseen)
overseer
oversight
oversleep (overslept)
overt
overtake (overtook,
  overtaken)
overthrow
overtime
overtness
overture
overturn
overview
overwhelm
overwork
oviduct
ovine
oviparity
oviparous
ovipositor
ovoid
ovoviviparity
ovoviviparous
ovulate

ovulation
ovule
ovum (*pl* ova)
owe
owing
owl
owlet
owlish
owlishly
owlishness
own
owner
ownership
ox (*pl* oxen)
oxalate
oxalic
oxalis
oxbow
Oxbridge
Oxford
oxidant
oxidation
oxide
oxidisation (*or* ~iz~)
oxidise (*or* ~ize)
oxlip
Oxonian
oxtail
oxyacetylene
oxygen
oxygenate
oxygenation
oxygenator
oxygenise (*or* ~ize)
oxymoron
oxytocic
oxytocin
oyster
oystercatcher
ozalid (O~, *tr*)
Ozark
ozone
ozonisation (*or* ~iz~)
ozonise (*or* ~ize)
ozoniser (*or* ~iz~)
ozonosphere

paca
pace
pacemaker
pacer
pacesetter
pacey (*or* ~cy)
pachyderm
Pacific *Ocean*
pacific *peaceful*
pacification
pacifier
pacifism
pacifist
pacify
pack
package
packager
packaging
packer
packet
packethorse
packing
packman (*pl* ~men)
pact
pacy (*or* ~cey)
pad (~dded, ~dding)
padded
padding
paddle
paddock
paddy
padlock
padre
padrone
paean (*US, also* pe~)
paediatric (*or* pe~)
paediatrician (*or* pe~)
paediatrics (*or* pe~)
paedologist (*or* pe~)

paedology (*or* pe~)
paedophile (*or* pe~)
paedophilia (*or* pe~)
paella
pagan
paganise (*or* ~ize)
paganism
page
pageant
pageantry
pageboy
pager
paginate
pagination
pagoda
pail (! pale) *bucket*
pain (! pane) *hurt*
painful
painfully
painfulness
painkiller
painless
painlessly
painlessness
painstaking
painstakingly
paint
paintball
paintbox
paintbrush
painter
paintwork
pair (! pare, pear) *two*
pairing
paisley (P~)
Pakistan
Pakistani
pakora
pal
palace
paladin
palaeoanthropology (*or* ~le~)
palaeobiology (*or* ~le~)
palaeobotany (*or* ~le~)
palaeocene (P~; *or* ~le~)
palaeoecology (*or* ~le~)
palaeographer (*or* ~le~)
palaeography (*or* ~le~)

palaeolithic (P~; *or* ~le~)
palaeomagnetism (*or* ~le~)
palaeontologist (*or* ~le~)
palaeontology (*or* ~le~)
palaeopathology (*or* ~le~)
palaeozoic (P~; *or* ~le~)
palaeozoological (*or* ~le~)
palaeozoology (*or* ~le~)
palamino (*or* palo~)
palatability
palatable
palatably
palatal
palatalisation (*or* ~iz~)
palatalise (*or* ~ize)
palatalised (*or* ~ized)
palatalising (*or* ~iz~)
palate (! palette, pallet) *mouth*
palatial
palatially
palatialness
palatinate (P~)
palatine (P~)
Palau
Palauan
palaver
palazzo (*pl* ~zzi)
pale (! pail) *colour, fence*
palely
paleness
Palestine
Palestinian
palette (! palate, pallet) *art*
palimony
palimpsest
palindrome
palindromic
palindromist
paling
palisade
pall
Palladian
pallbearer

pallet (! palate, palette) *platform, bed*
palliate
palliative
pallid
pallidness
pallium
pallor
pally
palm
palmaceous
palmar
palmate
palmer
palmetto (*pl* ~os, ~oes)
palmist
palmistry
palmitate
palmitic
palmitin
palmtop
palmy
palmyra
palomino (*or* pala~)
palp (*pl* ~ps, ~pi)
palpability
palpable
palpableness
palpably
palpate
palpation
palpitate
palpitation
palsied
palsy
paltrily
paltriness
paltry
paly
palynology
pampas
pamper
pamperer
pamphlet
pamphleteer
pan (~nned, ~nning)
panacea
panache
Panama *country*
panama *hat*

Panamanian
panatella (*or* ~ela)
pancake
pancetta
panchromatic
panchromatism
pancreas
pancreatic
panda (! pander) *animal*
pandemic
pandemonic
pandemonium
pander (! panda) *sexual*
Pandora
pane (! pain) *glass*
panegyric
panegyrical
panegyrist
panel (~lled, ~lling; *US*
  ~led, ~ling)
panelled (*US* ~eled)
panelling (*US* ~eling)
panellist
panettone
panful
pang
Pangaea (*or* ~gea)
pangolin
pangram
panhandle
panhellenic
panic (~cked, ~cking)
panicky
panicle
paniculate
Panjabi (*or* Pun~)
panjandrum
pannage
panne
pannier
pannus
panoply
panoptic
panoptical
panorama
panoramic
panoramically
panpipes
pansy
pant

pantaloons
pantechnicon
pantheism
pantheist
pantheistic
pantheistical
pantheon (P~)
panther
pantherine
pantherish
panties
pantihose
pantile
panto (*pl* ~os)
pantograph
pantographer
pantography
pantomime
pantomimic
pantomimical
pantothenic
pantothenol
pantry
pants
panzer
pap
papa
papacy
papain
papal
papally
Papanicolaou
paparazzo (*pl* ~zzi)
papaverine
papaw (*or* paw~)
papaya
paper
paperback
paperboy
paperclip
papergirl
paperiness
paperknife
paperless
paperweight
paperwork
papery
papier-mâché
papilla (*pl* ~ae)
papillary

papillate
papillectomy
papilliferous
papilloma (*pl* ~mata,
  ~as)
papillomatous
papillon
papillote
papism
papist
papistic
papistical
papistry
papoose (*US*)
pappadum (*or* po~,
  ~dom)
pappus (*pl* ~ppi, ~uses)
paprika
Papua
Papuan
papula
papular
papule (*pl* ~ules, ~lae)
papyrologist
papyrology
papyrus (*pl* ~ri, ~uses)
par
parabiosis
parabiotic
parable
parabola (*pl* ~ae, ~as)
parabolic
parabolically
paraboloid
parabrake
paracetamol
parachute
parachutist
Paraclete
parade
paradigm
paradisal
paradise
paradisiac
paradisiacal
parados
paradox
paradoxical
paradoxically
paradoxy

paraesthesia (*or* ~re~)
paraffin
paraffiny
paragenesia
paragenesis
paraglider
paragliding
paragon
paragraph
Paraguay
Paraguayan
parainfluenza
parakeet
paralanguage
paraldehyde
paralinguistics
parallax
parallel (~eled, ~eling)
parallelism
parallelogram
paralogism
Paralympics
paralyse (*US* ~yze)
paralysed (*US* ~yzed)
paralysing (*US* ~yz~)
paralysis (*pl* ~yses)
paralytic
paralytically
paramatta (*or* parra~)
paramecium (P~; *pl* ~ia)
paramedic
paramedical
parameter
parametric
parametrical
paramilitary
paramnesia
paramount
paramountcy
paramour
paranoia
paranoiac
paranoic
paranoid
paranormal
paranym
parapenting
parapet
paraph
paraphernalia

paraphrase
paraphrastic
paraphrastically
paraphysis
paraplegia
paraplegic
paraprofessional
parapsychological
parapsychologically
parapsychologist
parapsychology
parasail
parasailing
parascend
parascending
parascience
parasite
parasitic
parasitical
parasitically
parasiticide
parasitise (*or* ~ize)
parasitism
parasitoid
parasitologist
parasitology
parasol
parasuicide
parasynthesis
parataxis
parathion
parathyroid
paratrooper
paratroopers
parazoa (P~)
parazoan (P~; *pl*
   ~zoans, ~zoa)
parboil
parcel (~lled, ~lling; *US*
   ~led, ~ling)
parcelled (*US* ~eled)
parcelling (*US* ~eling)
parch
parchment
pardon
pardonable
pardonably
pardoner
pare (! pair, pear) *trim*
parenchyma

parent
parentage
parental
parenthesis (*pl* ~eses)
parenthesise (*or* ~ize)
parenthetic
parenthetical
parenthetically
parenthood
parenting
parentless
paresis
paretic
par excellence
parfait
parfumerie
parget (~eted, ~eting)
parheliacal
parhelic
parhelion (*pl* ~lia)
pariah
parietal
pari-mutuel
paring
paripinnate
Paris
parish
parishioner
Parisian
Parisienne
parity
park
parka
park-and-ride
parker
Parkinsonism
Parkinson's
parkland
parlance
parlando
parley
parliament (P~)
parliamentarian (P~)
parliamentarianism
parliamentarism
parliamentary
parlour (*US* ~or)
parlous
Parmesan
Parnassus

parochial
parochialism
parochiality
parochially
parodic
parodical
parodist
parody
parolable
parole
parolee
paronomasia
paronomastic
paronym
parotic
parotid
paroxysm
paroxysmal
paroxysmic
parquet
parquetry
parr
parramatta (*or* para~)
parricidal
parricide
parrot
parroter
parry
parse
parsec
Parsee (*or* Parsi)
parser
parsimonious
parsimoniously
parsimoniousness
parsimony
parsing
parsley
parsnip
parson
parsonage
part
partake (partook,
  partaking)
partaken
partaker
parterre
parthenogenesis
parthenogenetic
Parthenon

partial
partiality
partially
partialness
participant
participate
participation
participator
participial
participially
participle
particle
particoloured (*US* ~or~)
particular
particularisation (*or*
  ~iz~)
particularise (*or* ~ize)
particularism
particularity
particularly
particulate
partisan (*occ* ~zan)
partita
partite
partition
partitioner
partitionist
partly
partner (~ered, ~ering)
partnership
partook
partridge
part-time
part-timer
parturient
parturition
party
parvenu
parvenue
parvovirus
PASCAL (*or* Pascal)
  computing
pascal *unit of pressure*
paschal
pashmina
pasquinade
pass
passable (! passible) *quite
  good*
passableness

passably
passacaglia
passage
passageway
passant
passé
passenger
passe-partout (*or*
  passpartout)
passer
passer-by (*pl* passers-~)
passerine
passible (! passable)
  suffering
passim
passing
Passion *Christ*
passion *emotion*
passionate
passionately
passionateness
passionless
passive
passively
passiveness
passivity
Passover
passport
password
past
pasta
paste
pasteboard
pastel (! pastille) *crayon*
pastern
Pasteur
pasteurisation (*or* ~iz~)
pasteurise (*or* ~ize)
pasteurised (*or* ~ized)
pasteurising (*or* ~iz~)
pasticcio
pastiche
pastille (! pastel) *sweet*
pastily
pastime
pastiness
pastor
pastoral
pastorale
pastoralism

pastoralist
pastorally
pastrami
pastry
pasturage
pasture
pasty
pat (~tted, ~tting)
Patagonia
patch
patchable
patchily
patchiness
patchouli
patchwork
patchy
pate
pâté
patella (*pl* ~ae)
paten
patent
patentee
patently
patentor
pater
paterfamilias
paternal
paternalism
paternalist
paternalistic
paternalistically
paternally
paternity
paternoster (P~)
path
pathetic
pathetically
pathfinder
pathogen
pathogenesis
pathogenic
pathogenicity
pathogeny
pathological
pathologically
pathologist
pathology
pathos
pathway
patience

patient
patiently
patina
patinated
patination
patio (*pl* ~os)
patisserie
patois
patrial
patriarch
patriarchal
patriarchally
patriarchate
patriarchy
patrician
patricide
patrimonial
patrimonially
patrimony
patriot
patriotic
patriotically
patriotism
patristic
patrol (~lled, ~lling)
patron
patronage
patronal
patroness
patronise (*or* ~ize)
patronising (*or* ~iz~)
patronisingly (*or* ~iz~)
patronymic
patter
pattern
patty
paucal
paucity
Pauline
paunch
pauper
pauperisation (*or* ~iz~)
pauperise (*or* ~ize)
pauperism
pause
pavane (*or* ~van)
pave
pavement
pavilion
paving

pavlova
Pavlovian
paw
pawl
pawn
pawnbroker
pawnbroking
pawnshop
pawpaw (*or* pap~)
pax
pay (paid)
payable
pay-and-display
payback
payee
payload
paymaster
payment
pay-per-click
pay-per-view
payphone
payroll
pea
peace
peaceable
peaceably
peaceful
peacefully
peacefulness
peacekeeper
peacekeeping
peacemaker
peacemaking
peacetime
peach
peachiness
peachy
peacock
peafowl
peak (! peek) *summit*
peaked
peaky
peal (! peel) *bells*
peanut
peapod (*or* pea-~)
pear (! pair, pare) *fruit*
pearl (! purl) *gem*
pearliness
pearling
pearly

peasant
peasantry
peat
peaty
pebble
pebbledash (*UK*)
pebbly
pecan
peccadillo (*pl* ~os, ~oes)
peck
pecker
peckish
pectin
pectoral
peculiar
peculiarity
peculiarly
pecuniary
pedagogic
pedagogical
pedagogically
pedagogue
pedagogy
pedal (! peddle) *lever,
bicycle*
pedalled (*US* ~aled)
pedaller (*US* ~aler;
! peddler) *bicycle*
pedalling (*US* ~aling)
pedalo
pedant
pedantic
pedantry
peddle (! pedal) *sell*
peddler (! pedaller) *seller*
peddling
pederast
pederasty
pedestal
pedestrian
pedestrianisation (*or*
~iz~)
pedestrianise (*or* ~ize)
pedestrianised (*or* ~ized)
pediatric (*or* paed~)
pediatrician (*or* paed~)
pediatrics (*or* paed~)
pedicel
pedicle
pedicure

pedigree
pedigreed
pedlar (*US* peddler)
pedo~ *see* paedo~
pedometer
peduncle
peduncular
pedunculate
pee (peed, peeing)
peek (! peak) *glance*
peekaboo
peel (! peal) *skin*
peeler
peeling
peep
peeper
peephole
peepshow
peepul (*or* pipal, pipul)
peer (! pier) *noble, look*
peerage
peeress
peerless
peerlessly
peeve
peeved
peevish
peevishly
peevishness
peewit (*or* pew~)
peg (~gged, ~gging)
Pegasus
pegboard
pegmatite
peignoir
pejoration
pejorative
pejoratively
Peking (*now* Beijing)
Pekingese
pekoe
pelagic
pelargonium
pelerine
pelham
pelican
pellagra
pellagrous
pellet (~eted, ~eting)
pellicle

pellitory
pell-mell
pellucid
pellucidity
pellucidly
pellucidness
pelmanism (P~)
pelmet
Peloponnese
peloria
pelorus
pelota
pelt
peltate
pelvic
pelvis (*pl* ~ises, pelves)
Pembroke
pemmican (*or* pemi~)
pen (~nned, ~nning)
penal
penalisation (*or* ~iz~)
penalise (*or* ~ize)
penalised (*or* ~ized)
penalising (*or* ~iz~)
penalty
penance
pence
penchant
pencil (~lled, ~lling; *US*
~led, ~ling)
pendant (*n, occ* ~ent)
pendent (*adj, occ* ~ant)
pending
pendular
pendulous
pendulously
pendulousness
pendulum
penetrability
penetrable
penetrably
penetrate
penetrating
penetratingly
penetration
penetrative
penetratively
penetrativeness
penetrator
penguin

penicillin
penile
peninsula
peninsular
penis (*pl* ~ises, ~nes)
penitence
penitent
penitential
penitentially
penitentiary
penitently
penknife (*pl* ~knives)
penmanship
penna
pennant
pennate
penniless
pennilessness
pennon
penny
pennyroyal
pennyweight
pennywort
pennyworth
penological
penologist
penology
pensile
pensileness
pensility
pension
pensionability
pensionable
pensionary
pensioner
pensionless
pensive
pensively
pensiveness
pent
pentacle
Pentagon *USA*
pentagon *five sides*
pentagonal
pentagram
pentahedral
pentahedron (*pl* ~rons, ~ra)
pentamerous
pentameter

pentane
pentangular
pentaprism
Pentateuch
pentathlete
pentathlon
pentatonic
Pentecost
Pentecostal
Pentecostalism
penthouse
pentose
penultimate
penumbra (*pl* ~ae, ~as)
penumbral
penumbrous
penurious
penuriously
penuriousness
penury
peony (*occ* pae~)
people
pep (~pped, ~pping)
peperomia
peperoni (*or* pepp~)
pepper
peppercorn
pepperiness
peppermill
peppermint
pepperoni (*or* pepe~)
pepper-pot
peppery
peppy
pepsin
pepsinate
peptic
peptide
peptone
per annum
per capita
per cent
per diem
per se
peradventure
perambulate
perambulation
perambulator
perambulatory
percale

perceivable
perceive
perceivedness
perceiver
percentage
percentile
percept
perceptibility
perceptible
perceptibly
perception
perceptional
perceptive
perceptively
perceptiveness
perceptivity
perceptual
perch
perchance
percipience
percipient
percipiently
percolate
percolation
percolative
percolator
percuss
percussion
percussionist
percussive
percutaneous
perdition
peregrinate
peregrination
peregrinator
peregrine
pereira (P~)
peremptorily
peremptoriness
peremptory
perennial
perenniality
perennially
perestroika
perfect
perfecta
perfectibility
perfectible
perfection
perfectionism

perfectionist
perfectly
perfectness
perfidious
perfidiously
perfidiousness
perfidy
perforate
perforation
perforator
perforce
perform
performable
performance
performer
performing
perfume
perfumed
perfumeless
perfumer
perfumery
perfunctorily
perfunctoriness
perfunctory
perfuse
perfusion
perfusive
pergola
perhaps
perianth
pericardiac
pericardial
pericarditis
pericardium (pl ~ia)
pericarp
pericarpial
perichondrium (pl ~ria)
periclase
periderm
peridium
peridot
perigee
perihelion (pl ~lia)
peril
perilous
perilously
perilousness
perimeter
perimetric
perimetrical

perimetry
perinatal
perineal
perineum
period
periodate
periodic
periodical
periodically
periodicity
periodontal
periodontics
periodontist
periodontitis
periodontology
periosteal
periosteum
peripatetic
peripatetically
peripheral
peripherally
periphery
periphrasis
periphrastic
periphrastically
periscope
periscopic
perish
perishability
perishable
perisperm
perissodactyl
peristalsis (pl ~lses)
peristaltic
peristomal
peristome
peristyle
peritoneal
peritoneum
peritonitis
periwinkle
perjure
perjurer
perjury
perk
perkily
perkiness
perky
perm
permafrost

permalloy
permanence
permanency
permanent
permanganate
permeability
permeable
permeably
permeance
permeant
permeate
permeation
Permian
permissibility
permissible
permissibly
permission
permissive
permissively
permissiveness
permit (~tted, ~tting)
permutability
permutable
permutate
permutation
permute
permuting
pernicious
perniciously
perniciousness
pernickety
peroneal
perorate
peroration
peroxide
perpendicular
perpendicularity
perpendicularly
perpetrate
perpetration
perpetrator
perpetual
perpetually
perpetuate
perpetuation
perpetuator
perpetuity
perplex
perplexing
perplexingly

perplexity
perquisite
perron
perry
perse
persecute
persecution
persecutor
perseverance
perseverant
perseveration
persevere
persevering
perseveringly
Persia
Persian
persimmon
persist
persistence
persistency
persistent
persistently
person
persona (*pl* ~ae, ~as)
personable
personableness
personably
personage
personal
personalisation (*or* ~iz~)
personalise (*or* ~ize)
personalised (*or* ~ized)
personalising (*or* ~iz~)
personality
personally
personate
personation
personative
personator
personification
personifier
personify
personnel
perspective
perspectivism
Perspex (*tr*)
perspicacious
perspicaciously
perspicacity

perspicuity
perspicuous
perspicuously
perspicuousness
perspiration
perspire
perspiringly
persuadable
persuade
persuader
persuasible
persuasion
persuasive
persuasively
persuasiveness
pert
pertain
pertinacious
pertinaciously
pertinaciousness
pertinacity
pertinence
pertinency
pertinent
pertly
pertness
perturb
perturbable
perturbably
perturbation
perturbed
perturbedly
perturbingly
pertussis
Peru
perusal
peruse
peruser
Peruvian
pervade
pervader
pervasion
pervasive
pervasively
pervasiveness
perverse
perversely
perverseness
perversion
perversity

perversive
pervert
perverted
perverter
pervertible
pervious
perviousness
Pesach
peseta
peso (*pl* ~os)
pessary
pessimism
pessimist
pessimistic
pessimistically
pest
pester
pesterer
pestering
pesteringly
pesticidal
pesticide
pestiferous
pestilence
pestilent
pestilential
pestilentially
pestilently
pestle
pesto (*pl* ~os)
pet
petal
petaliferous
petalled (*US* ~aled)
petaloid
petard
peter
petersham
pethidine
petiolate
petiole
petit
petit four (*pl* petits fours)
petit mal
petite
petition
petitionary
petitioner
petits pois

petrel (! petrol) *bird*
petrifaction
petrification
petrifier
petrify
Petrine
petrochemical
petrochemistry
petrocurrency
petrodollar
petroglyph
petrographer
petrography
petrol (! petrel) *fuel*
petrolatum
petroleum
petrological
petrologist
petrology
petronel
petrosal
petrous
petted
petticoat
pettifogger
pettifogging
pettily
pettiness
petting
pettish
pettishly
pettishness
petty
petulance
petulancy
petulant
petulantly
petunia
pew
pewter
pewterer
peyote
phaeton
phage
phagocyte
phagocytic
phagocytical
phagocytosis
phalangeal
phalanger

phalanx (*pl* ~xes,
   ~anges)
phalarope
phallic
phallicism
phallicist
phallism
phallist
phallocentric
phallocentricity
phallocentrism
phallus (*pl* ~lli, ~uses)
Phanerozoic
phantasm
phantasmagoria
phantasmagoric
phantasmagorical
phantasmagorically
phantasmal
phantom
pharaoh (P~)
pharisaic (P~)
pharisaical
pharmaceutical
pharmaceutically
pharmaceutics
pharmacist
pharmacological
pharmacologically
pharmacologist
pharmacology
pharmacopoeia
pharmacy
pharyngal
pharyngeal
pharyngitis
pharyngologist
pharyngology
pharyngoscopy
pharyngotomy
pharynx (*pl* ~nges,
   ~xes)
phase
phases
phatic
pheasant
phenetics
phenobarbital (*US*)
phenobarbitone (*UK*)
phenol

phenological
phenologist
phenology
phenomenal
phenomenalism
phenomenalist
phenomenally
phenomenological
phenomenologist
phenomenology
phenomenon (*pl*
   ~mena)
phenotype
phenotypic
phenotypical
phenyl
phenylalanine
phenylketonuria
pheromone
phew!
phi
phial
Philadelphia
philadelphus
philander
philanderer
philanthropic
philanthropical
philanthropically
philanthropist
philanthropy
philatelic
philatelist
philately
philharmonic
philhellene
philhellenic
philhellenism
philippic
Philippines
philistine
philistinism
Phillips *screwdriver*
philodendron (*pl* ~rons,
   ~ra)
philogyny
philological
philologist
philology
philosopher

philosophic
philosophical
philosophically
philosophise (*or* ~ize)
philosophiser (*or* ~iz~)
philosophy
phimosis
phlebitic
phlebitis
phlebotomist
phlebotomy
phlegm
phlegmatic
phlegmatical
phlegmatically
phloem
phlox (*pl* ~ox, ~xes)
phobia
phobic
phocine
phoebe
Phoenicia
phoenix (P~)
phonate
phonation
phone
phonecard
phone-in
phoneme
phonemic
phonemically
phonemics
phonetic
phonetically
phonetics
phoney (*UK*; *US* ~ny; *pl*
  ~neys, ~nies)
phoneyness (*US* ~nin~)
phonic
phonically
phonics
phoniness (*UK* ~neyn~)
phonogram
phonograph
phonographer
phonographist
phonography
phonological
phonologically
phonologist

phonology
phonometer
phonon
phonotactics
phonotype
phonotypist
phonotypy
phony (*US*; *UK* ~ney)
phosgene
phosphate
phosphene
phosphide
phosphine
phosphite
phosphor
phosphoresce
phosphorescence
phosphorescent
phosphoric
phosphorite
phosphorous (*adj*)
phosphorus (*n*)
phot
photic
photo
photoactinic
photocell
photochemistry
photochromic
photocomposition
photocopiable
photocopier
photocopy
photocopying
photoelectric
photoelectricity
photofit (P~, *tr*)
photogenic
photogram
photogrammetry
photograph
photographer
photographic
photographically
photography
photogravure
photojournalism
photojournalist
photolithography
photoluminescence

photoluminescent
photolysis
photolytic
photometer
photometry
photomontage
photon
photophobia
photorealism
photoreceptor
photosensitive
photosensitivity
photosphere
photostat (P~, *tr*)
photosynthesis
photosynthesise (*or*
  ~ize)
photosynthetic
phototactic
phototaxis
phototropism
phototypesetter
phototypesetting
phrasal
phrasally
phrase
phraseologist
phraseology
phrasing
phreaker
phreaking
phrenic
phrenological
phrenologist
phrenology
Phrygian
phthisis
phut
phycologist
phycology
phylactery
phyletic
phyllite
phyllode
phylloid
phyllome
phylloxera (*pl* ~ae, ~as)
phylogenesis
phylogenetic
phylogeny

phylum (*pl* ~la)
physic
physical
physicalism
physicality
physically
physician
physicism
physicist
physics
physiognomic
physiognomical
physiognomist
physiognomy
physiographer
physiographic
physiography
physiological
physiologically
physiologist
physiology
physiotherapist
physiotherapy
physique
phytochemical
phytochemistry
phytogenesis
phytogeny
phytology
phytopathologist
phytopathology
phytophagy
phytoplankton
phytosociology
pi
pianissimo
pianist
piano (*pl* ~os)
pianoforte
pianola (P~, *tr*)
piassava
piazza
pica
picador
picaresque
picaroon
picayune
piccalilli
piccolo
pick

pick-'n'-mix
pickaback
pickable
pickaxe (*UK; US* ~ax)
picker
pickerel
picket (~eted, ~eting)
picketer
pickiness
pickings
pickle
pickled
pickler
picklock
pick-me-up
pickpocket
pick-up
picky
pick-your-own
picnic (~cked, ~cking)
picnicker
picot
picric
Pict
pictogram
pictograph
pictographic
pictography
pictorial
pictorially
picture
picturesque
picturesquely
picturesqueness
piddle
piddling
piddock
pidgin (! pigeon)
    language
pie
piebald
piece
pièce de résistance (*pl*
    pièces~)
piecemeal
piecework
piecrust
pied-à-terre (*pl* pieds-~)
piedmont (P~)
pier (! peer) *structure*

piercable
pierce
piercing
piercingly
pierrot (P~)
pietà
pietism
pietist
pietistic
piety
piezoelectric
piezoelectricity
piezometer
piffle
pig (~gged, ~gging)
pigeon (! pidgin) *bird*
pigeonhole
pigeon-toed
piggery
piggish
piggishly
piggishness
piggy (*or* ~ggie)
piggyback
pigheaded
pigheadedly
pigheadedness
piglet
pigment
pigmentary
pigmentation
pigmented
pigmy (*usu* pyg~)
pigskin
pigsticking
pigsty
pigswill
pigtail
pika
pike
pikestaff
pilaster
pilau
pilchard
pile
pileate
pile-driver
piles
pilfer
pilferage

pilferer
pilfering
pilgrim
pilgrimage
piliferous
pill
pillage
pillager
pillar
pillbox
pillion
pillory
pillow
pillowcase
pillowslip
pilose
pilosity
pilot
pilotage
pilotless
pimento (*pl* ~os)
pimiento (*pl* ~os)
pimp
pimpernel
pimple
pimpled
pimpliness
pimply
pin (~nned, ~nning)
pinaceous
pinafore
pinaster
pinball
pince-nez
pincer
pincers
pinch
pinchbeck
pinched
pincushion
pine
pineal
pineapple
pinewood
ping
pinger
pingo (*pl* ~os, ~oes)
ping-pong
pinguid
pinguidity

pinhead
pinheaded
pinhole
pinion
pink
pinkish
pinkness
pinky
pinna (*pl* ~ae)
pinnace
pinnacle
pinnate
pinnately
pinnation
pinochle (*or* ~ocle)
pinpoint
pinprick
pinscher
pinstripe
pinstriped
pint
pintail
pintle
pinto (*pl* ~os)
pin-up
pinwheel
pinyin
pioneer
pious
piously
piousness
pip (~pped, ~pping)
pipa
pipal (*or* pipul, peepul)
pipe
pipeclay
pipefish
pipeful
pipeline
piper
pipette
pipework
piping
pipistrelle
pipit
pipkin
pipless
pippin
pipsqueak
pipul (*or* pipal, peepul)

piquancy
piquant
piqué *fabric*
pique *pride*
piquet
piracy
piranha (*or* ~aña)
pirate
piratic
piratical
piratically
piri-piri
pirouette
piscatorial
Piscean
Pisces
piscicultural
pisciculture
pisciculturist
piscina (*pl* ~ae, ~as)
piscine
piscivorous
pisolite
piss
pistachio
piste
pistil (! pistol) *plant*
pistillate
pistol (! pistil) *gun*
pistolled (*US* ~oled)
pistolling (*US* ~oling)
piston
pit (~tted, ~tting)
Pitcairn
pitch
pitchblende
pitcher
pitchfork
pitchy
piteous
piteously
piteousness
pitfall
pith
pithead
pithecanthropine
pithecanthropus (P~)
pithily
pithiness
pithy

pitiable
pitiableness
pitiably
pitied
pitiful
pitifully
pitifulness
pitiless
pitilessly
pitilessness
piton
pitstop
pitta
pittance
pitter-patter
pittosporum
pituitary
pity
pitying
pityingly
pivot (~ted, ~ting)
pivotal
pixel
pixie (or pixy)
pixilated (or ~illa~)
pixilation (or ~illa~)
pixy (or pixie)
pizza
pizzeria
pizzicato (pl ~os)
placability
placable
placableness
placably
placard
placate
placation
place (! plaice) location
placeable
placebo (pl ~os, ~oes)
placement
placenta
placental
placer
placet
placid
placidity
placidly
placidness
placket

placoderm
placoid
plagiarise (or ~ize)
plagiarised (or ~ized)
plagiarising (or ~iz~)
plagiarism
plagiarist
plagioclase
plague
plaice (! place) fish
plaid
plain (! plane) pattern,
    land
plainish
plainly
plainness
plainsman (pl ~men)
plainsong
plaint
plaintiff
plaintive
plaintively
plaintiveness
plait
plan (~nned, ~nning)
planar
planarian
planation
Planck
plane (! plain) surface,
    tool, tree, aeroplane
planet
planetarium (pl ~iums,
    ~ia)
planetary
planetoid
planetologist
planetology
plangency
plangent
plangently
planimeter
planisphere
plank
planking
plankton
planktonic
planner
planning
planographic

planography
planometer
planometry
plant
plantable
Plantagenet
plantain
plantation
planter
plantigrade
planular
plaque
plasm
plasma
plasmapheresis
plasmid
plasmodium
plasmolysis
plaster
plasterboard
plastered
plasterer
plastic
plasticine (P~, tr)
plasticise (or ~ize)
plasticity
plastid
plat du jour
plate
plateau (pl ~us, ~ux)
plateful
platelayer
platelet
platen
plater
platform
platina
platinum
platitude
platitudinise (or ~ize)
platitudinous
platonic (P~)
platonically
Platonism
Platonist
platoon
platter
platypus
plaudit
plausibility

plausible
plausibleness
plausibly
plausive
play
playa
playability
playable
play-act
playback
playbill
playboy
player
playfellow
playful
playfully
playfulness
playground
playgroup
playhouse
playing
playlet
playlist
playmate
play-off
playpen
playschool
plaything
playtime
playwright
plaza
plea
plead
pleadable
pleader
pleading
pleadingly
pleasable
pleasant
pleasantly
pleasantness
pleasantry
please
pleasedly
pleaser
pleasurable
pleasurableness
pleasurably
pleasure
pleat

pleater
pleb
plebeian
plebiscite
plectrum (*pl* ~ra, ~ums)
pledge
pledgeable
pledgee
pledger
Pleiades
Pleiocene (*or* Plio~)
Pleistocene
plenary
plenipotentiary
plenitude
plenteous
plenteously
plenteousness
plentiful
plentifully
plentifulness
plenty
plenum (*pl* ~na, ~ums)
pleonasm
pleonastic
pleonastically
plesiosaur
plethora
pleura (*pl* ~ae)
pleural
pleurisy
pleuritic
plexiform
plexor
plexus
pliability
pliable
pliableness
pliably
pliancy
pliant
plié
plier
pliers
plight
Plimsoll *shipping*
plimsoll (*or* ~sole) *shoe*
plinth
Pliocene (*or* Pleio~)
plod (~dded, ~dding)

plodder
plodding
ploddingly
ploidy
plonk
plop (~pped, ~pping)
plosion
plosive
plot (~tted, ~tting)
plotter
plough (*US* plow)
ploughman (*US* plow~;
  pl ~men)
ploughshare (*US* plow~)
plover
plow (*US*; *UK* plough)
ploy
pluck
pluckily
pluckiness
plucky
plug (~gged, ~gging)
plughole
plum
plumage
plumate
plumb (! plum) *measure*
plumbable
plumbago
plumbeous
plumber
plumbism
plumbline
plumbum
plume
pluminess
plummet
plummy
plump
plumper
plumply
plumpness
plumule
plumy
plunder
plunderer
plunge
plunger
plunk
pluperfect

plural
pluralisation (*or* ~iz~)
pluralise (*or* ~ize)
pluralised (*or* ~ized)
pluralising (*or* ~iz~)
pluralism
pluralist
pluralistic
plurality
plurally
plus (*pl* ~ses, ~sses)
plush
plushness
plushy
Pluto
plutocracy
plutocrat
plutocratic
plutocratically
plutonic
plutonium
pluvial
pluviograph
pluviometer
pluviometry
ply
Plymouth
plywood
pneuma
pneumatic
pneumatically
pneumatics
pneumoconiosis
pneumonia
pneumonoconiosis
poach
poacher
poaching
pochard
pock
pocket
pocketable
pocketbook
pocketful
pockmark
pockmarked
pod (~dded, ~dding)
podgily
podginess
podgy

podiatry
podium (*pl* ~iums, ~ia)
poem
poesy
poet
poetess
poetic
poetical
poetically
poetry
pogo
pogrom
poi
poignancy
poignant
poignantly
poinsettia
point
point-blank
pointed
pointedly
pointedness
pointer
pointillism (P~)
pointillist (P~)
pointing
pointless
pointlessly
pointlessness
poise
poised
poison
poisoner
poisoning
poisonous
poisonously
poisonousness
poke
poker
pokily
pokiness
poky
Poland
polar
polarimetry
Polaris
polarisation (*or* ~iz~)
polarise (*or* ~ize)
polarised (*or* ~ized)
polarising (*or* ~iz~)

polarity
polaroid (P~, *tr*)
polder
Pole *Poland*
pole *rod, planet*
poleaxe
polecat
polemic
polemical
polemically
polemicist
polemics
polenta
pole-vault (*v*)
police
policeman (*pl* ~men)
policewoman (*pl*
  ~women)
policy
policyholder
polio
poliomyelitis
poliovirus
Polish *language*
polish *improve*
polisher
politburo (P~)
polite
politely
politeness
politesse
politic (~icked, ~icking)
political
politically
politician
politicise (*or* ~ize)
politicised (*or* ~ized)
politicising (*or* ~iz~)
politics
polity
polka (~kaed, ~kaing)
poll
pollack (*or* pollock)
pollen
pollinate
pollination
pollinator
polling
pollinosis
pollock (*or* pollack)

pollster
pollutant
pollute
polluter
pollution
pollyanna
polo
polonaise
polonium
polony
poltergeist
poltroon
polyacetylene
polyamide
polyandrous
polyandrously
polyanthus
polycarbonate
polychromatic
polychromatism
polychrome
polychromy
polycrystalline
polyester
polyethylene
polygamist
polygamous
polygamously
polygamy
polyglot
polyglottal
polygon
polygonal
polygraph
polygyny
polyhedral
polyhedron (*pl* ~rons,
  ~ra)
polymath
polymathic
polymathy
polymer
polymeric
polymerisation (*or*
  ~iz~)
polymerise (*or* ~ize)
polymorph
polymorphic
polymorphism
polymorphous

Polynesia
Polynesian
polyneuritis
polynomial
polyp
polyphone
polyphonic
polyphonically
polyphonous
polyphony
polyploid
polyploidy
polypod
polypous
polypropylene
polysaccharide
polysemic
polysemous
polysemy
polystyrene
polysyllabic
polysyllabically
polysyllable
polytechnic
polytheism
polytheist
polytheistic
polythene
polytonal
polyunsaturated
polyunsaturates
polyurethane
polyvalent
polyvinyl
polyzoic
pomace
pomaceous
pomade
pomander
pome
pomegranate
pomeranian (P~)
pomfret
pommel (~lled, ~lling;
  US ~led, ~ling)
pomp
pompadour
Pompeii
Pompeiian
pomposity

pompous
pompously
pompousness
ponce
poncho (*pl* ~os)
pond
ponder
ponderable
ponderer
ponderous
ponderousness
pondweed
pong
poniard
pons
pontiff
pontifical
pontificate
pontification
pontine
pontoon
pony
ponytail
pooch
poodle
poof (*tab*) gay
pooh-pooh
pool
poop
poor
poorly
poorness
pootle
pop (~pped, ~pping)
popcorn
pope
popedom
pop-eyed
popgun
popinjay
popish
popishness
poplar
poplin
poppadum (*or* ~dom,
  pa~)
popper
poppet
poppy
poppycock

populace
popular
popularisation (*or* ~iz~)
popularise (*or* ~ize)
popularised (*or* ~ized)
popularising (*or* ~iz~)
popularity
populate
population
populism
populist
populous
populousness
pop-up
porbeagle
porcelain
porcellaneous
porch
porcine
porcupine
pore
poriferan
pork
porker
porkiness
porky
porn
pornocracy
pornographer
pornographic
pornographically
pornography
porosity
porous
porousness
porphyria
porphyritic
porphyry
porpoise
porridge
porringer
port
portability
portable
portage
portakabin (P~, *tr*)
portal
portamento (*pl* ~ti)
portative
portcullis

portend
portent
portentous
portentously
portentousness
porter
porterage
porterhouse
portfolio
porthole
portico (*pl* ~oes, ~os)
portion
portliness
portly
portmanteau (*pl* ~us,
  ~ux)
portrait
portraitist
portraiture
portray
portrayable
portrayal
portrayer
Portugal
Portuguese
pose
Poseidon
poser
poseur
posh
posit (~ted, ~ting)
position
positional
positive
positively
positiveness
positivism
positivist
positron
posology
posse
possess
possessed
possession
possessive
possessively
possessiveness
possessor
posset
possibility

possible
possibly
possum
post
postage
postal
postbag
postbox
postbus
postcard
postcode
postcoital
postdate
poster
posterior
posterity
postern
postfix
postgraduate
posthaste
posthumous
postilion (*or* ~illion)
postimpressionism (P~)
postimpressionist (P~)
posting
post-it (P~, *tr*)
postman (*pl* ~men)
postmark
postmaster
postmeridian
postmistress
postmodern
postmodernism (P~)
postmodernist (P~)
postmortem
postnatal
post-operative
postponable
postpone
postponement
postponer
postscript
postulancy
postulant
postulate
postulation
postulator
postural
posture
posturer

postwar
postwoman (~women)
posy
pot (~tted, ~tting)
potability
potable
potage
potash
potassic
potassium
potation
potato (pl ~oes)
potboiler
potbound
poteen
potency
potent
potentate
potential
potentiality
potentially
potentiate
potentilla
potentiometer
potful
pother
pothole
potholer
potholing
potion
potlatch
potpourri (pl ~is)
potsherd
pottage
potted
potter
potterer
pottery
potting
potty
pouch
pouched
pouchy
pouf (or pouffe; ! poof)
 seat
poulard
poult
poulterer
poultice
poultry

pounce
pound
poundage
poundal
pounder
pour
pourer
poussin
pout
pouter
pouting
poutingly
poverty
powder
powderer
powdery
power
powerboat
powerful
powerfully
powerfulness
powerhouse
powerless
powerlessness
powwow
pox
poxy
practicability
practicable
practicableness
practicably
practical
practicality
practically
practice (n, UK & US)
practise (v, UK ~ised,
 ~ising; US ~ice,
 ~iced, ~icing)
practitioner
pragmatic
pragmatically
pragmatics
pragmatism
pragmatist
Prague
prairie
praise
praiseful
praiseworthily
praiseworthiness

praiseworthy
praline
pram
prance
prancer
prang
prank
prankish
prankster
prat (tab)
prate
prater
pratfall
pratincole
prattle
prattler
prawn
praxis
pray (! prey) request
prayer
prayerful
prayerfully
prayerfulness
praying
preach
preacher
preachify
preachiness
preachy
preamble
preambular
preamplifier
prearrange
prearrangement
prearranger
prebend
prebendal
prebendary
Precambrian
precancerous
precarious
precariously
precariousness
precast
precaution
precautionary
precede
precedence
precedent
precentor

precept
preceptive
preceptor
preceptress
precess
precession
precessional
precinct
preciosity
precious
preciousness
precipice
precipitance
precipitant
precipitate
precipitately
precipitation
precipitative
precipitator
precipitous
precipitously
precipitousness
precis (or pré~)
precise
precisely
preciseness
precision
preclinical
precludable
preclude
preclusion
preclusive
precocious
precociously
precociousness
precocity
precognition
precognitive
preconceive
preconceived
preconception
precondition
precursive
precursor
precursory
predacious
predate
predation
predator
predatorily

predatoriness
predatory
predecease
predecessor
predefine
predestinate
predestination
predestine
predeterminable
predeterminate
predetermination
predeterminative
predetermine
predicability
predicable
predicament
predicate
predication
predicative
predict
predictability
predictable
predictably
prediction
predictive
predictively
predictor
predilection
predisposal
predispose
predisposition
predominance
predominant
predominate
pre-eclampsia
pre-eminence
pre-eminent
pre-eminently
pre-empt
pre-emption
pre-emptive
pre-emptor
pre-emptory
preen
prefab
prefabricate
prefabrication
preface
prefatory
prefect

prefectorial
prefectural
prefecture
prefer (~rred, ~rring)
preferability
preferable
preferably
preference
preferential
preferentially
preferment
preferrer
prefigurative
prefigure
prefigurement
prefix
preflight
pregnability
pregnable
pregnancy
pregnant
preheat
preheated
prehensile
prehension
prehistoric
prehistorical
prehistorically
prehistory
pre-ignition
prejudge
prejudgement (or
  ~gm~)
prejudice
prejudicial
prejudicially
prelate
prelature
preliminarily
preliminary
prelude
preludial
premarital
premaritally
premature
prematurity
premedication
premeditate
premeditated
premeditatedly

premeditation
premeditative
premeditator
premenstrual
premier
premiere (*or* ~ère)
Premiership *football*
premiership *office*
premise (*or* ~miss)
premises
premiss (*or* ~mise)
premium
premolar
premonition
premonitory
premunition
prenatal
prenatally
prenup
preoccupation
preoccupy
preordain
preordination
prepack
prepackage
preparation
preparative
preparatory
prepare
prepared
preparedly
preparedness
prepay (prepaid)
prepayable
prepayment
preponderance
preponderant
preponderate
preposition
prepositional
prepositionally
prepositive
prepositor
prepossess
prepossession
preposterous
preposterously
preposterousness
prepotency
prepotent

preproduction
prepubescent
prepuce
prequel
Pre-Raphaelite
prerecord
prerequisite
prerogative
presage
presager
presbyopia
presbyopic
presbyter
presbyterian (P~)
Presbyterianism
presbytery
preschool
prescience
prescient
prescribe
prescriber
prescriptible
prescription
prescriptive
prescriptivism
presence
present
presentability
presentable
presentably
presentation
presentational
presentative
presenter
presentient
presentiment
presently
presentment
preservable
preservation
preservative
preserve
preserver
preset
presetting
preshrink
preshrunk
preside
presidency
president

presidential
presider
presiding
presidium (*pl* ~iums,
~ia)
press
pressed
presser
pressgang
pressing
press-up
pressure
pressurise (*or* ~ize)
pressurised (*or* ~ized)
pressurising (*or* ~iz~)
prestidigitation
prestidigitator
prestige
prestigious
prestigiously
prestigiousness
presto
presumable
presumably
presume
presumer
presumption
presumptive
presumptuous
presumptuously
presumptuousness
presuppose
presupposition
pretence (*US* ~nse)
pretend
pretender
pretension
pretentious
pretentiously
pretentiousness
preterite
preterm
preternatural
preternaturally
pretext
prettily
prettiness
pretty
pretzel
prevail

prevailer
prevalence
prevalent
prevalently
prevaricate
prevarication
prevaricator
prevent
preventable
preventative
preventer
prevention
preventive
preview
previous
previously
previousness
prevision
pre-war
prey (! pray) *hunting*
priapism
price
priceless
pricelessly
pricelessness
pricey (*or* ~cy)
prick
prickle
prickliness
prickly
pricy (*or* ~cey)
pride
priest
priestess
priesthood
priestliness
priestly
prig
priggery
priggish
priggishly
priggishness
prim (~mmer, ~mmest)
primacy
prima facie
primal
primarily
primary
primate
prime

primer
primeval (*or* ~maev~)
primevally (*or* ~maev~)
primiparous
primitive
primitively
primitiveness
primitivism
primitivist
primly
primness
primogenitor
primogeniture
primordial
primordially
primp
primrose
primula
primus (P~, *tr*)
prince
princedom
princeliness
princely
princess
principal (! principle)
    chief
principality
principally
principium (*pl* ~ia)
principle (! principal)
    rule
principled
prink
print
printability
printable
printer
printing
printout
prion
prior
prioress
prioritise (*or* ~ize)
prioritised (*or* ~ized)
prioritising (*or* ~iz~)
priority
priory
prise (*US* prize; ! prize)
    lever
prism

prismatic
prison
prisoner
prissily
prissiness
prissy
pristine
privacy
private
privateer
privation
privatisation (*US* ~iz~)
privatise (*US* ~ize)
privatised (*US* ~ized)
privatising (*US* ~iz~)
privative
privet
privilege
privileged
privily
privity
privy
prize (! prise) *award*
prizefight
prizefighter
prizefighting
pro
proactive
proactivity
probability
probable
probably
probate
probation
probationary
probationer
probative
probe
probeable
prober
probity
problem
problematic
problematical
problematically
proboscis (*pl* ~scises,
    ~scides)
procaine
procaryote (*or* ~ka~)
procaryotic (*or* ~ka~)

procedural
procedure
proceed
proceedings
proceeds
process
procession
processional
processor
proclaim
proclaimer
proclamation
proclamatory
proclitic
proclivity
procrastinate
procrastination
procrastinator
procreant
procreate
procreation
procreator
Procrustean
proctological
proctologist
proctology
proctor
proctorial
proctorship
proctoscopy
procurable
procuration
procurator
procure
procurement
procurer
prod (~dded, ~dding)
prodder
prodigal
prodigality
prodigally
prodigious
prodigiously
prodigiousness
prodigy
produce
producer
producibility
producible
product

production
productive
productively
productiveness
productivity
profanation
profanatory
profane
profanely
profaneness
profaner
profanity
profess
professedly
profession
professional
professionalism
professionalist
professionally
professor
professorial
professorship
proffer
profferer
proficiency
proficient
proficiently
profile
profit
profitability
profitable
profitably
profiteer
profiter
profiterole
profitless
profligacy
profligate
profluent
pro forma
profound
profoundly
profundity
profuse
profusely
profuseness
profusion
progenitor
progeny
progesterone

progestin
progestogen
prognosis (*pl* ~oses)
prognostic
prognostically
prognosticate
prognostication
prognosticative
prognosticator
program
programmable
programme (*US* ~gram;
  ~mmed, ~mming)
programmer
progress
progression
progressional
progressive
progressively
progressiveness
progressivism
progressivist
prohibit
prohibition
prohibitionary
prohibitionism
prohibitionist
prohibitive
prohibitively
prohibitiveness
prohibitor
project
projectile
projection
projectional
projectionist
projective
projector
prokaryote (*or* ~car~)
prokaryotic (*or* ~car~)
prolactin
prolapse
prolegomenon
prolepsis
proleptic
proletarian
proletarianism
proletarianness
proletariat
pro-life

pro-lifer
proliferate
proliferation
proliferative
proliferous
prolific
prolificacy
prolifically
prolificness
prolix
prolixity
prolixly
prologue (US ~log)
prolong
prolongation
prom
promenade
promenader
Prometheus
promethium
prominence
prominent
prominently
promiscuity
promiscuous
promiscuously
promiscuousness
promise
promisee
promiser (or ~or)
promising
promisingly
promissory
promontory
promotable
promote
promoter
promotion
promotional
promotive
promotively
promotiveness
prompt
prompter
promptitude
promptly
promptness
promulgate
promulgation
promulgator

promycelium (pl ~ia)
prone
pronely
proneness
prong
pronged
pronked
pronominal
pronominally
pronoun
pronounce
pronounceable
pronounced
pronouncedly
pronouncement
pronouncer
pronto
pronunciation
proof
proofread
proofreading
prop (~pped, ~pping)
propaganda
propagandise (or ~ize)
propagandist
propagatable
propagate
propagation
propagative
propagator
propane
propel (~lled, ~lling)
propellant (n)
propellent (adj)
propeller
propensity
proper
properly
properness
propertied
property
propfan
prophase
prophecy (n; ! prophesy)
prophesier
prophesy (v; ! prophecy)
prophet
prophetess
prophetic
prophetically

prophylactic
prophylaxis
propinquity
propitiable
propitiate
propitiation
propitiative
propitiator
propitious
propitiously
propitiousness
proponent
proportion
proportionability
proportionable
proportional
proportionality
proportionally
proportionate
proportionately
proportionateness
proportionment
proposable
proposal
propose
proposer
proposition
propositional
propound
propounder
proprietarily
proprietary
proprietor
proprietorial
proprietress
propriety
proprioceptor
propulsion
propulsive
propyl
propylaeum (or ~leum)
propylene
pro rata
prorogation
prorogue
prosaic
prosaically
proscenium (pl ~ia)
prosciutto
proscribe

proscriber
proscription
proscriptive
proscriptiveness
prose
prosecutable
prosecute
prosecution
prosecutor
proselyte
proselytic
proselytise (or ~ize)
proselytised (or ~ized)
proselytising (or ~iz~)
proselytism
prosily
prosimian
prosiness
prosodic
prosodist
prosody
prospect
prospective
prospector
prospectus
prosper (~ered, ~ering)
prosperity
prosperous
prosperously
prosperousness
prostate
prostatectomy
prostatic
prostatitis
prosthesis (pl ~eses)
prosthetic
prosthetically
prosthetics
prostitute
prostitution
prostitutor
prostrate
prostration
prostyle
prosy
protactinium
protagonism
protagonist
protamine
protea

protean
protease
protect
protection
protectionism
protectionist
protective
protectively
protectiveness
protector
protectorate
protectory
protectress
protégé
protégée
protein
pro tem
Proterozoic
protest
Protestant
Protestantism
protestation
protester (or ~or)
protestingly
prothesis
prothetic
prothetically
protist (P~)
protocol
protogynous
protogyny
proton
protoplasm
protoplasmic
protoplast
protoplastic
prototype
prototypic
prototypical
prototypically
protozoa (P~)
protozoan
protract
protracted
protractedly
protractedness
protractile
protraction
protractive
protractor

protrudable
protrude
protrusile
protrusion
protrusive
protrusively
protrusiveness
protuberance
protuberant
proud
proudly
proudness
provability
provable
prove
proven
provenance
provender
proverb
proverbial
proverbially
provide
providence (P~)
provident
providential
providentially
providently
provider
province
provincial
provincialise (or ~ize)
provincialism
provinciality
provincially
provision
provisional
provisionally
provisioner
provisions
proviso (pl ~sos)
provisorily
provisory
provocation
provocative
provocatively
provocativeness
provoke
provoking
provokingly
provost

prow
prowess
prowl
prowler
proximal
proximally
proximate
proximately
proximateness
proximation
proximity
proxy
Prozac (*tr*)
prude
prudence
prudent
prudential
prudently
prudentness
prudery
prudish
prudishly
prudishness
prunable
prune
prunella
pruner
prurience
prurient
prurigo
pruritic
pruritus
Prussia
Prussian
prussic
pry
psalm
psalmic
psalmist
psalmodic
psalmodist
psalmody
psalter
psalterium (*pl* ~ia)
psaltery
psephological
psephologically
psephologist
psephology
pseudo

pseudocarp
pseudomorph
pseudomorphic
pseudonym
pseudonymity
pseudonymous
psittacine
psittacosis
psoriasis
psoriatic
psyche
psychedelia
psychedelic
psychiatric
psychiatrically
psychiatrist
psychiatry
psychic
psychical
psycho
psychoanalyse (*US* ~yze)
psychoanalysis
psychoanalyst
psychoanalytic
psychoanalytically
psychobabble
psychobiological
psychobiologist
psychobiology
psychodrama
psychodramatic
psychodynamic
psychodynamics
psychogenesis
psychogenetic
psychogenetically
psychogenic
psychogenically
psychograph
psychographic
psychography
psychokinesis
psycholinguist
psycholinguistics
psychological
psychologically
psychologism
psychologist
psychology

psychometrics
psychometrist
psychometry
psychoneurosis
psychoneurotic
psychopath
psychopathic
psychopathological
psychopathologist
psychopathology
psychopathy
psychopharmacologist
psychopharmacology
psychopharmocological
psychophysical
psychophysics
psychophysiological
psychophysiologist
psychophysiology
psychosexual
psychosexuality
psychosis (*pl* ~oses)
psychosocial
psychosomatic
psychosurgery
psychotherapeutic
psychotherapist
psychotherapy
psychotic
psychotically
ptarmigan
pteridophyte
pterodactyl
pteropod
pterosaur
Ptolemaic
ptomaine
pub (~bbed, ~bbing)
puberty
puberulent
pubes
pubescence
pubescent
pubic
pubis (*pl* ~bes)
public
publican
publication
publicise (*or* ~ize)
publicised (*or* ~ized)

publicising (*or* ~iz~)
publicist
publicity
publicly
publish
publishable
publisher
publishing
puce
puck
pucker
puckish
puckishness
pudding
puddle
puddler
puddling
puddly
pudendum (*pl* ~da)
pudgily
pudginess
pudgy
puerile
puerilism
puerility
puerperal
puerperium
puff
puffball
puffer
puffily
puffin
puffiness
puffy
pug (~gged, ~gging)
puggish
pugilism
pugilist
pugilistic
pugilistically
pugnacious
pugnaciously
pugnaciousness
pugnacity
puissance
puke
pukka
pulchritude
pulchritudinous
puling

pull
pullet
pulley (*pl* ~eys)
Pullman
pullover
pullulate
pullulation
pulmonary
pulmonic
pulp
pulpiness
pulpit
pulpy
pulsar
pulsate
pulsation
pulsator
pulsatory
pulse
pulverable
pulverisation (*or* ~iz~)
pulverise (*or* ~ize)
pulverised (*or* ~ized)
pulveriser (*or* ~iz~)
pulverising (*or* ~iz~)
pulvinate
pulvinated
puma
pumice
pummel (~lled, ~lling;
  US ~led, ~ling)
pump
pumpernickel
pumpkin
pun (~nned, ~nning)
punch
punch-bag
punchball
punchbowl
puncheon
puncher
punchily
Punchinello
punchiness
punchline
punchy
punctilious
punctiliously
punctiliousness
punctual

punctuality
punctually
punctuate
punctuation
puncture
pundit
pungency
pungent
pungently
puniness
punish
punishability
punishable
punisher
punishingly
punishment
punition
punitive
punitively
punitiveness
Punjab
Punjabi (*or* Pan~)
punk
punka (*or* ~ah)
punner
punnet
punster
punt
punter
puny
pup
pupa (*pl* ~ae, ~as)
pupal
puparium
pupate
pupation
pupil
pupillage (*US* ~ilage)
pupillary
pupiparous
puppet
puppeteer
puppetry
puppy
purblind
purchasable
purchase
purchaser
purdah (*or* ~da)
pure

purée (puréed, puréeing)
purely
pureness
purgation
purgative
purgatorial
purgatory
purge
purification
purificator
purifier
purify
Purim
purin
purine
purism
purist
puristic
puristically
puritan (P~)
puritanical
puritanically
puritanicalness
puritanism (P~)
purity
purl (! pearl) *knit*
purler
purlieu (*pl* ~us)
purlin (*or* ~ine)
purloin
purloined
purple
purpleness
purplish
purport
purpose
purposeful
purposefully
purposefulness
purposeless
purposely
purposive
purposively
purposiveness
purr
purse
purser
pursuance
pursuant
pursue

pursuer
pursuit
purulence
purulent
purulently
purvey
purveyance
purveyor
purview
pus
push
pushchair
pusher
pushily
pushiness
pushover
pushy
pusillanimity
pusillanimous
pusillanimously
pussy
pussycat
pussyfoot
pustulant
pustular
pustulation
pustule
put
putative
putrefaction
putrefactive
putrefiable
putrefied
putrefier
putrefy
putrescence
putrescent
putrid
putridity
putridness
putsch
putt (~tted, ~tting)
puttee
putter
putty
puzzle
puzzlement
puzzler
puzzling
puzzlingly

pyaemia (*or* pye~)
pyaemic (*or* pye~)
pyelitic
pyelitis
pyelogram
pyelography
pygmy (*occ* pig~)
pyjamas (*US* paj~)
pyknic
pylon
pylorectomy
pyloric
pylorus
pyoderma
pyorrhoea (*US* ~hea)
pyosis
pyracantha
pyralid
pyramid
pyramidal
pyramidally
pyramidical
pyramidically
pyre
pyrene
Pyrenean
Pyrenees
pyrethrin
pyrethrum
pyretic
Pyrex (*tr*)
pyridine
pyridoxine
pyriform
pyrimidine
pyrite
pyritic
pyroclast
pyroclastic
pyrogen
pyrogenic
pyrography
pyrolysis
pyromancer
pyromancy
pyromania
pyromaniac
pyrometer
pyrometry
pyrosis

pyrotechnic
pyrotechnics
pyroxene
pyrrhic (P~)
Pythagoras
Pythagorean
python
Pythonesque
pythoness
pythonic
pyuria
pyx

Qabalah (*also* Qabba~,
   Ka~, Kabba~, Ca~,
   Cabba~, ~la)
Qaddish (*usu* Ka~)
qat (*or* khat)
Qatar
Qatari
qiblah (*or* ~la, kib~,
   keb~)
qigong (*also* chi~)
qua
quack
quackery
quackish
Quadragesima
quadrangle
quadrangular
quadrant
quadrantal
quadraphonic (*or* ~ro~)
quadraphonically (*or*
   ~ro~)
quadraphonics (*or*
   ~ro~)
quadraphony (*or* ~ro~)
quadraplex (*or* ~ri~)
quadratic

quadrature
quadrennial
quadrennially
quadrennium (*pl* ~ia,
   ~iums)
quadriceps
quadrilateral
quadrille
quadrillion
quadrillionth
quadripartite
quadriplegia
quadriplegic
quadroon
quadruped
quadrupedal
quadruple
quadruplet
quadruplicate
quadruplicated
quadruplication
quadruplicity
quadruply
quads
quaff
quaffable
quaffer
quagga
quagmire
quail
quaint
quaintly
quaintness
quake
Quaker
Quakerish
Quakerism
quaky
qualifiable
qualification
qualificatory
qualified
qualifier
qualify
qualitative
qualitatively
quality
qualm
qualmish
quandary

quango (*pl* ~os)
quanta *see* quantum
quantifiability
quantifiable
quantification
quantifier
quantify
quantisation (*or* ~iz~)
quantise (*or* ~ize)
quantitative
quantitatively
quantity
quantum (*pl* ~s; *phys*
   ~ta)
quarantine
quark
quarrel (~lled, ~lling;
   US ~led, ~ling)
quarreller
quarrelsome
quarry
quart
quarter
quarterback
quarterdeck
quartered
quartering
quarterly
quartermaster
quarters
quarterstaff (*pl* ~staves)
quartet (*occ* ~ette)
quarto (*pl* ~os)
quartz
quartzite
quasar
quash
quassia
quaternary
quaternion
quatrain
quatrefoil
quaver
quaverer
quavering
quaveringly
quay
quayside
queasily
queasiness

queasy
Quebec (*or French* Qué~)
Quebecer (*or* ~cker)
Quechua
Quechuan
queen (Q~)
queenliness
queenly
Queensberry
Queensland
Queenslander
queensware
queer
queerness
quell
queller
quench
quenchable
quencher
quenchless
quenelle
quern
quernstone
querulous
querulously
querulousness
query
quesadilla
quest
quester (*or* ~or)
question
questionability
questionable
questionableness
questionably
questioning
questionnaire
quetzal *bird*
quetzalcoatlus
queue (queued, queuing
  or queueing)
quibble
quibbler
quibbling
quibblingly
quiche
quick
quicken
quickening
quickie

quicklime
quickly
quickness
quicksand
quicksilver
quickstep (~pped,
  ~pping)
quick-witted
quick-wittedness
quid
quiddity
quiescence
quiescent
quiescently
quiet
quieten
quietism (Q~)
quietist (Q~)
quietly
quietness
quietude
quietus
quiff
quill
quilt
quilted
quilter
quilting
quinary
quince
quincentenary
quincentennial
quinine
quinone
quinquagenarian
Quinquagesima
quinquennial
quinquennially
quinquennium (*pl* ~ia,
  ~iums)
quins
quinsy
quintain *jousting target*
quintan *fever*
quintessence
quintessential
quintessentially
quintet (*occ* ~ette)
quintile
quintillion

quintillionth
quintuple
quintuplet
quintuplicate
quintuplication
quintuply
quip (~pped, ~pping)
quirk
quirkily
quirkiness
quirkish
quirky
quisling
quit (quit *or* quitted,
  quitting)
quite
quits
quittance
quitter
quiver
quiverer
quivering
quiveringly
quivery
quixotic
quiz (*n pl* quizzes; *v*
  quizzes, quizzed,
  quizzing)
quizmaster
quizzer
quizzical
quizzicality
quizzically
quizzicalness
Qumran
quoin
quoits
quorate
quorum
quota
quotability
quotable
quotation
quote
quoted
quotidian
quotient
Qu'ran (*or* Quran,
  occ Qoran; *usu*
  Koran)

rabbet (~eted, ~eting)
rabbi (*pl* ~is)
rabbinic
rabbinical
rabbinically
rabbit
rabbiter
rabble
Rabelasian
rabid
rabidity
rabidly
rabidness
rabies
raccoon (*or* raco~)
race
racecard
racecourse
racegoer
racegoing
racehorse
racemate
racemation
raceme
racemed
racemic
racemise (*or* ~ize)
racemose
racer
racetrack
racial
racialise (*or* ~ize)
racialism
racialist
racially
racily
raciness
racing
racism

racist
rack
racket (*or* racquet)
racketeer
racketeering
rackets
rackety
rack-rent
raconteur
racoon (*or* racc~)
racquet (*or* racket)
racquetball
racy
radar
radarscope
radial
radially
radian
radiance
radiant
radiate
radiation
radiator
radical (! radicle)
    fundamental
radicalisation (*or* ~iz~)
radicalise (*or* ~ize)
radicalism
radically
radicle (! radical) *plants*
radii (*sg* ~dius)
radio
radioactivate
radioactive
radioactivity
radiobiology
radiocarbon
radiochemistry
radiogram
radiographer
radiographic
radiography
radioisotope
radiological
radiologist
radiology
radioluminescence
radiometer
radio-pager
radiophonic

radioscopic
radioscopically
radioscopy
radiotherapist
radiotherapy
radish
radium
radius (*pl* ~dii, ~uses)
radix (*pl* ~ices)
radon
raffia (*or* raphia)
raffish
raffishly
raffishness
raffle
raft
rafter
rag
raga
ragamuffin
rag-bag
ragdoll
rage
ragged
raggedly
raggedness
raging
ragingly
raglan
ragout
ragstone
ragtag
ragtime
ragwork
ragworm
ragwort
raid
raider
raiding
rail
railcar
railcard
railhead
railing
raillery
railroad
railway
raiment
rain
rainbird

rainbow
raincloud
raincoat
raindrop
rainfall
rainforest
raining
rainmaker
rainmaking
rainproof
rainwater
rainy
raisable (or ~sea~)
raise
raised
raiser
raisin
raising
raison d'être (pl
  raisons~)
raita
raj (R~)
raja (or ~jah)
rake
rake-off
rakery
raki (or ~kee)
raking
rakish
rakishly
rakishness
raku
rallentando
rally
rallycross
rallying
RAM computing
ram sheep
ram (~mmed, ~mming)
  hit
Ramadan (or ~dhan)
ramapithecine
ramapithecus (R~)
ramate
ramble
rambler
rambling
Rambo
rambunctious
rambunctiously

rambunctiousness
ramification
ramiform
ramify
ramjet
ramp
rampage
rampageous
rampageousness
rampaging
rampancy
rampant
rampantly
rampart
ramrod
ramshackle
ramus
ranch
rancher
rancid
rancidity
rancidness
rancorous
rancorously
rancour
randily
randiness
random
randomness
randy
rang
range
rangefinder
ranger (R~)
ranginess
rangy
rank
ranking
rankle
rankly
rankness
ransack
ransacker
ransom
ransomable
ransomless
rant
ranter
ranting
rantingly

rap (~pped, ~pping)
rapacious
rapaciously
rapaciousness
rapacity
rape
raphia (or raffia)
rapid
rapidity
rapidly
rapidness
rapier
rapine
rapist
rapped (! rapt) knock,
  music
rapper
rapping
rapport
rapprochement
rapscallion
rapt (! rapped) entranced
raptly
raptor
raptorial
rapture
rapturous
rapturously
rare
rarebit
rarefaction
rarefactive
rarefiable
rarefied
rarefy
rarely
rareness
raring
rarity
rascal
rascally
rase (or raze)
rash
rasher
rasp
raspberry
rasper
rasping
raspingly
raspy

Rasta
Rastafarian
Rastafarianism
raster
rasterise (or ~ize)
rat (~tted, ~tting)
ratability (or ~tea~)
ratable (or ~tea~)
ratafia
ratatouille
ratchet
ratcheted
ratcheting
rate
rateability (or rata~)
rateable (or rata~)
ratepayer
rather
ratification
ratifier
ratify
rating
ratio
ration
rational (adj)
rationale (n)
rationalisation (or ~iz~)
rationalise (or ~ize)
rationalism
rationalist
rationalistic
rationalistically
rationality
rationally
ratpack
rattan (or ratan)
rattiness
rattle
rattler
rattlesnake
rattling
rattly
ratty
raucous
raucously
raucousness
raunchily
raunchiness
raunchy
rauwolfia

ravage
rave
ravel
ravelling
raven
ravening
ravenous
ravenously
ravenousness
raver
ravine
raving
ravioli
ravish
ravishing
ravishingly
raw
rawboned
rawhide
rawness
ray
rayon
raze (or rase)
razor
razorbill
razzamatazz (or
    razzma~)
razzle
reach
reachable
react
reactance
reactant
reaction
reactionary
reactionism
reactionist
reactivate
reactivation
reactive
reactivity
reactor
read
readability
readable
reader
readership
readily
readiness
reading

read-out
ready
ready-made
reagent
real
realgar
realisable (or ~iz~)
realisably (or ~iz~)
realisation (or ~iz~)
realise (or ~ize)
realism
realist
realistic
realistically
reality
really
realm
realpolitik
realtor
realty
ream
reamer
reap
reaper
reaping
rear
rearguard
rearmost
rearward
reason
reasonable
reasonableness
reasonably
reasoned
reasoning
reassurance
reassure
reassurer
reassuring
reassuringly
rebate
rebateable (or ~table)
rebel (~lled, ~lling)
rebellion
rebellious
rebelliously
rebelliousness
rebirth
rebirthing
reborn

rebound
rebuff
rebuke
rebuker
rebuking
rebukingly
rebus
rebut (~tted, ~tting)
rebuttable
rebuttal
recalcitrance
recalcitrant
recall
recallable
recant
recantation
recanter
recap (~pped, ~pping)
recapitulate
recapitulation
recapitulative
recapitulatory
recce
recede
receding
receipt
receivable
receivableness
receive
receiveability
received
receiver
receivership
receiving
recency
recension
recent
recently
recentness
receptacle
reception
receptionist
receptive
receptively
receptiveness
receptivity
receptor
recess
recessed
recession

recessional
recessive
recessively
recessiveness
recharge
réchauffé
recherché
recidivism
recidivist
recipe
recipient
reciprocal
reciprocality
reciprocally
reciprocate
reciprocating
reciprocation
reciprocative
reciprocator
reciprocity
recitable
recital
recitalist
recitation
recitative
recite
reciter
reckless
recklessly
recklessness
reckon
reckoner
reckoning
reclaim
reclaimable
reclaimant
reclaimer
reclamation
reclinable
reclinate
recline
recliner
recluse
reclusion
reclusive
reclusiveness
recognisable (or ~iz~)
recognisably (or ~iz~)
recognisance (or ~iz~)
recognise (or ~ize)

recogniser (or ~iz~)
recognition
recoil
recoiler
recoilless
recollect
recollected
recollecting
recollection
recollective
recollectively
recommend
recommendable
recommendably
recommendation
recommender
recompensable
recompense
recompenser
reconcilability
reconcilable
reconcilably
reconcile
reconcilement
reconciler
reconciliation
reconciliatory
reconciling
recondite
recondition
reconditioned
reconnaissance
reconnoitre (US ~ter)
record
recordable
recorder
recording
recount
recoup
recoupable
recourse
recover
recoverability
recoverable
recoverableness
recoverer
recovery
re-create
recreation
recreational

recriminate
recriminating
recrimination
recriminative
recriminator
recriminatory
recrudesce
recrudescence
recruit
recruitable
recruiter
recruiting
recruitment
recrystallisation (or ~iz~)
recrystallise (or ~ize)
rectal
rectangle
rectangular
rectangularity
rectangularly
rectifiable
rectification
rectified
rectifier
rectify
rectifying
rectilineal
rectilineally
rectilinear
rectilinearity
rectilinearly
rectitude
rector
rectorate
rectorial
rectorship
rectory
rectum (pl ~ums, ~ta)
recumbence
recumbency
recumbent
recumbently
recuperable
recuperate
recuperating
recuperation
recuperative
recur (~rred, ~rring)
recurrence

recurrent
recurrently
recurring
recurringly
recursion
recusance
recusancy
recusant
recyclable
recycle
red (adj ~dder, ~ddest)
redact
redaction
redactional
redactor
redactorial
redbreast
redbrick
redcoat
redcurrant
redden
reddish
redeem
redeemable
redeemer
redeeming
redemption
redemptive
redemptively
redemptory
red-eye
red-handed
redhead
redheaded
red-hot
redingote
redneck
redness
redolence
redolency
redolent
redolently
redoubt
redoubtable
redoubtably
redound
redress
redshank
redshift
reduce

reducing
reduction
reductionism
reductionist
reductive
reductively
reductiveness
redundancy
redundant
redundantly
reduplicate
reduplication
reduplicative
redwing
redwood
reebok
reed
reedmace
reedy
reef
reefer
reek
reel
refectory
refer
referee
refereed
refereeing
reference
referendum (pl ~ums, ~da)
referential
referentially
referral
referred
referring
refill
refillable
refinable
refine
refined
refinedly
refinedness
refinement
refiner
refinery
refining
refit (~tted, ~tting)
reflate
reflation

reflationary
reflect
reflectance
reflection (*or* ~exion)
reflective
reflectively
reflectiveness
reflectivity
reflector
reflex
reflexibility
reflexible
reflexion (*or* ~ection)
reflexive
reflexively
reflexiveness
reflexivity
reflexologist
reflexology
reflux
reform
reformability
reformable
Reformation *religion*
reformation *improvement*
reformative
reformatory
reformed
reformer
reformist
refract
refractable
refracted
refracting
refraction
refractive
refractivity
refractometer
refractor
refractorily
refractoriness
refractory
refrain
refresh
refresher
refreshing
refreshingly
refreshment
refrigerant
refrigerate

refrigerating
refrigeration
refrigerative
refrigerator
refrigeratory
refuel
refuelled (*US* ~eled)
refuelling (*US* ~eling)
refuge
refugee
refulgence
refulgency
refulgent
refulgently
refund
refundable
refunder
refurbish
refurbishment
refusal
refuse
refusenik (*or* ~snik)
refutability
refutable
refutably
refutation
refute
refuter
regain
regainable
regainer
regal
regale
regalement
regalia
regality
regally
regard
regarder
regardful
regardfully
regarding
regardless
regardlessly
regardlessness
regatta
regelate
regelation
regency (R~)
regenerable

regeneracy
regenerate
regeneration
regenerative
regeneratively
regenerator
regeneratory
regent
regentship
reggae
regicidal
regicide
regime (*or* rég~)
regimen
regiment
regimental
regimentally
regimentation
regimented
region
regional
regionalisation (*or* ~iz~)
regionalise (*or* ~ize)
regionally
register
registered
registrable
registrar
registrarship
registration
registry
regress
regression
regressive
regressively
regressiveness
regressivity
regret (~tted, ~tting)
regretful
regretfully
regretfulness
regrettable
regrettably
regroup
regular
regularisation (*or* ~iz~)
regularise (*or* ~ize)
regularity
regulate
regulation

regulative
regulatively
regulator
regulatory
reguline
regulo (*tr*)
regulus
regurgitant
regurgitate
regurgitation
rehab
rehabilitate
rehabilitating
rehabilitation
rehabilitative
rehabilitator
rehash
rehearsal
rehearse
rehearser
rehearsing
rehoboam (R~)
reification
reificatory
reifier
reify
reign (! rein) *period*
reimbursable
reimburse
reimbursement
reimburser
reimpose
reimposition
rein (! reign) *horse*
reincarnate
reincarnation
reincarnationism
reincarnationist
reindeer
reinforce
reinforcement
reinstate
reinstatement
reiterate
reiteration
reiterative
reject
rejectable (*or* ~ible)
rejection
rejector (*or* ~er)

rejig (~gged, ~gging)
rejoice
rejoicing
rejoicingly
rejoinder
rejuvenate
rejuvenating
rejuvenation
rejuvenator
rejuvenesce
rejuvenescence
rejuvenescent
relapse
relapser
relatable
relate
related
relatedness
relation
relational
relationally
relationship
relative
relatively
relativeness
relativise (*or* ~ize)
relativism
relativist
relativistic
relativity
relax
relaxant
relaxation
relaxed
relaxedly
relaxing
relay
releasable
release
releaser
relegatable
relegate
relegation
relent
relentless
relentlessly
relentlessness
relevance
relevancy
relevant

relevantly
reliability
reliable
reliably
reliance
reliant
relic
relict
relied
relief
relievable
relieve
relieved
reliever
religion
religiose
religiosity
religious
religiously
religiousness
relinquish
relinquishment
reliquary
relish
relishable
reluctance
reluctant
rely
rem
remain
remainder
remaindered
remains
remand
remanence
remanency
remanent
remark
remarkable
remarkableness
remarkably
remarker
remarque (*or* ~mark)
Rembrandt
remediable
remediably
remedial
remedially
remediless
remedy

remember
remembrance
remind
reminder
remindful
reminisce
reminiscence
reminiscent
reminiscently
reminiscing
remiss
remissibility
remissibly
remission
remissive
remissively
remissly
remissness
remit
remitment
remittal
remittance
remitted
remittee
remittent
remittently
remitter (*or* ~or)
remnant
remonstrance
remonstrant
remonstrate
remonstration
remonstrative
remonstrator
remora
remorse
remorseful
remorsefully
remorsefulness
remorseless
remorselessly
remorselessness
remote
remotely
remoteness
removability
removable
removal
remove
removed

remover
remunerable
remunerate
remuneration
remunerative
remunerator
Renaissance *historical*
    period
renaissance *revival*
renal
renascence
renascent
rend
render (~ered, ~ering)
renderable
renderer
rendering
rendezvous
rendition
renegade
renege (*or* ~egue)
renew
renewable
renewal
renewer
renewing
rennet
renounce
renouncement
renouncer
renovate
renovation
renovator
renown
renowned
renownedly
rent
rentability
rentable
rental
rented
renter
renunciation
renunciative
renunciatory
repair
repairable (! reparable)
    fix damage
repairer
reparability

reparable (! repairable)
    put right
reparably
reparation
repartee
repast
repatriate
repatriation
repeal
repealable
repealer
repeat
repeatable
repeated
repeatedly
repeater
repel (~pelled, ~pelling)
repellence
repellency
repellent (*or* ~ant)
repellently
repeller
repelling
repellingly
repent
repentance
repentant
repentantly
repenter
repercussion
repertoire
repertory
repetition
repetitious
repetitiously
repetitiousness
repetitive
repetitively
repetitiveness
replace
replaceable
replacement
replacer
replay
replenish
replenisher
replenishment
replete
repleteness
repletion

replica
replicate
replication
replicative
reply
report
reportable
reportage
reportedly
reporter
repose
reposed
reposedly
reposedness
reposeful
reposefully
repository
reprehend
reprehensible
reprehensibly
reprehension
reprehensory
represent
representability
representable
representation
representational
representative
representatively
representativeness
repress
repressed
represser (*or* ~or)
repressible
repressibly
repression
repressive
repressively
repressiveness
reprieve
reprimand
reprint
reprisal
reprise
reproach
reproachable
reproacher
reproachful
reproachfully
reproachfulness

reprobacy
reprobate
reprobation
reproduce
reproducible
reproducing
reproduction
reproductive
reproductively
reproductiveness
reprographer
reprographic
reprographically
reprography
reproof
reprovable
reproval
reprove
reprover
reproving
reprovingly
reptile
reptilian
reptiliferous
reptiloid
republic
republican (R~)
repudiable
repudiate
repudiation
repudiative
repudiator
repugnance
repugnant
repugnantly
repulse
repulsion
repulsive
repulsively
repulsiveness
reputability
reputable
reputably
reputation
repute
reputed
reputedly
request
requester
requiem (R~)

require
required
requirement
requirer
requisite
requisitely
requisiteness
requisition
requisitionary
requisitionist
requitable
requital
requite
requiter
reredos
rescind
rescindment
rescission
rescue
rescuer
rescuing
research
researcher
resemblance
resemble
resent
resentful
resentfully
resentment
reservation
reserve
reserved
reservedly
reservedness
reservist
reservoir
reside
residence
residency
resident
residential
residentiary
residentship
resider
residual
residually
residuary
residue
resign
resignation

resigned
resignedly
resignedness
resigner
resilience
resiliency
resilient
resiliently
resin
resinous
resinously
resist
Resistance *fighting*
resistance *opposition*
resistant
resister (! resistor)
  opposer
resistibility
resistible
resistibly
resistivity
resistor (! resister)
  electricity
resolubility
resoluble
resolubleness
resolute
resolutely
resoluteness
resolution
resolvability
resolvable
resolve
resolved
resolvent
resolver
resonance
resonant
resonantly
resonate
resonating
resonator
resorb
resorbence
resorbent
resorption
resort
resound
resounding
resoundingly

resource
resourceful
resourcefully
resourcefulness
resourceless
respect
respectability
respectable
respectably
respecter
respectful
respectfully
respectfulness
respecting
respective
respectively
respectiveness
respiration
respirator
respiratory
respire
respite
resplendence
resplendency
resplendent
resplendently
respond
respondence
respondent
responder
response
responseless
responsibility
responsible
responsibleness
responsibly
responsive
responsively
responsiveness
responsory
rest
restaurant
restaurateur
restful
restfully
restfulness
resting
restitution
restitutor
restitutory

restive
restively
restiveness
restless
restlessly
restlessness
restorable
Restoration *monarchy*
restoration *giving back*
restorative
restoratively
restore
restorer
restrain
restrained
restrainedly
restrainer
restraint
restrict
restricted
restriction
restrictive
restrictively
result
resultant
resumable
resume
résumé
resumption
resumptive
resumptively
resupinate
resupination
resurgence
resurgent
resurrect
Resurrection *Christ*
resurrection *back in use*
resurrectionary
resurrectionist
resurrector
resuscitable
resuscitatable
resuscitate
resuscitation
resuscitative
resuscitator
retable
retail
retailer

retain
retainable
retainer
retainment
retaliate
retaliation
retaliative
retaliator
retaliatory
retard
retardant
retardation
retardative
retardatory
retarded
retardment
retch (! wretch) *strain*
retention
retentionist
retentive
retentively
retentiveness
reticence
reticent
reticently
reticle
reticular
reticulate
reticulately
reticulation
reticulum (*pl* ~la)
retiform
retina (*pl* ~as, ~ae)
retinal
retinitis
retinoscope
retinoscopically
retinoscopist
retinoscopy
retinue
retiral
retire
retired
retirement
retiring
retiringly
retort
retrace
retract
retractable (*or* ~ible)

retraction
retractive
retractor
retreat
retrench
retrenchment
retribution
retributive
retributively
retrievability
retrievable
retrieval
retrieve
retriever
retro
retroactive
retroactively
retroactivity
retroflex
retroflexed
retroflexion (*or* ~ection)
retrogradation
retrograde
retrogradely
retrospect
retrospection
retrospective
retrospectively
retroversion
retroverted
retsina
return
returnable
reunification
reunify
reunion
rev (~vved, ~vving)
revamp
revanchism
revanchist
reveal
revealable
revealer
revealing
revealingly
reveille
revel
Revelation *bible*
revelation *revealing*
revelational

revelationist
revelatory
revelled (*US* ~eled)
reveller (*US* ~eler)
revelling (*US* ~eling)
revelry
revenge
revengeful
revengefully
revengefulness
revenger
revenue *money*
Revenue *tax*
reverb
reverberant
reverberantly
reverberate
reverberating
reverberation
reverberative
reverberator
reverberatory
revere
reverence (R~)
reverend (R~)
reverent
reverential
reverentially
reverently
reverer
reverie
reversal
reverse
reversed
reversedly
reversely
reverser
reversible
reversing
reversion
reversional
reversionally
reversionary
revert
revertible
review (! revue) *study*
reviewable
reviewal
reviewer
revile

revisable
revisal
revise
reviser
revision
revisional
revisionary
revisionism
revisionist
revisory
revivability
revivable
revivably
revival
revivalism
revivalist
revivalistic
revive
reviver
reviving
revivingly
revocability
revocable
revocably
revocation
revocatory
revoke
revoker
revolt
revolted
revolting
revoltingly
revolution
revolutionary
revolutionise (or ~ize)
revolutionism
revolutionist
revolvable
revolve
revolver
revolving
revue (! review)
  performance
revulsion
revulsive
reward
rewardable
rewarder
rewarding
rewardless

rhapsodic
rhapsodical
rhapsodically
rhapsodise (or ~ize)
rhapsodist
rhapsody
rhea
rhenium
rheological
rheologist
rheology
rheostat
rheostatic
rhesus
rhetoric
rhetorical
rhetorically
rhetorician
rheum
rheumatic
rheumatically
rheumaticky
rheumatism
rheumatoid
rheumatological
rheumatologist
rheumatology
rheumed
rheumy
rhinal
Rhine
rhinestone
rhinitis
rhino
rhinoceros (*pl* ~os,
  ~oses)
rhinological
rhinologist
rhinology
rhinoplastic
rhinoplasty
rhinoscope
rhinoscopy
rhinovirus
rhizocarp
rhizocarpic
rhizocarpous
rhizoid
rhizoidal
rhizomatous

rhizome
rho
rhodium
rhododendron (*pl* ~ons,
  ~dra)
rhodolite
Rhodon
rhodopsin
rhombic
rhomboid
rhombus (*pl* ~bi, ~uses)
rhubarb
rhyme (! rime) *poetry*
rhymed
rhymeless
rhymer
rhymester
rhyolite
rhyolitic
rhythm
rhythmic
rhythmical
rhythmicality
rhythmically
rhythmicity
rhythmist
rhytidectomy
rib (~bbed, ~bbing)
ribald
ribaldry
riband (or ribb~)
ribbed
ribbing
ribbon
ribbonfish
ribcage
ribless
riboflavin (or ~ine)
ribonucleic
ribose
ribosome
ribwort
rice
rich
richly
richness
Richter
ricin
rick
ricketiness

rickets
rickettsia (*pl* ~as, ~ae)
rickety
rickshaw
ricochet (~eted *or*
~etted, ~eting *or*
~etting)
ricotta
rictus
rid (~dded, ~dding)
riddance
riddle
riddler
ride
rider
riderless
ridge
ridged
ridgepiece
ridgepole
ridgeway
ridging
ridicule
ridiculer
ridiculous
ridiculously
ridiculousness
riding
rife
rifeness
riff
riffle
riffraff
rifle
rifleman (*pl* ~men)
rifling
rift
rig (~gged, ~gging)
rigger
right
rightable
righteous
righteously
righteousness
rightful
rightfully
rightism
rightist
rightly
rightness

rightward
rightwards
rigid
rigidify
rigidity
rigidly
rigidness
rigmarole
rigor (! rigour) *death*
rigor mortis
rigorous
rigorously
rigorousness
rigour (*US* ~or, ! rigor)
    strictness
rile
rill
rillet
rim (~mmed, ~mming)
rime (! rhyme) *frost*
rind
rinded
rindless
ring
ringbolt
ringed
ringent
ringer
ringing
ringingly
ringleader
ringlet
ringmaster
ringside
ringtail
ringworm
rink
rinse
riot (~tted, ~tting)
rioter
riotous
riotously
riotousness
rip (~pped, ~pping)
riparial
riparian
ripcord
ripe
ripely
ripen

ripeness
ripening
rip-off
riposte
ripper
ripping
rippingly
ripple
ripply
rip-roaring
ripsaw
ripsnorter
ripsnorting
ripsnortingly
riptide
rise (rose, risen, rising)
riser
risibility
risible
risibly
rising
risk
riskily
riskiness
risky
risorgimento (R~)
risorius
risotto (*pl* ~os)
risqué
rissole
ritardando
rite
riteless
ritenuto
ritual
ritualise (*or* ~ize)
ritualism
ritualist
ritualistic
ritualistically
ritually
ritziness
ritzy
rival (~lled, ~lling; *US*
    ~led, ~ling)
rivalless
rivalry
river
riverine
riverless

riverside
rivet (~eted ~eting)
riveter
riveting
rivetingly
riviera (R~)
rivulet
roach
road
roadbed
roadblock
road-hog
roadholding
roadhouse
roadie
roadside
roadstead
roadster
roadway
roadworks
roadworthiness
roadworthy
roam
roamer
roan
roar
roarer
roaring
roast
roaster
roasting
rob (~bbed, ~bbing)
robber
robbery
robe
robin
robinia
robot
robotic
robotise (or ~ize)
robust
robustly
robustness
roc (! rock) *bird*
rock
rockabilly
rocker
rockery
rocket
rocketry

rockfish
rockily
rockiness
rocking
rockling
rockrose
rocky
rococo (R~)
rod (~dded, ~dding)
rodent
rodenticidal
rodenticide
rodeo (*pl* ~os)
roe (! row) *fish, deer*
roentgen (or rönt~; R~)
rogation (R~)
rogue
roguery
roguish
roguishly
roguishness
roister
roistering
roisterous
roisterously
role (or rôle)
role-play
role-playing
rolfing (R~)
roll
roller
rollerblade (R~, *tr*)
rollercoaster
rollick
rollicking (or ~llock~)
rolling
rollneck
roll-on
rollover
roll-top
roly-poly
ROM *computing*
rom (R~) *gypsy*
romaine
Roman *Rome*
roman *print*
romance
romancer
romancing
Romanesque

Romani (or ~ny)
Romania (or Rum~, Rou~)
Romantic *arts*
romantic *love*
romantically
romanticisation (or ~iz~)
romanticise (or ~ize)
romanticism (R~)
romanticist
Romany (or ~ni)
Rome
Romeo (*pl* ~os)
romp
romper
rompers
rondeau (*pl* ~ux; ! rondo) *poem*
rondo (*pl* ~os; ! rondeau) *music*
röntgen (or roent~)
rood
roof (*pl* roofs)
roofing
rooftop
rooibos
rook
rookery
rookie (or ~ky)
room
roomful
roomily
roominess
roommate
roomy
roost
rooster
root
rooted
rootedly
rootedness
rootless
rootstock
rope
ropeable (or ~pa~)
ropeway
ropily
ropiness
ropy

Roquefort
ro-ro
rorqual
Rorschach
rosace
rosaceous
rosarian
rosarium
rosary (R~)
rose *flower*
rosé *wine*
roseate
rosebay
rosebud
rosehip
rosella
rosemary
roseola
roseolar
rosette
rose-water
rosewood
Rosicrucian
Rosicrucianism
rosily
rosin
rosiness
roster
rostrum (*pl* ~ra, ~ums)
rosy
rot (~tted, ~tting)
rota
Rotary *club*
rotary *turning*
rotate
rotateable
rotation
rotational
rotative
rotator
rotavator (R~)
rote
roti
rotifer
rotisserie
rotor
rotten
rottenly
rottenness
rotter

rotting
rottweiler (R~)
rotund
rotunda
rotundity
rotundness
rouble (*or* rub~)
rouge
rough
roughage
roughcast
roughen
roughhouse
roughly
roughneck
roughness
roughshod
roulade
roulette
Roumania (*or* Rom~,
  Rum~)
round
roundabout
rounded
roundel
roundelay
rounder
rounders
Roundhead
roundhouse
rounding
roundish
roundly
roundness
round-up
roundworm
rouse
rouser
rousing
rousingly
roustabout
rout
route
router
routine
routinely
routing
routinisation (*or* ~iz~)
routinise (*or* ~ize)
roux

rove
rover
roving
row (! roe) *line, boat*
rowan
rowboat
rowdily
rowdiness
rowdy
rowdyism
rower
rowing
rowlock
royal (R~)
royalist (R~)
royally
royalty
Ruanda (*or* Rwa~)
rub (~bbed, ~bbing)
rubato (*pl* ~os, ~ti)
rubber
rubberise (*or* ~ize)
rubberneck
rubbery
rubbing
rubbish
rubbishing
rubbishy
rubble
rubefacient
rubefaction
rubella
rubescence
rubescent
rubicon (R~)
rubicund
rubidium
Rubik
ruble (*or* roub~)
rubric
rubricate
rubrication
rubricator
ruby
ruche (*or* rouche)
ruck
rucksack
ruckus
ruction
rudbeckia

rudd
rudder
rudderless
ruddily
ruddiness
ruddock
ruddy
rude
rudely
rudeness
rudiment
rudimental
rudimentarily
rudimentariness
rudimentary
rue
rueful
ruefully
ruefulness
ruff
ruffian
ruffianly
ruffle
rug
rugby
rugged
ruggedly
ruggedness
rugger
rugose
rugosely
rugosity
ruin
ruination
ruinous
ruinously
ruinousness
rulable
rule
ruleless
ruler
ruling
rum (*adj* ~mmer,
  ~mmest)
Rumania (*or* Rom~,
  Roum~)
rumba
rumble
rumbling
rumbustious

rumbustiously
rumbustiousness
rumen (*pl* ~ens, ~mina)
ruminant
ruminantly
ruminate
ruminating
ruminatingly
rumination
ruminative
ruminatively
ruminator
rummage
rummager
rummy
rumour (*US* ~or)
rump
rumple
rumpled
rumply
rumpus
run
runabout
runaround
runaway
rune
rung
runic
runnable
runnel
runner
running
runny
run-off
runt
runtish
runtishness
runway
rupee
rupture
rural
ruralisation (*or* ~iz~)
ruralise (*or* ~ize)
ruralism
ruralist
rurally
Ruritanian
ruse
rush
rusher

rushing
rushy
rusk
russet
russetish
russety
Russia
Russian
russianise (R~; *or* ~ize)
russification (R~)
russify (R~)
russophile (R~)
russophobe (R~)
rust
rustic
rustically
rusticate
rusticated
rustication
rusticism
rusticity
rustily
rustiness
rustle
rustler
rustling
rustlingly
rustproof
rusty
rut (~tted, ~tting)
rutabaga (*US*)
rutaceous
ruthenium
rutherford
rutherfordium
ruthless
ruthlessly
ruthlessness
rutilated
rutile
ruttish
ruttishness
rutty
Rwanda (*or* Rua~)
rye

S

saag (or sag)
Saar
Saarland
sabadilla
sabayon
sabbat
sabbatarian (S~)
sabbatarianism (S~)
sabbath (S~)
sabbatical
sable
sablefish
sabot
sabotage
saboteur
sabre (US ~ber)
sabretooth
sac
saccade
saccadic
saccadically
saccaride
saccharin (n)
saccharine (adj)
sacerdotal
sacerdotalism
sacerdotally
sachet
sack
sackable
sackbut
sackcloth
sackful
sacking
sacklike
sack-race
sacral
sacralisation (or ~iz~)
sacralise (or ~ize)

sacrality
sacrament
sacramental
sacramentalise (or ~ize)
sacramentalism
sacramentality
sacramentally
sacrarium (pl ~ia)
sacred
sacredly
sacredness
sacrifice
sacrificial
sacrificially
sacrilege
sacrilegious
sacrilegiously
sacrist
sacristan
sacristy
sacroiliac
sacrosanct
sacrosanctity
sacrum (pl ~ra, ~ums)
sad (~dder, ~ddest)
sadden
saddhu (or sadhu)
saddish
saddle
saddleback
saddlebacked
saddlebag
saddlecloth
saddler
saddlery
Sadducee
sadhu (or saddhu)
sadism
sadist
sadistic
sadistically
sadly
sadness
sado-masochism
sado-masochist
sado-masochistic
safari (pl ~is)
safe
safe-breaker
safe-cracker

safe-deposit (adj)
safeguard
safekeeping
safety
saffian
safflower
saffron
saffrony
sag (~gged, ~gging)
saga
sagacious
sagaciously
sagaciousness
sagacity
sage
sagebrush
sagely
sageness
sagginess
saggital
saggitally
saggy
Sagittarian
Sagittarius
sago
saguaro
Sahara
Saharan
sahib
said
saiga
sail
sailable
sailboard
sailboarder
sailboarding
sailboat
sailcloth
sailed
sailer (! sailor) boat
sailfish
sailing
sailmaker
sailor (! sailer) crew
sailplane
sainfoin
saint (S~)
sainted
sainthood
saintliness

saintly
saintship
sake *benefit*
sake (*or* saki) *drink*
sal volatile
salaam
salable (*US; UK* ~lea~)
salacious
salaciously
salaciousness
salacity
salad
Saladin
salamander
salamandrine
salami (*pl* ~mi, ~mis)
salaried
salary
salchow
sale
saleability
saleable (*US* ~lab~)
saleableness (*US* ~lab~)
Salem
saleroom
salesgirl
salesman (*pl* ~men)
salesmanship
salespeople
salesperson
saleswoman (*pl* ~women)
salicylic
salience
saliency
salient
salientia (S~)
salientian
saliently
saline
salinisation (*or* ~iz~)
salinity
salinometer
saliva
salivary
salivate
salivating
salivation
Salk
sallow

sallowish
sallowness
sally *action*
salmagundi (*or* ~dy)
salmanazar
salmon
salmonella (S~; *pl* ~ae)
salon
saloon
salopettes
salsa
salsify
salt
SALT *treaty*
saltation
saltationism
saltationist
saltbox
saltcellar (*or* salt-~)
salted
salter
saltern
saltigrade
saltimbocca
saltiness
saltire (*or* ~tier)
saltpetre (*US* ~ter)
saltworks
saltwort
salty
salubrious
salubriously
salubriousness
salubrity
saluki
salutarily
salutariness
salutary
salutation
salutational
salutatory
salute
saluter
salvable
salvage
salvageable
salvager
salvation
salvationism (S~)
salvationist (S~)

salve
salver
salvia
salvo (*pl* ~os, ~oes)
salwar (*or* shal~)
Salyut
samadhi (*pl* ~his)
Samaritan
samarium
Samarkand (*or* ~qand)
samba (~bas, ~baed *or* ~ba'd, ~baing)
sambuca
same
sameness
sameyness
Samhain
samisen (*or* sha~)
samizdat
Samoa
Samoan
samosa
samovar
samoyed (S~)
sampan
samphire
sample
sampled
sampler
sampling
Samson
samurai
sanative
sanatorium (*pl* ~ia, ~iums)
sanctification
sanctified
sanctifier
sanctify
sanctimonious
sanctimoniously
sanctimoniousness
sanctimony
sanction
sanctionable
sanctioned
sanctitude
sanctity
sanctuary
sanctum

sand
sandal
sandalwood
sandbag (~gged, ~gging)
sandbagger
sandbank
sandbar
sandblast
sandblaster
sandbox
sandcastle
sand-dune
sander
sandfly
sandgrouse
sandhopper
sandiness
sanding
Sandinista
sandman
sandpaper
sandpiper
sandpit
sandshoe
sandstone
sandstorm
sandwich
sandwiched
sandy
sandyish
sane
sanely
saneness
sang
sangfroid (or sang-~)
sangria
sanguinary
sanguine
sanguinely
sanguineness
sanguineous
sanitarian
sanitarily
sanitariness
sanitary
sanitation
sanitisation (or ~iz~)
sanitise (or ~ize)
sanitised (or ~ized)

sanitiser (or ~iz~)
sanity
sans
sanserif (or sans serif)
Sanskrit
Sanskritic
Sanskritist
Santa
Santiago
sap (~pped, ~pping)
sapid
sapidity
sapience
sapient
sapiently
sapless
sapling
sapodilla
saponaceous
saponifiable
saponification
saponify
sapper
Sapphic
sapphire
sapphirine
sappily
sappiness
sapping
sappy
saprolite
saprophyte
saprozoic
saraband (or ~de)
Saracen
Saracenic
Sarajevo
sarcasm
sarcastic
sarcastically
sarcenet (or sarse~)
sarcoma (pl ~mata, ~as)
sarcomatosis (pl ~oses)
sarcomatous
sarcophagus (pl ~gi, ~uses)
sard
sardine
Sardinia
Sardinian

sardius
sardonic
sardonically
sardonicism
sardonyx
sargasso
sargassum
sari (or ~ree; pl ~is, ~rees)
sarin
sarong
saros
sarrusophone
sarsanet (or sarce~)
sarsaparilla
sartorial
sartorially
Sartre
sash
sashay
sashed
sashimi
sashless
sasquatch (S~)
sassafras
Sassenach
sassily
sassiness
sassy
sat
Satan
satanic
satanical
satanically
satanise (or ~ize)
satanism (S~)
satanist
satay (or ~tai, ~té)
satchel
sate
sated
satedness
sateen
satellite
satiability
satiable
satiate
satiation
satiety
satin

satined
satining
satinwood
satiny
satire
satiric
satirical
satirically
satirise (*or* ~ize)
satirist
satisfaction
satisfactorily
satisfactoriness
satisfactory
satisfiability
satisfiable
satisfice
satisfied
satisfy
satisfying
satisfyingly
satori
satsuma
saturability
saturable
saturant
saturate
saturated
saturation
Saturday
Saturn
saturnalia (S~)
saturnalian
Saturnian
saturnine
saturninely
satyagraha
satyr
satyriasis
satyrid
sauce
sauced
sauceless
saucepan
saucepanful
saucer
saucerful
saucerless
saucily
sauciness

saucisson
saucy
sauerkraut
sauna
saunter
saunterer
sauntering
saunteringly
saurian
saury
sausage
sauté (~tés, ~téed *or* ~téd, ~téing)
Sauvignon
savage
savagely
savageness
savagery
savannah (S~; *or* ~nna)
savant
savante
savate
save
saveable (*or* ~vab~)
saveloy
saver
saving
Saviour (*US* ~or) *Christ*
saviour (*US* ~or) *person who saves*
savoir-faire
savour (*US* ~or)
savouriness (US ~or~)
savourless (*US* ~or~)
savoury (*US* ~or~)
Savoy *opera, hotel*
savoy *cabbage*
savvy
saw (sawn)
sawdust
sawfish
sawfly
sawmill
sawn-off
sawtooth
sawtoothed
sawyer
saxhorn
saxifrage
Saxon

Saxonise (*or* ~ize)
saxophone
saxophonist
say (said)
saying
say-so
scab (~bbed, ~bbing)
scabbard
scabbed
scabbiness
scabby
scabies
scabrous
scabrously
scabrousness
scaffold
scaffolded
scaffolder
scaffolding
scalability
scalable
scalableness
scalably
scald
scalded
scalding
scale
scaled
scaleless
scalene
scaler
scaling
scallion
scallop (*or* sco~)
scalloped (*or* sco~)
scallywag (*US* scala~)
scaloppine (*pl* ~ni)
scalp
scalpel
scalper
scaly
scam (~mmed, ~mming)
scamp
scamper
scampi
scan (~nned, ~nning)
scanable (*or* ~anna~)
scandal
scandalise (*or* ~ize)

scandalmonger
scandalous
scandalously
scandalousness
Scandinavia
Scandinavian
scandium
scanner
scanning
scansion
scant
scantily
scantiness
scantly
scantness
scanty
scapegoat
scapegrace
scapula (*pl* ~ae, ~as)
scapular
scapulary
scar (~rred, ~rring)
scarab
scaramouch
scarce
scarcely
scarceness
scarcity
scare
scarecrow
scared
scaremonger
scaremongering
scarf (*pl* scarves, scarfs)
scarfed
scarification
scarifier
scarify
scarily
scariness
scarless
scarlet
scarp
scarper
scary
scat (~tted, ~tting)
scathing
scathingly
scatological
scatologically

scatter
scatterbrain
scatterbrained
scattered
scatterer
scattering
scattershot
scattily
scattiness
scatty
scavenge
scavenger
scenario
scene
scenery
scenic
scenically
scenographic
scenography
scent
scented
scentless
sceptic (*US* ske~)
sceptical (*US* ske~)
sceptically (*US* ske~)
scepticism (*US* ske~)
sceptre (*US* ~ter)
sceptred (*US* ~tered)
schadenfreude (S~)
schedule
scheduled
scheelite
Scheherazade
schema
schematic
schematisation (*or*
  ~iz~)
schematise (*or* ~ize)
scheme
schemer
scheming
scherzando (*pl* ~os, ~di)
scherzo (*pl* ~os, ~zi)
schism
schismatic
schist
schistosome
schistosomiasis
schizoid
schizophrenia

schizophrenic
schlock
schmaltz
schmooze
schnapps (*or* ~aps)
schnauzer (S~)
schnitzel
scholar
scholarly
scholarship
scholastic
scholastically
scholasticism (S~)
school
schoolboy
schoolchild
schooldays
schooled
schoolgirl
schoolhouse
schooling
schoolmaster
schoolmistress
schoolteacher
schooner
schottische
sciatic
sciatica
science
scientific
scientifically
scientism
scientist
Scientologist
Scientology
sci-fi
scimitar
scintilla
scintillate
scintillating
scintillation
scirocco (*or* sir~, S~)
scissor
scissors
sclera
sclerosis
sclerotic
sclerous
scoff

scold
scoliosis
scollop (*or* sca~)
sconce
scone
scoop
scoot
scooter
scope
scorch
scorcher
scorching
score
scoreboard
scorecard
scorer
scorn
scornful
Scorpio
scorpioid
scorpion
Scot
scotch
scot-free
Scotland
scotoma
Scots
Scotsman (*pl* ~men)
Scotswoman (*pl* ~women)
Scottish
scoundrel
scour
scourge
scouring
Scouse
scout
scouter
scouting
scoutmaster
scoutmistress
scowl
Scrabble (*tr*) *game*
scrabble *scratch*
scraggy
scram
scramble
scrambler
scramjet
scrap (~pped, ~pping)

scrapbook
scrape
scraper
scrapie
scrappy
scrapyard
scratch
scratchcard
scratching
scratchy
scrawl
scrawler
scrawniness
scrawny
scream
screamer
screaming
screamingly
scree
screech
screed
screen
screening
screenplay
screensaver
screenwriter
screw
screwball
screwdriver
screwed
screwing
screwy
scribble
scribbling
scribe
scrimmage
scrimp
scrimshaw
scrip
script
scriptural
scripture
scriptwriter
scrivener
scroll
scrolled
scrolling
Scrooge
scrotal
scrotum (*pl* ~ums, ~ta)

scrounge
scrounger
scrounging
scrub
scrubber
scrubbing
scrubby
scruff
scruffily
scruffiness
scruffy
scrum (~mmed, ~mming)
scrummage
scrummy
scrumptious
scrumptiously
scrumptiousness
scrunch
scrunchy
scruple
scrupulous
scrutinise (*or* ~ize)
scrutiny
scuba
scud (~dded, ~dding)
scuff
scuffing
scuffle
scull (! skull) *rowing*
sculler
scullery
sculling
scullion
sculpt
sculptor
sculptress
sculpture
sculpturesque
scum
scumble
scupper
scurf
scurfily
scurfiness
scurfy
scurrility
scurrilous
scurrilously
scurrilousness

scurry
scurvy
scutellum (*pl* ~lla)
scuttle
scuttlebutt
scuttleful
Scylla
scythe
sea
seabird
seaboard
seaborgium
seaborne
seafarer
seafaring
seafood
seafront
seagoing
seagull
seal
sealant
sealer
sealing-wax
sealskin
Sealyham
seam
seaman (*pl* ~men)
seamanly
seamanship
seaminess
seamless
seamlessly
seamstress
seamy
seance (*or* sé~)
seaplane
seaport
sear
search
searching
searchlight
seascape
seashell
seashore
seasick
seasickness
seaside
season
seasonable
seasonableness

seasonably
seasonal
seasonally
seasoned
seasoning
seat
seating
seaward
seawards
seaweed
seaworthiness
seaworthy
sebaceous
seborrhoea (*or* ~hea)
sebum
secant
secateurs
secede
secession
secessionism
secessionist
seclude
secluded
seclusion
seclusive
second
secondary
seconder
secondly
secondment
secrecy
secret
secretariat
secretary
secrete
secretion
secretive
secretory
sect
sectarian
sectarianism
section
sectional
sectionalism
sector
sectorial
secular
secularisation (*or* ~iz~)
secularise (*or* ~ize)
secularism

secularist
secularity
secularly
securable
secure
securely
securer
security
sedan
sedate
sedately
sedateness
sedation
sedative
sedentary
sedge
sediment
sedimentary
sedimentation
sedition
seditious
seduce
seducer
seducing
seduction
seductive
seductively
seductiveness
seductress
sedulity
sedulous
sedulousness
sedum
see
seed
seedbed
seeded
seeder
seediness
seedling
seedy
seeing
seek
seeker
seeking
seem
seeming
seemingly
seemly
seen

seep
seepage
seepy
seer
seesaw
seethe
see-through
segment
segmental
segmentally
segmentary
segmentation
segmented
segregate
segregated
segregation
segregational
segregationist
segue (~gued, ~gueing)
seine *net*
Seine *river*
seismic
seismicity
seismogram
seismograph
seismographer
seismography
seismologic
seismological
seismologically
seismologist
seismology
seize
seizing
seizure
seldom
select
selection
selective
selectively
selectiveness
selectivity
selectness
selector
selenite
selenium
selenographer
selenographic
selenographical
selenography

selenological
selenologist
selenology
self
self (*pl* selves)
self-abuse
self-addressed
self-catering
self-centred
self-centredness
self-confessed
self-confidence
self-conscious
self-consciousness
self-contained
self-control
self-controlled
self-defence
self-destruct
self-drive
self-effacing
self-employed
self-esteem
self-evident
self-explanatory
self-expressionism
self-fulfilling
self-government
self-help
self-image
self-important
self-imposed
self-indulgent
selfish
selfishness
selfless
selflessness
self-made
self-possessed
self-preservation
self-propelled
self-raising
self-reliant
self-respect
self-restraint
self-righteous
self-righteousness
self-sacrifice
selfsame
self-satisfied

self-seeking
self-service
self-starter
self-styled
self-sufficiency
self-sufficient
self-supporting
self-willed
Seljuk
sell
sell-by
seller
selling
sellotape (S~, *tr*)
sell-out
selva
selvage (*or* ~ege)
selves
semantic
semantically
semanticist
semanticity
semantics
semaphore
semaphoric
semblable
semblance
semen
semester
semiannual (*or* semi-~)
semiannually (*or* semi-~)
semiautomatic
semibreve
semicircle
semicircular
semicolon
semiconducting
semiconductivity
semiconductor
semidetached
semifinal (*or* semi-~)
semifinalist (*or* semi-~)
semilunar (*or* semi-~)
seminal
seminally
seminar
seminarian
seminarist
seminary

seminiferous
semiologist
semiology
semiotician
semiotics
semiquaver
Semite
Semitic
Semitism
semitone
semolina
Semtex (*tr*)
senate (S~)
senator (S~)
send
sender
sending
send-off
senescence
senescent
seneschal
senile
senility
senior
seniority
senna
sensation
sensational
sensationalise (*or* ~ize)
sensationalism
sensationalist
sensationalistic
sense
senseless
senselessly
senselessness
sensibility
sensible
sensing
sensitisation (*or* ~iz~)
sensitise (*or* ~ize)
sensitive
sensitivity
sensor
sensory
sensual
sensualism
sensualist
sensuality
sensually

sensuous
sensuously
sensuousness
sent
sentence
sentential
sententially
sententious
sententiously
sententiousness
sentience
sentient
sentiment
sentimental
sentimentalism
sentimentality
sentinel
sentry
Seoul
sepal
separability
separable
separableness
separably
separate
separated
separatedness
separation
separatism
separatist
separator
sepia
sepoy
sepsis (*pl* ~pses)
September
septennial
septet (*or* ~ette)
septic
septicaemia (*or* ~cem~)
septicaemic (*or* ~cem~)
septuagenarian
Septuagesima
Septuagint
septum
septuple
septuplet
sepulchral
sepulchre (*US* ~cher)
sepultural
sepulture

sequel
sequela (*pl* ~ae)
sequence
sequencer
sequencing
sequent
sequential
sequentiality
sequentially
sequester
sequestered
sequestrate
sequestration
sequestrator
sequin
sequined
sequoia
seraglio (*pl* ~os)
seraph (*pl* ~phs, ~phim)
seraphic
seraphical
seraphically
Serb
Serbia
Serbian
Serbo-Croat
serenade
serenader
serendipitous
serendipitousness
serendipity
serene
serenely
sereneness
serenity
serf
serfdom
serfhood
sergeant
sergeant-major
serial
serialisation (*or* ~iz~)
serialise (*or* ~ize)
serialised (*or* ~ized)
serialism
serialist
sericulture
series
serif
serigraph

serigrapher
serigraphy
seriocomic (*or* serio-~)
serious
seriously
seriousness
sermon
sermonise (*or* ~ize)
serologist
serologistical
serologistically
serology
serous
serpent
serpentine
serpigo
serrate
serrated
serration
serried
serum (*pl* ~ums, ~ra)
servant
serve
server
service
serviceability
serviceable
serviceably
serviceman
servicewoman
serviette
servile
servilely
servility
serving
servitude
servo
sesame
sesamoid
sessile
session
sestet
set
setback
settee
setter
setting
settle
settled
settlement

settler
settling
set-to
set-up
seven
sevenfold
seventeen
seventeenth
seventh
seventieth
seventy
sever
several
severance
severe
severely
severeness
severity
sew
sewage
sewer
sewerage
sewing
sewn
sex
sexagenarian
Sexagesima
sexed
sexiness
sexism
sexist
sexless
sexology
sexpert
sexploitation
sextant
sextet
sextillian
sextuple
sextuplet
sexual
sexualise (*or* ~ize)
sexuality
sexually
sexy
sforzando
sforzato
sfumato
sgraffito
shabbiness

shabby
shack
shacked
shackle
shaddock
shade
shadeless
shadiness
shading
shadoof (*or* ~duf)
shadow
shadowgraph
shadowy
shady
shaft
shag
shaggily
shagginess
shaggy
shah (S~)
shake
shakedown
shaken
shake-out
Shaker *sect*
shaker *container*
Shakespeare
Shakespearean (*or* ~rian)
shake-up
shakily
shakiness
shaking
shaky
shale
shallot (*or* shalot)
shallow
shallowly
shallowness
shalom
sham (~mmed, ~mming)
shaman
shamanism
shamanist
shamanistic
shamble
shambling
shambolic
shame

shamefaced
shamefacedly
shameful
shamefully
shamefulness
shameless
shamelessly
shamelessness
shamisen (*or* sam~)
shampoo
shamrock
shandy
shanghai
shanghaied
shanghaiing
Shangri-La
shank
shanty
shape
shapeless
shapeliness
shapely
shaper
shaping
shard (*or* sherd)
share
sharecropper
shareholder
shareware
sharia (*or* ~iah, ~iat)
shark
sharp
sharpen
sharper
sharpish
sharpness
sharpshooter
sharp-tongued
sharp-witted
shatter
shattered
shattering
shatterproof
shave
shaven
shaver
shaving
shawl
shawm
sheaf (*pl* sheaves)

shear (shorn *or* sheared)
shears
shearwater
sheath (*n*)
sheathe (*v*)
sheathing
sheaved
shed (~dding)
shedder
sheen
sheep
sheepdog
sheepfold
sheepish
sheepshank
sheepshearing
sheepskin
sheet
sheeting
sheikh (*or* shaikh,
    shaykh, sheik)
sheikhdom (*or* sheik~)
shelduck (*pl* ~ck, ~cks)
shelf (*pl* shelves)
shelf-life
shell
shellac
shellfire
shellfish
shelling
shellproof
shell-shock
shelter
sheltie (*or* ~ty)
shelve
shelved
shelving
shepherd
shepherdess
sherbet
sherd (*or* shard)
sheriff
Sherlock
Sherpa
sherry
Shetland
Shia (*or* ~iah, ~i'a)
shiatsu (*or* ~tzu)
shibboleth
shield

shielding
shift
shifter
shiftily
shiftiness
shifting
shiftless
shifty
shigella
shih-tzu
Shiite (*or* Shi'ite)
shilling
shillyshally
shimmer
shimmery
shimmy
shin
shinbone
shindig
shindy
shine (shone *or* shined,
    shining)
shiner
shingle
shingles
shingly
shininess
shining
Shinto
Shintoism
Shintoist
shinty
shiny
ship
shipboard
shipbuilder
shipbuilding
shipmate
shipment
shipping
shipshape
shipwreck
shipwright
shipyard
shire
shirk
shirker
shirt
shirtsleeve (*or* ~ves)
shirty

shish kebab
shit (*tab*)
shite (*tab*)
shiva (S~, *or* Siva)
shiver
shivering
shoal
shock
shocker
shocking
shockproof
shod
shoddiness
shoddy
shoe (shod)
shoehorn
shoelace
shoemaker
shoeshine
shoestring
shofar (*pl* ~fars, ~froth)
shogi
shogun
shogunate
shone
shoo
shook
shoot (shot)
shooter
shooting
shop
shopaholic
shopfitter
shopkeeper
shoplifter
shoplifting
shopper
shopping
shop-soiled
shopwalker
shore
shoreline
shorn
short
shortage
shortbread
shortcake
short-circuit (*v*)
short-circuited
shortcoming

shorten
shortening
shortfall
shorthand
short-handed
shorthorn
shortlist
short-lived
shortly
shortness
short-range
shorts
short-sighted
short-staffed
short-tempered
short-term
short-winded
shot
shot put
shotgun
shotputter
should
shoulder
shout
shove
shove-halfpenny
shovel
shovelboard
shovelful
shoveller (*US* ~eler)
show (shown *or* showed)
showbiz
showboat
showcase
showdown
shower
showery
showgirl
showhouse
showing
showjumper
showjumping
showman
showmanship
shown
show-off
showpiece
showplace
showroom
showy

shrank
shrapnel
shred (~dded, ~dding)
shredder
shrew
shrewd
shrewish
shriek
shrift
shrike
shrill
shrimp (*pl* ~mp, ~mps)
shrine
shrink (shrank, shrunk, shrunken)
shrinkable
shrinkage
shrive
shrivel (~lled, ~lling; *US* ~led, ~ling)
shriven
shroud
Shrovetide
shrub
shrubbery
shrubby
shrug (~gged, ~gging)
shrunk
shrunken
shudder
shuddering
shudderingly
shuddery
shuffle
shuffleboard
shun (~nned, ~nning)
shunt
shush
shut
shutdown
shuteye
shutter
shutting
shuttle
shuttlecock
shy
Shylock
shyness
shyster (*US*)
Siamese

Siberia
Siberian
sibilance
sibilancy
sibilant
sibling
sibylline
sic
Sicilian
Sicily
sick
sickbed
sicken
sickening
sickle
sickle-cell
sickliness
sickly
sickness
sidalcea
side
sideboard
sideburns
sidecar
sided
side-effect
sidekick
sidelight
sideline
sidelong
sidereal
side-saddle
sideshow
sideslip
sidesman
sidestep
sideswipe
sidetrack
sidewalk
sideways
sidewinder
siding
sidle
siege
siemens
sienna
siesta
sieve
sievert
sift

sigh
sight
sighted
sightless
sightlessly
sightsee
sightseeing
sightseer
sigil
sigillographer
sigillography
sigma
sign
signal (~lled, ~lling; *US*
    ~led, ~ling)
signally
signalman
signatory
signature
signet (! cygnet) *seal,*
    ring
significance
significant
significantly
signification
signified
signify
signing
signpost
Sikh
Sikhism
silage
silence
silencer
silent
silently
silentness
silhouette
silica
silicate
siliceous (*or* ~cious)
silicon
silicone
silicosis
silk
silken
silkiness
silk-screen
silkworm
silky

sill
sillabub (*or* syll~)
silliness
silly
silo (*pl* ~os)
silt
Silurian
silvan (*or* syl~)
silver
silverfish
silverside
silversmith
silverweed
silvery
silviculture
sima
simian
similar
similarity
simile
similitude
simmer
simony
simpatico
simper
simple
simple-minded
simple-mindedness
simpleton
simplicity
simplification
simplifier
simplify
simplistic
simplistically
simply
simulacrum (*pl* ~ums,
    ~cra)
simulate
simulated
simulation
simulator
simulcast
simultaneity
simultaneous
simultaneousness
sin (~nned, ~nning)
since
sincere
sincerely

sincerity
sine
sinecure
sine die
sine qua non
sinew
sinfonia
sinfonietta
sinful
sinfully
sinfulness
sing
singalong
Singapore
Singaporean
singe (singed, singeing)
singer
Singhalese (*or* Sinha~)
singing
single
single-handed
single-minded
single-mindedness
singleness
singles
singlet
singleton
singsong
singular
singularisation (*or* ~iz~)
singularise (*or* ~ize)
singularity
singularly
Sinhalese (*or* Singha~)
sinister
sinistral
Sinitic
sink
sinker
sinking
sinless
sinlessness
sinner
Sinologist
Sinology
sinter
sinuosity
sinuous
sinuously
sinuousness

sinus
sinusitis
sinusoid
sinusoidal
sinusoidally
Sion (*or* Z~)
Siouan
Sioux
sip (~pped, ~pping)
siphon (*or* sy~)
sir
sire (sired, siring)
Siren *sea-nymph*
siren *device*
Sirius
sirloin
sirocco (S~; *or* sci~)
sisal
siskin
sissy (*US*; *or* c~)
sister
sisterhood
sister-in-law
sisterliness
sisterly
sit
sitar
sitcom
site
sit-in
sitter
sitting
situate
situated
situation
Siva (*or* Shi~)
six
sixfold
six-pack
sixpence
sixpenny
sixteen
sixteenth
sixth
sixtieth
sixty
size
sizeable (*or* ~zab~)
sizzle
ska

skate
skateboard
skeet
skein
skeletal
skeleton
skeletonise (*or* ~ize)
skep
skepful
skeptic (*or* sc~)
skeptical (*or* sc~)
skepticism (*or* sc~)
skerry
sketch
sketchable
sketcher
sketchily
sketchiness
sketchy
skew
skewback
skewbald
skewer
skew-whiff
ski (*n pl* skis; *v* skis, skied
  or ski'd, skiing *or* skiing)
skid (~dded, ~dding)
skied
skier
skiff
skiffle
skiing
skilful
skilfully
skilfulness
skill
skilled
skillet
skim (~mmed,
  ~mming)
skimmer
skimp
skimpily
skimpiness
skimpy
skin (~nned, ~nning)
skincare
skin-deep
skindiver (*or* skin-~)

skindiving (*or* skin-~)
skinflint
skinhead
skink
skinned
skinner
skinny
skip (~pped, ~pping)
skipjack
skipper
skipping
skirl
skirmish
skirmisher
skirt
skirted
skirting
skirting-board
skit
skitter
skittish
skittishly
skittishness
skittle
skive
skiver
skivvy
skua
skulduggery (*or* skull~)
skulk
skull (! scull) *head*
skullcap
skunk
sky
skydiver (*or* sky-~)
skydiving (*or* sky-~)
Skye
skyer (*or* skier)
skyjack
skylark
skylight
skyline
skyscraper
skyward
skywards
slab
slack
slacken
slackener
slacks

slag (~gged, ~gging)
slain
slake
slalom
slam (~mmed, ~mming)
slammer
slander
slanderer
slanderous
slang
slanging
slant
slantways
slantwise
slap (~pped, ~pping)
slapdash
slap-happy
slapstick
slap-up
slash
slashing
slat
slate
slating
slattern
slatternliness
slatternly
slaughter
slaughterhouse
Slav
slave
slave-driver
slaver
slavering
slaveringly
slavery
Slavic
slaving
slavish
slavishly
slavishness
Slavonic
slay (slew)
sleaze
sleazily
sleaziness
sleazy
sled (~dded, ~dding)
sledge

sledgehammer
sledger
sledging
sleek
sleekily
sleekness
sleep (slept)
sleeper
sleepily
sleepiness
sleeping
sleepless
sleeplessly
sleeplessness
sleepwalk
sleepwalker
sleepwalking
sleepy
sleepyhead
sleet
sleeve
sleeved
sleeveless
sleeving
sleigh
sleighing
sleight
slender
slenderly
slenderness
slept
sleuth
slew (*occ* slue)
slewed
slice
slicing
slick
slicker
slickly
slickness
slid
slidable
slide (slid, sliding)
slider
slide-rule
slight
slighting
slightingly
slightly
slightness

slim (~mmed,
  ~mming)
slime
slimily
sliminess
slimly
slimness
slimy
sling
slinging
slingshot
slink
slinkily
slinkiness
slinky
slip (~pped, ~pping)
slipknot
slippage
slipped
slipper
slippered
slipperiness
slippery
slipping
slippy
slipshod
slipstream
slip-up
slipway
slit (~tted, ~tting)
slither
slithery
sliver
slivovitz
slob
slobber
slobbery
slobbish
slobby
sloe (! slow) *bush, gin*
slog
slogan
sloop
slop (~pped, ~pping)
slope
sloppily
sloppiness
sloppy
slosh
slot

sloth
slothful
slouch
sloucher
slouching
slouchy
slough
Slovak
Slovene
Slovenian
slovenliness
slovenly
slow
slowcoach
slowly
slowness
slowworm
sludge
slug
sluggard
sluggardliness
sluggardly
slugger
sluggish
sluggishly
sluggishness
sluice
slum (~mmed,
  ~mming)
slumber
slumberer
slumbering
slummy
slump
slumped
slung
slunk
slur (~rred, ~rring)
slurp
slurry
slush
slushiness
slushy
slut
sluttish
sly (slyer, slyest)
slyly (*or* slily)
slyness
smack
smacker

small
smallholding
small-minded
small-mindedly
small-mindedness
smallness
smallpox
smarmily
smarminess
smarmy
smart
smart alec (*or* ~ck)
smart-alecky
smarten
smartly
smartness
smarty (*or* ~tie)
smash
smash-and-grab
smashed
smasher
smashing
smash-up
smatter
smattering
smear
smearily
smeariness
smeary
smectic
smell (smelt *or* smelled)
smelliness
smelly
smelt
smelter
smidgen (*or* ~geon,
  ~gin)
smilax
smile
smiley (*pl* ~eys)
smiling
smirch
smirk
smirking
smirkingly
smite (smote, smitten,
  smiting)
smith
smithereens
smithy

smitten
smock
smocking
smog
smoggy
smokable
smoke
smoked
smokeless
smoker
smokescreen
smokestack
smokily
smokiness
smoking
smoky
smooch
smoocher
smoochy
smooth
smoothie
smorgasbord
smorzando
smote
smother
smoulder (*US* smol~)
smouldering (*US* smol~)
smudge
smudgily
smudginess
smudgy
smug
smuggle
smuggler
smuggling
smugly
smut
smuttily
smuttiness
smutty
snack
snaffle
snag (~gged, ~gging)
snaggletooth
snaggy
snail
snake
snakebite
snakily
snakiness

snaky
snap (~pped, ~pping)
snapdragon
snapper
snappily
snappiness
snapping
snappish
snappishness
snappy
snapshot
snare
snarer
snaring
snarl
snarler
snarling
snarlingly
snarl-up
snarly
snatch
snatcher
snatchily
snatching
snatchy
snazzily
snazziness
snazzy
sneak (sneaked *or US*
   snuck)
sneaker (*US*)
sneakily
sneakiness
sneaking
sneaky
sneck
sneer
sneerer
sneering
sneeringly
sneeze
sneezer
sneezewort
sneezing
snib
snick
snicker
snide
snidely
snideness

sniff
sniffer
sniffily
sniffiness
sniffle
sniffy
snifter
snigger
snip (~pped, ~pping)
snipe
sniper
snippet
snitch
snitcher
snivel (~lled, ~lling; *US*
   ~led, ~ling)
snob
snobbery
snobbish
snobbishly
snobbishness
snog (~gged, ~gging)
snood
snook
snooker
snoop
snooper
snoopy
snootily
snootiness
snooty
snooze
snoozer
snoozy
snore
snorkel (*or* schn~; *v*
   ~lled, ~lling; *US*
   ~led, ~ling)
snorkelling (*or* schn~;
   US ~eling)
snort
snorter
snorting
snortingly
snot
snottily
snottiness
snotty
snout
snouted

snouty
snow
snowball
snowberry
snowbird
snow-blind
snow-blindness
snowblower
snowboard
snowboarder
snowboarding
snowbound
snowcapped
snowcat
snowdrift
snowdrop
snowfall
snowflake
snowily
snowiness
snowline
snowman (pl ~men)
snowmobile
snowplough
snowshoe
snowstorm
snowy
snub (~bbed, ~bbing)
snubbing
snubbingly
snubby
snuck
snuff
snuffbox
snuffer
snuffle
snuffling
snuffy
snug (~gger, ~ggest)
snuggle
snugly
snugness
so
soak
soakaway
soaked
soaking
so-and-so (pl ~-sos)
soap
soapbox

soapstone
soapsuds
soapwort
soapy
soar
soaring
soaringly
sob (~bbed, ~bbing)
sobbing
sobbingly
sober
sobering
soberly
soberness
sobriety
sobriquet (or soub~)
so-called
soccer
sociability
sociable
sociableness
sociably
social
socialisation (or ~iz~)
socialise (or ~ize)
socialiser (or ~iz~)
socialism
socialist
socialite
sociality
socially
socialness
society
sociobiologist
sociobiology
socioeconomic
sociolinguistics
sociological
sociologist
sociology
sociometry
sociopath
sociopathic
sociopathy
sock
socket
socketed
sockeye
Socrates
Socratic

sod
soda
sodality
sodden
soddenness
sodium
sodomise (or ~ize)
sodomist
sodomite
sodomy
sofa
soffit
soft
softback
softball
soft-core
soften
softener
softening
soft-hearted
softie (or softy)
softness
software
softwood
softy (or ~tie)
soggily
sogginess
soggy
soil
soirée (or ~ree)
sojourn
solace
solar
solarise (or ~ize)
solarium (pl ~iums, ~ia)
sold
solder
solderer
soldering
soldier
soldiering
soldiery
sole
solecism
solecistic
solecistical
solecistically
solely
solemn
solemnisation (or ~iz~)

solemnise (or ~ize)
solemnity
solemnly
solemnness
solenoid
solenoidal
sol-fa
solicit
solicitation
soliciting
solicitor
solicitous
solicitously
solicitousness
solicitude
solid
solidarity
solidification
solidifier
solidify
solidity
solidly
solid-state
soliloquise (or ~ize)
soliloquiser (or ~iz~)
soliloquist
soliloquy
solipsism
solipsist
solipsistic
solitaire
solitary
solitude
solo (pl solos)
soloist
solstice
solstitial
solubility
soluble
solution
solvable
solvation
solve
solvency
solvent
solver
soma
Somali
somatic
somatogenic

somatype
sombre (US ~ber)
sombrely (US ~ber~)
sombreness (US ~ber~)
sombrero (pl ~os)
somebody
someday
somehow
someone
somersault (or summer~)
something
sometime
sometimes
somewhat
somewhere
sommelier
somnambulant
somnambulate
somnambulism
somnambulist
somnolence
somnolent
somnolently
son
sonar
sonata
sonatina
son et lumière (or ~ere)
song
songbird
songbook
songsmith
songster
songstress
songwriter
sonic
son-in-law
sonnet
sonneteer
sonny
sonorant
sonority
sonorous
sonorously
sonorousness
soon
sooner
soot
soothe

soother
soothing
soothingly
soothsayer
sootiness
sooty
sop
sophism
sophist
sophistical
sophistically
sophisticated
sophistication
sophistry
sophomore (US)
soporific
soppily
soppiness
sopping
soppy
soprano (pl ~os)
sorbet
sorbic
sorcerer
sorceress
sorcery
sordid
sordidly
sordidness
sordino
sore
sorely
soreness
sorghum
soroptimist (S~)
sorority
sorrel
sorrily
sorriness
sorrow
sorrower
sorrowful
sorrowfully
sorrowfulness
sorrowing
sorry
sort
sortable
sorted
sorter

sortie (~tied, ~tieing)
sorus (pl ~ri)
so-so
sostenuto
sot (~tted, ~tting)
soterial
soteriological
soteriology
sottish
sotto voce
soubriquet (or sob~)
souchong
soufflé
sough
sought
souk (or suk, sukh, suq)
soul
soulful
soulfully
soulfulness
soulless
soullessly
soullessness
soul-searching
sound
soundbite
soundboard
soundbox
soundcard
soundcheck
sounder
sounding
soundless
soundlessly
soundlessness
soundly
soundness
soundproof
soundscape
soundtrack
soup
soupçon
soupily
soupiness
soupy
sour
source
sourcebook
sourdough
soured

sourish
sourishly
sourly
sourness
sousaphone
sous-chef
souse
soused
sousing
souterrain
south
southbound
southeast
southeaster
southeasterly
southeastern
southeastward
southeastwardly
southeastwards
southerlies
southerly
southern
southerner
southernmost
southpaw
southward
southwardly
southwards
southwest
southwesterly
southwestern
southwestward
southwestwards
souvenir
souvlaki (pl ~ia, ~is)
sou'wester
sovereign
sovereignly
sovereignty
soviet (S~)
sovietologist
sow (sowed, sown)
sowing
sown
soy
soya
spa
space-bar
spacecraft

spaced
spacelab
spaceman (pl ~men)
spaceport
spacer
spaceship
spacesuit
spacewalk
spacewoman (pl ~women)
spacing
spacio-temporal
spacious
spaciously
spaciousness
spade
spadeful
spadework
spadille
spadix
spaghetti
Spain
spam (~med, ~mming)
spammer
span (~nned, ~nning)
spangle
spangled
spangly
Spaniard
spaniel
Spanish
spank
spanker
spanking
spanner
spar (~rred, ~rring)
spare
sparely
spareness
sparer
sparing
sparingly
sparingness
spark
sparkiness
sparkle
sparkler
sparkling
sparklingly
sparkly

sparky
sparrer
sparring
sparrow
sparrowhawk
sparse
sparsely
sparseness
sparsity
Spartan *from Sparta*
spartan *austere*
spasm
spasmodic
spasmodical
spasmodically
spastic
spastically
spasticity
spat (~tted, ~tting)
spatchcock
spate
spathaceous
spathe
spatial (*or* ~cial)
spatialisation (*or* ~iz~)
spatialise (*or* ~ize)
spatiality
spatially
spats
spatter
spatula
spatulate
spavin
spawn
spawner
spawning
spay
spayed
spaying
speak (spoke, spoken)
speakable
speaker
speakerphone
speaking
spear
spearhead
spearmint
spec
special
specialisation (or ~iz~)

specialise (*or* ~ize)
specialised (*or* ~ized)
specialism
specialist
speciality
specially
specialness
specialty
speciation
species
specifiable
specific
specifical
specifically
specification
specificity
specificness
specifics
specifier
specify
specimen
speciosity
specious
speciously
speciousness
speck
specked
speckle
speckled
speckless
specky
spectacle
spectacled
spectacles
spectacular
spectacularity
spectacularly
spectate
spectating
spectation
spectator
spectral
spectrality
spectrally
spectre (*US* ~ter)
spectrochemistry
spectrogram
spectrograph
spectrometer
spectroscope

spectrum (*pl* ~ra)
specular
speculate
speculating
speculation
speculative
speculatively
speculativeness
speculator
speculum
sped
speech
speechify
speechifying
speechless
speechlessly
speechlessness
speech-writer
speed (sped *or* speeded)
speedball
speedboat
speeder
speedily
speediness
speeding
speedometer
speedster
speedway
speedwell
speedy
speleological
speleologist
speleology
spell (spelt *or* spelled)
spellbind (spellbound)
spellbinder
spellbound
spellchecker (*or* spell-~)
speller
spelling
spelling-bee
spelt
spelunker
spelunking
spend (spent)
spendable
spender
spending
spendthrift
spent

sperm
spermaceti
spermatic
spermatid
spermatocyte
spermatogenesis
spermatogenetic
spermatophore
spermatophoric
spermatophyte
spermatophytic
spermatozoan
spermatozoic
spermatozoon (*pl* ~zoa)
spermicide
spermophyte
spew
spewer
spewing
sphagnum (*pl* ~na)
sphalerite
spheral
sphere
spheric
spherical
spherically
sphericalness
sphericity
spheroid
spheroidal
spheroidicity
sphincter
sphincteral
sphincterial
sphincteric
sphinx (S~)
sphygmograph
sphygmographical
sphygmographically
sphygmomanometer
sphymography
sphymometer
spica
spicate
spicated
spice
spiced
spicily
spiciness
spicule

spicy (*or* ~cey)
spider
spiderwort
spidery
spied
spiel
spigot
spike
spikelet
spikenard
spikily
spikiness
spiky
spill (spilt *or* spilled)
spillage
spiller
spillover
spilt
spin (spun, spinning)
spinach
spinal
spinally
spindle
spindly
spindrift
spin-dry
spin-dryer (*or* ~drier)
spine
spine-chiller
spine-chilling
spined
spinel
spineless
spinelessly
spinelessness
spinet
spininess
spinnaker
spinner
spinneret
spinney (*pl* ~eys)
spinning
spin-off
spinose
spinous
spinster
spinsterhood
spinsterish
spinsterly
spiny

spiral (~lled, ~lling; *US*
    ~led, ~ling)
spirally
spire
spirit
spirited
spiritedly
spiritedness
spiritism
spiritist
spiritistic
spiritless
spiritlessly
spiritlessness
spiritual
spiritualisation (*or* ~iz~)
spiritualise (*or* ~ize)
spiritualism
spiritualist
spiritualistic
spirituality
spiritually
spiritualness
spit (spat, spitting)
spitchcock
spite
spiteful
spitefully
spitefulness
spitfire
spitter
spitting
spittle
spittoon
spitz
splash
splashdown
splashed
splashily
splashiness
splashy
splat (~tted, ~tting)
splatter
splay
spleen
splendid
splendidly
splendidness
splendiferous
splendiferously

splendiferousness
splendour (*US* ~or)
splenectomy
splenetic
splenetical
splenetically
splenic
splenitis
splice
spliced
splicer
spline
splint
splinter
splintery
split (~tting)
split-level
splitter
splodge
splodgily
splodginess
splodgy
splosh
splotch
splotched
splotchy
splurge
splurgy
splurt
splutter
splutterer
spluttering
splutteringly
spluttery
spode (S~, *tr*)
spoil (spoilt *or* spoiled)
spoilage
spoilation
spoiled
spoiler
spoils
spoilsport
spoilt
spoke
spoked
spoken
spokesman (*pl* ~men)
spokesperson
spokeswoman (*pl* ~women)

spoliation
spoliator
spoliatory
spondaic
spondee
spondylitis
spondylosis
sponge (sponged, spongeing *or* sponging)
spongeable
sponger
spongily
sponginess
spongy
sponson
sponsor
sponsored
sponsorial
sponsorship
spontaneity
spontaneous
spontaneously
spoof
spoofer
spoofery
spook
spookily
spookiness
spookish
spooky
spool
spoon
spoonbill
spoonerism
spoonfeed
spoonful
spoor
sporadic
sporadically
sporangium (*pl* ~ia)
spore
sporophyll (*or* ~yl)
sporophyte
sporophytic
sporophytically
sporran
sport
sportif
sportily

sportiness
sporting
sportingly
sportive
sportively
sportiveness
sportsman (*pl* ~men)
sportsmanlike
sportsmanship
sportsperson
sportswoman (*pl* ~women)
sporty
spot (~tted, ~tting)
spotless
spotlessly
spotlessness
spotlight (~lit *or* ~lighted)
spotted
spottedness
spotter
spottily
spottiness
spotting
spotty
spot-weld
spot-welder
spot-welding
spousal
spouse
spout
spouted
spouter
spoutless
sprain
sprang
sprat (~tted, ~tting)
sprawl
sprawling
sprawlingly
spray
sprayable
sprayer
spray-gun
spray-paint
spread
spreadable
spreadeagle
spreadeagled

spreader
spreading
spreadsheet
spree
sprig (~gged, ~gging)
spriggy
sprightliness
sprightly
spring (sprang, sprung)
springboard
Springbok *sports team*
springbok (*or* ~buck)
  antelope
springe
springer
springily
springiness
springing
springless
spring-loaded
springtail
springtime
springy
sprinkle
sprinkler
sprinkling
sprint
sprinter
sprite
spritz
spritzer
sprocket
sprout
spruce
sprucely
spruceness
sprue
sprung
spry (spryer, spryest)
spryly
spryness
spud (~dded, ~dding)
Spumante
spume
spumy
spun
spunk
spunkily
spunkless
spunky

spur (~rred, ~rring)
spurious
spuriously
spuriousness
spurless
spurn
spurred
spurry
spurt
sputnik (S~)
sputter
sputterer
sputtery
sputum (*pl* ~ta)
spy
spyglass
spyhole
spymaster
squab
squabble
squabbler
squad
squadron
squalid
squalidity
squalidly
squalidness
squall
squally
squalor
squamose
squamous
squander
squanderer
square
squared
squarely
squareness
squarer
squarial (*UK*)
squarish
squash
squashed
squashily
squashiness
squashy
squat (~tter, ~ttest; *v*
  ~tted, ~tting)
squatly
squatness

squatter
squaw
squawk
squawker
squawkily
squawky
squeak
squeaker
squeakily
squeakiness
squeaky
squeal
squealer
squeamish
squeamishly
squeamishness
squeegee
squeezable
squeeze
squeezed
squeezer
squeezy
squelch
squelcher
squelchy
squib (~bbed, ~bbing)
squid
squidgily
squidgy
squiggle
squiggly
squill
squint
squinter
squint-eyed
squinting
squintingly
squinty
squire
squirm
squirmer
squirmy
squirrel (~lled, ~lling;
  US ~led, ~ling)
squirrelfish
squirrelly
squirt
squirter
squish
squishily

squishiness
squishy
Sri Lanka
stab (~bbed, ~bbing)
stabber
stabbing
stabilisation (or ~iz~)
stabilise (or ~ize)
stabiliser (or ~iz~)
stability
stable
stableful
stablemate
stableness
stabling
stably
staccato (pl ~os)
stack
stackable
stacked
stacker
stadium (pl ~ia, ~iums)
staff (pl staves)
staffed
stag
stage
stageability
stageable
stagecoach
stagecraft
stagehand
stage-struck
stagey (or ~gy)
stagflation
stagger
staggered
staggering
staggeringly
staghorn
stagily
staginess
staging
stagnancy
stagnant
stagnantly
stagnate
stagnating
stagnation
stagy (or ~gey)
staid

staidly
staidness
stain
stainable
stainer
stainless
stair
staircase
stairlift
stairway
stairwell
stake
stakeholder
stakeout
stalactite
stalactitic
stalagmite
stalagmitic
stale
stalely
stalemate
staleness
Stalinism
Stalinist
stalk
stalked
stalker
stalking
stalkless
stalklike
stalky
stall
stallholder
stallion
stalwart
stalwartly
stalwartness
stamen (pl ~ns, ~mina)
stamina
staminiferous
stammer
stammerer
stammering
stammeringly
stamp
stampede
stamper
stamping
stance

stanchion
stanchioned
stand (stood)
stand-alone
standard
standard-bearer
standardisable (or ~iz~)
standardisation (or ~iz~)
standardise (or ~ize)
standardiser (or ~iz~)
standby (or ~-by; pl ~bys, ~by's)
stand-in
standing
stand-off
stand-offish
stand-offishly
stand-offishness
standpipe
standpoint
standstill
stand-to
stand-up
stank
stannic
stannous
stanza
stanzic
staphylococcal
staphylococcus (pl ~cci)
staple
stapler
star (~rred, ~rring)
starboard
starburst
starch
starched
starcher
starchily
starchiness
starchy
star-crossed
stardom
stardust
stare
starfish
starfruit
stargaze
stargazer

stargazing
stark
starkly
starkness
starless
starlet
starlight
starling
starlit
starrily
starriness
starry
starry-eyed
star-studded
start
starter
starting
startle
startled
startler
startling
startlingly
start-up
starvation
starve
starved
starveling
starving
starwort
stash
stasis
statable (~eable)
state
statecraft
statehood
stateless
statelessness
stateliness
stately
statement
stateroom
statesman (*pl* ~men)
statesmanlike
statesmanship
statesperson
stateswoman (*pl* ~women)
static
statically
station

stationary (! stationery) *not moving*
stationer
stationery (! stationary) *writing materials*
stationmaster
statistic
statistical
statistically
statistician
statistics
statuary
statue
statuesque
statuesquely
statuesqueness
statuette
stature
statured
status
status quo
statute
statutorily
statutory
staunch
staunchly
staunchness
stave (staved *or* stove, staving)
staves
staving
stay
stayer
stead
steadfast
steadfastly
steadfastness
steadily
steadiness
steady
steak
steakhouse
steal (stole, stolen)
stealth
stealthily
stealthiness
stealthy
steam
steamboat
steamed

steamer
steamily
steaminess
steaming
steamroller
steamy
stearic
stearin (*or* ~ine)
steed
steel
steeliness
steelworker
steelworks
steely
steelyard
steep
steepen
steeper
steeping
steepish
steeple
steeplechase
steeplechaser
steeplechasing
steepled
steeplejack
steeply
steepness
steer
steerable
steerage
steerer
steering
stegosaurus
stela (*pl* ~ae)
stelar (! stellar) *stone*
stele
stellar (! stelar) *stars*
stellate
stem (~mmed, ~mming)
stemless
stemmed
stench
stencil (~lled, ~lling; US ~led, ~ling)
stenciller (US ~iler)
stenographer
stenographic
stenographical

stenographically
stenography
stenosis
stenotic
stentorian
step (~pped, ~pping)
stepbrother
stepchild
stepdad
stepdaughter
stepfamily
stepfather
stephanotis
stepladder
stepmother
stepmum
step-parent
steppe
stepped
stepping
stepsister
stepson
steradian
stereo (*pl* ~os)
stereochemical
stereochemically
stereochemist
stereochemistry
stereogram
stereograph
stereographic
stereographist
stereography
stereometer
stereometric
stereometrical
stereometrically
stereometry
stereophonic
stereophonically
stereophony
stereoscope
stereoscopic
stereoscopically
stereoscopy
stereotype
stereotyped
stereotyper
stereotypic
stereotypical

stereotypically
stereotypy
sterile
sterilely
sterilisable (*or* ~iz~)
sterilisation (*or* ~iz~)
sterilise (*or* ~ize)
sterilised (*or* ~ized)
steriliser (*or* ~iz~)
sterility
sterling
stern
sternal
sternly
sternmost
sternness
sternum (*pl* ~nums,
  ~na)
sternutation
sternutative
sternutator
sternutatory
sternwards
steroid
steroidal
stertorous
stertorously
stertorousness
stet
stethoscope
stethoscopic
stethoscopically
stetson
stevedore
stew
steward
stewardess
stewardship
stewed
stewing
stick (stuck)
stickability
sticker
stickily
stickiness
sticking
stickleback
stickler
sticky
stiff

stiffen
stiffening
stiffly
stiff-necked
stiffness
stifle
stifled
stifling
stiflingly
stigma
stigmata
stigmatic
stigmatically
stigmatise (*or* ~ize)
stigmatised (*or* ~ized)
stigmatism
stile (! style) *steps*
stiletto (*pl* ~os)
still
stillage
stillbirth
stillborn
stillness
stilt
stilted
stiltedly
stiltedness
Stilton
stimulable
stimulant
stimulate
stimulated
stimulating
stimulatingly
stimulation
stimulative
stimulator
stimulatory
stimulus
sting (stung)
stinger
stingily
stinginess
stingingly
stingless
stingray
stingy
stink (stank *or* stunk)
stinker
stinkhorn

stinkily
stinkiness
stinking
stinkingly
stinkweed
stinky
stint
stipe
stipend
stipendiary
stipes
stipple
stippler
stippling
stipulate
stipulating
stipulation
stipulator
stir (~rred, ~rring)
stir-fry
stirrer
stirring
stirringly
stirrup
stitch
stitched
stitcher
stitchery
stitching
stitchwort
stoat
stochastic
stochastically
stockade
stockaded
stockbreeder
stockbreeding
stockbroker
stockbrokerage
stockbrokering
stockbroking
stockfish
stockholder
stockholding
Stockholm
stockily
stockiness
stocking
stockinged
stockingless

stockist
stockless
stockman
stockpile
stockpiler
stockroom
stock-still
stocktake
stocktaker
stocktaking
stocky
stockyard
stodge
stodgily
stodginess
stodgy
stoic (S~)
stoical
stoically
stoicism (S~)
stoke
stoked
stoker
stole
stolen
stolid
stolidity
stolidly
stolidness
stolon
stoma
stomach
stomach-ache
stomached
stomachful
stomatology
stomp
stomper
stomping
stone
stonechat
stoned
stonefruit
Stonehenge
stonemason
stonemasonry
stonewall
stonewalled
stonewalling
stoneware

stonewash
stonewashed
stonework
stoney (or ~ny)
stonily
stoniness
stony (or ~ney)
stony-hearted
stood
stooge
stook
stool
stool-pigeon
stoop
stooped
stooping
stoopingly
stop (~pped, ~pping)
stopcock
stopgap
stop-go
stopover
stoppable
stoppage
stopper
stoppered
stopping
stopwatch
storable
storage
storax
store
storefront
storehouse
storekeeper
storeman
storer
storeroom
storey (US story; pl ~reys, ~ries)
stork
storm
stormbound
stormily
storminess
stormtrooper
stormy
story
storyboard
storybook

storyline
storyteller
storytelling
stoup
stout
stout-hearted
stout-heartedly
stout-heartedness
stoutish
stoutly
stoutness
stove
stow
stowage
stowaway
strabismal
strabismic
strabismical
strabismus
straddle
straddler
Stradivarius
strafe
strafer
straggle
straggler
straggling
straggly
straight
straightaway
straightedge
straighten
straightener
straightforward
straightforwardly
straightforwardness
straightish
straightjacket
straight-laced (or strait-
  ~)
straightly
straightness
strain
strained
strainer
straining
strait
straiten
straitened
straitjacket

strait-laced (or straight-
  ~)
straitly
straits
strand
stranded
strange
strangely
strangeness
stranger
strangle
strangled
stranglehold
strangler
strangulate
strangulated
strangulation
strap (~pped, ~pping)
strapless
strap-on
strapping
strata
stratagem
stratal
strategic
strategical
strategically
strategise (or ~ize)
strategist
strategy
strathspey (pl ~eys)
stratification
stratiform
stratify
stratigrapher
stratigraphic
stratigraphical
stratigraphically
stratigraphist
stratigraphy
stratocumulus
stratose
stratosphere
stratospheric
stratospherically
stratum (pl ~ta)
straw
strawberry
strawy
stray

strayer
streak
streaked
streaker
streakily
streakiness
streaking
streaky
stream
streamer
streaming
streamline
streamlined
streamlining
streamy
street
streetcar
streetlamp
streetlight
streetwalker
streetwalking
streetwise
strength
strengthen
strengthener
strengthless
strenuosity
strenuous
strenuously
strenuousness
streptococcal
streptococcic
streptococcus (pl ~cci)
streptomycin
stress
stressed
stressful
stressfully
stressfulness
stressless
stressor
stretch
stretchability
stretchable
stretched
stretcher
stretchiness
stretching
stretchy
strew (strewn or strewed)

stria (*pl* ~iae)
striate
striated
striation
stricken
strict
strictish
strictly
strictness
stricture
strictured
stride (strode, stridden, striding)
stridence
stridency
strident
stridently
stridor
strife
strike (struck, striking)
strikebound
strikebreaker
striking
strikingly
strimmer
string (strung)
stringed
stringency
stringent
stringently
stringer
stringiness
stringing
stringy
strip (~pped, ~pping)
stripe
striped
stripey (*or* ~py)
stripling
stripper
strippergram (*or* ~ppag~)
stripping
striptease
stripy (*or* ~pey)
strive (strove *or* strived, striving)
strobe
strobic
strobing

stroboscope
stroboscopic
stroboscopically
strode
stroganoff
stroke
stroll
stroller
strong
strongarm
strongbox
stronghold
strongish
strongly
strongman (*pl* ~men)
strong-minded
strong-mindedness
strongroom
strontium
strop (~pped, ~pping)
strophe
strophic
stroppily
stroppiness
stroppy
strove
struck
structural
structuralism
structuralist
structurally
structure
structured
structureless
strudel
struggle
struggler
struggling
strugglingly
strum (~mmed, ~mming)
strung
strut (~tted, ~tting)
strychnine
stub (~bbed, ~bbing)
stubbily
stubbiness
stubble
stubbled
stubbly

stubborn
stubbornly
stubbornness
stubby
stucco
stuccoed (*or* ~o'd)
stuck
stuck-up
stud (~dded, ~dding)
studding
student
studentship
studied
studio (*pl* ~os)
studious
studiously
studiousness
study
stuff
stuffed
stuffily
stuffiness
stuffing
stuffy
stultification
stultifier
stultify
stultifying
stumble
stumbling
stumblingly
stump
stumpily
stumpiness
stumpy
stun (~nned, ~nning)
stung
stunner
stunning
stunningly
stunt
stunted
stuntedness
stuntman (*pl* ~men)
stuntwoman (*pl* ~women)
stupa
stupe
stupefacient
stupefaction

stupefactive
stupefier
stupefy
stupefying
stupefyingly
stupendous
stupendously
stupendousness
stupid
stupidity
stupidly
stupidness
stupor
sturdily
sturdiness
sturdy
sturgeon
stutter
stutterer
stuttering
stutteringly
sty (! stye) *pigs*
stye (*or* sty; *pl* sties, styes) *eyes*
Stygian
style (! stile) *manner*
styler
styling
stylisation (*or* ~iz~)
stylise (*or* ~ize)
stylised (*or* ~ized)
styliser (*or* ~iz~)
stylish
stylishly
stylishness
stylist
stylistic
stylistically
stylometrics
stylometrist
stylometry
stylus (*pl* ~li, ~uses)
stymie (~mieing *or* ~mying)
styptic
Styx
suability
suable
suasive
suave

suavely
suaveness
suavity
sub (~bbed, ~bbing)
subacute
subadult
subalpine
subaltern
subantarctic
subaqua
subaquatic
subaqueous
subarctic
subatomic
Subbuteo (*tr*)
subcategorise (*or* ~ize)
subcategory
subclass
sub-clause
subcommittee
subconscious
subconsciously
subconsciousness
subcontinent
subcontinental
subcontract
subcontractor
subcultural
subculture
subcutaneous
subcutaneously
subcutaneousness
subdeacon
subdirectory
subdivide
subdivisible
subdivision
subdivisional
subdivisive
subdominant
subduable
subduably
subdual
subdue
subdued
subedit
subeditor
subeditorial
subeditorialship
subframe

subfusc
subglacial
subharmonic
subheading
subhuman
subito
subjacency
subjacent
subject
subjected
subjection
subjective
subjectively
subjectiveness
subjectivise (*or* ~ize)
subjectivism
subjectivist
subjectivistic
subjectivistically
subjectivity
subjectless
subjoin
sub judice
subjugate
subjugation
subjugator
subjunctive
subjunctively
sublease
sublessee
sublessor
sublet (~tted, ~tting)
sublieutenant
sublimate
sublimation
sublime
sublimely
sublimeness
subliminal
subliminally
subliminated
sublimity
submachine-gun
submarine
submariner
submerge
submerged
submergence
submergibility
submergible

submerse
submersibility
submersible
submersion
submission
submissive
submissively
submissiveness
submit (~tted, ~tting)
submittable
submitted
submitter
submitting
submultiple
subnormal
subnormality
subnormally
subordinacy
subordinate
subordinately
subordination
suborn
subornation
suborner
subplot
subpoena (~nas, ~naed
or ~na'd, ~naing)
subrogate
subrogation
subroutine
subscribable
subscribe
subscriber
subscript
subscription
subsea
subsequence
subsequent
subsequently
subservience
subserviency
subservient
subserviently
subset
subside
subsidence
subsidiarity
subsidiary
subsidise (or ~ize)
subsidy

subsist
subsistence
subsistent
subsoil
subsonic
subsonically
subspecies
substance
substantial
substantialise (or ~ize)
substantiality
substantially
substantiate
substantiation
substantival
substantivally
substantive
substantively
substantiveness
substation
substituent
substitutability
substitutable
substitute
substitution
substitutional
substitutionally
substitutionary
substitutive
substitutively
substratal
substrate
substrative
substratum
substructural
substructure
subsumable
subsume
subsumed
subsumption
subsumptive
subsurface
subtenancy
subtenant
subtend
subterfuge
subterranean
subterraneously
subtext
subtitle

subtle
subtlely
subtleness
subtlety
subtopia (*UK*)
subtopian (*UK*)
subtotal (~lled, ~lling;
US ~led, ~ling)
subtract
subtracter
subtraction
subtractive
subtropic
subtropical
subtropically
subtropics
suburb
suburban
suburbanisation (*or*
~iz~)
suburbanise (*or* ~ize)
suburbanite
suburbia
subvention
subventionary
subversion
subversive
subversively
subversiveness
subvert
subverter
subway
subzero
succedaneous
succedaneum
succeed
success
successful
successfully
successfulness
succession
successional
successionally
successionless
successive
successively
successiveness
successor
succinct
succinctly

succinctness
succinic
Succoth (or Sukkoth)
succour (US ~or)
succourer
succourless
succuba (pl ~ae)
succubus (pl ~bi)
succulence
succulent
succulently
succumb
succursal
such
suck
sucker
sucking
suckle
suckler
suckling
sucrose
suction
Sudan
Sudanese
Sudanic
sudden
suddenly
suddenness
sudoriferous
sudorific
suds
sudsy
sue
suede
suet
suety
suffer
sufferable
sufferance
sufferer
suffering
suffice
sufficer
sufficiency
sufficient
sufficiently
suffix
suffixation
suffocate
suffocating

suffocatingly
suffocation
suffocative
suffragan
suffraganship
suffrage
suffragette
suffragism
suffragist
suffuse
suffusion
suffusive
sugar
sugar-coated
sugarcraft
sugared
sugariness
sugaring
sugarless
sugarloaf
sugary
suggest
suggestibility
suggestible
suggestion
suggestive
suggestively
suggestiveness
suicidal
suicidally
suicide
sui generis
suit
suitability
suitable
suitableness
suitably
suitcase
suitcaseful
suite
suited
suiting
suitor
sukiyaki
Sukkoth (or Succoth)
sulcus (pl ~ci)
sulk
sulkily
sulkiness
sulky

sullen
sullenly
sullenness
sully
sulphate (US ~fate)
sulphide (US ~fide)
sulphonamide (US ~fon~)
sulphur (US ~fur)
sulphuric (US ~fur~)
sulphurous (US ~fur~)
sultan
sultana
sultanate
sultanic
sultrily
sultriness
sultry
sum (~mmed, ~mming)
sumac (or ~ach)
Sumatra
summarily
summariness
summarisation (or ~iz~)
summarise (or ~ize)
summary
summation
summer
summersault (or somer~)
summertime
summery
summing-up
summit
summiteer
summitless
summon
summonable
summoner
summons
sumo
sump
sumptuous
sumptuosity
sumptuously
sumptuousness
sun (~nned, ~nning)
sunbaked
sunbathe
sunbather

sunbathing
sunbeam
sunbed
sunbelt
sunbird
sunblock
sunburn (~burned *or* ~burnt)
sunburst
suncream
sundae
Sunday
sundeck
sunder
sundew
sundial
sundown
sundress
sun-dry *preserve*
sundry *various*
sunfish
sunflower
sung
sunglasses
sunhat
sunk
sunken
sun-kissed
sunlamp
sunless
sunlight
sunlit
Sunni (*pl* ~ni, ~nis)
sunnily
sunniness
sunny
sunrise
sunroof
sunscreen
sunset
sunshade
sunshine
sunshiny
sunspot
sunstroke
suntan
suntanned
suntrap
sup (~pped, ~pping)
super

superable
superabound
superabundance
superabundant
superabundantly
superannuable
superannuate
superannuated
superannuation
superb
superbly
superbness
superbug
supercargo
supercede (*or* ~rse~)
supercharge
supercharger
superciliary
supercilious
superciliously
superciliousness
superconduct
superconducting
superconductive
superconductivity
superconductor
supercritical
supercriticality
supererogation
superficial
superficiality
superficially
superficialness
superfine
superfluidity
superfluity
superfluous
superfluously
superfluousness
supergiant
superglue (~gluing *or* ~glueing)
superhero (*pl* ~oes)
superheterodyne
superhighway
superhuman
superhumanly
superimpose
superimposition
superintend

superintendence
superintendency
superintendent
superior
superiority
superiorly
superlative
superlatively
superlativeness
superman (*pl* ~men)
supermarket
supermodel
supernatural
supernaturally
supernova (*pl* ~ae, ~as)
supernumerary
superordinate
superphosphate
superplastic
superpower
superscribe
superscript
supersede (*or* ~rce~)
supersedence (*or* ~rce~)
superseder (*or* ~rce~)
supersonic
supersonically
superstar
superstardom
superstition
superstitious
superstitiously
superstitiousness
superstore
superstring
superstructure
supertanker
supervene
supervention
supervise
supervision
supervisor
supervisory
superwoman (*pl* ~women)
supinate
supinated
supination
supinator
supine

supinely
supineness
supper
supperless
supplant
supplantation
supplanter
supple
supplely
supplement
supplemental
supplementally
supplementarily
supplementary
supplementation
suppleness
suppliant
suppliantly
supplicant
supplicate
supplicating
supplicatingly
supplication
supplicatory
supplier
supply
support
supportability
supportable
supporter
supporting
supportive
supportively
supportiveness
supportless
supposable
supposably
suppose
supposed
supposedly
supposer
supposition
suppositional
suppositionally
suppository
suppress
suppressant
suppressed
suppressible
suppression

suppressive
suppressively
suppressor
suppurate
suppuration
suppurative
supranational
supranationalism
supranationality
suprarenal
supremacist
supremacy
supreme
supremely
supremeness
supremo (pl ~os)
sura (or ~rah)
surcharge
surcharged
surcoat
surd
sure
sure-footed
sure-footedly
sure-footedness
surely
sureness
surety
surf
surface
surfactant
surfboard
surfeit
surfer
surfing
surge
surgeon
surgery
surgical
surgically
Suriname (or ~nam)
surlily
surliness
surly
surmisable
surmise
surmiser
surmising
surmount
surmountable

surmounted
surmounter
surmounting
surname
surpass
surpassable
surpassed
surpassing
surpassingly
surplice
surpliced
surplus
surprise
surprised
surpriser
surprising
surprisingly
surprisingness
surreal
surrealism
surrealist
surrealistic
surrealistically
surreally
surrender
surreptitious
surreptitiously
surreptitiousness
surrogacy
surrogate
surround
surrounded
surrounding
surtax
surtitles
surveillance
surveillant
survey
surveying
surveyor
survivability
survivable
survival
survive
surviving
survivor
susceptibility
susceptible
susceptibleness
susceptibly

susceptive
sushi
suspect
suspend
suspended
suspender
suspense
suspenseful
suspension
suspensive
suspensory
suspicion
suspicious
suspiciously
suspiciousness
suss
sustain
sustainability
sustainable
sustained
sustainedly
sustainer
sustaining
sustainment
sustenance
susurration
susurrus
sutra
suttee (or sati; pl ~tees, ~tis)
suture
suzerain
suzerainty
svelte
Svengali
swab (~bbed, ~bbing)
swaddle
swaddling
swag
swagger
swaggerer
swaggering
swaggeringly
Swahili
swallow
swallowable
swallowtail
swam
swami
swamp

swampily
swampiness
swampy
swan (~nned, ~nning)
swank
swankily
swankiness
swanky
swansong
swap (or swop; ~pped, ~pping)
swappable (or swo~)
swapper (or swo~)
sward
swarf
swarm
swarthily
swarthiness
swarthy
swash
swashbuckler
swashbuckling
swastika
swat (~tted, ~tting ! swot) swipe
swatch
swathe (pl ~thes, ~ths)
swatter (or swo~)
sway
swaying
Swaziland
swear (swore, sworn)
swearer
swearing
sweat
sweatband
sweated
sweater
sweatily
sweatiness
sweating
sweatshirt
sweatshop
sweatsuit
sweaty
Swede from Sweden
swede plant
Sweden
Swedish
sweep (swept)

sweeper
sweeping
sweepingly
sweepstake
sweet
sweetbread
sweetcorn
sweeten
sweetener
sweetening
sweetheart
sweetmeat
sweetness
sweety
swell (swollen)
swelling
swelter
sweltering
swelteringly
swept
sweptback
swerve
swerver
swift
swiftly
swiftness
swig (~gged, ~gging)
swill
swiller
swim (swam, swum, swimming)
swimmable
swimmer
swimming
swimmingly
swimsuit
swimwear
swindle
swindler
swine
swineherd
swing (swung)
swingeing
swingeingly
swinging
swingingly
swing-wing
swinish
swinishly
swinishness

swipe
swirl
swirling
swish
swishy
Swiss
switch
switchable
switchback
switchblade
switchboard
swivel (~lled, ~lling; US ~led, ~ling)
swizzle
swollen
swoon
swoop
swoosh
swop (or swap, ~pped, ~pping)
swoppable (or swa~)
swopper (or swa~)
sword
sword-bearer
swordfish
swordplay
swordsman (pl ~men)
swordsmanship
swordstick
swordtail
swore
sworn
swot (~tted, ~tting ! swat) study
swum
swung
sybarite
sybaritic
sybaritism
sycamore
sycophancy
sycophant
sycophantic
sycophantically
Sydney
syllabary
syllabic
syllabically
syllabicity
syllabification

syllabify
syllable
syllabub (or sill~)
syllabus (pl ~uses, ~bi)
syllogism
syllogistic
syllogistically
sylph
sylvan
symbiont
symbiosis (pl ~oses)
symbiotic
symbiotically
symbol
symbolic
symbolical
symbolically
symbolisation (or ~iz~)
symbolise (or ~ize)
symboliser (or ~iz~)
symbolism
symbolist
symbology
symmetric
symmetrical
symmetrically
symmetry
sympathetic
sympathise (or ~ize)
sympathiser (or ~iz~)
sympathy
symphonic
symphonically
symphony
symposium (pl ~iums, ~ia)
symptom
symptomatic
symptomatically
symptomatology
symptomless
synagogue
synapse
synapsis (pl ~pses)
synaptic
synaptically
synch (or sync)
synchromesh
synchronic
synchronically

synchronicity
synchronisation (or ~iz~)
synchronise (or ~ize)
synchroniser (or ~iz~)
synchronism
synchronous
synchronously
synchrony
synchrotron
syncline
syncopate
syncopated
syncopation
syncope
syncretic
syncretisation (or ~iz~)
syncretise (or ~ize)
syncretism
syncretist
syncretistic
syndicalism
syndicalist
syndicate
syndication
syndicator
syndrome
synecdoche
synergetic
synergic
synergism
synergy
synod
synodic
synodical
synonym
synonymous
synonymously
synopsis (pl ~pses)
synoptic
synoptical
synoptically
synovia
synovial
synovitis
syntactic
syntactical
syntactically
syntax
synthesis (pl ~eses)

synthesise (*or* ~ize)
synthesiser (*or* ~iz~)
synthetic
synthetical
synthetically
syphilis
syphilitic
syphon (*or* siphon)
syringa
syringe
syrinx (*pl* ~xes, ~inges)
syrup (*US* sirup)
syrupy (*US* sirupy)
system
systematic
systematically
systematics
systematisation (*or* ~iz~)
systematise (*or* ~ize)
systematiser (*or* ~iz~)
systematist
systemic
systole
systolic
syzygy

T t

tab (~bbed, ~bbing)
tabard
tabaret
Tabasco (*tr*)
tabbouleh
tabby
tabernacle
tabes
tabescent
tabla
tablature
table
tableau (*pl* ~ux)

tablecloth
table-d'hôte (*pl* tables~)
tableful
tableland
tablespoon
tablespoonful
tablet
tabletop
tableware
tabloid
taboo (*or* ~bu; *n pl*
  ~boos, ~bus; *v* ~boos,
  ~booed, ~booing *or*
  ~bus, ~bued, ~buing)
tabor
tabouret (*US* ~or~)
tabular
tabula rasa
tabulate
tabulated
tabulating
tabulation
tabulator
tacet
tachograph
tachometer
tachycardia
tachygrapher
tachygraphic
tachygraphical
tachygraphy
tachymeter
tachymetric
tachyon
tacit
tacitly
taciturn
taciturnity
taciturnly
tack
tackily
tackiness
tackle
tackling
tacky
taco (*pl* ~os)
tact
tactful
tactfully
tactfulness

tactic
tactical
tactically
tactician
tacticity
tactics
tactile
tactility
tactless
tactlessly
tactlessness
tactual
tad
tadpole
Tadzhikistan (*or* Taji~)
taekwondo
taffeta
tag (~gged, ~gging)
tagging
tagliatelle
Tagus
Tahiti
Tahitian
tahr
Tai (! Thai) *languages*
t'ai chi ch'uan (*or* tai chi
  chuan)
taiga
tail
tailback
tailboard
tailcoat
tailgate
tailing
tailless
tailor
tailorbird
tailored
tailoring
tailor-made
tailpiece
tailpipe
tailplane
tailspin
tailstock
tailwater
tailwheel
tailwind
taint
tainted

taintless
taipan
Taipei
Taiwan
Taiwanese
Tajikistan (or Tadzhi~)
take (took, taken, taking)
takeaway
taken
takeoff (or take-~)
takeover
taker
take-up
taking
talapoin
talc
talcum
tale
tale-bearer
tale-bearing
talent
talented
talentless
Taliban
talisman
talismanic
talk
talkathon
talkative
talkatively
talkativeness
talkback
talkie
talking
talktime
tall
tallboy
taller
tallish
tallith
tallness
tallow
tallowy
tally
Talmud
Talmudic
Talmudical
Talmudism
Talmudist

talon
tamable (or ~meab~)
tamagotchi
tamale
tamari
tamarillo
tamarin
tamarind
tamarisk
tambour
tambourine
tambourinist
tame
tameable (or ~mab~)
tamely
tameness
tamer
Tamil
taming
tamo'shanter
tamp
tamper
tamperer
tampon
tam-tam
tan (~nned, ~nning)
tanager
tandem
tandoori (pl ~is)
tang
Tanganyika
tangelo
tangency
tangent
tangential
tangentially
tangerine
tangibility
tangible
tangibleness
tangibly
tanginess
tangle
tangled
tangly
tango (n pl ~gos; v ~goes, ~goed, ~going)
tangram
tangy

tank
tankard
tanker
tankful
tanner
tannery
tannic
tannin
tannoy (T~, tr)
tansy
tantalisation (or ~iz~)
tantalise (or ~ize)
tantaliser (or ~iz~)
tantalising (or ~iz~)
tantalisingly (or ~iz~)
tantalum
tantamount
tantra (T~)
tantrum
Tanzania
Tanzanian
tanzanite
Tao
Taoiseach
Taoism
Taoist
Taoistic
tap (~pped, ~pping)
tapas
tape
taper
tapestried
tapestry
tapeworm
tapioca
tapir
tapotement
tappet
tapping
taproom
taproot
tapster
taqueria
tar (~rred, ~rring)
taramasalata
tarantella (or ~lle)
tarantula
tardigrade
tardily
tardiness

tardy
tare
targa
target
targum (T~)
tariff
tarmac (v ~acked,
  ~acking)
tarmacadam (T~ tr)
tarn
tarnish
tarnishable
taro
tarot
tarpaulin
tarpon
tarragon
tarry
tarsal
tarsier
tarsus (pl ~si)
tart
tartan
Tartar (or Tatar) people
tartar
tartare
tartaric
Tartarus
tartily
tartiness
tartlet
tartrazine
Tartuffe
tarty
taser
task
taskmaster
taskmistress
Tasmania
tassel (~lled, ~lling; US
  ~led, ~ling)
taste
tasteful
tastefully
tastefulness
tasteless
tastelessly
taster
tastevin
tastily

tastiness
tasting
tasty
Tatar (or Tartar)
tatter
tattered
tatters
tattily
tattiness
tattle
tattler
tattletale
tattoo
tattooer
tattooist
tatty
tau
taught
taunt
taupe
taurine
tauromachian
tauromachic
tauromachy
Taurus
taut
tauten
tautly
tautness
tautological
tautologically
tautologise (or ~ize)
tautologous
tautology
tautomerism
tavern
taverna
tawdrily
tawdriness
tawdry
tawny
tax
taxable
taxation
taxer
taxi (n pl ~is, ~ies; v
  ~iing or ~ying)
taxicab
taxidermal
taxidermically

taxidermist
taxidermy
taximeter
taxing
taxman (pl ~men)
taxonomic
taxonomist
taxonomy
taxpayer
tayberry
Tchaikovsky
te (or ti; pl tes, tis) note
tea
teacake (or tea-~)
teach
teachable
teacher
teach-in
teaching
teacup
teacupful
teahouse
teak
teal
team
teammate
teamster
teamwork
teapot
tear
tearable
tearaway
teardrop
tearer
tearful
tearfully
tearfulness
tearing
tearless
tearoom (or tea-~)
tearstained (or tear-~)
tease
teasel (or teazle, teazel)
teaser
teashop
teasing
teasingly
teaspoon
teaspoonful
teat

tea-table
tea-time
teazel (*or* ~sel, ~zle)
technetium
technical
technicality
technically
technicalness
technician
Technicolor (*tr*)
technique
technobabble
technocracy
technocrat
technocratic
technocratically
technological
technologically
technologist
technology
technophile
technophobe
tectonic
tectonically
tectonics
ted (~dded, ~dding)
tedder
teddy
tedious
tediously
tediousness
tedium
tee (teed)
teem
teeming
teen
teenage
teenager
teensy
teeny
teenybopper
teepee (*or* tepee)
teeter
teeth (*n*)
teethe (*v*)
teething
teetotal
teetotalism
teetotaller (*US* ~aler)
tefillin (*or* teph~)

teflon (T~, *tr*)
Tehran (*or* Teheran)
telaesthesia (*or* ~les~)
telamon (*pl* ~ones)
telebanking
telecast
telecaster
telecommunication
telecommute
telecommuter
telecommuting
teleconference
teleconferencing
teleconverter
telecottage
telecottaging
telefax
telefilm
telegenic
telegram
telegraph
telegrapher
telegraphese
telegraphic
telegraphically
telegraphist
telegraphy
telekinesis
telekinetic
telemarketer
telemarketing
telematics
telemessaging
telemeter
telemetric
telemetry
teleological
teleologically
teleologism
teleologist
teleology
teleoperate
teleoperation
teleoperator
telepath
telepathic
telepathically
telepathise (*or* ~ize)
telepathist
telepathy

telephone
telephoner
telephonic
telephonically
telephonist
telephony
telephoto (*pl* ~os)
telephotographic
telephotography
teleport
teleportation
telepresence
teleprinter
teleprompter (T~, *tr*)
telesales
telescope
telescopic
telescopically
teleselling
teleshopping
teletext
telethon
teletype (T~, *tr*)
televangelist
televisable
televise
televised
televising
television
televisual
televisually
teleworker
teleworking
telex (T~, *tr*)
tell
teller
telling
tellingly
telltale
tellurian
telluric
tellurium
telly
telophase
temazepam
temerarious
temerity
temper
tempera
temperament

temperamental
temperamentally
temperance
temperate
temperately
temperateness
temperature
temperer
tempest
tempestuous
tempestuously
tempestuousness
Templar
template (occ ~plet)
temple
tempo (pl ~pi, ~pos)
temporal
temporality
temporally
temporarily
temporariness
temporary
temporisation (or ~iz~)
temporise (or ~ize)
temporiser (or ~iz~)
tempt
temptability
temptable
temptation
tempted
tempter
tempting
temptingly
temptress
tempura
ten
tenable
tenacious
tenaciously
tenaciousness
tenacity
tenancy
tenant
tenanted
tenantless
tenantry
tench
tend
tendency
tendentious

tendentiously
tendentiousness
tender
tenderer
tenderfoot
tender-hearted
tender-heartedly
tender-heartedness
tenderise (or ~ize)
tenderiser (or ~iz~)
tenderloin
tenderly
tenderness
tendon
tendonitis (or ~din~)
tendril
tenebrous
tenement
Tenerife
tenet
tenfold
Tennessee
tennis
tenor
tenosynovitis
tenotomy
tenpin
tense
tensely
tenseness
tensile
tension
tensional
tensionally
tensioner
tensionless
tent
tentacle
tentacled
tentacular
tentaculate
tentative
tentatively
tentativeness
tenter
tenterhook
tenth
tenthly
tenuity
tenuous

tenuously
tenuousness
tenure
tenured
tepee (or teepee, tipi)
tephillin (or tefi~)
tepid
tepidity
tepidly
tepidness
tequila
terabyte
teratogen
teratogenic
terbium
tercel (or tier~)
tercentenary
tercentennial
terebinth
tergiversate
tergiversation
tergiversator
term
termagent
terminability
terminable
terminableness
terminably
terminal
terminally
terminate
termination
terminator
terminological
terminologically
terminologist
terminology
terminus (pl ~uses, ~ni)
termitarium (pl ~ia)
termite
termly
tern
ternary
terpene
Terpsichore
Terpsichorean
terra
terrace
terraced
terracing

terracotta
terra firma
terrain
terrapin
terrazzo (*pl* ~os)
terrene (! terrine) *of earth*
terrestrial
terrestrially
terrible
terribleness
terribly
terrier
terrific
terrifically
terrifier
terrify
terrifying
terrifyingly
terrine (! terrene) *dish*
territorial
territoriality
territorially
territory
terror
terrorisation (*or* ~iz~)
terrorise (*or* ~ize)
terroriser (*or* ~iz~)
terrorism
terrorist
terry
terse
tersely
terseness
tertiary
tesla
tessellate
tessellated
tessellation
tessera (*pl* ~ae)
tesseral
tessitura
test
testability
testable
Testament *bible*
testament *statement*
testate
testation
testator

testatrix (*pl* ~trices, ~trixes)
testee
tester
testicle
testicular
testifier
testify
testily
testimonial
testimony
testiness
testing
testis (*pl* ~tes)
testosterone
testy
tetanus
tetchily
tetchiness
tetchy
tête-à-tête (*pl* ~tes; *or* tete-a-tete)
tether
tetra
tetracycline
Tetragrammaton
tetrahedral
tetrahedron (*pl* ~rons, ~ra)
tetralogy
tetraplegia
tetraplegic
tetrapod
Teutonic
Texan
Texas
text
textbook
textile
textless
textual
textualism
textualist
textuality
textually
textural
texturally
texture
textured
texturing

texturise (*or* ~ize)
Thai (*pl* Thai, Thais; ! Tai) *people*
Thailand
thalamic
thalamus (*pl* ~mi)
thalassaemia (*or* ~sem~)
thalassic
thalassotherapy
thali (*pl* ~is)
Thalia
thalidomide
thallium
thallus (*pl* ~uses, ~lli)
Thames
than
thanatological
thanatologist
thanatology
thank
thankful
thankfully
thankfulness
thankless
thanklessly
thanklessness
Thanksgiving *US holiday*
thanksgiving *giving thanks*
thatch
thatched
thatcher
thaw
thawing
theatre (*US* ~ter)
theatrical
theatricalisation (*or* ~iz~)
theatricalise (*or* ~ize)
theatricalism
theatricality
theatrically
theft
their (! there) *belonging to them*
theirs
theirselves
theism
theist
theistic

thematic
thematically
thematics
thematise (or ~ize)
theme
themed
themselves
then
thence
thenceforth
thenceforward
theocentric
theocracy
theocrat
theocratic
theocratically
theodicy
theodolite
theologian
theological
theologically
theologist
theology
theophany
theorbo (pl ~os)
theorem
theoretic
theoretical
theoretically
theoretician
theorisation (or ~iz~)
theorise (or ~ize)
theoriser (or ~iz~)
theorist
theory
theosopher
theosophical
theosophically
theosophist
theosophy
therapeutic
therapeutical
therapeutically
therapeutics
therapist
therapy
Theravada
there (! their) *at a place*
thereabouts
thereafter

thereby
therefore
therein
theremin
thereof
thereon
thereto
thereunder
thereupon
therewith
therm
thermal
thermic
thermion
thermionic
thermionics
thermistor
thermocouple
thermodynamic
thermodynamical
thermodynamically
thermodynamicist
thermodynamics
thermoelectric
thermoelectrically
thermoelectricity
thermogenesis
thermograph
thermographic
thermography
thermoluminescence
thermoluminescent
thermolysis
thermometer
thermometric
thermometrical
thermometrically
thermometry
thermonuclear
thermoplastic
thermos (T~, *tr*)
thermosphere
thermostat
thermostatic
thermostatically
thesaurus (pl ~ri, ~uses)
thesis (pl theses)
thespian
theta
theurgy

thiamine (or ~min)
thick
thicken
thickener
thickening
thicket
thickness
thickset
thief (pl thieves)
thieve
thievery
thieving
thigh
thimble
thimbleful
thin (v ~nned, ~nning;
    adj ~nner, ~nnest)
thing
think
thinkable
thinker
thinking
thin-skinned
third
third-rate
thirst
thirstily
thirstiness
thirsty
thirteen
thirteenth
thirtieth
thirty
thistle
thong
Thor
thoracic
thoracotomy
thorax (pl ~aces, ~axes)
thorium
thorn
thornily
thorniness
thornless
thorny
thorough
thoroughbred
thoroughfare
thoroughgoing
thoroughly

thoroughness
though
thought
thoughtful
thoughtfully
thoughtfulness
thoughtless
thoughtlessly
thoughtlessness
thousand
thousandfold
thousandth
thraldom (*or* thrall~)
thrall
thrash
thrasher
thrashing
thread
threadbare
threader
threadworm
thready
threat
threaten
threatening
threateningly
three
three-dimensional
threefold
threepence
threepenny
three-ply
three-quarters
threescore
threesome
threnodial
threnodic
threnodist
threnody
thresh
thresher
threshing
threshold
threw
thrice
thrift
thriftily
thriftiness
thriftless
thriftlessly

thriftlessness
thrifty
thrill
thriller
thrilling
thrillingly
thrips
thrive (throve *or* thrived,
   thriven, thriving)
thriving
throat
throated
throatily
throatiness
throaty
throb (~bbed, ~bbing)
throes
thrombosis (*pl* ~oses)
thrombus
throne
throng
throttle
through
throughout
throughput
throw (threw, thrown)
throwaway
throwback
thrower
throw-in
throwing
thrown
thrum (~mmed,
   ~mming)
thrush
thrust
thruster
thrusting
thud (~dded, ~dding)
thudding
thuddingly
thug
thuggery
thuggish
thuggishly
thuggishness
thulium
thumb
thumbed
thumbless

thumbnail
thumbprint
thumbscrew
thump
thumper
thumping
thunder
thunderbolt
thunderclap
thundercloud
thunderer
thunderflash
thundering
thunderingly
thunderous
thunderously
thunderousness
thunderstorm
thunderstruck
thundery
Thursday
thus
thwack
thwacking
thwart
thyme
thymine
thymus (*pl* ~mi)
thyroid
thyroxine (*or* ~in)
tiara
Tiber
Tibet
Tibetan
tibia (*pl* ~ae, ~as)
tibial
tic
tick
ticker
ticket (~eted, ~eting)
ticketing
ticketless
ticking
tickle
tickled
tickling
ticklish
ticklishly
ticklishness
tidal

tidally
tidbit (*US*; *UK* titbit)
tiddly
tiddlywinks
tide
tideline
tidemark
tidewater
tideway
tidily
tidiness
tidings
tidy
tie
tied
tie-in
tie-pin
tier
tiff
tiger
tight
tighten
tightness
tightrope
tights
tigress
tikka
tilde
tile
tiled
tiler
tiling
till
tiller
tilt
timber *wood*
timbre (*US* ~ber) *tone*
timbrel
time
time-consuming
time-honoured (*US* ~nor~)
timekeeper
timekeeping
time-lapse
timeless
timeliness
timely
timepiece
timer

timescale
timeshare
time-sharing
timetable
timeworm
timid
timidity
timidly
timing
timorous
timorously
timorousness
timpani (*or* tym~)
timpanist (*or* tym~)
tin (~nned, ~nning)
tincture
tinder
tinderbox
tine
tinfoil
tinful
tinge
tingle
tinker
tinkle
tinned
tinnily
tinniness
tinnitus
tinny
tin-opener
tinpot
tinsel
tinselled
tinselly
tint
tintinnabulation
tiny
tip (~pped, ~pping)
tipex (*or* Tipp-Ex, *tr*)
tip-off
tippet
Tipp-Ex (*tr*; *or* tipex)
tipple
tippler
tipsiness
tipster
tipsy
tiptoe
tiptop

tirade
tiramisu
tire (! tyre) *weary*, (*US*) *wheel*
tired
tiredly
tiredness
tireless
tirelessness
tiresome
tiresomely
tiresomeness
tiro (*or* tyro)
Tirolean (*or* Tyr~)
tissue
tit
titan
titanic
titanium
titbit (*UK*; *US* tidbit)
tithe
tithing
Titian
titillate
titillating
titillation
titivate (*or* titt~)
title
titled
titling
titrate
titration
titre (*UK*; *US* ~ter)
titter
tittivate (*or* titi~)
tittle-tattle
titular
titularly
T-junction
toad
toad-in-the-hole
toadstool
toady
toadyish
toadyism
toast
toasted
toaster
toastie
toastmaster

toastmistress
toasty
tobacco
tobacconist
toboggan
tobogganer
tobogganing
tobogganist
toccata
tocopherol
tocsin
today
toddle
toddler
toddy
to-do
toe
toecap
toehold
toenail
toff
toffee
tofu
tog (~gged, ~gging)
toga (~gaed, ~ga'd)
together
togetherness
toggle
toil
toilet (! toilette) *lavatory*
toiletry
toilette (! toilet)
  cleansing
toilsome
tokamak
token
tokenism
tolbooth (*or* toll~)
told
tolerability
tolerable
tolerableness
tolerably
tolerance
tolerant
tolerantly
tolerate
tolerating
toleration
toll

tollbooth (*or* tolb~)
tollbridge
toll-free
tollgate
toluene
tomahawk
tomato (*pl* ~oes)
tomb
tombola
tomboy
tomboyish
tomboyishness
tombstone
tomcat
tome
tomfool
tomfoolery
tommygun
tomography
tomorrow
tom-tom
ton
tonality
tone
tone-deaf
tone-deafness
toneless
tonelessly
toner
Tonga
Tongan
tongs
tongue (~gued, ~guing)
tonic
tonight
tonnage
tonne
tonsil
tonsillectomy
tonsillitis
tonsorial
tonsure
took
tool
toolbox
toolkit
toolmaker
toot
tooth (*pl* teeth)
toothache

toothbrush
toothily
toothiness
toothless
toothpaste
toothpick
toothpowder
toothsome
toothy
tootle
top
topaz
top-heavy
topi (*or* topee)
topiarian
topiarist
topiary
topic
topical
topicality
topically
topknot
topless
toplessness
topmast
topmost
topographer
topographic
topographical
topographically
topography
topological
topologically
topologist
topology
toponymic
toponymy
topper
topping
topple
topsail
topside
topsoil
topspin
topsy-turvily
topsy-turviness
topsy-turvy
tor
Torah
torc (*or* torque)

torch
torchbearer
torchlight
tore
toreador
torment
tormentedly
tormentil
tormenting
tormentingly
tormentor
torn
tornadic
tornado (*pl* ~oes)
Toronto
torpedo (*pl* ~os, ~oes)
torpefy
torpid
torpidity
torpidly
torpor
torque (*occ* torc)
torr
torrent
torrential
torrentially
torrid
torridity
torridly
torsion
torsional
torsionally
torsionless
torso (*pl* ~os)
tort *law*
torte *cake*
tortellini
torticollis
tortilla
tortoise
tortoiseshell
tortuous
tortuousity
tortuously
tortuousness
torture
torturer
torturous
torturously
torus (*pl* ~ri)

Tory
Toryism
tosa
tosh
toss
tot (~tted, ~tting)
total (~lled, ~lling; *US* ~led, ~ling)
totalisation (*or* ~iz~)
Totalisator (*or* ~iz~)
totalise (*or* ~ize)
totaliser (*or* ~iz~)
totalitarian
totalitarianism
totality
totally
totem
totemic
totemism
totemist
totter
totterer
tottering
totteringly
tottery
toucan
toucanet
touch
touchdown
touché
touched
touchily
touchiness
touching
touchingly
touchingness
touchline
touchpaper
touchstone
touch-tone
touch-type
touch-typing
touch-typist
touch-up
touchwood
touchy
touchy-feely
tough
toughen
toughener

toughening
toughish
toughness
toupee (*or* ~pet)
tour
tour de force
tourer
touring
tourism
tourist
touristic
touristically
touristy
tourmaline
tournament
tournedos
tourniquet
tousle
tousled
tout
touted
touter
tow
towable
towage
toward
towards
towel
towelling (*US* ~eling)
tower
towered
towering
towing
towline
town
townscape
townsfolk
township
townsman (*pl* ~men)
townspeople
townswoman (*pl* ~women)
towpath
toxaemia (*US* ~xem~)
toxic
toxically
toxicant
toxicity
toxicological
toxicologically

toxicologist
toxicology
toxigenic
toxigenicity
toxin
toxocara
toxocariasis
toxophilite
toxophily
toxoplasmosis
toy
toyboy
toytown
trace
traceability
traceable
traceably
traceless
tracer
traceried
tracery
trachea (*pl* ~ae, ~as)
tracheal
tracheate
tracheated
tracheitis
tracheostomy
tracheotomy
trachoma
trachomatous
tracing
track
trackball
tracker
trackerball
tracking
trackless
tracklist
tracksuit
trackway
trackwork
tract
tractability
tractable
tractably
tractate
traction
tractive
tractor
tradable (*or* ~deab~)

trade
tradeable (*or* ~dab~)
trademark
trademarked
trader
tradescantia
tradesman (*pl* ~men)
tradespeople
tradeswoman (*pl*
  ~women)
trading
tradition
traditional
traditionalism
traditionalist
traditionalistic
traditionality
traditionally
traditionary
traditionist
traditionless
traduce
traducement
traducer
traffic
trafficker
trafficking
tragacanth
tragedian
tragedienne
tragedy
tragic
tragical
tragically
tragicomedy
tragicomic
tragicomical
tragicomically
trail
trailblazer
trailblazing
trailer
train
trainability
trainable
trained
trainee
traineeship
trainer
training

trainload
trainsick
trainspotter
trainspotting
traipse (*occ* trapse)
trait
traitor
traitorous
traitorously
trajectory
tram
tramcar
tramlines
trammel (~lled, ~lling;
  US ~led, ~ling)
tramontane
tramp
trample
trampled
trampler
trampoline
trampolining
trampolinist
tramway
trance
tranche
tranquil
tranquilise (*or* ~ize,
  ~ll~)
tranquiliser (*or* ~iz~,
  ~ll~)
tranquilising (*or* ~iz~,
  ~ll~)
tranquillity (*or* ~ility)
tranquilly
tranquilness
transact
transactinide
transaction
transactional
transactionally
transactor
transalpine
transatlantic
Transcaucasia
transceiver
transcend
transcendence
transcendency
transcendent

transcendental
transcendentalise (*or* ~ize)
transcendentalism
transcendentalist
transcendentally
transcendently
transcode
transcontinental
transcontinentally
transcribe
transcriber
transcribing
transcript
transcription
transcriptional
transcriptionally
transcriptionist
transcriptive
transcutaneous
transdermal
transduce
transducer
transduction
transect
transection
transept
transeptal
transfer
transferability
transferable
transferee
transference
transferor
transferral
transfiguration
transfigure
transfigured
transfigurement
transfiguring
transfix
transfixed
transfixion
transform
transformability
transformable
transformation
transformational
transformative
transformed

transformer
transforming
transfuse
transfuser
transfusing
transfusion
transgenic
transgenics
transglobal
transgress
transgression
transgressional
transgressive
transgressor
tranship (*or* ~nssh~)
transhipment
transhipper
transhipping
transhumance
transience
transient
transilluminate
transillumination
transistor
transistorisation (*or* ~iz~)
transistorise (*or* ~ize)
transistorised (*or* ~ized)
transit (~ited, ~iting)
transition
transitional
transitionally
transitionary
transitive
transitively
transitorily
transitoriness
transitory
translatability
translatable
translate
translation
translational
translationally
translator
transliterate
transliteration
transliterator
translocate
translucence

translucency
translucent
translucently
transmigrate
transmigration
transmigrator
transmigratory
transmissibility
transmissible
transmission
transmissional
transmissive
transmissivity
transmit (~tted, ~tting)
transmittable
transmittal
transmitter
transmogrification
transmogrified
transmogrify
transmutability
transmutable
transmutably
transmutation
transmutational
transmutationist
transmutative
transmute
transmuter
transnational
transnationalism
transnationalist
transnationally
transoceanic
transom
transpacific
transparence
transparency
transparent
transparently
transparentness
transpirable
transpiration
transpire
transpiring
transplant
transplantable
transplantation
transplanter
transplanting

transponder
transport
transportability
transportable
transportation
transported
transporter
transposable
transposal
transpose
transposer
transposing
transposition
transpositional
transputer
transsexual (*or* ~nse~)
transsexualism (*or* ~nse~)
transsexuality (*or* ~nse~)
transubstantiate
transubstantiated
transubstantiation
transuranic
Transvaal
transversal
transversality
transversally
transverse
transversely
transvestist
transvestite
transvestitism
Transylvania
trap (~pped, ~pping)
trapdoor
trapeze
trapezium
trapeziums
trapezoid
trapezoidal
trapper
trappings
Trappist
trapse (*usu* traipse)
trash
trashed
trashiness
trashy
trattoria

trauma (*pl* ~as, ~mata)
traumatic
traumatically
traumatisation (*or* ~iz~)
traumatise (*or* ~ize)
traumatism
travail
travel (~lled, ~lling; *US* ~led, ~ling)
travelator (*or* ~vol~)
travelled
traveller (*US* ~eler)
travelling (*US* ~eling)
travelogue (*US* ~log)
traversable
traversal
traverse
traversed
traverser
traversing
travesty
travolator (*or* ~vel~)
trawl
trawler
tray
trayful
treacherous
treacherously
treacherousness
treachery
treacle
treacly
tread (trod, trodden)
treadle
treadmill
treason
treasonable
treasonableness
treasonably
treasonous
treasure
treasured
treasurer
treasurership
treasure-trove
treasury
treat
treatable
treater
treatise

treatment
treaty
treble
trebly
trebuchet
tree
treeless
treelessness
treeline
tree-lined
treetop
treetops
trefoil
trek (~kked, ~kking)
trekker
Trekkie
trellis (~ised, ~ising)
trellised
trellising
trelliswork
trematode
trembler
trembling
tremblingly
trembly
tremendous
tremendously
tremendousness
tremolando (*pl* ~os, ~di)
tremolo (*pl* ~os)
tremor
tremulant
tremulous
tremulously
tremulousness
trench
trenchancy
trenchant
trenchantly
trencher
trencherman (*pl* ~men)
trend
trendily
trendiness
trendsetter
trendsetting
trendy
trepan
trepanation

trepidation
trepidatory
trespass
trespasser
tress
tressed
tressy
trestle
trestletree
trestlework
trews (*UK*)
triad
triadic
trial (~lled, ~lling; *US* ~led, ~ling)
triallist (*US* ~alist)
triangle
triangular
triangularity
triangularly
triangulate
triangulation
Triassic
triathlete
triathlon
triaxial
tribal
tribalism
tribalist
tribalistic
tribally
tribe
tribesman (*pl* ~men)
tribespeople
tribeswoman (*pl* ~women)
tribologist
tribology
triboluminescence
triboluminescent
tribometer
tribulation
tribunal
tribune
tributary
tribute
trice
tricentenary
triceps
triceratops

trichiasis
trichinosis
trichological
trichologist
trichology
trichomoniasis
trichosis
trichotomous
trichotomously
trichotomy
trichromatic
trichromatism
trick
trickery
trickily
trickiness
trickle
trickling
tricksiness
trickster
tricksy
tricky
tricolour (*US* ~or)
tricoloured (*US* ~or~)
tricorne (*or* ~rn)
tricuspid
tricycle
trident
tridental
tridentate
Tridentine
tried
triennial
triennially
triennium (*pl* ~ia, ~iums)
trier
trifle
trifler
trifling
trifocal
trifoliate
trifurcate
trifurcation
trigeminal
trigger
triggered
triggerfish
trigger-happy
triglyceride

trigon
trigonal
trigonally
trigonometric
trigonometrical
trigonometry
trigram
trigraph
trihedral
trihedron (*pl* ~rons, ~ra)
trike
trilateral
trilateralism
trilateralist
trilaterally
trilby
trilinear
trilingual
trilingualism
trill
trilling
trillion
trillionth
trillium
trilobite
trilobitic
trilogy
trim (*adj* ~mmer, ~mmest; *v* ~mmed, ~mming)
trimaran
trimester
trimestral
trimestrial
trimmer
trimming
trimness
trimonthly
trimurti (T~)
trine
Trinidad
Trinidadian
Trinitarian
trinitrotoluene
Trinity *Christian*
trinity *group of three*
trinket
trinketry
trinomial

trio (*pl* ~os)
triode
trip (~pped, ~pping)
tripartite
tripartitely
tripartition
tripe
triphthong
triphthongal
triplane
triple
triplet
triplicate
triplication
triplicity
triply
tripod
tripodal
Tripoli
tripper
tripping
triptych
tripwire
trireme
trisect
trisyllabic
trisyllable
trite
tritely
triteness
triticum
tritium
Triton
triumph
triumphal
triumphalism
triumphalist
triumphalistic
triumphant
triumphantly
triumviral
triumvirate
triune
trivet
trivia
trivial
trivialisation (*or* ~iz~)
trivialise (*or* ~ize)
triviality
trivially

trivialness
trochaic
trochee
trod
trodden
troglodyte
troglodytic
troglodytical
troglodytism
trogon
troika
troilism
Trojan
troll
trolley (*pl* ~eys)
trollop
trombone
trombonist
troop
trooper
troopship
trope
trophic
trophy
tropic (T~)
tropical
tropics (T~)
tropism
troposphere
trot (~tted, ~tting)
troth
Trotskyism
Trotskyist
Trotskyite
trotter
trotting
troubadour
trouble
troubled
troublemaker
troublemaking
troubleshoot
troubleshooter
troubleshooting
troublesome
troublesomely
troublesomeness
trough
trounce
trouncer

troupe
trouper
trousered
trousers
trout
trove
trowel
Troy *Homer*
troy *weight*
truancy
truant
truce
truck
trucker
trucking
truckle
truculence
truculent
truculently
trudge
trudger
true (truer, truest)
truffle
truism
truistic
truly
trump
trumped-up
trumpery
trumpet (~eted, ~eting)
trumpeted
trumpeter
trumpetfish
trumpeting
truncate
truncated
truncating
truncation
truncheon
trundle
trunk
trunkful
trunkless
trunks
truss
trussed
trusser
trust
trusted
trustee

trusteeship
trustful
trustfully
trustfulness
trustily
trustiness
trusting
trustingly
trustingness
trustworthily
trustworthiness
trustworthy
trusty
truth
truthful
truthfully
truthfulness
try (tries, tried, trying)
tryst
tsar (*UK, occ* tzar, *also* czar; T~, C~)
tsarina (*or* cza~, tza~; T~, C~)
tsarism (*or* cza~, tza~)
tsarist (*or* cza~, tza~)
tsetse
T-shirt (*or* tee-~)
tsunami (*pl* ~mi, ~mis)
Tuareg
tub
tuba
tubal
tubbiness
tubby
tube
tubed
tubeless
tubelike
tuber
tubercle
tubercular
tuberculation
tuberculin
tuberculoid
tuberculosis
tuberculous
tuberose
tuberous
tubful

tubiform
tubing
tubular
tubule
tuck
tucked
tucker
tucking
Tudor
Tuesday
tuff (! tough) *rock*
tuffet
tuft
tufted
tufting
tufty
tug (~gged, ~gging)
tug-of-war
tuile
tuition
tuitional
tuitionary
tulip
tulle
tumble
tumbled
tumbledown
tumble-drier (*or* ~dryer)
tumble-dry
tumbler
tumblerful
tumbleweed
tumbling
tumefacient
tumefaction
tumefy
tumescence
tumescent
tumescently
tumid
tumidity
tumidly
tumidness
tummy
tumorous
tumour (*US* ~or)
tumult
tumultuous
tumultuously
tumultuousness

tumulus (*pl* ~li)
tun
tuna
tunable (*or* ~nea~)
tundra
tune
tuneable (*or* ~na~)
tuned
tuneful
tunefully
tunefulness
tuneless
tunelessly
tunelessness
tuner
tunesmith
tungsten
tunic
tuning
Tunisia
Tunisian
tunnel (~lled, ~lling; *US* ~led, ~ling)
tunneller (*US* ~eler)
tupelo (*pl* ~os)
turban
turbaned (*or* ~nned)
turbid
turbidity
turbidly
turbidness
turbinate
turbine
turbo (*pl* ~os)
turboboost
turbocharge
turbocharged
turbocharger
turbofan
turbojet
turboprop
turbot
turbulence
turbulent
turbulently
turd
tureen
turf (*pl* turfs, turves)
turfy
turgescence

turgescent
turgid
turgidity
turgidly
Turk
Turkey *country*
turkey *bird*
Turkish
Turkmenistan
Turkoman (*or* Turco~)
turmeric
turmoil
turn
turnabout
turnaround
turncoat
turner
turning
turnip
turnipy
turn-off
turn-on
turn-out
turnover
turnpike
turnstile
turnstone
turntable
turpentine
turpitude
turquoise
turret
turreted
turtle
turtledove
turtleneck
Tuscany
tusk
tusked
tusker
tuskless
tusser (*or* ~ssore)
tussive *relating to coughing*
tussle
tussock
tussocked
tussocky
tussore (*or* ~sser)
tut (~tted, ~tting)

Tutankhamen (*or* ~mun)
tutelage
tutelary
tutor
tutorage
tutorial
tutorially
tutoring
tutti-frutti
tut-tut
tutu
Tuvalu
tu-whit tu-whoo
tuxedo (*US; pl* ~os, ~oes)
twaddle
twaddler
twain
twang
twanging
twangingly
twangy
tweak
twee (*UK*)
tweed
tweedily
tweediness
tweedy
tweeness
tweet
tweeter
tweezers
twelfth
twelfthly
twelve
twelvefold
twentieth
twenty
twentyfold
twerp (*or* twirp)
twice
twiddle
twiddler
twiddly
twig
twigged
twiggy
twilight
twilit (*or* twilighted)

twin (~nned, ~nning)
twine
twiner
twinge
twingeing (*or* ~ging)
twinkle
twinkle-toed
twinkletoes
twinkling
twinkly
twinned
twinning
twinset
twinspot
twiny
twirl
twirly
twirp (*or* twerp)
twist
twistable
twisted
twister
twisting
twisty
twit (~tted, ~tting)
twitch
twitcher
twitchily
twitchiness
twitching
twitchy
twitter
twitterer
twittering
twitteringly
twittery
twizzle
two
two-dimensional
two-edged
twofold
two-handed
two-handedly
twoness
twopence
twopenny (*occ* tuppenny)
two-piece
two-ply
two-seater

two-sided
twosome
two-star
two-step
two-stroke
two-time
two-timing
two-tone
two-way
two-wheeler
tycoon
tying
tyke (*or* tike)
tympani (*or* tim~)
tympanist (*or* tim~)
tympanum (*pl* ~na)
type
typecast
typeface
typescript
typesetter
typewriter
typewriting
typewritten
typhoid
typhoidal
typhonic
typhoon
typhus
typical
typicality
typically
typification
typifier
typify
typing
typist
typo (*pl* ~os)
typographer
typographic
typographical
typographically
typography
typological
typologist
typology
tyrannic
tyrannical
tyrannically
tyrannicidal

tyrannicide
tyrannise (*or* ~ize)
tyrannosaur
tyrannosaurus
tyrannous
tyrannously
tyranny
tyrant
tyre (*UK*, ! tire; *US* tire)
  wheel
tyro (*or* tiro)
Tyrolean (*or* Tir~)
tyrrannise (*US* ~ize)
tzar (*UK*, *usu* tsar, *also*
  czar; T~, C~)

ubiquitous
ubiquitously
ubiquitousness
ubiquity
U-boat
udder
Uffizi
UFO (*pl* UFOs; *or* ufo)
ufological
ufologist
ufology
Uganda
Ugandan
ugh
ugli (! ugly) *fruit*
uglification
uglify
ugliness
ugly
uillean
ukiyo-e
Ukraine
Ukrainian
ukulele

ulcer
ulcerate
ulceration
ulcerative
ulcered
ulcerous
ullage
ulna (*pl* ~ae, ~as)
Ulster
ulterior
ultimate
ultimately
ultimateness
ultimatum (*pl* ~ums,
  ~ta)
ultra
ultrahigh
ultralight
ultramarine
ultramicroscope
ultramicroscopic
ultramontane
ultramundane
ultrasaurus
ultrasonic
ultrasonically
ultrasonics
ultrasound
ultraviolet
ululant
ululate
ululation
Ulysses
umbellifer
umbelliferous
umber
umbilical
umbilically
umbilicus (*pl* ~ci,
  ~uses)
umbo
umbra (*pl* ~ae)
umbrage
umbrageous
umbrella
umbriferous
umlaut
umpirage
umpire
umpireship

umpteen
umpteenth
unabashed
unabashedly
unabated
unabatedly
unable
unabridged
unabsorbed
unacceptability
unacceptable
unacceptably
unaccompanied
unaccomplished
unaccountability
unaccountable
unaccountably
unaccounted
unaccustomed
unaccustomedly
unaccustomedness
unacknowledged
unacquainted
unaddressed
unadjusted
unadorned
unadulterated
unadventurous
unadventurously
unadvertised
unadvisable
unadvisableness
unadvisably
unaesthetic (*or* ~nes~)
unaffected
unaffectedly
unaffectedness
unaffectionate
unaffiliated
unaffordable
unafraid
unaggressive
unaided
unalike
unalleviated
unalloyed
unalterable
unalterableness
unalterably
unaltered

unambiguity
unambiguous
unambiguously
unambitious
unambitiously
unambitiousness
unambivalent
unambivalently
unamiable
unamused
unanimity
unanimous
unanimously
unannounced
unanswerable
unanswerably
unanswered
unanticipated
unapologetic
unappealing
unappealingly
unappetising (*US* ~iz~)
unappetisingly (*US*
 ~iz~)
unappreciated
unappreciative
unapproachability
unapproachable
unapproachably
unapt
unarguable
unarguably
unarmed
unarticulated
unashamed
unashamedly
unashamedness
unasked
unassailability
unassailable
unassailably
unassigned
unassisted
unassociated
unassuageable
unassuaged
unassuming
unassumingly
unassumingness
unattached

unattainable
unattainableness
unattainably
unattempted
unattended
unattractive
unattractively
unauthenticated
unauthorised (*US* ~ized)
unavailability
unavailable
unavailableness
unavoidability
unavoidable
unavoidably
unavowed
unaware
unawareness
unawares
unbalance
unbalanced
unbar (~rred, ~rring)
unbearable
unbearably
unbeatable
unbeatably
unbeaten
unbecoming
unbelief
unbelievability
unbelievable
unbelievably
unbeliever
unbelieving
unbelievingly
unbend (unbent)
unbendable
unbendingly
unbendingness
unbiased (*or* ~assed)
unbiasedly
unbiasedness
unbind
unblinking
unblinkingly
unblock
unblushing
unblushingly
unbolt
unborn

unbosom
unbound
unbounded
unboundedly
unboundedness
unbowed
unbreachable
unbreakable
unbridled
unbroken
unbrokenly
unbrokenness
unbuckle
unburden
unbutton
uncaged
uncalled
uncannily
uncanny
uncap (~pped, ~pping)
uncaring
uncaringly
unceasing
unceasingly
unceremonious
unceremoniously
unceremoniousness
uncertain
uncertainly
uncertainty
uncertified
unchain
unchallenged
unchangeability
unchangeable
unchangeableness
unchangeably
unchanged
unchanging
uncharacteristic
uncharacteristically
uncharted
unchecked
unchivalrous
unchivalrously
unchivalrousness
unchristian
uncial
uncircumcised
uncircumcision

uncivil
uncivilised (*US* ~ized)
uncivility
uncivilly
unclasp
unclassifiable
unclassified
uncle (U~ *for the title*)
unclean
uncleanliness
uncleanly
uncleanness
unclear
unclearly
unclearness
unclench
unclimbable
unclog
unclothe
uncluttered
uncoil
uncombed
uncomely
uncomfortable
uncomfortableness
uncomfortably
uncomfy
uncommitted
uncommon
uncommonly
uncommonness
uncommunicative
uncommunicativeness
uncomplaining
uncomplainingly
uncomplicated
uncomplicatedly
uncomplimentary
uncomprehending
uncomprehendingly
uncompromising
uncompromisingly
uncompromisingness
unconcealed
unconcern
unconcerned
unconcernedly
unconditional
unconditionality
unconditioned

unconditionally
unconfessed
unconfirmed
unconformability
unconformable
unconformably
uncongenial
unconnected
unconnectedly
unconnectedness
unconquerable
unconquerably
unconscionable
unconscionably
unconscious
unconsciously
unconsciousness
unconsecrated
unconstitutional
unconstitutionality
unconstitutionally
uncontaminated
uncontrollable
uncontrollably
unconventional
unconventionality
unconventionally
unconverted
unconvinced
unconvincing
unconvincingly
uncooked
uncool
uncooperative
uncooperatively
uncoordinated
uncork
uncorroborated
uncounted
uncouple
uncouth
uncouthly
uncouthness
uncover
uncovered
uncreate
uncreated
uncredited
uncritical
uncritically

uncross
uncrossable
uncrossed
uncrowned
unction
unctuosity
unctuous
unctuously
unctuousness
uncultured
uncured
uncurl
uncut
undamaged
undated
undaunted
undauntedly
undauntedness
undead
undeceivable
undeceive
undeceived
undeceiver
undecidability
undecideable
undecided
undecidedly
undecipherable
undecipherableness
undecorated
undefeated
undefended
undefiled
undefinable
undefinably
undefined
undelivered
undemanding
undemocratic
undemocratically
undemonstrative
undemonstratively
undemonstrativeness
undeniable
undeniableness
undeniably
undented
undependable
under
underachieve

underachievement
underachiever
underact
underactive
under-age
underarm
underbelly
underbid
underbite
underbody
undercapitalisation (*or* ~iz~)
undercapitalise (*or* ~ize)
undercarriage
undercharge
underclothes
underclothing
undercoat
undercook
undercooked
undercover
undercroft
undercurrent
undercut (~tting)
underdeveloped
underdevelopment
underdog
underdone
underdressed
underemphasis (*pl* ~ases)
underemphasise (*or* ~ize)
underemphasised (*or* ~ized)
underemployed
underemployment
underestimate
underestimated
underestimation
underexpose
underexposure
underfed
underfelt
underfloor
underfoot
underfund
underfunded
underfunding
undergarment

undergird
undergo (~goes, ~went, ~gone, ~going)
undergraduate
Underground *tube trains*
underground *beneath the ground*
undergrowth
underhand
underhanded
underhandedly
underhandedness
underhang
underhung
underinsured
underinvest
underinvestment
underlay (underlaid)
underlie (underlay, underlain, underlying)
underline
underling
underlying
underman (~nned, ~nning)
undermine
underneath
undernourished
undernourishment
underpaid
underpants
underpart
underpass
underpay (underpaid)
underperform
underpin (~nned, ~nning)
underplay
underpopulated
underprepared
underpriced
underprivileged
underquote
underrate
underrated
under-rehearsed
underrepresented
underripe
underscore
undersea

underseal
undersecretary (*or* under-~)
undersell (undersold)
undershirt
undershoot (undershot)
underside
undersigned
underslung
underspend
understaff
understaffed
understaffing
understand
understandability
understandable
understandably
understanding
understandingly
understate
understated
understatement
understood
understudy
undersubscribed
undertake (undertook, undertaken, undertaking)
undertaker
undertaking
undertone
undertow
underuse
underutilise (*or* ~ize)
undervaluation
undervalue
underwater
underwear
underweight
underwhelm
underworld
underwrite (underwrote, underwriting)
underwriter
undeserve
undeserved
undeservedly
undeserving
undeservingly
undesirability

undesirable
undesirableness
undesirably
undesired
undetectability
undetectable
undetectably
undetected
undetermined
undeterred
undeveloped
undiagnosed
undid
undigested
undignified
undiluted
undiminished
undisciplined
undisclosed
undiscovered
undisputed
undisturbed
undivided
undo (undoes, undid, undone, undoing)
undock
undoer
undoing
undomesticated
undone
undramatic
undreamed (*or* undreamt)
undress
undressed
undue
undulant
undulate
undulating
undulation
undulatory
undying
undyingly
unearned
unearth
unearthliness
unearthly
unease
uneasily
uneasiness

uneasy
uneaten
uneconomic
uneconomical
uneconomically
unedifying
unedifyingly
unedited
uneducable
uneducated
unelected
unembarrassed
unemotional
unemotionally
unemphatic
unemphatically
unemployability
unemployable
unemployed
unemployment
unencumbered
unending
unendurable
unendurably
unenforceability
unenforceable
unenjoyable
unenlightened
unenlightening
unenlightenment
unenterprising
unenthusiastic
unenthusiastically
unenviable
unenviably
unequal
unequalled (*US* ~aled)
unequally
unequipped
unequivocal
unequivocally
unequivocalness
unerring
unerringly
unerringness
unescapable
UNESCO
unessential
unethical
uneven

unevenly
unevenness
uneventful
uneventfully
uneventfulness
unexceptionable
unexceptionably
unexceptional
unexceptionally
unexpected
unexpectedly
unexpectedness
unexplainable
unexplainably
unexplained
unexploded
unexploited
unexplored
unexpressed
unexpurgated
unfaceable
unfading
unfadingly
unfailing
unfailingly
unfair
unfairly
unfairness
unfaithful
unfaithfully
unfaithfulness
unfaltering
unfamiliar
unfamiliarity
unfamiliarly
unfashionable
unfashionableness
unfashionably
unfasten
unfastened
unfathomable
unfathomably
unfathomed
unfavourable (*US* ~or~)
unfavourableness (*US*
~or~)
unfavourably (*US* ~or~)
unfazable (*or* ~zeab~)
unfazed
unfeasibility

unfeasible
unfeasibly
unfeeling
unfeelingness
unfettered
unfiltered
unfinished
unfit
unfitness
unfitting
unflagging
unflappability
unflappable
unflappably
unflattering
unfledged
unflinching
unfold
unfolded
unforced
unforgettable
unforgettably
unforgivable
unforgivably
unforgiven
unforgiveness
unforgiving
unforgivingly
unforseeable
unforseen
unforthcoming
unfortold
unfortunate
unfortunately
unfounded
unfoundedly
unfoundedness
unfreeze (unfroze,
unfrozen, unfreezing)
unfrequented
unfriendliness
unfriendly
unfrock
unfruitful
unfruitfulness
unfulfillable
unfulfilled
unfulfilling
unfunnily
unfunniness

unfunny
unfurl
unfurnished
unfussy
ungainliness
ungainly
unget-at-able (*or*
ungetatable)
ungodliness
ungodly
ungovernability
ungovernable
ungovernably
ungoverned
ungraceful
ungracefully
ungracefulness
ungracious
ungraciously
ungraciousness
ungrateful
ungratefully
ungratefulness
ungrounded
ungual
unguarded
unguardedly
unguardedness
unguent
unguessable
ungulate
unhallowed
unhampered
unhand
unhandsome
unhandy
unhappily
unhappiness
unhappy
unharmed
unharmonious
unhealthily
unhealthiness
unhealthy
unheard
unheeded
unheeding
unhelpful
unheralded
unheroic

unheroically
unhesitating
unhesitatingly
unhindered
unhinge
unhinged
unhistoric
unhistorical
unhistorically
unholiness
unholy
unhook
unhorse
unhoused
unhurried
unhurriedly
unhurt
unhygienic
unhygienically
unicameral
UNICEF
unicellular
unicolour (*US* ~or)
unicoloured (*US*
~or~)
unicorn
unicuspid
unicycle
unicyclist
unidentifiable
unidentifiably
unidentified
unidimensional
unidiomatic
unidirectional
unidirectionality
unidirectionally
unifiable
unification
unified
unifier
uniform
uniformed
uniformitarian
uniformity
uniformly
unify
unilateral
unilateralism
unilateralist

unimaginable
unimaginably
unimaginative
unimaginatively
unimaginativeness
unimodal
unimpaired
unimpeachable
unimpeachably
unimportance
unimportant
unimposing
unimpressed
unimpressionable
unimpressive
unimpressively
unimpressiveness
unimproved
uninfected
uninflected
uninfluenced
uninfluential
uninformative
uninformed
uninhabitable
uninhabited
uninhibited
uninitiated
uninjured
uninspired
uninspiring
uninspiringly
uninsulated
uninsurable
uninsured
unintelligence
unintelligent
unintelligently
unintelligibility
unintelligible
unintelligibly
unintentional
unintentionally
uninterested
uninterestedly
uninterestedness
uninteresting
uninterestingly
uninterrupted
uninventive

uninventively
uninvited
uninviting
uninvitingly
uninvolved
union
unionisation (*or* ~iz~)
unionise (*or* ~ize)
unionised (*or* ~ized)
unionism
unionist
unionistic
uniparous
uniped
unipod
unipolar
unique
uniquely
uniqueness
unisex
unisexual
unisexually
unison
unissued
unit
unitard
unitarian (U~)
unitarianism (U~)
unitary
unite
united
unitedly
unitedness
uniter
unitive
unity
universal
universalise (*or* ~ize)
universalism
universalist
universalistic
universality
universe
university
UNIX (*or* Unix)
unjoin
unjoined
unjointed
unjust
unjustifiable

unjustifiably
unjustified
unjustly
unjustness
unkempt
unkemptly
unkemptness
unkept
unkind
unkindly
unkindness
unknit (~tted, ~tting)
unknot (~tted, ~tting)
unknowability
unknowable
unknowing
unknowingly
unknowingness
unknown
unlace
unladen
unladylike
unlamented
unlatch
unlawful
unlawfully
unleaded
unlearn
unlearned (or unlearnt)
unleash
unleavened
unless
unlettered
unlicensed (*UK; US*
~nced)
unlike
unlikeable (or ~kab~)
unlikelihood
unlikeliness
unlikely
unlikeness
unlimited
unlined
unlisted
unlit
unlived-in
unload
unloader
unlock
unlockable

unlocked
unlooked-for
unloose
unloosen
unlovable (or ~vea~)
unloved
unloveliness
unlovely
unloving
unlovingly
unluckily
unluckiness
unlucky
unmade
unmaidenly
unmake
unman (~nned,
~nning)
unmanageable
unmanageably
unmanaged
unmanliness
unmanly
unmanned
unmannerly
unmapped
unmarked
unmarried
unmask
unmasked
unmasker
unmatchable
unmatched
unmeasurable
unmeasured
unmediated
unmentionable
unmentionableness
unmentionably
unmerciful
unmercifully
unmercifulness
unmet
unmindful
unmindfully
unmindfulness
unmissable
unmistakability
unmistakable (or
~kea~)

unmistakably (or
~kea~)
unmitigated
unmitigatedly
unmixed
unmodified
unmotivated
unmovable (or ~vea~)
unmoving
unmown
unmusical
unmuzzle
unmuzzled
unnamable (or ~mea~)
unnatural
unnaturally
unnaturalness
unnecessarily
unnecessariness
unnecessary
unnerve
unnerving
unnervingly
unnilennium
unnilhexium
unnilloctium
unnilpentium
unnilquadium
unnilseptium
unnoticeable
unnoticeably
unnoticed
unnumbered
unobjectionable
unobjectionably
unobliging
unobscured
unobservable
unobservant
unobserved
unobstructed
unobtainable
unobtrusive
unobtrusively
unobtrusiveness
unoccupied
unoffended
unoffending
unofficial
unofficially

unopposed
unorganised (or ~ized)
unoriginal
unornamental
unorthodox
unorthodoxy
unostentatious
unostentatiously
unostentatiousness
unowned
unpack
unpacker
unpaid
unpalatable
unparalleled
unpardonable
unpardonableness
unpardonably
unparliamentary
unpatriotic
unpeel
unpeeled
unpeg
unperturbed
unpick
unpin
unplaced
unplanned
unplayable
unpleasant
unpleasantly
unpleasantness
unplug (~gged, ~gging)
unpolished
unpopular
unpopularity
unpopularly
unpractical
unpracticality
unpractically
unpractised (*UK; US*
  ~iced)
unprecedented
unpredictability
unpredictable
unpredictably
unprejudiced
unprepared
unpreparedness
unprepossessing

unpretentious
unprincipled
unprintable
unproductive
unproductiveness
unprofessional
unprofessionally
unprofitability
unprofitable
unpromising
unprompted
unpronounceable
unprotected
unprovoked
unputdownable
unqualifiable
unqualified
unqualifiedly
unquantifiable
unquenchable
unquenchably
unquestionable
unquestionably
unquestioned
unquestioning
unquestioningly
unquiet
unquietly
unquietness
unquote
unravel (~lled, ~lling;
  US ~led, ~ling)
unread
unreadability
unreadable
unreadableness
unreadily
unreadiness
unready
unreal
unrealised (or ~ized)
unreality
unreason
unreasonable
unreasonableness
unreasonably
unreasoning
unreasoningly
unreceptive
unreciprocated

unrecognisable (or
  ~iz~)
unrecognised (or ~ized)
unreconciled
unredeemable
unredeemed
unrefined
unregeneracy
unregenerate
unregenerately
unrelated
unrelatedness
unreleased
unrelenting
unrelentingly
unrelentingness
unreliability
unreliable
unreliably
unreligious
unreligiously
unremarkable
unremembered
unremitting
unremittingly
unremittingness
unremunerative
unrepeatable
unrepentant
unrequited
unreserved
unreservedly
unreservedness
unresolved
unrest
unrestrained
unrestricted
unrewarded
unrewarding
unrighteous
unrighteously
unrighteousness
unripe
unripened
unripeness
unrivalled (*US* ~aled)
unroadworthy
unroll
unromantic
unrounded

unruffled
unruliness
unruly
unsaddle
unsafe
unsaid
unsanitary
unsatisfactory
unsatisfied
unsatisfying
unsaturated
unsavoury (*US* ~ory)
unscathed
unscented
unscheduled
unschooled
unscientific
unscramble
unscrambler
unscrew
unscripted
unscriptural
unscrupulous
unscrupulously
unscrupulousness
unseal
unsealed
unsearchable
unsearchableness
unseasonable
unseasonably
unseasonal
unseasoned
unseat
unsecured
unseeded
unseemliness
unseemly
unseen
unselfish
unselfishly
unselfishness
unsettle
unsettled
unsettledness
unsettling
unshackle
unshakeability
unshakeable
unshaken

unshaped
unshaven
unsheathe
unshrinking
unsightliness
unsightly
unsinkable
unskilled
unsling
unsmoked
unsnap
unsnarl
unsociability
unsociable
unsociableness
unsocial
unsocially
unsold
unsolicited
unsophisticated
unsophisticatedly
unsophisticatedness
unsophistication
unsoundly
unsoundness
unsparing
unsparingly
unsparingness
unspeakable
unspeakably
unspecific
unspecified
unspoilt
unstable
unsteadily
unsteadiness
unsteady
unstick
unstinting
unstop
unstoppable
unstoppably
unstring
unstructured
unstrung
unstuck
unstudied
unsubstantial
unsubstantiality
unsubstantially

unsubstantiated
unsuitable
unsuited
unsullied
unsung
unsupervised
unsupportable
unsure
unsurpassed
unsuspected
unsuspectedly
unsuspectedness
unsuspecting
unsustainable
unsustained
unsweetened
unswerving
unswervingly
untalented
untangle
untaught
unteachable
unteachableness
untenability
untenable
untenableness
untenably
untether
unthinkable
unthinkableness
unthinkably
unthinking
unthinkingly
unthinkingness
unthread
untidily
untidiness
untidy
untie
until
untimeliness
untimely
untold
untouchability
untouchable
untouchableness
untouchably
untoward
untowardly
untowardness

untraceable
untractability
untractable
untreatable
untreated
untrue
untrustworthiness
untrustworthy
untruth
untruthful
untruthfully
untruthfulness
untuned
untying
unuse
unused
unusual
unusually
unusualness
unutterability
unutterable
unutterably
unvarnished
unvarying
unvaryingness
unveil
unvoiced
unwaged
unwanted
unwantedness
unwarily
unwariness
unwarrantable
unwarrantably
unwarranted
unwary
unwashed
unwatchable
unwelcome
unwell
unwholesome
unwholesomeness
unwieldiness
unwieldy
unwilling
unwillingly
unwillingness
unwind
unwise
unwisely

unwitting
unwittingly
unwittingness
unwomanliness
unwomanly
unwonted
unworkable
unworkably
unworldliness
unworldly
unworthiness
unworthy
unwound
unwrap (~pped,
  ~pping)
unwritten
unyielding
unyoke
unzip (~pped, ~pping)
up-and-coming
Upanishad
upbeat
upbraid
upbringing
updatable (or ~tea~)
update
updated
upend
upended
upfront (or up-~)
upgrade
upgradeability (or
  ~dab~)
upgradeable (or ~dab~)
upheaval
uphill
uphold (~held)
upholster
upholstered
upholsterer
upholstery
upkeep
upland
uplift
uplifted
uplifting
uplighting
uplink
upload
up-market

upmost
upper
uppercut
uppermost
upping
uppish
uppishly
uppishness
uppitiness
uppity
upraise
upraised
uprate
upright
uprightly
uprightness
uprising
upriver
uproar
uproarious
uproariously
uproariousness
uproot
upset (~tting)
upsetting
upsettingly
upshot
upside
upsilon
upstage
upstaging
upstairs
upstanding
upstart
upstream
upstroke
upsurge
upswing
uptake
upthrust
uptight
uptightness
upturn
upward
upwardly
upwardness
upwards
upwind
uraemia (or ~rem~)
uraemic (or ~rem~)

ural
uranic
uranium
uranographer
uranographic
uranographical
uranography
Uranus
urban
urbane
urbanely
urbaneness
urbanisation (or ~iz~)
urbanise (or ~ize)
urbanism
urbanist
urbanite
urbanity
urchin
Urdu
urea
uremia (or urae~)
uremic (or urae~)
ureter
urethra
urethral
urethritis
urge
urgency
urgent
urgently
urger
uric
urinal
urinary
urinate
urination
urine
urinogenital
urn
urogenital
urologic
urological
urologist
urology
ursine
urtica
urticaria
urticate
urticating

urtication
Uruguay
Uruguayan
usability
usable (or useable)
usage
use
useable (or usable)
useful
usefully
usefulness
useless
uselessly
uselessness
user
user-friendliness
user-friendly
username
usher
usherette
usual
usually
usualness
usurer
usurious
usuriously
usurp
usurpation
usurper
usury
Utah
utensil
uterus (pl ~uses, ~ri)
utilisable (or ~iz~)
utilisation (or ~iz~)
utilise (or ~ize)
utilising (or ~iz~)
utilitarian
utilitarianism
utility
utmost
utopia (U~)
utopian (U~)
utter
utterable
utterance
utterer
utterly
uttermost
U-turn

uvea
uveal
uvula (pl ~ae)
uvular
uxorial
uxorious
uxoriously
uxoriousness
Uzbekistan
Uzi

vacancy
vacant
vacantly
vacatable
vacate
vacation
vacationist
vaccinal
vaccinate
vaccination
vaccinator
vaccine
vaccinia
vacillate
vacillating
vacillatingly
vacillation
vacillator
vacuity
vacuolar
vacuolation
vacuole
vacuous
vacuously
vacuousness
vacuum (pl ~uums,
  ~cua)
vade-mecum
vagabond

vagabondage
vagal
vagarious
vagary
vagina (*pl* ~as, ~ae)
vaginal
vaginismus
vaginitis
vaginosis
vagrancy
vagrant
vagrantly
vague
vaguely
vagueness
vaguish
vagus
vail
vain
vainglorious
vaingloriously
vaingloriousness
vainglory
vainly
vainness
valance
valanced
vale
valediction
valedictorian
valedictory
valence
valency
valentine (V~)
valerian
valet
valeta (*or* vel~)
valetudinarian
valetudinarianism
valetudinary
Valhalla
valiant
valiantly
valid
validate
validation
validity
validly
valise
Valium

Valkyrie
vallecula (*anat*)
Valletta
valley (*pl* ~eys)
vallium (V~, *tr*)
valorisation (*or* ~iz~)
valorise (*or* ~ize)
valorous
valorously
valour (*US* ~or)
valuable
valuableness
valuables
valuably
valuation
valuational
value
valued
valueless
valuelessness
valuer
valve
valved
valveless
valvular
valvulitis
vamoose (*US*)
vamp
vampire
vampiric
vampirism
vampish
vampishly
vampy
van
vanadium
Vancouver
Vandal *people*
vandal *damager*
vandalise (*or* ~ize)
vandalism
vandalistic
vandalistically
vandyke (V~)
vane
vaned
vaneless
vanguard
vanguardism
vanilla

vanillin
vanish
vanishing
vanishingly
vanitas
vanity
vanquish
vanquishable
vanquisher
vantage
Vanuatu
vapid
vapidity
vapidly
vapidness
vapor (*US*; *UK* ~our)
vaporable
vaporetto (*pl* ~os, ~tti)
vaporisable (*or* ~iz~)
vaporisation (*or* ~iz~)
vaporise (*or* ~ize)
vaporiser (*or* ~iz~)
vaporous
vaporousness
vapour (*US* ~or)
vapourish (*US* ~or~)
vapoury (*US* ~ory)
variability
variable
variableness
variably
variance
variant
variation
variational
variationist
varicoloured (*US* ~or~)
varicose
varicosed
varicosity
varied
variedly
variegated
variegation
varietal
variety
varifocal
variform
variola
variolar

variolous
variorum
various
variously
variousness
varix
varlet
varmint (*US*)
varnish
varnisher
varnishing
varve
vary
varying
varyingly
vas
vasal
vascular
vascularisation (*or* ~iz~)
vascularise (*or* ~ize)
vascularity
vasculature
vasculitis
vase
vasectomise (*or* ~ize)
vasectomy
vaseline (V~, *tr*)
vasoactive
vasoconstriction
vasoconstrictive
vasoconstrictor
vasodilatation
vasodilation
vasodilator
vasodilatory
vasopressin
vassal
vassalage
vast
vastly
vastness
VAT *tax*
vat (~tted, ~tting) *store*
Vatican
vaudeville
vaudevillian
vault
vaulted
vaulter
vaulting

vaunt
vaunted
vaunter
vaunting
vauntingly
veal
vector
vectorial
vectorially
vectorisation (*or* ~iz~)
vectorise (*or* ~ize)
Veda
Vedanta
Vedantic
Vedantist
Vedic
veduta
veer
vegan
veganism
vegeburger
Vegemite (*tr*)
vegetable
vegetal
vegetarian
vegetarianism
vegetate
vegetation
vegetational
vegetative
vegetatively
veggie (*or* ~ggy)
vehemence
vehement
vehemently
vehicle
vehicular
veil
veiled
veiling
veilless
vein
veined
veinless
veinlet
veinous
veiny
velar
velaric
velarisation (*or* ~iz~)

velarise (*or* ~ize)
Velcro (*tr*)
veld (*or* ~dt)
veleta (*or* val~)
vellum
velocipede
velociraptor
velocity
velodrome (V~)
velour (*or* ~rs)
velouté (*or* ~tée)
velum (*pl* ~la, ~ums)
velvet
velveted
velveteen
velvety
venal
venality
venally
venation
venational
vend
vendetta
vendibility
vendible
vendor (*US* ~er)
veneer
veneerer
veneering
venepuncture (*or* veni~)
venerability
venerable (V~)
venerableness
venerably
venerate
venerated
veneration
venerator
venereal
venereally
venereological
venereologist
venereology
Venetian
Venezuela
vengeance
vengeful
vengefully
vengefulness
venial

veniality
venially
Venice
venipuncture (*or* vene~)
venison
Venn
venom
venomed
venomous
venomously
venomousness
venose
venosity
venous
venously
vent
venter
ventiduct
ventifact
ventil
ventilable
ventilate
ventilated
ventilation
ventilative
ventilator
ventilatory
ventless
ventral
ventrally
ventricle
ventricular
ventriloquial
ventriloquise (*or* ~ize)
ventriloquism
ventriloquist
ventriloquy
venture
venturer
venturesome
venturesomely
venturesomeness
venue
venule
Venus
Venusian
veracious
veraciously
veraciousness
veracity

veranda (*or* ~dah)
verandaed
verb
verbage
verbal
verbalisable (*or* ~iz~)
verbalisation (*or* ~iz~)
verbalise (*or* ~ize)
verbaliser (*or* ~iz~)
verbalism
verbalist
verbalistic
verbally
verbatim
verbena
verbiage
verbless
verbose
verbosely
verboseness
verbosity
verdancy
verdant
verdantly
verdict
verdigris
verdure
verdured
verdureless
verdurous
verge
verger
vergership
verglas
veridical
veridicality
veridically
verifiability
verifiable
verifiably
verification
verifier
verify
verily
verisimilar
verisimilitude
verism
verismo
verist
veristic

veritable
veritably
vérité
verity
verjuice
vermeil
vermian
vermicelli
vermicide
vermicular
vermiculate
vermiculated
vermiculite
vermiculture
vermiform
vermilion (*or* ~illi~)
vermin
verminate
verminating
vermination
verminous
vermis
vermouth
vernacular
vernacularise (*or* ~ize)
vernacularism
vernacularity
vernacularly
vernal
vernalisation (*or* ~iz~)
vernalise (*or* ~ize)
vernally
vernissage
vernix
veronica
verruca (*pl* ~ae, ~as)
verrucose
verrucous
Versailles
versal
versant
versatile
versatilely
versatileness
versatility
verse
versed
verselet
verset
versicle

versicoloured (*US* ~or~)
versicular
versification
versifier
versify
versifying
version
versional
vers libre
verso (*pl* ~os)
versus
vert
vertebra (*pl* ~ae)
vertebral
vertebrate
vertebration
vertex (*pl* ~tices, ~xes)
vertical
verticalise (*or* ~ize)
verticality
vertically
vertiginous
vertiginously
vertiginousness
vertigo
vertu (*or* vir~)
vervain
verve
vervet
very
Very (*or* ~rey) *light*
Vesak (*or* Wes~)
vesica
vesical
vesicant
vesicate
vesication
vesicatory
vesicle
vesicular
vesiculated
vesiculation
vespers (V~)
vespertine
vessel
vest
vesta
vestal
vested
vestiary

vestibular
vestibule
vestibuled
vestige
vestigial
vestigially
vestimentary
vestiture
vestment
vestry
Vesuvius
vet (~tted, ~tting)
vetch
veteran
veterinarian (*US*)
veterinary
vetiver
veto (*pl* ~oes)
vetoer
vetted
vetting
vex
vexation
vexatious
vexatiously
vexatiousness
vexed
vexedly
vexer
vexillological
vexillologist
vexillology
vexillum (*pl* ~lla)
vexing
via
viability
viable
viably
viaduct
vial
viaticum (*pl* ~ums, ~ca)
vibe
vibex (*pl* ~bices)
vibrancy
vibrant
vibrantly
vibraphone
vibraphonist
vibrate
vibration

vibrational
vibrationless
vibrato
vibrator
vibratory
vibrio
vibrissa (*pl* ~ae)
vibrotactile
viburnum
vicar
vicarage
vicarial
vicariate
vicarious
vicariously
vicariousness
vicarship
vice *evil*
vice (*US* vise) *tool*
vicegerency
vicegerent
viceless
viceregal
vicereine
viceroy
viceroyal
viceroyalty
viceroyship
vicesimal (*or* vige~)
vichyssoise
vicinage
vicinal
vicinity
vicious
viciously
viciousness
vicissitude
vicissitudinous
vicountess
victim
victimisation (*or* ~iz~)
victimise (*or* ~ize)
victimiser (*or* ~iz~)
victor
Victorian
victoriana (V~)
victorious
victoriously
victoriousness
victory

victual (~lled, ~lling;
  US ~led, ~ling)
victualler (US ~aler)
vicuna (or ~ña)
vide *look*
video (pl ~eos)
videoconference
videoconferencing
videodisc (or ~k)
videofit
videogram
videographer
videographics
videography
videophone
videotape
videotext
vie
vielle
Vienna
Viennese
Vietcong
Vietminh
Vietnam
Vietnamese
view
viewable
viewdata
viewer
viewership
viewfinder
viewing
viewless
viewpoint
vigesimal (or vice~)
vigil
vigilance
vigilant
vigilante
vigilantism
vigilantly
vignette
vignettist
vigorous
vigorously
vigorousness
vigour (US ~or)
vihara
Viking
vile

vilely
vileness
vilification
vilifier
vilify
villa
village
villager
villagey
villain
villainous
villainously
villainousness
villainy
villiform
villous
villus (pl ~li)
vim
vin
vinaceous
vinaigrette
vincibility
vincible
vindaloo
vindicable
vindicate
vindication
vindicative
vindicator
vindicatory
vindictive
vindictively
vindictiveness
vine
vinegar
vinegarish
vinegary
vinery
vineyard
vinicultural
viniculture
viniculturist
vinification
vinify
vino (pl ~os)
vinosity
vinous
vint
vintage
vintner

viny
vinyl
viol
viola
violable
violate
violation
violator
violence
violent
violently
violet
violin
violinist
violist
violoncellist
violoncello
viper
viperfish
viperine
viperish
viperous
viraemia (or ~em~)
viraemic (or ~em~)
virago (pl ~os, ~oes)
viral
virally
virement
virescence
virescent
virescently
virga (pl ~ae)
Virgin *mother of Jesus*
virgin *no sexual
  intercourse*
virginal
virginalist
virginally
virginals
Virginia
virginity
Virgo
virgule
viridescence
viridescent
virile
virility
viroid
virological
virologically

virologist
virology
virtu (*or* ver~)
virtual
virtuality
virtually
virtue
virtueless
virtuosic
virtuosity
virtuoso (*pl* ~osi, ~os)
virtuous
virtuously
virtuousness
virulence
virulent
virulently
virus
visa
visage
visaged
visagist
vis-à-vis
viscacha (*or* viz~)
visceral
viscid
viscidity
viscose
viscosity
viscount
viscountcy
viscountship
viscounty
viscous
viscously
viscousness
viscus (*pl* viscera)
vise (*US*; *UK* vice)
Vishnu
visibility
visible
visibly
Visigoth
Visigothic
vision
visional
visionariness
visionary
visionless
visit (~ited, ~iting)

visitable
visitation
visitatorial
visiting
visitor
visitorial
visor (*or* ~zor)
visored (*or* ~zor~)
vista
visual
visualisable (*or* ~iz~)
visualisation (*or* ~iz~)
visualise (*or* ~ize)
visuality
visually
visuals
vital
vitalisation (*or* ~iz~)
vitalise (*or* ~ize)
vitalism
vitalist
vitalistic
vitality
vitamin
vitiate
vitiation
vitiator
viticultural
viticulture
viticulturist
vitiligo
vitreous
vitreousness
vitrescence
vitrescent
vitrifaction
vitrifiable
vitrification
vitriform
vitrify
vitriol
vitriolic
vituperate
vituperation
vituperative
vituperator
viva
vivace
vivacious
vivaciously

vivaciousness
vivacity
vivarium (*pl* ~ia, ~iums)
viva voce
vivid
vividly
vividness
vivification
vivify
viviparity
viviparous
viviparously
viviparousness
vivisect
vivisection
vivisectional
vivisectionist
vivisector
vixen
vixenish
vixenly
vizcacha (*or* vis~)
vizier
vizierate
vizierial
viziership
vizor (*or* vis~)
vocable
vocabulary
vocal
vocalese
vocalic
vocalisation (*or* ~iz~)
vocalise (*or* ~ize)
vocaliser (*or* ~iz~)
vocalism
vocalist
vocality
vocally
vocation
vocational
vocationalise (*or* ~ize)
vocationalism
vocationally
vocative
vociferant
vociferate
vociferation
vociferous

vociferously
vociferousness
Vodafone (*tr*)
vodka
vogue
vogueish
voice
voiced
voiceful
voiceless
voicelessly
voicelessness
voicemail
voice-over
voiceprint
void
voidable
voidance
voided
voidness
volant
volatile
volatilisable (*or* ~iz~)
volatilisation (*or* ~iz~)
volatilise (*or* ~ize)
volatility
vol-au-vent
volcanic
volcanically
volcanicity (*or* vul~)
volcanism (*or* vul~)
volcano (*pl* ~oes, ~os)
volcanological (*or* vul~)
volcanologist (*or* vul~)
volcanology (*or* vul~)
vole
Volga
volition
volitional
volitionality
volitionally
volitive
volley (*pl* ~eys)
volleyball
volleyer
volt
Volta
voltage
voltaic
volte (*or* volt) *movement*

volte-face
voltmeter
volubility
voluble
volubleness
volubly
volume
volumetric
voluminous
voluminously
voluminousness
volumise (*or* ~ize)
volumiser (*or* ~iz~)
voluntarily
voluntariness
voluntarism
voluntarist
voluntary
voluntaryism
volunteer
volunteerism
voluptuary
voluptuous
voluptuously
voluptuousness
volute
voluted
volution
volva
volvulus (*pl* ~li, ~uses)
vomer
vomit (~tted, ~tting)
vomiter
voodoo
voodooism
voodooist
Voortrekker
voracious
voraciously
voraciousness
voracity
vortex (*pl* ~tices)
vortical
vortically
vorticism
vorticity
vorticose
vorticular
votarist
votary

vote
voteless
voter
voting
votive
vouch
voucher
vouchsafe
vow
vowel
vowelless
vox
vox pop
voyage
voyager
voyeur
voyeurism
voyeuristic
voyeuristically
vroom
V-sign
Vulcan
vulcanicity (*or* vol~)
vulcanisable (*or* ~iz~)
vulcanisation (*or* ~iz~)
vulcanise (*or* ~ize)
vulcaniser (*or* ~iz~)
vulcanism (*or* vol~)
vulcanite
vulcanological (*or* vol~)
vulcanologist (*or* vol~)
vulcanology (*or* vol~)
vulgar
vulgarian
vulgarisation (*or* ~iz~)
vulgarise (*or* ~ize)
vulgarism
vulgarity
Vulgate *bible*
vulgate *common speech*
vulnerability
vulnerable
vulnerableness
vulnerably
vulnerary
vulpine
vulture
vulturine
vulturish
vulturous

vulva
vulval
vulvar
vulvitis
vying

wackily (*or* wha~)
wackiness (*or* wha~)
wacky (*or* wha~)
wad
wadding
waddle
waddler
waddling
wade
wader
wadi (*or* wady; *pl* ~dis,
~dies)
wading
wafer
wafery
waffle
waffler
waffling
waft
wag
wage
waged
wager
wagerer
waggish
waggishly
waggishness
waggle
waggler
waggly
waggon (*or* wagon)
Wagner
Wagnerian
wagon (*or* waggon)

wagoner
wagonload
wagtail
waif
wail
wailer
wailing
wailingly
wainscot
wainscoting (*or* ~tting)
wainwright
waist
waistband
waistcoat
waistcoated
waistline
wait
waiter
waiting
waiting-list
waiting-room
waitress
waive
waiver
wake
wakeboard
wakeboarding
wakeful
wakefully
wakefulness
waken
wake-up
wale
Wales
walk
walkabout
walker
walkie-talkie (*or* ~ky-
~ky)
walk-in
walking
walking-frame
walking-stick
Walkman (*pl* ~mans,
men)
walk-on
walkout (*or* walk-~)
walkover
walk-through
walk-up

walkway
walky-talky (*or* ~kie-
~kie)
wall
wallaby
wallet
walleye
walleyed
wallflower
Walloon
wallop (~ped, ~ping)
walloping
wallow
wallower
wallpaper
walnut
walrus
waltz
waltzer
wan
wand
wander
wanderer
wandering
wanderingly
wanderlust
wane
wangle
wank
wanly
wannabe (*or* ~bee)
wanness
want
wanted
wanting
wanton
wantonly
wantonness
wap
wapiti
war
warble
warbler
ward
warden
warder
wardress
wardrobe
wardroom
ware

warehouse
warehouseman
warehousing
warfare
warfarin
warhead
warhorse
warily
wariness
warlike
warlock
warlord
warm
warmer
warm-hearted
warm-heartedly
warm-heartedness
warmonger
warmth
warm-up
warn
warner
warning
warp
warpaint
warpath
warping
warplane
warrant
warrantable
warrantably
warrantee
warrantor (*or* ~er)
warranty
warren
warring
warrior
warship
wart
warthog
wartime
Warwick
wary
wash
washable
washbag
washbasin
washboard
washcloth
washday

washer
washerwoman (*pl*
~women)
washeteria
wash-house
washily
washiness
washing
Washington
washing-up
washout
washroom
wash-up
washy
wasp
waspish
waspishly
waspishness
wassail
wassailer
wastage
waste
wasted
wasteful
wastefully
wastefulness
wasteland
wastepaper
waster
wastrel
watch
watchability
watchable
watchdog
watcher
watchful
watchfully
watchfulness
watchmaker
watchman (*pl* ~men)
watchspring
watchstrap
watchtower
watchword
water
waterage
waterbed
waterborne
watercolour (*US* ~or)
watercourse

watercress
waterer
waterfall
waterfowl
waterfront
Watergate *scandal*
watergate *floodgate*
waterhole
wateriness
watering
waterline
waterlog (~gged,
~gging)
Waterloo
waterman (*pl* ~men)
watermark
watermelon
watermill
waterproof
water-rat
watershed
waterside
waterspout
watertight
waterway
waterwheel
waterwings
waterworks
watery
watt
wattage
wattle
wattmeter
waul (*or* wawl)
wave
waveband
waveform
wavelength
waver
waverer
wavering
waveringly
wavily
waviness
wavy
wawl (*or* waul)
wax
waxbill
waxcloth
waxen

waxily
waxiness
waxwing
waxwork
waxy
way
wayfarer
wayfaring
waylaid
waylay
waylayer
wayside
wayward
waywardly
waywardness
weak
weaken
weak-kneed
weakliness
weakling
weakly
weak-minded
weak-mindedness
weakness
weak-willed
weal
wealth
wealthily
wealthiness
wealthy
wean
weapon
weaponless
weaponry
wear
wearability
wearable
weariness
wearing
wearisome
wearisomely
wearisomeness
weary
weasel (~lled, ~lling; US ~led, ~ling)
weather
weatherbeaten
weatherboard
weatherboarding
weathercock

weathergirl
weathering
weatherliness
weatherly
weatherman
weatherproof
weathervane
weave
weaver
weaverbird
Web *internet*
web *spider*
webbed
webbing
weber
webwork
wed
wedding
wedge
wedged
wedging
Wedgwood
wedgy
wedlock
Wednesday
wee
weed
weeder
weedily
weediness
weeding
weedkiller
weedless
weedy
week
weekday
weekend
weekender
weekly
weeknight
weeny
weep
weeper
weepie
weepily
weepiness
weeping
weepy (*or* ~pie)
weever
weevil

weft
weigela
weigh
weighable
weighbridge
weigher
weighing
weight
weightily
weightiness
weighting
weightless
weightlessness
weightlifter
weightlifting
weightwatcher
weil
weir
weird
weirdie
weirdly
weirdness
weirdo
welch (*or* welsh)
welcome
welcomer
welcoming
welcomingly
weld
weldable
welder (*or* ~or)
welding
welfare
well
wellhead
wellington
well-nigh
wellspring (*or* well-~)
well-wisher
welly (*or* ~llie)
welsh (*or* welch) *cheat*
Welsh *Wales*
Welshman (*pl* ~men)
Welshness
Welshwoman (*pl* ~women)
welt
welter
welterweight
wen

wench
wend
Wensleydale
went
wept
werewolf (*pl* ~wolves; *or* werw~)
Wesleyan
west
westbound
westerling
westerly
western
westerner
westernisation (*or* ~iz~)
westernise (*or* ~ize)
westerniser (*or* ~iz~)
westernmost
Westminster
westward
wet (*adj* ~tter, ~ttest; *v* ~tted, ~tting)
wether
wetting
whack
whackiness (*or* wa~)
whacking
whacky (*or* wa~)
whale
whaleback
whaleboat
whalebone
whaler
whaling
wham (~mmed, ~mming)
whammy
whang
wharf (*pl* wharves)
what
whatever
whatnot
whatsoever
wheat
wheaten
wheatgerm
wheatmeal
Wheatstone
wheedle
wheel

wheelbarrow
wheelbase
wheelchair
wheeler
wheelhouse
wheelie (*UK*)
wheelwright
wheeze
wheezer
wheezily
wheeziness
wheezy
whelk
whelp
when
whence
whenever
whensoever
where
whereabouts
whereas
whereby
wherefore
wherein
whereof
whereon
wheresoever
whereupon
wherever
wherewith
wherewithal
wherry
whet (~tted, ~tting)
whether
whetstone
whey
which
whichever
whichsoever
whidah (*or* why~)
whiff
whiffle
whiffy
while
whilst
whim
whimper
whimperer
whimpering
whimperingly

whimsical
whimsicality
whimsically
whimsily
whimsiness
whimsy (*or* ~sey)
whinchat
whine
whiner
whinge
whinger
whinging
whining
whiningly
whinny
whip
whipcord
whiplash
whipped
whipper
whippersnapper
whippet
whippiness
whipping
whippoorwill
whippy
whip-round
whipsaw
whipstitch
whipstock
whirl
whirler
whirligig
whirling
whirlpool
whirlwind
whirr (*or* whir)
whisk
whisker
whiskered
whiskery
whisky (*or* ~key; *pl* ~keys, ~kies)
whisper
whisperer
whispering
whist
whistle
whistler
whistle-stop

whistling
Whit *Whitsun*
whit *bit*
white
whitebait
whitebeam
whiteboard
Whitechapel
white-collar
whited
whitefly
Whitehall
white-hot
white-knuckle
whiten
whitener
whiteness
whitening
white-out
whitewash
whitewood
whitey (*tab*)
whither
whiting
whitish
whitleather
whitling
whitlow
Whitsun
Whitsuntide
whittle
whittler
whiz (*or* whizz)
who
whodunit (*or* ~dunnit)
whoever
whole
wholefood
wholegrain
wholehearted
wholeheartedly
wholemeal
wholesale
wholesome
wholesomely
wholesomeness
wholewheat
wholism
wholly
whom

whomever
whomp
whomsoever
whoop
whoopee
whooper
whooping
whoops
whoosh
whop (~pped, ~pping)
whopper
whore
whorehouse
whorish
whorishly
whorishness
whorl
whorled
whortleberry
whosoever
why
whydah (*or* whi~)
wick
wicked
wickedly
wickedness
wicker
wickerwork
wicket
wicketkeeper (*or* wicket-
  ~)
wide
wide-angle
wide-awake
wide-eyed
widely
widen
wideness
widescreen
widespread
widgeon (*or* wig~)
widget
widish
widow
widower
width
wield
wielder
wieldy
wife (*pl* wives)

wifehood
wifeliness
wig
wigeon (*or* widg~)
wiggle
wiggly
wigwam
wild
wildcat
wildebeest
wilderness
wildfire
wildfowl
wildish
wildlife
wildly
wildness
wile
wilful (*UK*; *US* will~)
wilfullness (*UK*; *US*
  will~)
wilfully (*UK*; *US* will~)
wiliness
will
willful (*US*; *UK* wilf~)
will-o'-the-wisp
willow
willowiness
willowy
willpower
wilt
wily
Wimbledon
wimp
wimpily
wimpiness
wimpish
wimpishness
wimple
Wimpy (*tr*) *hamburger*
wimpy *feeble*
win
wince
wincer
winch
wincing
wincingly
wind
windage
windbag

windborne
windbreak
windcheater
windchill
winded
windedness
winder
windfall
windily
windiness
winding
windlass
windmill
window
windowpane
window-shopping
windowsill
windpipe
windpower
windscreen
windsock
windsurf
windsurfer
windsurfing
windswept
wind-up
windward
windy
wine
wineglass
winepress
winery
wing
wingbeat
winged
winger
wingman
wingspan
wink
winker
winking
winnable
winner
winning
winningly
winnow
winnower
wino (*pl* ~os)
winsome
winsomely

winsomeness
winter
winterage
wintergreen
wintering
wintertide
wintertime
wintry (*or* ~tery)
winy (*or* ~ney)
wipe
wipe-out
wiper
wire
wirecutter
wire-haired
wireless
wiretapper (*or* wire-~)
wireworm
wiring
wiry
Wisconsin
wisdom
wise
wiseacre
wisecrack
wisely
wish
wishbone
wishful
wishfully
wishfulness
wishing
wishy-washy
wisp
wispily
wispiness
wispy
wisteria
wistful
wistfully
wistfulness
wit
witch
witchcraft
witchery
witching
with
withdraw (~drew)
withdrawal
withdrawn

wither
withered
withering
witheringly
withers
withhold (~held)
withholder
withholding
within
without
withstand (~stood)
withstander
witless
witlessly
witlessness
witness
witter
wittering
witticism
wittily
wittiness
witting
witty
wizard
wizardry
wizen
wizened
woad
wobble
wobbler
wobbliness
wobbly
wodge
woe
woebegone
woeful
woefulness
woggle
wok
woke
woken
wold
wolf (*pl* wolves)
wolfcub
wolfhound
wolfish
wolfsbane
wolverine (*or* ~rene)
wolves
woman (*pl* women)

womanhood
womanise (*or* ~ize)
womaniser (*or* ~iz~)
womanish
womankind
womanliness
womanly
womb
wombat
womenfolk
won
wonder
wonderful
wonderfully
wonderfulness
wondering
wonderingly
wonderland
wonderment
wondrous
wondrously
wondrousness
wonkily
wonkiness
wonky
wont
woo
wood
woodbine
woodblock
woodcarver
woodcarving
woodchuck
woodcock
woodcraft
woodcut
woodcutter
wooden
woodgrain
woodiness
woodland
woodlouse (*pl* ~lice)
woodpecker
woodpigeon
woodpile
woodruff
woodscrew
woodshed
woodsman (*pl* ~men)
woodwind

woodwork
woodworm
woody
woodyard
wooer
woof
woofer
wooing
wool
woollen (*US* woolen)
woolly (*US* wooly)
wool-pack
woolsack (W~)
woozily
wooziness
woozy
Worcester
Worcestershire
word
wordage
wordgame
wordily
wordiness
wording
wordless
wordlessly
wordlessness
wordplay
wordsearch
wordsmith
wordy
wore
work
workability
workable
workableness
workaday
workaholic
workbasket
workbench
workbook
workbox
workday
worked
worker
workforce
workhorse
workhouse
working
workload

workman (*pl* ~men)
workmanlike
workmanship
workmate
workout
workpeople
workplace
workroom
worksheet
workshop
work-shy
workspace
workstation
worktop
world
worldliness
worldly
worldly-minded
worldly-wise
world-shaking
worldweariness
worldweary
worldwide
worm
worm-eaten
wormer
wormhole
worminess
wormwood
wormy
worn
worried
worriedly
worrier
worrisome
worry
worrying
worryingly
worse
worsen
worship (~pped,
~pping)
worshipful
worshipper
worst
worsted
wort
worth
worthily
worthiness

worthless
worthlessness
worthwhile
worthwhileness
worthy
would
would-be
wound
wounded
woundedness
wounding
woundwort
wove
woven
wow
wrack
wraith
wrangle
wrangler
wrangling
wrap (~pped, ~pping)
wraparound
wrapped
wrapper
wrapping
wrasse
wrath
wrathful
wrathfully
wrathfulness
wreak
wreath (*n*)
wreathe (*v*)
wreck
wreckage
wrecker
wrecking
Wren *navy*
wren *bird*
wrench
wrest
wrestle
wrestler
wrestling
wretch
wretched
wriggle
wriggler
wriggling
wriggly

wring
wringer
wringing
wrinkle
wrinkled
wrinkly
wrist
wristband
wristlet
wristwatch
writ
write
write-off
writer
write-up
writhe
writhing
writhingly
writing
written
wrong
wrongdoer
wrongdoing
wrongfoot
wrongful
wrong-headed
wrong-headedly
wrong-headedness
wrongly
wrongness
wrote
wrought
wrung
wry
wrybill
wryly
wryneck
wryness
wunderkind (*pl* ~ds,
   ~der)
wurst
wuss
WYSIWYG (*or* wysiwyg)

Xanadu
xanthoma (*pl* ~mata,
   ~as)
xebec (*occ* ze~,
   ~eck)
xenobiotic
xenoglossia
xenon
xenophobe
xenophobia
xenophobic
Xenophon
xeroderma
xerographer
xerographic
xerographically
xerography
xerophilous
xerophyte
xerox (X~ *tr*)
Xerxes
Xhosa
xi
Xmas
X-ray (*occ* x-ray)
xylem
xylene
xyloid
xylophagous
xylophone
xylophonic
xylose

yabby
yacht
yachting
yachtsman (*pl* ~men)
yachtsmanship
yachtswoman (*pl*
~women)
yack (*or* yak) *talk*
yahoo
yahooism
yahrzeit
Yahweh (*occ* ~veh)
yak *mammal*
yak (*or* yack; v ~kked,
~kking) *talk*
yakuza
Yale
yam
yammer (~mmered,
~mmering)
yang
Yangtze
Yank *American*
yank *tug*
Yankee
yap (~pped, ~pping)
yappy
yarborough (Y~)
yard
yardage
yardarm (*or* yard-~)
yardbird
yardie
yardstick
yarmulke (*or* ~ka)
yarn
yarrow
yashmak (*occ* ~mac,
~mack)

yatagan (*or* ~ghan)
yatter (~ttered,
~ttering)
yaw
yawl
yawn
yawner
yawniness
yawning
yawningly
yaws
year
yearbook
yearling
yearn
yearner
yearning
yearningly
yeast
yeastily
yeastiness
yeasty
yell
yellow
yellow-belly
yellowed
yellowfin
yellowing
yellowish
yellowly
yellowness
Yellowstone
yellowy
yelp
Yeltsin
Yemen
Yemeni (*pl* ~is)
Yemenite
yen
yeoman (*pl* ~men)
yeomanly
yeomanry
Yerevan
yes (*pl* yeses, yesses)
yesterday
yester-year
yet
yeti
yew
Yggdrasil

Yiddish
Yiddisher
Yiddishism
Yiddishkeit
yield
yieldable
yielder
yielding
yieldingly
yieldingness
yin
ylang-ylang (*or* ilang-
ilang)
ylem
yob
yobbish
yobbishly
yobbishness
yobbo (*pl* ~os, ~oes)
yobby
yod
yodel (~lled, ~lling; *US*
~led, ~ling)
yodeller (*US* ~ler)
yoga
yoghurt (*esp UK; US esp*
~gurt; *also* ~hourt,
~gourt)
yogi (*pl* ~is, ~in)
yogic
yogism
yogurt *see* yoghurt
yoicks
yoke (! yolk) *frame*
yokel
Yokohama
yokozuna
yolk (! yoke) *egg*
yolkless
yolky
yomp
yonder
yoni
yonks
yoo-hoo
yore
York
yorker
Yorkie
Yorkshire

Yoruba
Yosemite
young
youngish
youngling
youngster
your
yours
yourself (*pl* ~selves)
youth
youthful
youthfully
youthfulness
yowl
yowler
yo-yo (*pl* ~yos)
Ypres
ytterbium
yuan
yucca (*occ* yuca)
yuck (*or* yuk)
yuckiness (*occ* yukk~)
yucky (*also* yukky)
Yugoslav
Yugoslavia
Yugoslavian
yuk (*or* yuck)
yukata (*pl* ~ta, ~tas)
yukky (*or* yucky)
Yukon
Yukoner
Yule
Yuletide
yummy
yum-yum
yuppie (*occ* ~ppy)
yuppiedom
yuppification
yuppify
yurt

Z

zabaglione
Zagreb
Zaire (*or* ~ïre)
Zairean (*or* ~ian)
zakat
Zambezi
Zambia
Zambian
Zamboanga
zambra
zamindar
zander
zanily
zaniness
zany
Zanzibar
Zanzibari
zap (~pped, ~pping)
zapateado (*pl* ~os)
zapper
zappy
Zarathustra
Zarathustrian
zarzuela
zazen
zeal
Zealand
zealot
zealotry
zealous
zealously
zealousness
zebec *see* xebec
zebra (*pl* ~as, ~ra)
zebu (*pl* ~bu, ~bus)
    cattle
Zebulun (*or* ~on)
Zechariah
zed (*US* zee)

zeitgeist (Z~)
Zen
Zend
zener (Z~)
Zenist (*or* Zennist)
zenith
zenithal
Zennist (*or* Zenist)
Zeno
zeolite
Zephaniah
zephyr
zeppelin
zero (*n pl* ~ros, ~roes;
    v ~roes, ~roed,
    ~roing)
zeroth
zest
zester
zestful
zestfully
zestfulness
zesty
zeta
zeugma
zeugmatic
zeugmatically
Zeus
zho (*or* dzo)
zig (~gged, ~gging)
ziggurat
zigzag (~gged,
    ~gging)
zigzaggedly
zilch
zillion
zillionaire
zillionth
Zimbabwe
Zimbabwean
zimmer (Z~)
zinc
zincked (*occ* zinced)
Zinfandel
zing
zinnia
Zion (*or* Sion)
Zionism
Zionist
zip (~pped, ~pping)

ziplock
zipper
zippily
zippiness
zippy
zircon
zirconia
zirconic
zirconium
zit
zither
zitherist
ziti
zloty (*pl* ~ty, ~tys,
~ties)
zodiac
zodiacal
zombie (*occ* ~bi)
zombielike
zombified
zombify
zonal

zonally
zonation
zone
zoned
zoning
zoo
zoogeography
zoolater
zoolatrous
zoolatry
zoological
zoologist
zoology
zoom
zoomorphic
zoomorphism
zoonosis (*pl* ~oses)
zoonotic
zoophyte
zorbing
Zoroaster
Zoroastrian

Zoroastrianism
zorro (*pl* ~os)
Zouave
zouk
zucchetto (*pl* ~os)
zucchini (*pl* ~ni, ~nis)
zugzwang
Zulu
Zululand
Zurich (*or* Zü~)
zwieback
Zwingli
Zwinglian
zwitterion
zydeco
zygoma (*pl* ~mata)
zygomatic
zygomorphic
zygomorphy
zygote
zygotic
zymurgy